The **Car** Book

19

The Definitive Buyer's Guide to Car Safety, Fuel Economy, Maintenance and Much More

by

with Daniel Gustafson and Ailis Aaron

graphics and design
by Amy B. Curran

foreword by Clarence M. Ditlow
Center for Auto Safety

HarperPerennial

A Division of HarperCollins Publishers

Acknowledgments

...up the complex process of compiling the information you need ...car choice. Dan Gustafson has stepped in as lead researcher and joined computer graphics maven Amy Curran to compile and package more information than we've ever before presented. Thanks to his willingness to dig in, Dan was able to assemble one of the most complex consumer guides available—and make an on time delivery. As always, Amy's ability to make graphical sense out of all of this data is the key ingredient in successfully providing this important information to the American car buyer. Accompanying Amy every step of the way was a new little bundle due to arrive shortly after The Car Book! These two professionals were able to accomplish this increasingly complex feat with the talented assistance of co-author Ailis Aaron, now a Car Book Veteran who now knows much more about cars than her Dad! Rounding out the team was the hard working and skilfull Meaghan Farrell, the newest member of the team, who helped with research, copyediting, data collection and photo selection.

Many, many talented professionals enabled Amy, Dan and Ailis to successfully accomplish this effort. This year's edition would not have been possible without essential contributions from many talented individuals. Most significant was Clarence Ditlow and the staff of the Center for Auto Safety. In addition, valuable insight and information was provided by safety expert David Biss, president of Automotive Safety Analysis; legal expert Phil Nowicki, president of Nowicki and Associates; Carolyn Gorman of the Insurance Information Institute; Martha Casey, U.S. EPA; Pete Packer, Runzheimer International; Kim Hazelbaker, Highway Loss Data Institute; Debbie Bindeman, Insurance Services Organization; John DeCicco and Martin Thomas, American Council for an Energy-Efficient Economy. Very special thanks go to my friend, terrific literary agent, and most importantly, father-to-be, Stuart Krichevsky.

As always, the most important factor in being able to bring this information to the American car buyer for 19 years is the encouragement, support, and love from my brilliant and beautiful wife, Marilyn Mohrman-Gillis.

J.G.

As Always,

for Marilyn &
Katie, John, Brian and Brennan

ISSN: 0893-1208
ISBN: 0-06-27-3448-2
99 00 CW 5 4 3 2

Cover design ©Gillis and Associates.
Photo credits: Chrysler Corporation, Dodge Division; General Motors Corporation, Buick Division; General Motors Corporation, Pontiac Division; Nissan Motor Corp. USA; Toyota Motor Sales, USA, Inc.; Volvo Cars of North America

Cover Photo of Jack Gillis: Donna Cantor-MacLean

Contents

Foreword

by Clarence M. Ditlow,
Executive Director, Center for Auto Safety

Ralph Nader and Consumers Union founded the Center for Auto Safety (CAS) in 1970 to be a voice for the consumer in Washington against the powerful auto lobby. When auto company lobbyists killed the first Car Book in 1980, CAS was there to help former government worker Jack Gillis publish it privately. To the chagrin of the auto companies, this year marks the 19th edition of *The Car Book* helping consumers buy safe cars and avoid unsafe cars. This year also marks the beginning of the Center's 30th year fighting for consumers. On a shoe string budget, half what Ford or GM pay for one Super Bowl commercial, CAS has gotten lemon laws in every state, numerous recalls including the infamous Ford Pinto, while making cars safer, less polluting, more reliable and fuel efficient.

Ominous signs from the auto industry indicate CAS' job of watching out for the consumer will get more difficult in the future. Used car dealers want Congress to pass a law legalizing the sale of rebuilt wrecks and taking away the consumer's right to sue when they buy undisclosed wrecks. Ford withheld information in numerous safety investigations that enabled it to avoid costly recalls. After Consumer Reports rates the Samurai and Trooper unacceptable as prone to rollover, Suzuki and Isuzu spend millions on lawyers to sue Consumer Reports rather than on engineers for recalls. Shades of GM and Ralph Nader, Suzuki even sends teams of detectives across the county to check out former CAS employees because we had the audacity to seek a recall of its tipsy Samurai.

Children are often the innocent victims of auto executives' decisions that value profits over lives. CAS repeatedly asked the government to install releases in trunks so people trapped inside can get out. In one month this summer, 11 children died after being trapped inside trunks. In 1984 a federal official denied a petition for a interior trunk release saying, "The agency is not aware of any accident data indicating there is much likelihood of accidental entrapment in a vehicle's trunk." Today that official works for the American Automobile Manufacturers Association and cites his 1984 statement as a reason not to install trunk releases. Chrysler lobbied Congress to block a safety recall of its minivans for defective tailgate latches which popped open in moderate crashes and killed over 35 children.

General Motors did a cost benefit analysis that found it was not worth more than $2.20 per vehicle to prevent a fire death even though 500 people died each year in fire crashes in GM vehicles like its 1973-87 full size pickups with side saddle gas tanks which have killed 1600 people in fire crashes. Although a GM Vice President called a $23 safety shield for the pickups "a probable easy fix," it flunked GM's cost benefit analysis. GM's lawyers called the engineer who did the cost benefit analysis "an individual whom we would [not] ever, in any conceivable circumstance, want to be identified [as] the documents he generated are undoubtedly some of the potentially most harmful and damaging were they ever to be produced." Why? Because they showed GM's callous disregard for the lives of its customers.

Big companies who hold themselves above the law are getting even bigger. GM owns significant shares of Isuzu and Saab. Ford bought Jaguar. Chrysler merges with Mercedes and Chrysler Chairman Robert Eaton stands to gain over $100 million in the merger. No one deserves that much money, let alone some one who was responsible for the minivan latch debacle.

These changes in the auto industry are a clarion call to consumers—get sharper or get run over. Every dollar you pay for overpriced vehicles, lemon repairs, and accident costs goes to pay multi-million dollar salaries for fat cat auto executives rather than for safer and more reliable vehicles. Find out how your politicians vote on auto issues and vote them out if they support anticonsumer legislation like allowing rebuilt wrecks and laundered lemons to be sold without notice. Demand that federal regulators issue standards that prevent children from suffocating in trunks. Learn to use the Internet to spot auto hazards and find better auto values. If you get ripped off, complain. Support CAS and your local consumer group. Get your friends and neighbors to join as a form of lemon insurance—lemons are life's great levelers, sooner or later everyone gets one.

CAS is committed to bringing you the best in consumer advocacy including the 1999 *Car Book* to meet these new challenges. We're tough and we're smart. We don't flinch when auto companies file lawsuits and subpoenas by the dozens to try to intimidate. We are building a Website, www.autosafety.org, for consumers who want to fight back, buy a better car, save money, reduce the impact of autos on society, and improve the quality of their life by having an auto information resource that is ready with whatever they need whenever they need it. The two most important things consumers can do to advance safety are to become CAS supporters and go into the marketplace armed with *The Car Book*.

For 19 years, *The Car Book* has been providing the information you need to purchase a safe, reliable and economical car. Each year we prepare and offer more data, beginning in 1980, when we were first to provide you with the valuable and life-saving crash test results to last year when we were your source for the first-ever government *side* crash test results. New in this year's edition, you'll find the "Green Ratings" complied by the American Council for an Energy-Efficient Economy. With this information, there is no reason why your next car can't be safe, reliable and environmentally responsible.

When it comes to buying a car, the best weapon you have to protect yourself is information. You now have in your hands the best arsenal of facts available to help you wade through the claims and hype from auto companies. If you use the information in *The Car Book,* there is no reason why your next car shouldn't last at least 100,000 miles. To help make your selection easy, we've completely updated the 19th edition of *The Car Book* with more data and information than ever!

Your continued use of the information in *The Car Book* dramatically influences how car companies build their cars. You are voting with your dollars for safer, better performing and longer lasting cars. As a result, today's cars are better than ever. And you don't have to be afraid to buy American, that is if you can find a truly U.S. built car! Foreign companies are now building cars in the U.S. and traditional domestic companies are selling cars built elsewhere. The distinction between domestic and foreign is now blurred beyond recognition. No better is that exemplified by the recent merger of Chrysler and Mercedes!

The good news is that, after record profits, car makers are finally giving us a break. Many have held the line on prices and some have even lowered them. Republic Industries is out to change the industry by buying auto dealerships, offering non-commissioned sales people and no-haggle pricing. This is putting competitive pressure on the entire industry to change traditional ways of doing business to more consumer friendly transactions.

Since last year's edition, the news has contained stories about people injured by air bags. Particularly tragic are the injuries to children. For the first time, safety advocates, auto makers and government officials are frantically working together to implement the best possible solution: smart airbags.

Unfortunately, we will not see smart airbags until at least next year. Until then, auto makers will be de-powering the passenger-side airbags on their vehicles. Beware - de-powered airbags can still be fatal to out-of-position children (children who are not sitting up straight and properly buckled in). Worse, de-powered airbags lowers the protection for adult passengers.

In other words, always buckle up and put your children in back.

So how do you buy for safety? Many consumers mistakenly be-

What's Really New

TIP Most consumers have a difficult time identifying one car from another or even knowing the cars' model year. In fact, today's cars are really more alike than different. This is the result of two factors: aerodynamic styling and manufacturing efficiencies.

To eke out extra miles per gallon, car companies are designing cars to be less wind resistant. This explains the smooth shapes and rounded styling of the new models. As a result cars are losing the distinctive features that made it easy to tell one from another.

Most people over 45 can remember the Fall introductions when dealers pulled the covers off of the new designs and it was easy to tell which cars were the new models. Today, by keeping essentially the same model car for a number of years, manufacturers dramatically reduce their expenses.

Because of these changes, each year there are very few truly new models. This year, for example, there are only nineteen. While not as true as it used to be, the old adage of not buying a car during its first model year of production is a still a good rule of thumb. This is when the most recalls usually occur and when the manufacturer is subject to the most assembly problems. Hopefully, after building the same model for a year, the manufacturer will have worked most of the bugs out of the process and you'll get a better car.

To help you make a choice based on the car's model age, our Vehicle Pages will tell you how long the car has been in production.

lieve that handling and performance are the key elements in the safety of a car. While an extremely unresponsive car could cause an accident, most new cars meet basic handling requirements. In fact, many people actually feel uncomfortable driving high performance cars because the highly responsive steering, acceleration, and suspension systems can be difficult to get used to. But the main reason handling is overrated as a safety measure is that automobile collisions are, by nature, accidents. Once they've begun, they are beyond human capacity to prevent, no matter how well your car handles. So the key to protecting yourself is to purchase a car that offers a high degree of crash protection.

As our concern for safety has influenced car makers' attitudes, so have our demands for quality. The result-U.S. cars in the '90s continue to be better built than those of the '80s. And, because we're demanding that companies stand behind their products, we're seeing better warranties, too. Since *The Car Book* began comparing warranties in 1986, a number of car makers have told us that they've been forced to improve their warranties now that consumers can tell the difference.

Consumers are learning that they can get better-performing and safer cars by buying the ones with good safety records, low maintenance costs, long warranties, and insurance discounts. Use the "Buying Guide" to compare cars, and read the chapters to learn more about each model. This year, the "Buying Guide" is loaded with new and important information. You'll find everything from crash test results to an ease-of-parking rating.

The "safety" chapter rates crash safety, describes your options for protection, and is where you'll find vital information on airbags, the detailed frontal and side crash test results, tips on avoiding unsafe child seats, and a review of safety belt and child seat laws.

The "fuel economy" chapter uncovers the money-saving gas misers and offers advice on buying "green".

The "maintenance" chapter allows you to compare those inevitable repair costs *before* you buy. You'll also find advice on dealing with mechanics and how to make your car last longer.

The "warranties" chapter offers a critical comparison of the new warranties and lets you know the best and worst before you get into trouble down the road. If you do have trouble, we'll let you know which companies offer roadside assistance and we'll tip you off to secret warranties.

The "insurance" chapter will help you save money on an expense that is often forgotten in the showroom.

Because most of us can't tell one tire from another, we've included the "tire" chapter to help you select the best.

The "complaint" chapter provides a road map to resolving inevitable problems quickly and efficiently. We provide consumers with their only

access to about 300,000 car complaints on file with the U.S. government. Thanks to the efforts of the Center for Auto Safety, we continue to include this otherwise unavailable information.

Review the "showroom strategies" chapter for tips on getting the best price-for many of us one of the hardest and most distasteful aspects of car buying.

Finally, our "ratings" chapter provides a detailed review of each of the 1999 cars and minivans. These pages provide, at a glance, an overview of all the criteria you need to make a good choice. Here, you'll be able to quickly assess key features and see how the car you're interested in stacks up against its competition so you can make sure your selection is the best car for you. Car prices have more than doubled since 1980, so we've also included the percent of *dealer* markup to help you negotiate the very best price.

The information in *The Car Book* is based on data collected and developed by our staff, the U.S. Department of Transportation, and the Center for Auto Safety. With all of this data in hand, you'll find some great choices for 1999. *The Car Book* will guide you through the trade-offs, promises, facts, and myths to the car that will best meet your needs.

—Jack Gillis

Questions, Comments

If you have any suggestions, questions, or comments, you may e-mail us at JAGillis@aol.com

BUYING GUIDE

The Buying Guide provides an overall comparison of the 1999 cars in terms of safety, fuel economy, maintenance, insurance costs, warranty, complaint ratings, and other key items. The cars are arranged by size class based on weight.

Based on these comparisons, we have developed *The Car Book's* Best Bets for 1999—these vehicles rated tops when all of these categories were considered. In general, there are five key steps to buying a car.

1 Narrow your choice down to a particular class of car–sports, station wagon, minivan, sedan, large luxury, or economy car. These are general classifications and some cars may fit into more than one category. In most cases, *The Car Book* presents the vehicles by size class.

2 Determine what features are really important to you. Most buyers consider safety on the top of their list, which is why the "safety" chapter is right up front in *The Car Book*. Airbags, power options, ABS, and the number of passengers, as well as "hidden" elements such as maintenance and insurance costs, should be considered at this stage in your selection process.

3 Find 3 or 4 cars that meet the needs you outlined above *and* your pocketbook. It's important not to narrow your choice down to one car because then you lose all your bargaining power in the showroom. In fact, because cars today are more similar than dissimilar, it's not hard to keep three or four choices in mind. On the car rating pages in the back of the book, we suggest some competitive choices for your consideration. For example, if you are interested in the Honda Accord, you should also consider the Toyota Camry and Ford Taurus.

4 Make sure you take a good, long test drive. The biggest car buying mistake most of us make is to overlook those nagging problems that seem to surface only after we've brought the car home. Spend at least an hour driving the car without a dealer in the car. If a dealership won't allow you to test drive a car without a dealer, go somewhere else. This includes time on the highway, parking, taking the car in and out of your driveway or garage, sitting in the back seat, and using the trunk or storage area. Whatever you do, *don't talk price until you're ready to buy!*

5 This is the stage most of us dread–negotiating the price. While price negotiation is a car buying tradition, a few car makers and dealers are trying to break tradition by offering so called "no-haggle pricing." Since they're still in the minority and, because it's almost impossible to establish true competition between dealers as individuals, we offer a new means to avoid negotiating altogether by using the non-profit CarBargains pricing service.

Now that you have a quick guide to the steps necessary in making a good choice, use the tables that follow to quickly review the new cars and the pages in the back for a detailed critique of each model. See the "showroom strategies" chapter for more details on getting the best price.

Using the Buying Guide

The "Buying Guide" will allow you to quickly compare the 1999 models.

To fully understand these summary charts, it is important to read the appropriate section of the book. You will note that here and throughout the book, some of the charts contain empty boxes. This indicates that data were unavailable at the time of printing.

Here's how to understand what's included in the "Buying Guide."

Page Reference: The page in the back of the book where you'll find all the details for this car.

Overall Rating: This is the "bottom line." It shows how well this car stacks up on a scale of 1 to 10 when compared to all others on the market. The overall rating considers safety, maintenance, fuel economy, warranty, insurance costs and complaints. Due to the importance of crash tests, cars with no results as of our publication date cannot be given an overall rating. More recent results may be available from the Auto Safety Hotline at 1-800-424-9393 (see page 77).

Car Book Crash Test Rating: This indicates how well the car performed in the U.S. Government's 35-mph frontal crash test program. We have analyzed and compared all of the crash test results to date and have given them a rating from *very good* to *very poor*. These ratings allow you to compare the test results of one car with another. A car with a poor rating may have done well according to government injury ratings, but still be among the worst performers of cars being offered in 1999.

Airbags: Here we tell you if the car is equipped with dual and side airbags, dual with optional side airbags, or only dual airbags.

Green Rating: This rating is based on data from the American Council for an Energy-Efficient Economy. It incorporates the fuel economy and the emissions of a vehicle to derive an environmental impact rating.

Fuel Economy: This is the EPA-rated fuel economy for city and highway driving measured in miles per gallon. A single model may have a number of fuel economy ratings because of different engine and transmission options. We have included the figure for what is expected to be the most popular model.

Repair Rating: This rating is based on nine typical repairs after the warranty expires and the cost of following the manufacturer's preventive maintenance schedule during the warranty period.

Warranty Rating: This is an overall assessment of the car's warranty when compared to all other warranties. The rating considers the important features of each warranty, with emphasis on the length of the basic and powertrain warranties.

Best Bets for 1999

Based on information in the *Buying Guide*, this list shows the highest-rated cars in each of the size categories. Ratings are based on expected performance in eight important categories (crash tests, safety features, fuel economy, maintenance and repair costs, warranties, insurance costs, and complaints), with the heaviest emphasis on crash test performance and complaints.

Subcompact
Saturn SL/SW (8)
Nissan Sentra (6)
Subaru Impreza (5)
Suzuki Swift (5)

Compact
Subaru Legacy (7)
Ford Contour (6)
Mercury Mystique (6)

Intermediate
Audi A4 (10)
Lexus ES300 (10)
Volvo S70 (10)
Audi A8 (9)

Intermediate (cont.)
Toyota Avalon (9)
Buick Regal (8)
Ford Taurus (8)
Merc.-Benz C-Class (8)
Mercury Sable (8)

Large
Buick LeSabre (9)
Cadillac DeVille (9)
Chevrolet Lumina (9)
Infiniti I30 (9)

Minivan
Ford Windstar (5)
Pontiac Montana (5)

Complaint Rating: This rating is based on the number of complaints about that car on file at the U.S. Department of Transportation. The complaint index will give you a general idea of experiences others have had with models which are essentially unchanged for this model year. All-new vehicles for 1999 are given an *average* complaint rating as it is unknown how many complaints they will receive.

Insurance Rating: Many automobile insurance companies use ratings based on the car's accident and occupant injury history to determine whether or not the insurance premium of a car should be *discounted* or *surcharged*. (Your insurance company may or may not participate in a rating program.) If the car is likely to receive neither, we label it *regular*.

Parking Index: This rating of *very easy* to *very hard* is an indicator of how much difficulty you will typically have parking. If you regularly parallel park, or find yourself maneuvering in and out of tight spaces, this can be an important factor in your choice of a car. This rating is based on the car's wheelbase, length, and turning circle.

Typical Price: This price range will give you a general idea of the "sticker," or asking price of a car. It is based on the lowest to highest retail price of the various models, and it does not include options or the discount that you should be able to negotiate using a service such as CarBargains (see page 92).

Typical Operating Costs

As you can probably guess, buying a 1999 luxury car rather than an economy model will cost considerably more—not only due to higher initial cost, but also higher fuel, maintenance, tire replacement, insurance and finance costs. Also, higher priced cars often decrease faster in value.

The table below shows the *annual* operating costs for fifteen popular cars. Costs include operating expenses (fuel, oil, maintenance and tires) and ownership expenses (insurance, depreciation, financing, taxes, and licensing) and are based on keeping the car for 3 years, driving 20,000 miles per year.

Annual Costs*

Vehicle	Operating	Ownership	Total
Mercedes 320 S	$2,610	$16,100	$18,710
Lincoln Town Car Exec.	$2,460	$12,404	$14,864
Cadillac DeVille	$2,680	$12,154	$14,834
Oldsmobile Aurora	$2,580	$11,363	$13,943
Buick Riviera	$2,390	$10,557	$12,947
Buick LeSabre Limited	$2,160	$8,443	$10,603
Merc. Grand Marquis GS	$2,450	$7,853	$10,303
Nissan Maxima GXE	$2,190	$7,603	$9,793
Dodge Intrepid	$2,160	$7,168	$9,328
Ford Taurus SE	$2,180	$6,880	$9,060
Chevy Lumina	$2,080	$6,765	$8,845
Toyota Camry CE	$1,820	$5,909	$7,729
Dodge Neon	$1,790	$5,767	$7,557
Honda Accord DX	$2,040	$5,421	$7,461
Chevrolet Metro LSI	$1,550	$5,363	$6,913
Saturn SL2 Sedan	$1,850	$4,906	$6,756

Source: Runzheimer International, Rochester, Wisconsin.
*Costs are based on four-door models, with automatic transmission, power steering, power disc brakes, air conditioning, tinted glass, AM-FM stereo, body side molding, cruise control, left-hand remote control mirror, rear window defogger, pulse windshield wipers, ABS, dual air bags and tilt-steering.

1999 Buying Guide

Car	See Pg.	Overall Rating[1] Poor ⇔ Good	Crash Test	Airbags[2]	Green Rating	Fuel Economy	Repair Rating
Subcompact							
Chevrolet Metro	126		Good	Dual	Good	41/47	Very Poor
Dodge/Plym Neon	139		Good	Dual	Good	28/39	Very Good
Ford Escort	143		Average	Dual	Average	28/37	Very Good
GM EV1	147		Poor	Dual	Very Good	3.3/4.0[4]	N/A
Honda Civic	150		Good	Dual	Very Good	32/37	Good
Honda EV Plus	151		No Test	Dual	Very Good	2.0/2.0[4]	N/A
Hyundai Accent	154		Average	Dual	Average	28/37	Very Good
Kia Sephia	162		Good	Dual	Average	24/31	Average
Mazda Miata	170		No Test	Dual	Average	25/29	Average
Mazda Protegé	172		No Test	Dual	Average	29/34	Poor
Mercury Tracer	179		Average	Dual	Average	28/37	Very Good
Mitsubishi Mirage	184		No Test	Dual	Good	33/40	Average
Nissan Sentra	188		Average	Dual	Average	29/39	Average
Saturn SC	205		No Test	Dual	Good	29/40	Very Good
Saturn SL/SW	206		Very Good	Dual	Good	29/40	Very Good
Subaru Impreza	207		Good	Dual	Average	22/29	Average
Suzuki Esteem	210		No Test	Dual	Good	30/37	Very Poor
Suzuki Swift	211		Good	Dual	Good	39/43	Poor
VW New Beetle	220		No Test	Dual & Side	Average	24/31	Poor
Compact							
Acura Integra	103		Average	Dual	Average	25/32	Poor
BMW 3 Series	109		No Test	Dual & Side[3]	Average	23/32	Poor
BMW Z3	111		No Test	Dual & Side	Average	19/26	Poor
Chevrolet Cavalier	123		Good	Dual	Average	24/34	Good
Chevrolet Prizm	128		Good	Dual/Opt. Side	Average	31/37	Poor
Chrysler Sebring	134		Very Good	Dual	Average	22/31	Good
Dodge Avenger	136		Very Good	Dual	Poor	22/32	Good
Ford Contour	141		Very Good	Dual	Average	24/34	Good
Honda Prelude	153		No Test	Dual	Poor	22/27	Average
Hyundai Elantra	155		No Test	Dual	Average	24/33	Very Good
Hyundai Tiburon	157		No Test	Dual	Average	22/31	Very Good
Infiniti G20	158		No Test	Dual & Side	Poor	23/31	Poor
Mazda 626	169		No Test	Dual	Average	26/33	Good

[1]Due to the importance of crash tests, cars with no crash test results as of publication date cannot be given an overall rating.
[2]Underline denotes next generation, de-powered airbags. [3]Rear side opt. [4]Values given in miles per kilowatt hour.

Warranty	Complaint Rating	Insurance Rating	Parking Index	Typical Price $	Overall Rating* Poor ⟺ Good	See Pg.	Car
							Subcompact
Very Poor	Average	Very Poor	Very Easy	8-11,000		126	Chevrolet Metro
Very Poor	Poor	Very Poor	Easy	11-12,000		139	Dodge/Plym Neon
Very Poor	Average	Very Poor	Very Easy	11-15,000		143	Ford Escort
Poor	Average	Average	Very Easy	33-34,000		147	GM EV1
Very Poor	Good	Very Poor	Very Easy	10-15,000		150	Honda Civic
Very Poor	Average	Average	Very Easy	53-54,000		151	Honda EV Plus
Average	Poor	Very Poor	Very Easy	9-12,000		154	Hyundai Accent
Average	Average	Very Poor	Very Easy	9-11,000		162	Kia Sephia
Poor	Average	Average	Very Easy	19-20,000		170	Mazda Miata
Poor	Average	Average	Very Easy	12-16,000		172	Mazda Protegé
Very Poor	Poor	Very Poor	Very Easy	11-15,000		179	Mercury Tracer
Average	Very Poor	Very Poor	Very Easy	11-15,000		184	Mitsubishi Mirage
Poor	Very Good	Very Poor	Very Easy	11-17,000		188	Nissan Sentra
Poor	Average	Very Poor	Easy	11-16,000		205	Saturn SC
Poor	Average	Average	Easy	10-15,000		206	Saturn SL/SW
Poor	Good	Very Poor	Very Easy	15-20,000		207	Subaru Impreza
Very Poor	Average	Very Poor	Very Easy	12-24,000		210	Suzuki Esteem
Very Poor	Very Good	Very Poor	Very Easy	9-10,000		211	Suzuki Swift
Very Good	Average	Average	Very Easy	15-17,000		220	VW New Beetle
							Compact
Average	Very Good	Very Poor	Very Easy	16-22,000		103	Acura Integra
Good	Average	Average	Easy	23-35,000		109	BMW 3 Series
Good	Good	Very Good	Very Easy	29-43,000		111	BMW Z3
Very Poor	Good	Average	Easy	11-15,000		123	Chevrolet Cavalier
Very Poor	Average	Very Poor	Very Easy	12-15,000		128	Chevrolet Prizm
Very Poor	Very Poor	Very Poor	Hard	17-27,000		134	Chrysler Sebring
Very Poor	Poor	Very Poor	Hard	15-18,000		136	Dodge Avenger
Very Poor	Average	Average	Easy	14-23,000		141	Ford Contour
Very Poor	Very Good	Very Poor	Easy	23-26,000		153	Honda Prelude
Average	Very Poor	Very Poor	Very Easy	11-14,000		155	Hyundai Elantra
Average	Very Poor	Average	Very Easy	13-16,000		157	Hyundai Tiburon
Very Good	Average	Average	Easy	20-24,000		158	Infiniti G20
Poor	Average	Very Poor	Easy	15-24,000		169	Mazda 626

[1] Due to the importance of crash tests, cars with no crash test results as of publication date cannot be given an overall rating.

Car	See Pg.	Overall Rating[1] (Poor ⇔ Good)	Crash Test	Airbags[2]	Green Rating	Fuel Economy	Repair Rating
Compact (cont.)							
Mercury Mystique	177		Very Good	Dual	Average	24/34	Good
Mitsubishi Eclipse	182		Good	Dual	Average	22/33	Good
Mitsubishi Galant	183		No Test	Dual/Opt. Side	Average	23/31	Very Good
Oldsmobile Alero	190		No Test	Dual	Poor	22/30	Average
Pontiac Grand Am	199		No Test	Dual	Average	22/30	Average
Pontiac Sunfire	202		Good	Dual	Average	24/34	Good
Subaru Legacy	208		Good	Dual	Average	22/29	Average
Toyota Celica	214		No Test	Dual	Average	22/28	Poor
Toyota Corolla	215		Good	Dual/Opt. Side	Average	31/38	Poor
Volkswagen Golf	218		No Test	Dual/Opt. Side	Average	24/31	Average
Volkswagen Jetta	219		No Test	Dual/Opt. Side	Average	24/31	Average
Intermediate							
Audi A4	106		Very Good	Dual & Side	Poor	23/32	Very Poor
Audi A8	108		Very Good	Dual & Side[3]	Very Poor	17/26	Very Poor
Buick Century	112		Good	Dual	Poor	20/29	Good
Buick Regal	115		Good	Dual	Poor	19/30	Good
Cadillac Catera	117		No Test	Dual	Very Poor	18/24	Very Poor
Chevrolet Camaro	122		Very Good	Dual	Poor	19/30	Poor
Chrysler 300M	130		No Test	Dual	Very Poor	18/27	N/A
Chrysler Cirrus	131		Average	Dual	Poor	19/27	Good
Chrysler Concorde	132		No Test	Dual	Poor	21/30	Very Good
Dodge Intrepid	138		No Test	Dual	Poor	21/30	Very Good
Dodge Stratus	140		Average	Dual	Average	26/37	Very Good
Ford Mustang	144		Very Good	Dual	Poor	20/29	Good
Ford Taurus	145		Very Good	Dual	Poor	20/28	Good
Honda Accord	149		Gd. (2dr/4dr)	Dual	Average	25/31	Average
Hyundai Sonata	156		Average	Dual	Poor	21/30	Good
Lexus ES300	163		Good	Dual & Side	Poor	19/26	Poor
Mazda Millenia	171		Very Good	Dual	Poor	20/28	Very Poor
Merc-Benz C-Class	173		Good	Dual & Side	Poor	21/27	Very Poor
Mercury Sable	178		Very Good	Dual	Poor	20/28	Very Good
Nissan Altima	185		Poor	Dual	Average	24/31	Average
Nissan Maxima	186		Good	Dual/Opt. Side	Poor	22/27	Very Poor

[1] Due to the importance of crash tests, cars with no crash test results as of publication date cannot be given an overall rating.
[2] Underline denotes next generation, de-powered airbags. [3] Side airbags for rear occupants also standard on the A8.

Warranty	Complaint Rating	Insurance Rating	Parking Index	Typical Price $	Overall Rating[1] Poor ⇔ Good	See Pg.	Car
							Compact (cont.)
Very Poor	Poor	Average	Average	16-18,000		177	Mercury Mystique
Average	Very Poor	Very Poor	Easy	15-27,000		182	Mitsubishi Eclipse
Average	Average	Average	Easy	16-25,000		183	Mitsubishi Galant
Poor	Average	Average	Easy	16-19,000		190	Oldsmobile Alero
Very Poor	Average	Average	Average	15-20,000		199	Pontiac Grand Am
Very Poor	Good	Very Poor	Easy	12-20,000		202	Pontiac Sunfire
Poor	Good	Average	Easy	19-24,000		208	Subaru Legacy
Poor	Very Good	Very Poor	Very Easy	20-25,000		214	Toyota Celica
Poor	Average	Very Poor	Very Easy	12-15,000		215	Toyota Corolla
Very Good	Average	Average	Very Easy	13-21,000		218	Volkswagen Golf
Very Good	Average	Average	Very Easy	14-21,000		219	Volkswagen Jetta
							Intermediate
Very Good	Good	Average	Easy	23-32,000		106	Audi A4
Very Good	Average	Average	Hard	57-65,000		108	Audi A8
Very Poor	Average	Very Good	Average	18-20,000		112	Buick Century
Very Poor	Good	Very Good	Average	21-24,000		115	Buick Regal
Good	Poor	Average	Easy	29-30,000		117	Cadillac Catera
Very Poor	Poor	Very Poor	Hard	16-28,000		122	Chevrolet Camaro
Very Poor	Average	Average	Average	28-29,000		130	Chrysler 300M
Very Poor	Very Poor	Average	Average	19-20,000		131	Chrysler Cirrus
Very Poor	Average	Very Good	Hard	21-22,000		132	Chrysler Concorde
Very Poor	Average	Very Good	Hard	19-23,000		138	Dodge Intrepid
Very Poor	Poor	Average	Easy	15-19,000		140	Dodge Stratus
Very Poor	Good	Very Poor	Easy	16-25,000		144	Ford Mustang
Very Poor	Average	Very Good	Average	17-29,000		145	Ford Taurus
Very Poor	Average	Very Good	Easy	15-22,000		149	Honda Accord
Average	Poor	Very Poor	Easy	14-18,000		156	Hyundai Sonata
Good	Very Good	Very Good	Easy	30-31,000		163	Lexus ES300
Poor	Very Good	Average	Average	28-37,000		171	Mazda Millenia
Poor	Very Good	Very Good	Easy	31-53,000		173	Merc-Benz C-Class
Very Poor	Average	Very Good	Hard	18-21,000		178	Mercury Sable
Poor	Average	Very Poor	Easy	14-20,000		185	Nissan Altima
Poor	Very Good	Very Poor	Easy	21-27,000		186	Nissan Maxima

[1]Due to the importance of crash tests, cars with no crash test results as of publication date cannot be given an overall rating.

Car	See Pg.	Overall Rating[1] Poor ⇔ Good	Crash Test	Airbags[2]	Green Rating	Fuel Economy	Repair Rating
Intermediate (cont.)							
Oldsmobile Cutlass	192		Good	Dual	Average	22/30	Good
Oldsmobile Intrigue	193		Average	Dual	Poor	19/27	Very Good
Plymouth Breeze	195		Average	Dual	Average	26/37	Very Good
Pontiac Firebird	198		Very Good	Dual	Poor	19/30	Average
Pontiac Grand Prix	200		Good	Dual	Poor	20/29	Good
Saab 9-3	203		No Test	Dual & Side	Very Poor	20/27	Very Poor
Saab 9-5	204		No Test	Dual & Side	Poor	21/30	Very Poor
Subaru Outback	209		No Test	Dual	Average	22/29	Average
Toyota Avalon	212		Very Good	Dual & Side	Average	21/29	Poor
Toyota Camry	213		Very Good	Dual & Side	Average	23/32	Poor
Toyota Solara	217		No Test	Dual/Opt. Side	Poor	23/32	Poor
VW Passat	221		No Test	Dual & Side	Average	23/32	Poor
Volvo S70	222		Very Good	Dual & Side[3]	Poor	20/28	Average
Volvo S80	223		No Test	Dual & Side	Very Poor	18/27	Average
Large							
Acura CL	102		No Test	Dual	Poor	24/31	Average
Acura RL	104		No Test	Dual & Side	Poor	18/24	Very Poor
Acura TL	105		No Test	Dual	Poor	19/27	Very Poor
Audi A6	107		No Test	Dual & Side	Poor	17/27	Very Poor
BMW 5 Series	110		No Test	Dual & Side	Poor	20/29	Poor
Buick LeSabre	113		Good	Dual	Poor	19/30	Very Good
Buick Park Avenue	114		Average	Dual	Poor	19/28	Very Good
Buick Riviera	116		Average	Dual	Poor	18/27	Good
Cadillac DeVille	118		Very Good	Dual & Side	Very Poor	17/26	Very Poor
Cadillac Eldorado	119		No Test	Dual	Very Poor	17/26	Very Poor
Cadillac Seville	120		Average	Dual & Side	Very Poor	17/26	Very Poor
Chevrolet Lumina	124		Very Good	Dual	Poor	20/29	Good
Chevrolet Malibu	125		Good	Dual	Average	22/30	Very Poor
Chev. Monte Carlo	127		Very Good	Dual	Poor	20/29	Good
Chrysler LHS	133		No Test	Dual	Very Poor	18/27	Very Good
Ford Crown Victoria	142		Very Good	Dual	Average	17/24	Average
Infiniti I30	159		Good	Dual & Side	Poor	21/26	Very Poor
Infiniti Q45	160		No Test	Dual & Side	Very Poor	17/24	Very Poor

[1] Due to the importance of crash tests, cars with no crash test results as of publication date cannot be given an overall rating.
[2] Underline denotes next generation, de-powered airbags. [3] New style.

Warranty	Complaint Rating	Insurance Rating	Parking Index	Typical Price $	Overall Rating[1] Poor ⇔ Good	See Pg.	Car
							Intermediate (cont.)
Poor	Very Poor	Very Good	Easy	17-20,000		192	Oldsmobile Cutlass
Poor	Average	Average	Average	20-25,000		193	Oldsmobile Intrigue
Very Poor	Good	Average	Easy	14-15,000		195	Plymouth Breeze
Very Poor	Average	Very Poor	Average	18-26,000		198	Pontiac Firebird
Very Poor	Poor	Very Good	Average	18-21,000		200	Pontiac Grand Prix
Good	Average	Average	Easy	25-42,000		203	Saab 9-3
Good	Average	Average	Easy	29-37,000		204	Saab 9-5
Poor	Good	Average	Easy	22-24,000		209	Subaru Outback
Poor	Very Good	Very Good	Average	24-29,000		212	Toyota Avalon
Poor	Average	Average	Easy	17-25,000		213	Toyota Camry
Poor	Average	Average	Average	18-25,000		217	Toyota Solara
Very Good	Average	Very Good	Average	21-31,000		221	VW Passat
Very Good	Average	Very Good	Average	26-39,000		222	Volvo S70
Very Good	Average	Average	Easy	35-41,000		223	Volvo S80
							Large
Average	Good	Average	Hard	22-23,000		102	Acura CL
Average	Very Good	Very Good	Average	41-42,000		104	Acura RL
Average	Average	Average	Average	30-34,000		105	Acura TL
Very Good	Average	Very Good	Average	33-37,000		107	Audi A6
Good	Average	Average	Average	38-53,000		110	BMW 5 Series
Very Poor	Good	Very Good	Very Hard	22-26,000		113	Buick LeSabre
Very Poor	Poor	Very Good	Hard	30-36,000		114	Buick Park Avenue
Very Poor	Average	Very Good	Hard	32-33,000		116	Buick Riviera
Good	Good	Very Good	Very Hard	37-43,000		118	Cadillac DeVille
Good	Poor	Very Good	Hard	38-43,000		119	Cadillac Eldorado
Good	Average	Very Good	Very Hard	42-49,000		120	Cadillac Seville
Very Poor	Very Good	Very Good	Average	17-20,000		124	Chevrolet Lumina
Very Poor	Poor	Very Good	Easy	15-19,000		125	Chevrolet Malibu
Very Poor	Average	Average	Average	17-21,000		127	Chevrolet Monte Carlo
Very Poor	Average	Average	Hard	28-29,000		133	Chrysler LHS
Very Poor	Poor	Very Good	Very Hard	21-24,000		142	Ford Crown Victoria
Very Good	Very Good	Average	Easy	28-33,000		159	Infiniti I30
Very Good	Very Good	Very Good	Average	47-50,000		160	Infiniti Q45

[1]Due to the importance of crash tests, cars with no crash test results as of publication date cannot be given an overall rating.

Car	See Pg.	Overall Rating[1] Poor ⇔ Good	Crash Test	Airbags[2]	Green Rating	Fuel Economy	Repair Rating
Large (cont.)							
Lexus GS300/400	164		No Test	Dual & Side	Poor	20/25	Poor
Lexus LS400	165		No Test	Dual & Side	Poor	18/25	Very Poor
Lexus SC300/400	166		No Test	Dual	Poor	19/24	Poor
Lincoln Continental	167		No Test	Dual & Side	Very Poor	17/25	Poor
Lincoln Town Car	168		No Test	Dual & Side	Poor	17/24	Very Poor
Merc-Benz E-Class	174		No Test	Dual & Side	Poor	21/30	Very Poor
Mercury Cougar	175		No Test	Dual	Poor	24/34	Poor
Merc. Grand Marquis	176		Very Good	Dual	Poor	17/24	Very Poor
Mitsubishi Diamante	181		No Test	Dual	Poor	18/24	Very Poor
Oldsmobile 88	189		Good	Dual	Poor	19/29	Very Good
Oldsmobile Aurora	191		Average	Dual	Very Poor	17/26	Average
Pontiac Bonneville	197		Good	Dual	Poor	19/28	Very Good
Minivan							
Chevrolet Astro	121		Poor	Dual	Very Poor	16/21	Good
Chevrolet Venture	129		Good	Dual & Side	Very Poor	18/25	Average
Chrys. Town and Cntry	135		Good	Dual	Very Poor	18/24	Very Good
Dodge Caravan	137		Good	Dual	Average	20/26	Very Good
Ford Windstar	146		Very Good	Dual	Very Poor	17/23	Average
GMC Safari	148		Poor	Dual	Very Poor	16/21	Good
Honda Odyssey	152		No Test	Dual	Poor	18/26	Poor
Isuzu Oasis	161		No Test	Dual	Poor	21/26	Poor
Mercury Villager	180		No Test	Dual	Very Poor	17/24	Average
Nissan Quest	187		No Test	Dual	Very Poor	17/24	Average
Oldsmobile Silhouette	194		Good	Dual & Side	Very Poor	18/25	Average
Plymouth Voyager	196		Good	Dual	Very Poor	20/26	Very Good
Pontiac Montana	201		Good	Dual & Side	Very Poor	18/25	Average
Toyota Sienna	216		Very Good	Dual	Very Poor	18/24	Very Poor

[1]Due to the importance of crash tests, cars with no crash test results as of publication date cannot be given an overall rating.
[2]Underline denotes next generation, de-powered airbags.

Warranty	Complaint Rating	Insurance Rating	Parking Index	Typical Price $	Overall Rating[1] Poor ⇔ Good	See Pg.	Car
							Large (cont.)
Good	Average	Very Good	Average	36-45,000		164	Lexus GS300/400
Good	Very Good	Very Good	Easy	53-54,000		165	Lexus LS400
Good	Good	Very Poor	Easy	41-53,000		166	Lexus SC300/400
Average	Average	Very Good	Very Hard	38-39,000		167	Lincoln Continental
Average	Average	Very Good	Very Hard	38-43,000		168	Lincoln Town Car
Poor	Very Good	Very Good	Average	46-52,000		174	Merc-Benz E-Class
Very Poor	Average	Average	Easy	16-17,000		175	Mercury Cougar
Very Poor	Average	Very Good	Very Hard	22-25,000		176	Merc. Grand Marquis
Average	Very Poor	Average	Average	27-34,000		181	Mitsubishi Diamante
Poor	Good	Very Good	Very Hard	22-25,000		189	Oldsmobile 88
Good	Average	Very Good	Very Hard	36-37,000		191	Oldsmobile Aurora
Very Poor	Good	Very Good	Hard	22-30,000		197	Pontiac Bonneville
							Minivan
Very Poor	Average	Very Good	Average	19-21,000		121	Chevrolet Astro
Very Poor	Very Poor	Very Good	Average	20-23,000		129	Chevrolet Venture
Very Poor	Very Poor	Very Good	Average	30-35,000		135	Chrys. Town and Cntry
Very Poor	Very Poor	Very Good	Average	17-23,000		137	Dodge Caravan
Very Poor	Very Poor	Very Good	Very Hard	20-30,000		146	Ford Windstar
Very Poor	Poor	Very Good	Hard	19-23,000		148	GMC Safari
Very Poor	Average	Average	Hard	23-26,000		152	Honda Odyssey
Good	Good	Average	Average	23-26,000		161	Isuzu Oasis
Very Poor	Average	Average	Hard	22-26,000		180	Mercury Villager
Poor	Average	Average	Hard	23-27,000		187	Nissan Quest
Poor	Very Poor	Very Good	Average	24-31,000		194	Oldsmobile Silhouette
Very Poor	Very Poor	Very Good	Average	17-23,000		196	Plymouth Voyager
Very Poor	Poor	Very Good	Hard	20-24,000		201	Pontiac Montana
Poor	Average	Average	Hard	21-28,000		216	Toyota Sienna

[1]Due to the importance of crash tests, cars with no crash test results as of publication date cannot be given an overall rating.

Corporate Twins

"Corporate twin" is a term for similar cars sold under different names. In many cases, the cars are identical, such as the Dodge and Plymouth Neon. Sometimes the difference is in body style and luxury items, as with the Buick Regal and Pontiac Grand Prix. Generally, twins have the same mechanics, engine, drive train, size, weight, and internal workings. In addition to corporate twins, there are what we call "Asian cousins." These are Asian imports marketed under a U.S. name. In most cases, the main difference is the name plate and price; sometimes you will find differences in style.

Twins

Chrysler

Dodge Caravan
Plymouth Voyager

Chrysler Town & Country
Dodge Grand Caravan
Plymouth Grand Voyager

Chrysler Cirrus
Dodge Stratus
Plymouth Breeze

Chrysler Concorde
Dodge Intrepid

Chrysler Sebring
Dodge Avenger

Dodge Neon
Plymouth Neon

Volkswagen
VW Golf
VW Jetta

Toyota
Lexus ES 300
Toyota Camry

Nissan
Infiniti I30
Nissan Maxima

Infiniti G20
Nissan Sentra

Ford

Ford Crown Victoria
Lincoln Town Car
Mercury Grand Marquis

Ford Taurus
Mercury Sable

Ford Escort
Mercury Tracer

Ford Contour
Mercury Mystique

General Motors

Buick Park Avenue
Buick Riviera
Cadillac Seville
Oldsmobile Aurora

Buick LeSabre
Oldsmobile 88
Pontiac Bonneville

Chevrolet Astro
GMC Safari

Chevrolet Camaro
Pontiac Firebird

Chevrolet Cavalier
Pontiac Sunfire

Buick Century
Buick Regal
Pontiac Grand Prix

Chevrolet Venture
Oldsmobile Silhouette
Pontiac Montana

Chevrolet Lumina
Chevrolet Monte Carlo

Chevrolet Malibu
Oldsmobile Cutlass

Oldsmobile Alero
Pontiac Grand Am

Asian Cousins

Chevrolet Metro-*Suzuki Swift*
Chevrolet Prizm-*Toyota Corolla*
Mercury Villager-*Nissan Quest*

SAFETY

For most of us, safety is one of the most important factors in choosing a new car, yet it is one of the most difficult items to evaluate. To provide the greatest possible protection, a car should have a variety of safety features including dual airbags, side airbags, safety belt adjusters and pretensioners, 4-wheel anti-lock brakes (ABS) and built-in child safety seats.

Another key factor in occupant protection is how well the car performs in a crash test. In order for you to easily use the government crash tests, we have analyzed the results and presented them in a easy-to-understand format. In the past, crash tests have measured protection in a frontal crash. The government is now testing the performance of cars in *side* crash tests. Where available, we have included these results on the following charts.

Also in this chapter, you'll find a review of the current safety features in this year's models including ABS and a state-by-state list of the safety belt and child restraint laws. We also provide a detailed look at an important, and often overlooked, safety feature—the child safety seat. Our section on children and airbags is a must-read for any parent.

Crash Test Program: In 1979, the U.S. Department of Transportation began a crash test program to compare the occupant protection of cars called the New Car Assessment Program. These crash tests show significant differences in how well various vehicles protect belted occupants in crashes.

In the frontal crash test, an automobile is sent forward into a concrete barrier at 35-mph, causing an impact similar to two identical cars crashing head on at 35-mph. The car contains electronically monitored dummies in the driver and passenger seats. This electronic data is analyzed to measure the impact of such a collision on a human being.

For the new side crash tests, a moving barrier is smashed into the vehicle on both sides at 38.5-mph. This test simulates a typical intersection collision between two vehicles. The dummies in the side crash tests are also electronically monitored and the data collected measures the impact on a human being.

Note that in both crash tests, the dummies are securely belted. Therefore, these test results do not apply to unbelted occupants.

To make it easy for you to use this important data to compare vehicles, we have analyzed and presented the results using our *Car Book Crash Test Index*. Using this Index, you can easily compare the crash test performance among vehicles.

It is best to compare the results within the same weight class, such as compacts to compacts. Do not compare cars with differing weights. For example, a subcompact that is rated "Good" may not be as safe as a large car with the same rating.

We rate the crash test results of each car relative to all of the cars ever crash tested to give you a better idea of the true top performers among the '98 models and identify those cars which have room for improvement.

The Car Book's crash test rating is intended to stimulate competition. You, the buyer, now know which are the best performers. Manufacturers who have chosen to build better performing cars will likely be rewarded with your decision to purchase their models.

1999 cars missing from this list have not been tested at the time of printing.

Crash Tests: How the Cars Are Rated

A car's ability to protect you in a crash depends on its ability to absorb the force of impact rather than transfer it to the occupant. This is a function of the car's size, weight and, most importantly, design. Frontal and side crash tests measure the amount of crash forces transferred to the head, chest and legs of occupants in a 35-mph (frontal) or 38.5-mph (side) crash.

The table on the following pages indicate how this year's cars can be expected to perform in crash tests. They are listed by weight class, then alphabetically by manufacturer. We only included a vehicle if its design has not changed enough to dramatically alter previous results. Twins that are structurally the same, like the Dodge Caravan and Plymouth Voyager, can be expected to perform similarly.

The first column provides *The Car Book*'s overall Crash Test Index. This number represents all the forces measured by the test. Lower index numbers are better. The Index is best used to compare cars within the same size and weight class.

The second column provides an overall rating of *Very Good*, *Good*, *Average*, *Poor*, or *Very Poor*. These reflect the car's performance compared to all other models ever tested. The overall crash test ratings let you compare, at a glance, the performance of the cars you'll find in the showroom.

The next two columns indicate the likelihood of each occupant sustaining a life-threatening injury, based on the dummies' head and chest scores. Lower percentages mean a lower likelihood of being seriously injured. This information is taken directly from the government's analysis of the crash test results.

The last two columns indicate how the dummies' legs fared in the crash test. Legs labeled *Poor* did not meet the government's standards. Those that did meet the standards are rated *Moderate*, *Good*, and *Very Good*, reflecting performance relative to all other cars ever tested. The leg injury ratings are not weighted as heavily as the head and chest in determining overall performance.

Crash test results may vary due to differences in the way cars are manufactured, in how models are equipped, and in test conditions. There is no absolute guarantee that a car which passed the test will adequately protect you in an accident. Keep in mind that some two-door models may not perform exactly like their four-door counterparts.

Crash Tests: The Best

Here is a list of the best crash test performers among the 1999 cars for which crash test information is available. Lower Crash Test Index numbers indicate better performance. See the following tables for more results.

Front Tests

Subcompact
Honda Civic 2dr. (2344)
Saturn SL/SW (2524)

Compact
Chrysler Sebring (1760)
Dodge Avenger (1760)
Ford Contour (2536)
Mercury Mystique (2536)

Minivan
Ford Windstar (1671)
Toyota Sienna (1863)

Intermediate
Chevrolet Camaro (1783)
Pontiac Firebird (1783)

Intermediate (cont.)
Volvo S70 (1794)
Ford Mustang Conv. (1915)
Ford Taurus (1992)
Mercury Sable (1992)
Ford Mustang (2046)
Toyota Camry (2057)
Mazda Millenia (2084)
Toyota Avalon (2291)
Audi A4 (2385)

Large
Ford Crown Victoria (1832)
Mercury Grand Marquis (1832)
Chevrolet Lumina (2491)
Cadillac DeVille (2515)

Side Tests*

Compact
Ford Contour (1540)
Mercury Mystique (1540)

Intermediate
Lexus ES300 (1282)

Large
Cadillac DeVille (1196)
Ford Crown Victoria (1484)
Mercury Grand Marquis (1484)

*No scores for subcompacts or minivans rated above good.

Crash Test Performance		Crash Test Index	Car Book Rating	Likelihood of Life Threatening Injury		Leg Injury Rating	
				Driver	Passenger	Driver	Passenger
Subcompact							
Chevrolet Metro	FRONT	3080	Good	15	16	Moderate	Good
Dodge /Plymouth Neon	FRONT	3424	Good	22	15	Good	Good
Ford Escort	FRONT	4389	Average	31	18	Moderate	Good
	SIDE	2733	Average	18	14	Moderate	Good
GM EV1	FRONT	4642	Poor	21	35	Very Good	Very Good
Honda Civic 2dr	FRONT	2344	Very Good	11	12	Good	Good
	SIDE	2979	Average	22	14	Good	Good
Honda Civic 4dr	FRONT	3148	Good	16	18	Good	Good
	SIDE	2557	Average	15	14	Moderate	Poor
Hyundai Accent	FRONT	3764	Average	30	12	Good	Good
Kia Sephia	FRONT	3418	Good	19	15	Moderate	Moderate
Mercury Tracer (Escort)	FRONT	4389	Average	31	18	Moderate	Good
	SIDE	2733	Average	18	14	Moderate	Good
Nissan Sentra	FRONT	3546	Average	22	19	Very Good	Very Good
	SIDE	3153	Average	19	18	Moderate	Good
Saturn SL/SW	FRONT	2524	Very Good	13	13	Very Good	Good
	SIDE	3158	Average	18	19	Moderate	Good
Subaru Impreza	FRONT	2930	Good	15	17	Very Good	Good
Suzuki Swift (Metro)	FRONT	3080	Good	15	16	Moderate	Good
Toyota Tercel 2dr	FRONT	3155	Good	15	20	Very Good	Good
Toyota Tercel 4dr	FRONT	3705	Average	24	17	Good	Good
Compact							
Acura Integra	FRONT	3543	Average	16	21	Moderate	Good
Chevrolet Cavalier 2dr	FRONT	3313	Good	22	14	Good	Good
	SIDE	5496	Very Poor	49	22	Moderate	Good

Parentheses indicate actual model tested. *A version of this vehicle is scheduled to be tested later this year. Results are expected to be similar.

HOW TO READ THE CHARTS:

| 1234 | **Crash Test Index** is the overall numerical injury rating for front occupants in a frontal and side crash. *Lower numbers mean better performance.*

| 00% | **Likelihood of Life Threatening Injury** is the chance that the occupants would be seriously injured in a frontal and side crash. *Lower percentages mean better performance.*

| Very Good | **Car Book Rating** shows how the vehicle compares among all cars tested to date. The range is very good, good, average, poor and very poor.

| Good | **Leg Injury Rating** compares occupant leg protection in a frontal and side crash for all cars tested to date.

Note: Side crash ratings are included when available.

Crash Test Performance		Crash Test Index	Car Book Rating	Likelihood of Life Threatening Injury		Leg Injury Rating	
				Driver	Passenger	Driver	Passenger
Compact (cont.)							
Chevrolet Cavalier 4dr	FRONT	3248	Good	17	17	Good	Good
	SIDE	3857	Poor	31	15	Poor	Moderate
Chevrolet Prizm	FRONT	2735	Good	15	13	Good	Good
	SIDE	2381	Good	14	14	Moderate	Good
Chrysler Sebring (Avenger)	FRONT	1760	Very Good	9	6	Good	Moderate
Dodge Avenger	FRONT	1760	Very Good	9	6	Good	Moderate
Ford Contour	FRONT	2536	Very Good	10	15	Good	Good
	SIDE	1540	Very Good	11	6	Good	Good
Hyundai Elantra	FRONT	4467	Average	21	29	Good	Moderate
	SIDE	5083	Very Poor	18	46	Moderate	Good
Mazda 626	SIDE	2557	Average	14	16	Poor	Good
Mercury Mystique (Contour)	FRONT	2536	Very Good	10	15	Good	Good
	SIDE	1540	Very Good	11	6	Good	Good
Mitsubishi Eclipse	FRONT	3012	Good	18	13	Good	Good
	SIDE	—	—	48	—	Moderate	—
Pontiac Sunfire 2dr (Cavalier)	FRONT	3313	Good	22	14	Good	Good
	SIDE	5496	Very Poor	49	22	Moderate	Good
Pontiac Sunfire 4dr (Cavalier)	FRONT	3248	Good	17	17	Good	Good
	SIDE	3857	Poor	31	15	Poor	Moderate
Subaru Legacy	FRONT	2804	Good	15	15	Very Good	Good
	SIDE	—	—	18	—	Poor	—
Toyota Corolla	FRONT	2735	Good	15	13	Good	Good
	SIDE	2381	Good	14	14	Moderate	Good

Parentheses indicate actual model tested.
*A version of this vehicle is scheduled to be tested later this year. Results are expected to be similar.

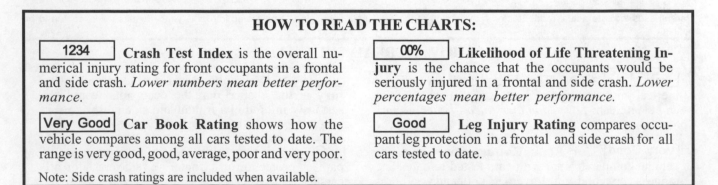

HOW TO READ THE CHARTS:

1234 **Crash Test Index** is the overall numerical injury rating for front occupants in a frontal and side crash. *Lower numbers mean better performance.*

Very Good **Car Book Rating** shows how the vehicle compares among all cars tested to date. The range is very good, good, average, poor and very poor.

Note: Side crash ratings are included when available.

00% **Likelihood of Life Threatening Injury** is the chance that the occupants would be seriously injured in a frontal and side crash. *Lower percentages mean better performance.*

Good **Leg Injury Rating** compares occupant leg protection in a frontal and side crash for all cars tested to date.

Crash Test Performance		Crash Test Index	Car Book Rating	Likelihood of Life Threatening Injury		Leg Injury Rating	
				Driver	Passenger	Driver	Passenger
Intermediate							
Audi A4	FRONT	2385	Very Good	14	9	Good	Good
Audi A8	FRONT	1845	Very Good	10	8	Good	Good
Buick Century (Grand Prix)	FRONT	3194	Good	20	14	Good	Good
	SIDE	2814	Average	15	18	Moderate	Good
Buick Regal (Grand Prix)	FRONT	3194	Good	20	14	Good	Good
	SIDE	2814	Average	15	18	Moderate	Good
Chevrolet Camaro	FRONT	1783	Very Good	11	7	Very Good	Good
	SIDE	2345	Good	17	10	Good	Moderate
Chrysler Cirrus (Stratus)	FRONT	3901	Average	25	19	Good	Good
	SIDE	3094	Average	12	25	Moderate	Good
Dodge Stratus	FRONT	3901	Average	25	19	Good	Good
	SIDE	3094	Average	12	25	Moderate	Good
Ford Mustang	FRONT	2046	Very Good	9	11	Good	Good
	SIDE	2561	Average	18	12	Good	Very Good
Ford Mustang Convertible	FRONT	1915	Very Good	9	8	Good	Good
Ford Taurus	FRONT	1992	Very Good	11	9	Very Good	Good
	SIDE	2429	Good	11	17	Good	Good
Honda Accord 2dr	FRONT	2688	Good	15	15	Very Good	Very Good
Honda Accord 4dr	FRONT	2880	Good	16	17	Very Good	Very Good
	SIDE	1595	Good	9	8	Very Good	Very Good
Hyundai Sonata	FRONT	4034	Average	25	20	Moderate	Good
	SIDE	4235	Very Poor	29	24	Moderate	Good
Lexus ES300	FRONT	2521	Good	14	13	Good	Very Good
	SIDE	1282	Very Good	6	8	Moderate	Good
Mazda Millenia	FRONT	2084	Very Good	11	8	Good	Good
Mercedes-Benz C-Class	FRONT	3420	Good	18	19	Good	Good
Mercury Sable (Taurus)	FRONT	1992	Very Good	11	9	Very Good	Good
	SIDE	2429	Good	11	17	Good	Good
Nissan Altima	FRONT	4869	Poor	23	36	Very Good	Good
	SIDE	3012	Average	18	18	Good	Good
Nissan Maxima	FRONT	3174	Good	14	19	Good	Good
	SIDE	1856	Good	9	11	Good	Good
Oldsmobile Cutlass (Malibu)	FRONT	2633	Good	13	14	Good	Good
	SIDE	3699	Poor	27	18	Moderate	Good

Parentheses indicate actual model tested.
*A version of this vehicle is scheduled to be tested later this year. Results are expected to be similar.

Crash Test Performance		Crash Test Index	Car Book Rating	Likelihood of Life Threatening Injury		Leg Injury Rating	
				Driver	Passenger	Driver	Passenger
Intermediate (cont.)							
Oldsmobile Intrigue	FRONT	4168	Average	14	34	Good	Good
	SIDE	4469	Very Poor	16	39	Good	Very Good
Plymouth Breeze (Stratus)	FRONT	3901	Average	25	19	Good	Good
	SIDE	3094	Average	12	25	Moderate	Good
Pontiac Firebird (Camaro)	FRONT	1783	Very Good	11	7	Very Good	Very Good
	SIDE	2345	Good	17	10	Good	Moderate
Pontiac Grand Prix	FRONT	3194	Good	20	14	Good	Good
	SIDE	2814	Average	15	18	Moderate	Good
Toyota Avalon	FRONT	2291	Very Good	14	9	Good	Very Good
Toyota Camry	FRONT	2057	Very Good	12	8	Good	Good
	SIDE	2344	Good	15	12	Good	Good
Volvo S70	FRONT	1794	Very Good	10	8	Very Good	Good
Large							
Buick LeSabre	FRONT	2673	Good	12	15	Good	Good
	SIDE	3202	Poor	16	22	Moderate	Moderate
Buick Park Avenue (Aurora)	FRONT	4381	Average	23	26	Good	Good
Buick Riviera (Aurora)	FRONT	4381	Average	23	26	Good	Good
Cadillac DeVille	FRONT	2515	Very Good	14	12	Good	Good
	SIDE	1196	Very Good	6	7	Good	Good
Cadillac Seville	FRONT	4381	Average	23	26	Good	Good
Chevrolet Lumina	FRONT	2491	Very Good	16	9	Good	Good
	SIDE	1793	Good	7	13	Very Good	Moderate

Parentheses indicate actual model tested.
*A version of this vehicle is scheduled to be tested later this year. Results are expected to be similar.

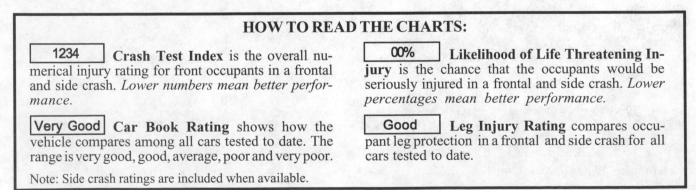

HOW TO READ THE CHARTS:

`1234` **Crash Test Index** is the overall numerical injury rating for front occupants in a frontal and side crash. *Lower numbers mean better performance.*

`Very Good` **Car Book Rating** shows how the vehicle compares among all cars tested to date. The range is very good, good, average, poor and very poor.

Note: Side crash ratings are included when available.

`00%` **Likelihood of Life Threatening Injury** is the chance that the occupants would be seriously injured in a frontal and side crash. *Lower percentages mean better performance.*

`Good` **Leg Injury Rating** compares occupant leg protection in a frontal and side crash for all cars tested to date.

Crash Test Performance		Crash Test Index	Car Book Rating	Likelihood of Life Threatening Injury		Leg Injury Rating	
				Driver	Passenger	Driver	Passenger
Large (cont.)							
Chevrolet Malibu	FRONT	2633	Good	13	14	Good	Good
	SIDE	3699	Poor	27	18	Moderate	Good
Chevrolet Monte Carlo	FRONT	2491	Good	16	9	Good	Good
	SIDE	1793	Good	7	13	Very Good	Moderate
Ford Crown Victoria	FRONT	1832	Very Good	10	8	Good	Very Good
	SIDE	1484	Very Good	9	7	Good	Good
Infiniti I30 (Maxima)	FRONT	3174	Good	14	19	Good	Good
	SIDE	1856	Good	9	11	Good	Good
Mercury Grand Marquis (Cr. Vic.)	FRONT	1832	Very Good	10	8	Good	Very Good
	SIDE	1484	Very Good	9	7	Good	Good
Oldsmobile 88 (LeSabre)	FRONT	2673	Good	12	15	Good	Good
	SIDE	3202	Poor	16	22	Moderate	Moderate
Oldsmobile Aurora	FRONT	4381	Average	23	26	Good	Good
Pontiac Bonneville (LeSabre)	FRONT	2673	Good	12	15	Good	Good
	SIDE	3202	Poor	16	22	Moderate	Moderate
Minivan							
Chevrolet Astro	FRONT	5091	Poor	25	34	Moderate	Good
Chevrolet Venture	FRONT	3227	Good	17	17	Moderate	Good
Chrysler T&C (Caravan)	FRONT	2996	Good	20	11	Moderate	Good
Dodge Caravan	FRONT	2996	Good	20	11	Moderate	Good
Ford Windstar	FRONT	1671	Very Good	9	7	Good	Good
GMC Safari (Astro)	FRONT	5091	Poor	25	34	Moderate	Good
Olds Silhouette (Venture)	FRONT	3227	Good	17	17	Moderate	Good
Plymouth Voyager (Caravan)	FRONT	2996	Good	20	11	Moderate	Good
Pontiac Montana (Venture)	FRONT	3227	Good	17	17	Moderate	Good
Toyota Sienna	FRONT	1863	Very Good	10	9	Very Good	Good

Parentheses indicate actual model tested.
*A version of this vehicle is scheduled to be tested later this year. Results are expected to be similar.

Automatic Crash Protection

The concept of automatic protection is not new—automatic fire sprinklers in public buildings, automatic release of oxygen masks in airplanes, purification of drinking water, and pasteurization of milk are all commonly accepted forms of automatic safety protection. Ironically, of all the products we buy, the one most likely to kill us has only recently been equipped with automatic safety protection. In fact, we often incorporate better technology in safely transporting electronic equipment, eggs, and china than we do in packaging humans in automobiles.

Over twenty years ago, in cooperation with the federal government, the automobile industry developed two basic forms of automatic crash protection: airbags and automatic safety belts. These devices will not prevent all deaths, but they will halve your chances of being killed or seriously injured in a car accident.

The idea behind automatic crash protection is to protect people from what is called the "second collision" when the occupant comes forward and collides with the interior of their own car. Because the "second collision" occurs within milliseconds, and because so many people do not use seat belts, providing automatic rather than manual protection dramatically improves the chances of escaping injury.

Federal law now requires all new cars to be equipped with some form of automatic crash protection that will protect the driver and front seat passenger in a 30-mph frontal collision into a fixed barrier and a 33.5-mph side collision. To meet the standard, auto makers now opt for airbags and no longer use automatic belts.

Airbags: Hidden in the steering wheel hub and the right side of the dashboard, airbags provide unobtrusive and effective protection in frontal crashes. When needed, they inflate instantly to cushion the driver and the front seat passenger. By spreading crash forces over the head and chest, airbags protect the body from violent contact with the hard surfaces of the car. Cars with airbags also provide manual seat belts to protect occupants in nonfrontal crashes and to keep them in the best position to benefit from an airbag. However, airbags offer protection in frontal crashes even if the safety belt is not fastened.

Side airbags work the same way, except they come out of the doors in order to spread crash forces across the driver or passenger's legs, side and arms.

Should I Turn My Airbag Off?
In short, no. Approximately, 3,100 people have been saved by airbags. In spite of the tragic stories you have no doubt heard, airbags save lives. If properly belted, an airbag will reduce your risk of a serious head injury by 75 percent!

Because of concern for their children's safety, parents may be considering turning off their airbag—a far better alternative is to keep your children in the back seat and keep the airbag ready to save a larger passenger.

De-Powered Airbags: In an effort to lower the number of improperly buckled children killed by airbag deployment, the government is allowing auto makers to de-power their airbags for new models. As a result, almost all the auto makers are de-powering their airbags on 1999 models, which has safety advocates concerned. Please be warned: de-powered airbags can still be fatal to out-of-position children (children who are not sitting upright and properly buckled in). Additionally, de-powering airbags lowers the amount of protection for adults. De-powering airbags, unfortunately, is weak solution to a serious problem.

Airbag Cutoff Switches: One option presently available is the airbag cutoff switch. The government will only allow a cutoff switch

---

A Note for Pregnant Women:

The American College of Obstetricians and Gynecologists strongly urges pregnant women to always wear a safety belt, including on the ride to the hospital to deliver the baby! In a car crash, the most serious risk to an unborn baby is that the mother may be injured. Obstetricians recommend that the lap and shoulder belts be used, with the lap belt as low as possible on the hips, under the baby.

When packing your things for the hospital, make sure you include an infant car safety seat to bring your baby home. As the American Academy of Pediatrics says, "Make the first ride a safe ride!"

in vehicles without a back seat like the F-Series and C/K Series Pick-ups. However, the cutoff switch has it's own danger — it only takes that one time to forget to turn the airbag back on when an adult sits in the seat for tragedy to occur.

Smart Airbags: The solution to airbag concerns lies with smart airbags. Mercedes-Benz offers a special child seat system which, when installed in the passenger-side seat, has a sensor that emits an electronic signal to turn the airbag off. It will even inform you if you've installed the seat improperly. When the seat is removed, the airbag turns back on.

Most auto makers are developing smart airbag systems which will differentiate between an adult, a child, a rear-facing child seat or an empty seat, using various heat, ultrasonic sound wave and infrared sensors. Not only will smart airbags save lives, but by preventing the passenger-side airbag from deploying when the seat is empty, they will save thousands in repair costs. When will they be available? Probably not before the year 2000, but we hope the car companies will prove us wrong.

Consumers with questions about airbags often find dealers do not know the facts about these safety devices. Here are the correct answers to typical airbag questions from the Insurance Institute for Highway Safety:

Is the gas that inflates airbags dangerous? Nitrogen, which makes up 79.8 percent of the air we breathe, is the gas that inflates the bags. A solid chemical, sodium azide, generates this nitrogen gas. Sodium azide does not present a safety hazard in normal driving, in crashes, or in disposal. In fact, occupants of the car will never even come in contact with the sodium azide.

Will airbags inflate by mistake? Airbags will inflate only in frontal impacts equivalent to hitting a solid wall at about 10-mph or higher. They will not inflate when you go over bumps or potholes or when you hit something at low speed. Even slamming on your brakes will not cause the airbags to inflate unless you hit something.

In the unlikely event of an inadvertent airbag deployment, you would not lose control of the car. Airbags are designed to inflate and deflate in fractions of a second. GM tested driver reaction by inflating airbags without warning at speeds of up to 45-mph. GM reported that "without exception, the drivers retained control of the automobile."

Will airbag systems last very long? Airbags are reliable and require no maintenance. Only one part moves, the device that senses the impact, so there is nothing to wear out. They work throughout the life of the car although some manufacturers suggest inspections at anywhere from two to ten years.

In a study of 228 cars in which airbags were deployed, 40 had traveled more than 40,000 miles. One car had traveled almost 115,000 miles at the time of the crash. In every case, the airbags worked as they were designed to.

Are airbags reliable? According to the U.S. Department of Transportation, airbags have saved over 3,100 lives since they were introduced in the early 1980s. General Motors installed airbags in over 10,000 cars from 1974 to 1976. These cars traveled over 600 million miles, and the death and injury rate of the occupants was 50 percent lower than the rate for non-airbag cars. Studies of the operation of the airbags reported no cases of failure to deploy or malfunction of the inflator. This reliability rate (99.995 percent) is far higher than that of such safety features as brakes, tires, steering, and lights, which show failure rates of up to 10 percent.

Will airbags protect occupants without seat belts? Airbags are designed to protect unbelted front-seat *adult* in 30-mph frontal crashes into a wall. However, airbags are *not* designed to protect unbelted children or elderly. Equipping cars with airbags reduced the average injury severity for adults in serious frontal crashes by 64 percent, even though over 80 percent of the occupants were unbelted. The best protection, however, is provided by a combination of airbags and lap and shoulder safety belts. With airbags and seat belts, you'll be protected in the event of side impact and roll-over crashes, as well as in frontal crashes.

Airbag Deployment

In the fall of 1997, the Center for Auto Safety (CAS) revealed major differences in passenger-side airbag design which may affect their safety. The study found auto manufacturers generally chose one of two methods to deploy passenger-side airbags, vertically or horizontally. The horizontally deploying airbags shoot straight out of the dashboard toward the passenger. Vertically deploying airbags mounted in the top of the dash move upward towards the windshield and reflect off the windshield towards the passenger. Vertically deploying airbags can also be mounted from the edge of the dash creating a safety zone between the occupant and the deploying airbag. According to CAS, all passenger-side airbag deaths have been from horizontally deploying airbags and there have been no deaths from vertically deploying airbags. It appears that vertically deploying airbags may be more effective.

Based on data collected by CAS and responses received from auto companies, we have listed below those manufacturers who have chosen to use vertically deploying airbags. Some models may be missing due to lack of information available — the government presently does not require auto companies to disclose this information.

It is our hope that with the implementation of smart airbags, the information presented here will become obsolete. Please note that while no deaths have occurred due to vertically deploying airbags, you still must keep your children in the back seat, even with a vertically deploying passenger-side airbag. And whoever does sit up front, *always* buckle up and sit back.

Vertically Deploying Passenger Side Airbags

Acura CL	Lexus LS400
Acura Integra	Mercury Sable
Acura RL	Mitsubishi Galant
Acura TL	Nissan Sentra
BMW 318ti	Oldsmobile Alero
Cadillac DeVille	Oldsmobile Aurora
Cadillac Eldorado	Oldsmobile Cutlass
Cadillac Seville	Pontiac Sunfire
Chevrolet Cavalier	Saturn EV1
Chevrolet Malibu	Subaru Legacy
Chevrolet Prizm	Toyota Camry
Ford Taurus	Toyota Celica
Honda Accord	Toyota Corolla
Honda Civic	Toyota Sierra
Infiniti G20	Toyota Solara
Infiniti Q45	Volvo C70/S70/V70
Lexus ES300	Volvo S80
Lexus GS300/400	

Saved by the Airbag

Do airbags save lives? Here is how Kathleen Jones Carlisle of Blacksburg, VA, and one of over 3,100 people who've been saved by airbags, described her experience:

"On Wednesday, August 21, 1996, while traveling at approximately 55 mph, another car swerved into my lane. I braced for impact, closed by eyes and prayed. Immediately upon impact my seat belt pinned me tightly to my seat and my airbag exploded. I slowly opened my eyes. I couldn't believe I was alive. I could not move, but I was able to carefully glance around to see I was in one piece. My red 1991 Mercury Capri sustained a head-on collision and I was alive to tell the world. I later learned the driver of the car who hit me died horribly at the scene. He wasn't wearing his seat belt, nor did he have an airbag."

Kathleen is a member of Advocates for Highway and Auto Safety's "Saved by the Airbag" group. If you or someone you know has been protected from death and/or serious injury by an airbag, please call Cathy Hickey at 1-800-659-BAGS (2247) to find out how you can help promote the lifesaving benefits of airbags.

Children and Airbags

Will airbags protect children? Studies of actual crashes indicate that children can be protected by airbags—but only if they are properly buckled up! A deploying airbag can be deadly to an unrestrained child. Properly buckling your child has never been more important now that virtually all cars and minivans, and most trucks and sport utilities, offer airbags on the passenger's side where children often sit.

According to government estimates, airbags have saved the lives of approximately 3,100 people. However, to date, 61 children under the age of 12 have been killed by the deployment of an airbag. The National Highway Traffic Safety Administration estimates about one child per month is killed by airbag deployment and, if certain measures are not implemented, the number could increase to one per week.

Remember—*most children killed by airbags are not properly belted*. The majority of the children killed were either completely unrestrained or improperly restrained. To protect the occupant, an airbag must inflate in a fraction of a second before the occupant hits the dashboard. For an full-size adult, the result is coming forward into a cushion of air. For a child who isn't properly buckled, it can be deadly, especially if the child is standing up or leaning on the dashboard.

How to Best Protect Your Child (and Yourself)

Never place a rear-facing child seat in front of a passenger side airbag. Even front facing child seats should be used on a rear seat. The best spot for your children is in the center of the back seat. If you do not have a back seat, here are some tips for keeping your child (and yourself) safe while seated in an airbag seat:

- ☑ Push the seat as far back as it will go.
- ☑ Make sure your child is sitting up straight and not leaning forward against the dash.
- ☑ If you are an adult, sit at least 10-12 inches away from the steering wheel. In the passenger side, slide the seat back as far as it will go.

For tips on how to use a child seat and how to properly buckle up your child, see pages 34-40.

Young Drivers

Each year, teenagers accounted for about 15 percent of highway deaths. According to the Insurance Institute for Highway Safety (IIHS), the highest driver death rate per 100,000 people is among 18 year olds. Clearly, parents need to make sure their children are fully prepared to be competent, safe drivers before letting them out on the road. All states issue learner's permits. However, only 35 states and the District of Columbia *require* permits before getting a driver's license. It isn't difficult for teenagers to get a license and only fourteen states prohibit teenagers from driving during night and early morning. Call your MVA for your state's young driver laws.

Anti-Lock Brakes

After airbags, one of the best safety features available is an anti-lock braking system (ABS). ABS shortens stopping distance on dry, wet, and even icy roads by preventing wheel lock-up and keeps you from skidding out of control when you "slam" on the brakes.

The ABS works by sensing the speed of each wheel. If one or more of the wheels begins to lock up or skid, it releases that wheel's brakes, allowing the wheel to roll normally again, thus stopping the skid. When the wheel stops skidding, the hydraulic pressure is reapplied instantly. This cycle can be repeated several times per second, keeping each wheel at its optimum braking performance even while your foot keeps pushing on the brake pedal. Although ABS is typically connected to all four wheels, in some light trucks and vans it is connected to only the rear wheels.

The ABS is only active when it senses that the wheels are about to lock up. When an ABS is active, you may notice that the brake pedal pulsates slightly. This pulsation is normal, and it indicates that the brakes are being released and reapplied. *Don't pump your brakes—* the ABS is doing it for you. If there is a failure in the ABS, the vehicle reverts to its conventional braking system and a warning light indicates that the ABS needs repair.

Note: Using tires other than the ones originally on the vehicle may affect the anti-lock braking system. If you are planning to change the size of the tires on your vehicle, first consult your owner's manual.

You'll find ABS on all 1999 models, but unfortunately, mostly as an option.

Don't Buy Add-On ABS Brakes

Adding "so-called" ABS brakes to your car can be dangerous. These products use a variety of deceptive names that incorporate the letters ABS, such as ABS-Trax (Automotive Breakthrough Science—the company's name) and Brake-Guard ABS (Advanced Braking System). These add-on systems "have virtually no effect on stopping distances, vehicle stability or control," according to government tests. You should *not* purchase or install these systems. Only *electronic* ABS systems are capable of preventing wheel skid in panic braking situations. Currently, true electronic anti-lock brakes are only available as factory installed systems.

What Happens in a Collision

A car crash typically involves two collisions. First, the car hits another object and second, the occupant collides with the inside of the car. Injuries result from this *second collision.* The key to surviving an auto accident is protecting yourself from the second collision. Always wearing your safety belt is the most important defense while having an airbag is a very close second. The whole purpose of the airbag is to protect you in this second collision.

Upon impact, in a typical 35-mph crash, the car begins to crush and slow down. Within 1/10 of a second, the car comes to a stop, but the person keeps moving forward at 35-mph. 1/50 of a second after the car has stopped, the unbelted person slams into the dashboard or windshield.

According to government reports prepared before the widespread use of belts and airbags, these were the major causes of injury in the *second collision:*

Steering wheel	27%
Instrument panel	11%
Side (doors)	10%
Windshield	5%
Front roof pillar	4%
Glove box area	3%
Roof edges	3%
Roof	2%

About 60 percent of occupants killed or injured in auto crashes would have been saved from serious harm had they been wearing safety belts. Yet many Americans do not use these life-saving devices.

Safety belts are particularly important in minivans, 4x4s and pickups because there is a greater chance of being killed or seriously injured in a rollover accident. The simple precaution of wearing your belt greatly improves your odds of survival.

Why don't people wear their belts? They simply don't know the facts. Once you know the facts, you should be willing to buckle up.

While most safety advocates welcome the passage of safety belt usage laws, the ones passed to date are weak and generally unenforced. In addition, most of the laws are based on "secondary" enforcement—meaning that you cannot be stopped for failing to wear your belt. If you are stopped for another reason and the officer notices you don't have your belt on by the time he or she reaches the vehicle, you may be fined. In states with "primary" enforcement, you can be stopped for not wearing a safety belt. Yet, in many cases the fines are less than a parking ticket. In Arkansas, however, you can get a $10 credit toward a primary violation if you are wearing a seat belt and in Wyoming, a $5 credit.

Another unusual feature of these laws is that most of them allow drivers to avoid buckling up if they have a doctor's permission. This loophole was inserted to appease those who were not really in favor of the law. However, many doctors are wondering if they will be held responsible for the injuries of unbuckled patients. In fact, the State of New York Medical Society cautions doctors never to give medical dispensation from the law because "no medical condition has yet been found to warrant a medical exemption for seat belt use."

Even though most state laws are weak, they have heightened awareness and raised the level of usage. Belt use in states that have passed a safety belt law tends to rise sharply after the law is enacted. However, after the law has been on the books a few months, safety belt use drops.

The tables on the following pages describe the current safety belt laws. In some cases, the driver is responsible for all or some of the passengers as noted; otherwise, occupants are responsible for themselves. All states are listed, even those that do not yet have safety belt laws. We hope that the blank following New Hampshire will soon be filled with new laws.

Safety Belt Myths and Facts

Myth: *"I don't want to be trapped by a seat belt. It's better to be thrown free in an accident."*

Fact: The chance of being killed is 25 times greater if you're ejected. A safety belt will keep you from plunging through the windshield, smashing into trees, rocks, or other cars, scraping along the ground, or getting run over by your own or another's vehicle. If you are wearing your belt, you're far more likely to be conscious after an accident to free yourself and other passengers.

Myth: *"Pregnant women should not wear safety belts."*

Fact: According to the American Medical Association, "Both the pregnant mother and the fetus are safer, provided the lap belt is worn as low on the pelvis as possible."

Myth: *"I don't need it. In case of an accident, I can brace myself with my hands."*

Fact: At 35 mph, the impact of a crash on you and your passengers is brutal. There's no way your arms and legs can brace you against that kind of collision; the speed and force are just too great. The force of impact at only 10 mph is roughly equivalent to the force of catching a 200-pound bag of cement dropped from a first floor window.

Myth: *"I just don't believe it will ever happen to me."*

Fact: Every one of us can expect to be in a crash once every 10 years. For one out of 20 of us, it will be a serious crash. For one out of 60 born today, it will be fatal.

Safety Belt Laws

	Law Applies To:	Driver Fined For:	Enforcement	Max. Fine 1st Offense
Alabama	Front seat only	6 year olds and up	Secondary	$25
Alaska*	All occupants	16 year olds and up	Secondary	$15
Arizona	Front seat only	5 year olds and up	Secondary	$10
Arkansas	Front seat only	5 year olds and up	Secondary	$25[1]
California*	All occupants	16 year olds and up	Primary	$20[2]
Colorado	Front seat only	4 year olds and up	Secondary	$15
Connecticut	Front seat only	4 year olds and up	Primary	$15
Delaware	Front seat only	All occupants	Secondary	$240
Dist. of Columbia	All occupants	16 year olds and up	Primary	$50**
Florida	Front seat[6]	6 year olds and up	Secondary	$25
Georgia	All occupants	4 to 17 year olds	Primary	$15[2]
Hawaii	Front seat only	4 year olds and up	Primary	$20
Idaho	Front seat only	4 year olds and up	Secondary	$5
Illinois	Front seat only	6 year olds and up	Secondary	$25
Indiana	Front seat only	5 year olds and up	Primary	$25
Iowa	Front seat only	6 year olds and up	Primary	$10
Kansas	Front seat only	14 year olds and up	Secondary	$10
Kentucky*	All occupants	Over 40 inches	Secondary	$25
Louisiana	Front seat only	13 year olds and up	Primary	$25[1]
Maine	All occupants	4 year olds and up	Secondary	$50
Maryland	Front seat only	16 year olds and up	Primary	$25
Massachusetts*	All occupants	12 year olds and up	Secondary	$25
Michigan	All occupants	4 to 15 year olds	Secondary	$25
Minnesota	All occupants	3 to 10 year olds[3]	Secondary	$25
Mississippi	Front seat only	4 year olds and up	Secondary	$25
Missouri	Front seat only	4 year olds and up	Secondary	$10

* In these states driver can be held liable in court for *all* passengers.
**Driver gets 2 points on license.
  See next page for footnotes.

Safety Belt Laws

	Law Applies To:	Driver Fined For:	Enforcement	Max. Fine 1st Offense
Montana*	All occupants	4 years old and up	Secondary	$20
Nebraska	Front seat	5 year olds and up	Secondary	$25
Nevada*	All occupants	5 year olds and up	Secondary	$25
New Hampshire	No law			
New Jersey	Front seat only	5 year olds and up	Secondary	$20
New Mexico	Front seat only	11 year olds and up	Primary	$25
New York	Front seat[4]	16 year olds and up	Primary	$50
North Carolina	Front seat only	12 year olds and up	Primary	$25
North Dakota	Front seat only	3 year olds and up	Secondary	$20
Ohio	Front seat only	4 year olds and up	Secondary	$25[7]
Oklahoma	Front seat only	All occupants	Primary	$20
Oregon*	All Occupants	16 year olds and up	Primary	$50
Pennsylvania	Front seat only	4 year olds and up	Secondary	$10
Rhode Island*	All Occupants	13 year olds and up	Secondary	None
South Carolina	All Occupants[5]	6 year olds and up	Secondary	$10
South Dakota	Front seat	5 year olds and up	Secondary	$20
Tennessee	Front seat only	13 year olds and up	Secondary	$50
Texas	Front seat only	4 year olds and up	Primary	$50
Utah	Front seat only	10 year olds and up	Secondary	$10
Vermont*	All occupants	13 year olds and up	Secondary	$10
Virginia	Front seat only	16 year olds and up	Secondary	$25
Washington*	All occupants	All occupants	Secondary	$66
West Virginia	Front seat[6]	9 year olds and up	Secondary	$25
Wisconsin	All occupants[5]	4 year olds and up	Secondary	$10
Wyoming	Front seat only	3 year olds and up	Secondary	None[1]

* In these states driver can be held liable in court for *all* passengers.
[1] In Arkansas, reward for buckling up is a $10 reduction in primary violation fine; in Wyoming, a $5 reduction. In Louisiana, 10% reduction in fine for moving violation.
[2] $25 fine if driver is a minor. In Georgia, driver is responsible for 18 year olds and those in front seat.
[3] Parent driver is responsible for all occupants in front seat.
[4] Driver responsible for 4 to 10 year olds riding in rear seat.
[5] Covers rear seat occupants where shoulder belts are available.
[6] In West Virginia driver responsible for occupants 9 to 17 years old in rear seat; in Florida occupants 6-15 years old in rear seat also covered.
[7] $15 passenger fine.

Child Safety Seats

How many times have you gone out of your way to prevent your children from being injured by keeping household poisons out of reach, watching carefully as they swam, or keeping a good grip on their hand while crossing a street or parking lot? Probably quite often. Yet, parents ignore the biggest danger of all when they allow their children to lay down in the back of a minivan or roam unrestrained in their car. Ironically, it's your automobile that poses the greatest threat to your child's health.

Child safety seats are the best and only reliable way to protect your child in a vehicle. Automobile crashes remain the leading cause of death in children over one year old. Sadly, over 100,000 children are injured unnecessarily each year. Research on the effectiveness of child safety seats has found that they reduce the risk of fatal injury by 69% for infants (less than one year old) and by 47% for toddlers (1-4 years old) if used correctly.

Never place a child in your lap. At 30 mph, a crash or sudden stop will wrench a ten pound child from your arms with a force of nearly 300 pounds! If you aren't wearing a seat belt, then your own body will be thrown forward with enough force to crush your child against the dashboard or the back of the front seat.

Hand-Me-Down Seats: To insure that a second hand child seat will adequately protect your child, see if its identification stickers, belt instructions and date of manufacture are still visible. Only use seats less than 5 years old. Make sure no parts or instructions are missing. Most importantly, know the history of the child seat—never use seats that have been in crashes, no matter how perfect they look.

Buying Tips: Purchasing a new child seat for your child is always money well spent. Many vehicles now have built-in child seats which are an excellent option. Child seats with an automatic retracting harness and a shield are typically the easiest to use. Here are some additional tips when shopping for a child safety seat:

☑ Try before you buy. Your car's seat belts and the shape of its seats will determine which child seats fit your car so make sure it can be properly installed.

☑ Determine how many straps or buckles must be fastened to use a child seat. The less complicated the seat, the less chance for misuse. The easiest seats require only one strap or buckle after fastening the seat belt around the child seat.

☑ Make sure the seat is wide enough for growth and bulky winter clothes. If possible, let your child sit in the seat to measure for fit.

☑ Is your child comfortable? Can your child move his or her arms freely, sleep in the seat, or see out a window?

Locking Clips

Locking clips come with most child safety seats and are needed if the latch plate on the car's seat belt slides freely along the belt. If you don't properly install the locking clip, the child seat can move or tip over. Look for *heavy-duty locking clips*, available at Ford, Toyota and Nissan dealers. The safest way to use a heavy-duty locking clip is to pull the seat belt entirely out and attach the clip so the child seat is secure with no retracting involved. For more information, contact Safety Belt Safe at 800-745-SAFE.

Register Your Child Seat

Last year, the U.S. Department of Transportation recalled millions of child safety seats for serious safety defects. Tragically, most parents never heard about these recalls and the majority of these problem seats are still being used. You can do two things to protect your children—first, call the Auto Safety Hotline at 800-424-9393 and find out if your seat has been recalled. If so, they will tell you how to contact the manufacturer for a resolution. Second, make sure you fill out the registration card that must come with all new seats. This will enable the company to contact you should there be a recall. If you currently own a seat, ask the Hotline for the address of your seat's manufacturer and send them your name, address and seat model, asking them to keep it on file for recall notices.

Child Safety Seat Types

There are six types of child seats: *infant-only, convertible, toddler-only, child/booster, booster* and *built-in*.

Infant-Only Seats: Infant-only seats can be used from birth until your baby reaches a weight of 17-20 pounds. This type of seat must be installed facing the rear in a semi-reclined position. In a collision, the crash forces are spread over the baby's back, the strongest body surface. The seat's harness should come from below the child's shoulders in the rear-facing position.

One benefit of an infant-only seat is that you can easily install and remove the seat with the baby in place. Most infant car seats can also be used as household baby seats. Caution: Some household baby seats look remarkably similar to infant safety seats. These are not crash worthy and should *never* be used as car safety seats.

Convertible Seats: Buying a convertible seat can save you the expense of buying both an infant and a toddler seat. Most convertible seats can be used from birth until the child reaches four years and 40 pounds. When used for an infant, the seat faces rearward in a semi-reclined position. When the child is at least a year old and 20 pounds or more, the frame can be adjusted upright and the seat turned to face forward.

As with any safety seat, it is extremely important that the straps fit snugly over the child's shoulders. A good way to ensure that the straps are adjusted correctly is to buy a seat with an automatically adjusting harness. Like a car safety belt, these models automatically adjust to fit snugly on your child.

Convertible seats come in three basic types:

The *five-point harness* consists of two shoulder and two lap straps that converge at a buckle connected to a crotch strap. These straps are adjustable, allowing for growth and comfort.

The *T-shield* has a small pad joining the shoulder belts. With only one buckle, many parents find this the simplest and easiest-to-use type of convertible seat; but, it will not fit newborns properly.

The *tray shield* is another convenient model, since the safety harness is attached to the shield. As the shield comes down in front of the child, the harness comes over the child's shoulders. The shield is an important part of the restraint system, but like the T-shield, it will not fit small infants.

Toddler-Only Seats: These are really booster child seats and they may take the place of convertible seats when a child is between 20 and 30 pounds. Weight and size limits vary greatly among seats.

Child/Booster Seats: Some manufacturers are now making a variety of combination child/booster seats. For example, one model can be converted from a 5-point harness to a high-backed, belt-positioning booster seat. They can be used for children ranging from 20 to 40 pounds, making them a very economical choice.

Booster Seats: Booster seats are used when your child is too big for a convertible seat, but too small to use safety belts. Most car lap/shoulder belts do not adequately fit children with a seating height less than 28". Booster seats can be used for children over 30 pounds and come in three types:

Belt-positioning booster seats raise the child for a better fit with the car's safety belts. If your child is under 3 years old, do not use belt-positioning booster seats because your child may be able to unbuckle him or herself.

The *removable-shield booster seat* can be used with a lap/shoulder belt with the shield removed, or with a lap belt with the shield on. This seat can be adapted to different cars and seating positions, making it a good choice.

The *shield-type booster seat* has a small plastic shield with no straps and can be used only with lap belts. Typically, the safety belt fastens in front of the shield, anchoring it to the car. Most safety experts recommend using these seats until a child is 4 years old and 40 pounds.

Built-in Seats: Chrysler, Ford, GM, Volvo and other auto companies offer the option of a fold-out toddler seat on some of their models. These seats are only for children older than one and come as either a five-point harness or a booster with 3-point belt; however, the 3-point booster is not recommended for children under 3 years old. This built-in seat is an excellent feature because it is always in the car and does not pose the problem of compatability that often occurs with separate child seats.

Name of Seat	Price	Comments
Infant Safety Seats		
Century Assura 565 Series	$29-39	3-pt.; up to 20 lbs., correct recline indicator
Century Assura Premiere	$49-59	3-pt.; separate base stays in car; can be used without base; correct recline indicator
Cosco Arriva	$35-55	3-pt.; up to 22 lbs.; detachable base with some models
Cosco Dream Ride Plus	$59	3-pt.; up to 17-20 lbs. (depending on mfg date); use as car seat rear facing; converts to swing
Cosco TLC	$20-25	3-pt.
Evenflo Joy Ride	$25-45	3-pt.; harness adjuster located in compartment behind seat.
Evenflo On My Way	$55-65	3-pt.; detachable base; can use without base
Evenflo Travel Tandem	$45-55	3-pt.; separate base stays in car; can be used without base; harness adjuster behind seat.
Gerry Guard with Glide	$50-55	3-pt.; use as glider in house; must be converted to in-car position
Gerry Secure Ride	$40	3-pt.; tilt-indicator
Kolcraft Travel About	$60-70	3-pt.; detachable base; can use without base
Kolcraft Infant Rider	$50-60	3-pt.
Kolcraft Rock 'N Ride	$30-35	3-pt.; no harness height adjustment
Convertible Safety Seats		
Babyhood Baby Sitter	$89-99	5-pt.
Century 1000 STE, 1500 Prestige	$49-75	5-pt.; adjustable crotch strap positions
Century 2000 STE, 2500 Prestige	$59-85	T-shield; adjustable crotch strap positions
Century 3000 STE, 3500 Prestige	$69-89	Tray shield; 5-position adjustable shield
Century Smart Move	$109-139	5-pt./ Tray shield; adjustable shield grows with child
Cosco Regal Ride	$65-85	5-pt./ T-shield/ Tray shield; use rear-facing up to 22 lbs.
Cosco Touriva 5-pt.	$40-60	5-pt./ T-Shield/ Tray shield; use rear facing up to 22 lbs.
Early Development Guardian Comfort	$80-100	5-pt./ T-shield/ Tray shield; harness designed like vehicle seat belts; lock upon impact.

Based on data collected by the American Academy of Pediatrics.

Name of Seat	Price	Comments
Convertible Seats (cont.)		
Evenflo Champion	$50-70	Tray shield; optional tether available
Evenflo Scout	$39-60	5-pt./ T-shield; optional tether available
Evenflo Trooper	$60-70	5-pt./ Tray shield; adjustable shield; optional tether available
Evenflo Ultara I	$80-100	Tray shield; adjustable shield; optional tether available
Evenflo Ultara V	$80-100	5-pt.; optional tether available
Gerry One-Click	$80-90	Tray shield; automatic harness adjustment; optional tether available
Gerry Pro-Tech	$60-65	5-pt.; optional tether available
Kolcraft Auto-Mate	$50-60	5-pt.; requires 2-handed operation
Safeline Sit 'N Stroll	$159-169	5-pt.; converts to stroller
Toddler-Only Vests and Built-In Seats		
Chrysler Built-In Seat	$100-200	5-pt. (20-65 lbs.); 2 built in option in minivans; one seat available in most sedans
E-Z-On Vest	$74-90	4-pt. (25+ lbs.); tether strap must be installed in vehicle
Ford Built-In	$135-240	5-pt. (20-60 lbs.); two seats optional in minivans; one seat optional in Explorer, Escort, and Tracer
GM Built-In	N/A	5-pt. (20-40 lbs., Booster 40-60 lbs.); seats optional in minivans and some sedans.
Little Cargo Travel Vest	$39-49	5-pt. (25-40 lbs.); simplified strap-buckle system; auto lap belt attached through padded stress plate
Booster		
Century Breverra Classic	$49-59	High-backed; use 5-point shield with lap belt only; remove shield when using vehicle lap/shoulder belt
Cosco Grand Explorer/Adventurer	$20-35	Must use shield if vehicle has lap belts only; use as a belt-positioning booster with lap/shoulder belt
Evenflo Sidekick	$20-30	Must use shield if vehicle has lap belts only; use as a belt-positioning booster with lap/shoulder belt
Gerry Evolution	$54-60	High-backed; optional tether available

Based on data collected by the American Academy of Pediatrics.

Tips for Using Your Child Safety Seat

The incorrect use of child safety seats has reached epidemic proportions. A stunning 95% of parents misuse their child's safety seat. Problems fall into two categories: incorrect installation of the seat and incorrect use of the seat's straps to secure the child. In most cases, the car's safety belt was improperly routed through the seat.

Incorrect use of a child safety seat prevents lifesaving protection and may even contribute to further injury. In addition to following your seat's installation instructions, here are some important usage tips:

☑ The safest place for the seat is the center of the back seat.

☑ Use a locking clip when needed. Check the instructions that come with your seat and those in your car owner's manual.

☑ Keep your child rear-facing for at least a year.

☑ Regularly check the seat's safety harness and the car's seat belt for a tight, secure fit because the straps will stretch on impact.

☑ Don't leave sharp or heavy objects or groceries loose in the car. Anything loose can be deadly in a crash.

☑ In the winter, dress your baby in a legged suit to allow proper attachment of the harness. If necessary, drape an extra blanket over the seat after your baby is buckled.

☑ Be sure all doors are locked.

☑ Do not give your child lollipops or ice cream on a stick while riding. A bump or swerve could jam the stick into his or her throat.

Seat Belts for Kids: How long should children use car seats? For school age children, a car seat is *twice* as effective in preventing injury than an adult lap and shoulder harness — use a booster as long as possible. Most children can start using seat belts at 65 pounds and when tall enough for the shoulder belt to cross the chest, not the neck. The lap section of the belt should be snug and as low on the hips as possible. If the shoulder belt does cross the face or neck, use a booster.

Never:

➜ Use the same belt on two children.

➜ Move a shoulder belt behind a child's back or under an arm.

➜ Buckle in a pet or any large toys with the child.

➜ Recline a seat with a belted child.

➜ Use a twisted seat belt. The belt must be straight and flat.

➜ Use pillows or cushions to boost your child.

➜ Place a belt around you with a child in your lap. In an accident or sudden stop, your child would absorb most of the crash force.

TIP

Buckled Up = Better Behavior

Medical researchers have concluded that belted children are better behaved. When not buckled up, children squirm, stand up, complain, fight, and pull at the steering wheel. When buckled into safety seats, however, they displayed 95 percent fewer incidents of bad behavior.

When buckled up, children feel secure. In addition, being in a seat can be more fun because most safety seats are high enough to allow children to see out the window. Also, children are less likely to feel carsick and more likely to fall asleep in a car seat.

Make the car seat your child's own special place, so he or she will enjoy being in it. Pick out some special soft toys or books that can be used only in the car seat to make using the seat a positive experience.

Set a good example for your child by using your own safety belt every time you get in the car.

Rear-Facing Child Safety Seats

Never use a rear-facing child safety seat in a seating position that has an airbag. To deploy fast enough to protect adult occupants, an airbag inflates with enough force to potentially cause serious head and chest injuries to a child in a rear-facing safety seat. And remember, airbags do not take the place of child safety seats.

Child Restraint Laws

Every state now requires children to be in safety seats or buckled up when riding in automobiles. The following table provides an overview of the requirements and penalties in each state. Note that most states use the child's age to define the law, although some states have height or weight requirements as well. Also, in most states, the laws are not limited to children riding with their parents, but require that any driver with child passengers makes sure those children are buckled up.

	Law Applies To:	Child Restraint Required:	Max Fine 1st Offense:	Safety Belt Required:
Alabama	Resident drivers	0-3 yrs.	$10	4-5 yrs.
Alaska	All drivers	0-3 yrs.	$50	4-15 yrs.
Arizona	All drivers	0-4 yrs.	$50	See Safety Belt Laws
Arkansas	Resident drivers	0-3 yrs. and <40 lbs.	$50	4 yrs. or >40 lbs.
California	All drivers	0-3 yrs. and <40 lbs.	$100	4-15 yrs. or >40 lbs.
Colorado	All drivers	0-3 yrs. and <40 lbs.	$11	4-15 yrs. or >40 lbs.
Connecticut	All drivers	0-3 yrs. and <40 lbs.	$90	4-15 yrs. or >40 lbs.
Delaware	All drivers	0-3 yrs.	$29	4-15 yrs.
Dist. of Columbia	All drivers	0-3 yrs.	$55	4-16 yrs.
Florida	All drivers	0-3 yrs.	$60	4-5 yrs.[1]
Georgia	All drivers	0-2 yrs.	$50	3-4 yrs.
Hawaii	All drivers	0-2 yrs.	$100	3 yrs. only
Idaho	All drivers	0-3 yrs. and <40 lbs.	$52	See Safety Belt Laws
Illinois	All drivers	0-3 yrs.	$25	4-5 yrs.
Indiana	Resident drivers	0-2 yrs.	$500	3-4 yrs.
Iowa	Resident drivers	0-2 yrs.	$10	3-5 yrs.
Kansas	All drivers	0-3 yrs.	$20	4-13 yrs.
Kentucky	All drivers	0-40 inches	$50	See Safety Belt Laws
Louisiana	Resident drivers	0-2 yrs.	$50	3-12 yrs.
Maine	All drivers	0-3 yrs.	$55	4-18 yrs.
Maryland	All drivers	0-3 yrs. and <40 lbs.	$25	4-15 yrs. or >40 lbs.
Massachusetts	All drivers	0-4 yrs.	$25	5-12 yrs.
Michigan	All drivers	1-3 yrs. in front[2]	$10	1-3 yrs. in rear
Minnesota	All drivers	0-3 yrs.	$50	See Safety Belt Laws
Mississippi	Resident drivers	0-3 yrs.	$25	4-7 yrs.

Child Restraint Laws

	Law Applies To:	Child Restraint Required:	Max. Fine 1st Offense	Safety Belt Required:
Missouri	All drivers	0-3 yrs.	$25	4-15 yrs.
Montana	Resident drivers	0-1 yr.	$25	2-3 yrs. or <40 lbs.
Nebraska	Resident drivers	0-3 yrs. and <40 lbs.	$25	4 yrs. or >40 lbs.
Nevada	All drivers	0-4 yrs. and <40 lbs.	$100	See Safety Belt Laws
New Hampshire	All drivers	0-3 yrs.	$500	4-11 yrs.
New Jersey	All drivers	1 ½-4 yrs. in front[3]	$25	1 ½-4 yrs. in rear
New Mexico	All drivers	1-4 yrs. in front[2]	$25	1-4 yrs. in rear[4]
New York	All drivers	0-3 yrs.	$100	10-15 in front[5]
North Carolina	All drivers	0-3 yrs.	$25	4-11 yrs.
North Dakota	All drivers	0-2 yrs.	$20	3-10 yrs.
Ohio	Resident drivers	0-3 yrs. or <40 lbs.	$100	See Safety Belt Laws
Oklahoma	Resident drivers	0-3 yrs. or <60 lbs.	$25	4-5 yrs.
Oregon	All drivers	0-3 yrs. or <40 lbs.	$50	4-15 yrs. or >40 lbs.
Pennsylvania	All drivers	0-3 yrs.	$25	See Safety Belt Laws
Rhode Island	All drivers	0-2 yrs.	$30	3-12 yrs.[6]
South Carolina	Resident drivers	1-4 yrs. in front[2]	$25	4-5 yrs. in front[7]
South Dakota	All Drivers	0-1 yr.	$20	2-4 yrs.
Tennessee	All drivers	0-3 yrs.	$50	See Safety Belt Laws
Texas	All drivers	0-1 yr.	$50	2-3 yrs.
Utah	All drivers	0-1 yr.	$75	2-9 yrs.
Vermont	All drivers	0-4 yrs.	$25	5-12 yrs.
Virginia	All drivers	0-3 yrs.	$50	4-15 yrs.
Washington	All drivers	0-2 yrs.	$75	3-9 yrs.
West Virginia	All drivers	0-2 yrs.	$20	3-8 yrs.
Wisconsin	All drivers	0-3 yrs.	$75	4-7 yrs.
Wyoming	All drivers	0-4 yrs. and <40 lbs.	$25	See Safety Belt Laws

[1] Under 16 must ride in rear.
[2] 0-1 yr. in all seats.
[3] 0-1 ½ yrs. in all seats.
[4] 5-10 yrs. in all seats.
[5] 4-9 yrs. in all seats.
[6] Under 6 yrs. must be in rear.
[7] 1-5 yrs. in rear.

FUEL ECONOMY

A car's fuel efficiency affects both our environment and our wallets—which is why comparative mileage ratings are an important factor to most consumers. To save money and the environment, the first and most obvious step is to select a car that gets high mileage, so we've included the Environmental Protection Agency's fuel economy ratings for all 1999 vehicles. We also discuss numerous factors that affect your car's fuel efficiency, and caution you against the many products that falsely promise more gas mileage.

Using EPA ratings is an excellent way to incorporate fuel efficiency in selecting a new car. By comparing these ratings, even among cars of the same size, you'll find that fuel efficiency varies greatly. One compact car might get 36 miles per gallon (mpg) while another gets only 22 mpg. If you drive 15,000 miles a year and you pay $1.20 per gallon for fuel, the 36 mpg car will save you $319 a year over the "gas guzzler."

Octane Ratings: Once you've purchased your car, you'll be faced with choosing the right gasoline. Oil companies spend millions of dollars trying to get you to buy so-called higher performance or high octane fuels. Because high octane fuel can add considerably to your gas bill, it is important that you know what you're buying.

The octane rating of a gasoline is *not* a measure of power or quality. It is simply a measure of the gas's resistance to engine knock, which is the pinging sound you hear when the air and fuel mixture in your engine ignites prematurely during acceleration.

The octane rating appears on a yellow label on the fuel pump. Octane ratings vary with different types of gas (premium or regular), in different parts of the country (higher altitudes require lower octane ratings), and even between brands (Texaco's gasolines may have a different rating than Exxon's).

Determining the Right Octane Rating for Your Car: Using a lower-rated gasoline saves money. Most cars are designed to run on a posted octane rating of 87. The following procedure can help you select the lowest octane level for your car.

1 Have your engine tuned to exact factory specifications by a competent mechanic, and make sure it is in good working condition.

2 When the gas in your tank is very low, fill it up with your usual gasoline. After driving 10 to 15 miles, find a safe place to come to a complete stop and then accelerate rapidly. If your engine knocks during acceleration, switch to a higher octane rating. If there is no knocking sound, wait until your tank is very low and fill up with a lower rated gasoline. Repeat the test. When you determine the level of octane that causes your engine to knock during the test, use gasoline with the next highest rating.

Note: Your engine may knock when accelerating a heavily loaded car uphill or when the humidity is low. This is normal and does not call for a higher-octane gasoline.

Factors Affecting Fuel Economy

Fuel economy is affected by a number of factors that you can consider before you buy.

Transmission: Manual transmissions are generally more fuel-efficient than automatic transmissions. In fact, a 5-speed manual transmission can add up to 6.5 miles per gallon over a three-speed automatic. However, the incorrect use of a manual transmission wastes gas, so choose a transmission that matches your preference. Many transmissions now feature an overdrive gear, which can improve a vehicle's fuel economy by as much as 9 percent for an automatic transmission and 3 percent for a manual transmission.

Engine: The size of your car's engine greatly affects your fuel economy. The smaller your engine, the better your fuel efficiency. A 10-percent increase in the size of an engine can increase fuel consumption by 6 percent.

Cruise Control: Cruise control can save fuel because driving at a constant speed uses less fuel than changing speeds frequently.

Air Conditioning: Auto air conditioners add weight and require additional horsepower to operate. They can cost up to 3 miles per gallon in city driving. At highway speeds, however, an air conditioner has about the same effect on fuel economy as the air resistance created by opening the windows.

Trim Package: Upgrading a car's trim, installing soundproofing, and adding undercoating can increase the weight of a typical car by 150 pounds. For each 10 percent increase in weight, fuel economy drops 4 percent.

Power Options: Power steering, brakes, seats, windows, and roofs reduce your mileage by adding weight. Power steering alone can cause a 1-percent drop in fuel economy.

Here are some tips for after you buy:

Tune-Up: If you have a 2- to 3- mpg drop over several fill-ups that is not due to a change of driving pattern or vehicle load, first check tire pressure, then consider a tune-up. A properly tuned engine is a fuel saver.

Tire Inflation: For maximum fuel efficiency, tires should be inflated to the pressure range found on the label in your door well. The tire's maximum pressure may not be suitable for your car. Be sure to check the tire pressure when the tires are cold before you've driven a long distance.

Short Trips: Short trips can be expensive because they usually involve a "cold" vehicle. For the first mile or two before the engine gets warmed up, a cold vehicle only gets 30 to 40 percent of the mileage it gets at full efficiency.

Warning: Products that Don't Work

Hundreds of products on the market claim to improve fuel economy. Not only are most of these products ineffective, some may even damage your engine.

Sometimes the name or promotional material associated with these products implies they were endorsed by the federal government. *In fact, no government agency endorses any gas saving products.* Many of the products, however, *have* been tested by the U.S. EPA and rarely do they offer any fuel savings.

For copies of reports on these products, write Test and Evaluation Branch, U.S. EPA, 2565 Plymouth Rd., Ann Arbor, MI 48105.

The good news is that, slowly, cars are becoming environmentally friendlier. But how do you know which ones? Engine size, fuel type and emission system all contribute to fuel efficiency and the amount of pollution that your car emits. You do have choices and knowing the different emission options will allow you to better control the impact your car has on our environment. Buying "green" not only lowers air pollution, but sends a strong signal to manufacturers that building "green" cars pays off.

Because it is not easy to evaluate the impact your car has on the environment, experts at the American Council for an Energy-Efficient Economy have developed *The Green Car Rating* system. This rating system considers a wide variety of items that measure the environmentally friendliness of a particular car. Listed in the box are the most and least environmentally friendly cars based on ACEEE's *Green Car Rating*. You can check our Vehicle Pages and Buying Guide for more rating information from ACEEE. We strongly recommend that you get the full story on the green ratings and the details for virtually every new model in ACEEE's "Green Guide to Cars and Trucks". Copies are available for $8.95 from ACEEE, 1001 Connecticut Ave. NW, Washington, DC 20036 by calling 202-429-0063, or visit www.aceee.org.

Emissions Options: California has traditionally lead the country in requiring environmentally sensible vehicles. These CA certified vehicles are available nationwide. Buy checking ACEEE's "Green Guide to Cars and Trucks" you can find the emission rating for the cars you are considering. Here is what the ratings mean.

Federal Certification:

Tier 1: Current National Standard, the weakest, and therefore most polluting of the standards.

California Certification:

TLEV: Transitional Low Emission Vehicle, slightly stronger than the Federal Standard.

LEV: Low Emission Vehicle, an intermediate California standard, about twice as strong as Tier 1.

ULEV: Ultra Low Emission Vehicle, emphasizes very low emissions of compounds that cause smog and are toxic and carcinogenic.

ZEV: Zero Emission Vehicle, prohibits any tailpipe emissions.

Green Machines

Ten Greenest Vehicles	Greenest Engine Option (eng/cyl/trans)	Green Rating
GM EV1	All-Electric	Very Good
Honda Civic	1.6L CNG[2]/4/A, ULEV	Very Good
Honda EV Plus	All-Electric	Very Good
Chevrolet Metro	1.0L/3/M, LEV	Good
Ford Crown Victoria	4.6L CNG[2]/8/A, ULEV	Good
Suzuki Swift	1.3L/4/M, LEV	Good
Dodge Caravan	Electric "Epic" Model	Good
Mitsubishi Mirage	1.5L/4/M, LEV	Good
Mazda Protegé	1.5L/4/M, ULEV	Good
Dodge/Plymouth Neon	2.0L/4/M, LEV	Good

Ten Brownest Vehicles[1]		
Chevrolet Astro	4.3L/6/A, LEV	Very Poor
GMC Safari	4.3L/6/A, LEV	Very Poor
Mercury Villager	3.3L/6/A, TLEV	Very Poor
Chevrolet Venture	3.3L/6/A, TLEV	Very Poor
Chrysler T & C	3.3L/6/A, LEV	Very Poor
Nissan Quest	3.3L/6/A, LEV	Very Poor
Oldsmobile Silhouette	3.3L/6/A, TLEV	Very Poor
Pontiac Montana	3.3L/6/A, TLEV	Very Poor
Toyota Sienna	3.0L/4/A	Very Poor
Ford Windstar	3.0L/6/A, LEV	Very Poor

[1] The brownest of the green, these vehicles are still better than models without emissions options.
[2] Engine Runs on Compressed Natural Gas

Fuel Economy Ratings

Every year the Department of Energy publishes the results of the Environmental Protection Agency's (EPA) fuel economy tests in a comparative guide. In the past, millions of these booklets have been distributed to consumers who are eager to purchase fuel-efficient automobiles. However, the government has recently limited the availability of the guide. Because the success of the EPA program depends on consumers' ability to compare the fuel economy ratings easily, we have reprinted the EPA mileage figures for this year's misers and guzzlers.

1999 Fuel Economy Winners and Losers

The Misers	MPG City/Highway	Annual Fuel Cost[1]
Volkswagen New Beetle (1.9L/4/M5)[2]	42/49	$345
Volkswagen Jetta (1.9L/4/M5)[2]	42/49	$345
Volkswagen Golf (1.9L/4/M5)[2]	42/49	$345
Chevrolet Metro (1L/3/M5)	41/47	$360
Suzuki Swift (1.3L/4/M5)	39/43	$387
Chevrolet Metro (1.3L/4/M5)	39/43	$387
Volkswagen Golf (1.9L/4/L4)[2]	34/45	$396
Volkswagen Jetta (1.9L/4/L4)[2]	34/45	$396
Volkswagen New Beetle (1.9L/4/L4)[2]	34/45	$396
Honda Civic HX (1.6L/4/M5)	35/43	$407
Mitsubishi Mirage (1.5L/4/M5)	33/40	$440
Honda Civic HX (1.6L/4/AV)	34/38	$440

The Guzzlers[3]	MPG City/Highway	Annual Fuel Cost[1]
Mercedes-Benz CL600 (6L/12/L5)	13/19	$991
GMC Safari AWD (pass) (4.3L/6/L4)	15/19	$933
Chevrolet Astro AWD (pass) (4.3L/6/L4)	15/19	$933
GMC Safari 2WD (4.3L/6/L4)	16/20	$881
Chevrolet Astro AWD (cargo) (4.3L/6/L4)	16/20	$881
BMW 540I (4.4L/8/L5)	15/21	$881
Mercedes-Benz CL500 (5L/8/L5)	15/22	$881
Chevrolet Astro 2WD (4.3L/6/L4)	16/21	$881
GMC Safari AWD (cargo) (4.3L/6/L4)	16/20	$881
BMW 540I Touring (4.4L/8/L5)	15/21	$881
BMW 540I (4.4L/8/M6)	15/23	$881
Chevrolet Camaro (5.7L/8/L4)	17/24	$793
Ford Mustang (4.6L/8/L4)	17/23	$793
Infiniti Q45 (4.1L/8/L4)	17/24	$793
Lexus GS300/GS400 (4L/8/L5)	17/24	$793
Ford Taurus (3.4L/8/L4)	16/25	$793
Ford Crown Victoria (4.6L/8/L4)	17/24	$793
Lincoln Town Car (4.6L/8/L4)	17/24	$793
Mercury Grand Marquis (4.6L/8/L4)	17/24	$793

Based on 1999 EPA figures. (Engine size/number of cylinders/transmission type)
[1] Based on driving 15,000 miles per year.
[2] Diesel vehicles.
[3] Based on popular models.

The following pages contain the EPA mileage ratings and the average annual fuel cost for most of the cars and many popular trucks sold in the United States. We have arranged the list in alphabetical order. After the car name, we have listed the engine size in liters, the number of cylinders, and some other identifiers: A = automatic transmission; L = lockup transmission; M = manual transmission.

The table includes the EPA city (first) and highway (second) fuel economy ratings. The city numbers will most closely resemble your expected mileage for everyday driving. The third column presents your average annual fuel cost. Reviewing this number will give you a better idea of how differences in fuel economy can affect your pocketbook. The amount is based on driving 15,000 miles per year.

Car (eng./# of cyl./trans.)	City	Hwy	Cost	Car (eng./# of cyl./trans.)	City	Hwy	Cost
Acura 2.3CL (2.3L/4/M5)	24	31	$566	BMW 540I (4.4L/8/L5)	15	21	$881
Acura 2.3CL (3L/6/L4)	20	28	$661	BMW 540I (4.4L/8/L5)	18	24	$755
Acura 2.3CL (2.3L/4/L4)	22	30	$610	BMW Z3 coupe (2.8L/6/M5)	19	26	$721
Acura 3.0CL (2.3L/4/M5)	24	31	$566	BMW Z3 coupe (2.8L/6/L4)	19	26	$721
Acura 3.0CL (3L/6/L4)	20	28	$661	BMW Z3 Roadster (2.5L/6/L4)	19	26	$721
Acura 3.0CL (2.3L/4/L4)	22	30	$610	BMW Z3 Roadster (2.8L/6/L4)	19	26	$721
Acura 3.2TL (3.2L/6/L4)	19	27	$689	BMW Z3 Roadster (2.5L/6/M5)	20	27	$661
Acura 3.5RL (3.5L/6/L4)	18	24	$755	BMW Z3 Roadster (2.8L/6/M5)	19	26	$721
Acura Integra (1.8L/4/L4)	24	32	$566	Buick Century (3.1L/6/L4)	20	29	$661
Acura Integra (1.8L/4/M5)	25	32	$566	Buick LeSabre (3.8L/6/L4)	19	30	$661
Acura Integra (1.8L/4/M5)	25	31	$566	Buick Park Avenue (3.8L/6/L4)	19	28	$661
Audi A4 (2.8L/6/M5)	20	29	$661	Buick Park Avenue (3.8L/6/L4)	18	27	$721
Audi A4 (1.8L/4/L5)	21	31	$610	Buick Regal (3.8L/6/L4)	18	27	$721
Audi A4 (2.8L/6/L5)	18	29	$661	Buick Regal (3.8L/6/L4)	19	30	$661
Audi A4 (1.8L/4/M5)	23	32	$566	Buick Riviera (3.8L/6/L4)	18	27	$721
Audi A4 Quattro (1.8L/4/L5)	18	27	$721	Cadillac DeVille (4.6L/8/L4)	17	26	$721
Audi A4 Quattro (2.8L/6/M5)	19	27	$689	Cadillac Eldorado (4.6L/8/L4)	17	26	$721
Audi A4 Quattro (2.8L/6/L5)	17	27	$721	Cadillac Seville (4.6L/8/L4)	17	26	$721
Audi A4 Quattro (1.8L/4/M5)	21	29	$634	Chev. Astro 2WD (cargo) (4.3L/6/L4)	16	21	$881
Audi A6 (2.8L/6/L5)	17	27	$721	Chev. Astro AWD (cargo) (4.3L/6/L4)	16	20	$881
Audi A6 Avant Quattro (2.8L/6/L5)	17	26	$721	Chev. Camaro (3.8L/6/L4)	19	29	$661
Audi A6 Quattro (2.8L/6/L5)	17	26	$721	Chev. Camaro (5.7L/8/M6)	19	28	$661
BMW 318TI (1.9L/4/L4)	23	31	$587	Chev. Camaro (5.7L/8/L4)	17	24	$793
BMW 318TI (1.9L/4/M5)	23	32	$566	Chev. Camaro (3.8L/6/M5)	19	30	$661
BMW 323I (2.5L/6/L5)	19	28	$661	Chev. Cavalier (2.2L/4/L4)	23	31	$587
BMW 323I (2.5L/6/M5)	20	29	$661	Chev. Cavalier (2.4L/4/L4)	22	30	$610
BMW 323I Conv. (2.5L/6/L4)	19	27	$689	Chev. Cavalier (2.2L/4/M5)	24	34	$547
BMW 323I Conv. (2.5L/6/M5)	21	31	$610	Chev. Cavalier (2.2L/4/L3)	23	29	$610
BMW 323IS (2.5L/6/L4)	19	27	$689	Chev. Cavalier (2.4L/4/M5)	23	33	$566
BMW 323IS (2.5L/6/M5)	21	31	$610	Chev. Lumina (3.8L/6/L4)	19	30	$661
BMW 328I (2.8L/6/M5)	20	29	$661	Chev. Lumina (3.1L/6/L4)	20	29	$661
BMW 328I (2.8L/6/L5)	19	27	$689	Chev. Malibu (3.1L/6/L4)	20	29	$661
BMW 328I CONV (2.8L/6/L4)	20	27	$661	Chev. Malibu (2.4L/4/L4)	22	30	$610
BMW 328I CONV (2.8L/6/M5)	20	29	$661	Chev. Metro (1.3L/4/M5)	39	43	$387
BMW 328IS (2.8L/6/L4)	20	27	$661	Chev. Metro (1.3L/4/A3)	30	34	$495
BMW 328IS (2.8L/6/M5)	20	29	$661	Chev. Metro (1L/3/M5)	41	47	$360
BMW 528I (2.8L/6/L4)	18	26	$721	Chev. Monte Carlo (3.1L/6/L4)	20	29	$661
BMW 528I (2.8L/6/M5)	20	29	$661	Chev. Monte Carlo (3.8L/6/L4)	19	30	$661
BMW 540I (4.4L/8/M6)	15	23	$834	Chev. Prizm (1.8L/4/M5)	31	37	$466

Car (eng./# of cyl./trans.)	City	Hwy	Cost	Car (eng./# of cyl./trans.)	City	Hwy	Cost
Chev. Prizm (1.8L/4/L4)	28	36	$495	Ford Taurus Wgn. (3L/6/L4)	18	26	$721
Chev. Prizm (1.8L/4/L3)	28	33	$528	Ford Windstar FWD Wgn. (3.8L/6/L4)	17	23	$793
Chev. Venture FWD (3.4L/6/L4)	18	25	$721	Ford Windstar FWD Van (3.8L/6/L4)	18	23	$793
Chrysler 300 M (3.5L/6/L4)	18	27	$721	Ford Windstar FWD Van (3L/6/L4)	17	23	$793
Chrysler Cirrus (2.5L/6/L4)	19	27	$689	Ford Windstar FWD Wgn. (3L/6/L4)	17	23	$793
Chrysler Cirrus (2.5L/6/L4)	19	27	$689	GMC Safari 2WD (cargo) (4.3L/6/L4)	16	21	$881
Chrysler Concorde (2.7L/6/L4)	21	30	$610	GMC Safari AWD (cargo) (4.3L/6/L4)	16	20	$881
Chrysler Concorde (3.2L/6/L4)	19	29	$661	Honda Accord (3L/6/L4)	20	28	$661
Chrysler LHS (3.5L/6/L4)	18	27	$721	Honda Accord (2.3L/4/M5)	25	31	$566
Chrysler Sebring (2L/4/L4)	21	30	$610	Honda Accord (2.3L/4/M5)	25	31	$566
Chrysler Sebring (2.5L/6/L4)	19	27	$689	Honda Accord (2.3L/4/L4)	22	29	$610
Chrysler Sebring (2L/4/M5)	22	31	$610	Honda Accord (2.3L/4/L4)	23	30	$610
Chrysler Sebring Conv. (2.5L/6/L4)	19	27	$689	Honda Civic (1.6L/4/M5)	32	37	$466
Chrysler Sebring Conv. (2.5L/6/L4)	19	27	$689	Honda Civic (1.6L/4/L4)	28	35	$495
Chrysler Sebring Conv. (2.4L/4/L4)	21	30	$610	Honda Civic (1.6L/4/M5)	26	31	$566
Chrysler T&C 2WD (3.3L/6/L4)	18	24	$755	Honda Civic (1.6L/4/M5)	29	35	$495
Chrysler T&C 2WD (3.8L/6/L4)	17	24	$793	Honda Civic (1.6L/4/L4)	28	35	$495
Chrysler T&C AWD (3.8L/6/L4)	16	23	$793	Honda Civic HX (1.6L/4/AV)*	34	38	$440
Dodge Avenger (2L/4/L4)	21	30	$610	Honda Civic HX (1.6L/4/M5)	35	43	$407
Dodge Avenger (2L/4/M5)	22	32	$587	Honda Prelude (2.2L/4/L4)	21	26	$661
Dodge Avenger (2.5L/6/L4)	19	27	$689	Honda Prelude (2.2L/4/M5)	22	27	$661
Dodge Caravan 2WD (2.4L/4/L3)	20	26	$689	Hyundai Accent (1.5L/4/L4)	26	36	$511
Dodge Caravan 2WD (3L/6/L4)	19	26	$721	Hyundai Accent (1.5L/4/M5)	28	37	$495
Dodge Caravan 2WD (3.3L/6/L4)	18	24	$755	Hyundai Elantra (2L/4/L4)	22	31	$610
Dodge Caravan 2WD (3.8L/6/L4)	17	23	$793	Hyundai Elantra (2L/4/M5)	24	33	$566
Dodge Caravan 2WD (3.8L/6/L4)	17	24	$793	Hyundai Sonata (2.5L/6/M5)	20	29	$661
Dodge Caravan AWD (3.8L/6/L4)	16	23	$793	Hyundai Sonata (2.4L/4/M5)	21	30	$610
Dodge Caravan AWD (3.8L/6/L4)	16	23	$793	Hyundai Sonata (2.5L/6/L4)	20	28	$661
Dodge Intrepid (2.7L/6/L4)	21	30	$610	Hyundai Sonata (2.4L/4/L4)	21	28	$661
Dodge Intrepid (3.2L/6/L4)	18	28	$689	Hyundai Tiburon (2L/4/L4)	22	29	$610
Dodge Neon (2L/4/L3)	23	32	$566	Hyundai Tiburon (2L/4/M5)	22	31	$610
Dodge Neon (2L/4/M5)	28	39	$466	Infiniti G20 (2L/4/L4)	22	28	$634
Dodge Stratus (2.4L/4/L4)	21	30	$610	Infiniti G20 (2L/4/M5)	23	31	$587
Dodge Stratus (2.5L/6/L4)	19	27	$689	Infiniti I30 (3L/6/L4)	21	28	$661
Dodge Stratus (2.5L/6/L4)	19	27	$689	Infiniti I30 (3L/6/M5)	21	26	$661
Dodge Stratus (2L/4/M5)	26	37	$495	Infiniti Q45 (4.1L/8/L4)	17	24	$793
Ford Contour (2.5L/6/M5)	20	28	$661	Isuzu Oasis (2.3L/4/L4)	21	26	$661
Ford Contour (2L/4/L4)	23	31	$587	Kia Sephia (1.8L/4/M5)	24	31	$566
Ford Contour (2.5L/6/L4)	20	29	$661	Kia Sephia (1.8L/4/L4)	23	31	$587
Ford Contour (2L/4/M5)	24	34	$547	Lexus ES 300 (3L/6/L4)	19	26	$721
Ford Crown Victoria (4.6L/8/L4)	17	24	$793	Lexus GS 300/GS 400 (3L/6/L5)	20	25	$721
Ford Escort (2L/4/L4)	25	34	$528	Lexus GS 300/GS 400 (4L/8/L5)	17	24	$793
Ford Escort (2L/4/M5)	28	37	$495	Lexus LS 400 (4L/6/L5)	18	25	$721
Ford Escort ZX2 (2L/4/L4)	25	33	$547	Lexus SC 300/SC 400 (4L/6/L5)	18	25	$721
Ford Escort ZX2 (2L/4/M5)	25	33	$547	Lexus SC 300/SC 400 (3L/6/L4)	19	24	$721
Ford Mustang (3.8L/6/ M5)	20	29	$661	Lincoln Continental (4.6L/8/L4)	17	25	$755
Ford Mustang (4.6L/8/L4)	17	23	$793	Lincoln Town Car (4.6L/8/L4)	17	24	$793
Ford Taurus (3.4L/8/L4)	16	25	$793	Mazda 626 (2L/4/L4)	22	29	$610
Ford Taurus (3L/6/L4)	18	26	$721	Mazda 626 (2.5L/6/M5)	21	27	$661
Ford Taurus (3L/6/L4)	20	28	$661	Mazda 626 (2.5L/6/L4)	20	26	$689
Ford Taurus Wgn. (3L/6/L4)	18	27	$721	Mazda 626 (2L/4/M5)	26	33	$528

*AV=Automatic variable transmission.

Car (eng./# of cyl./trans.)	City	Hwy	Cost
Mazda Millenia (2.5L/6/L4)	20	27	$661
Mazda Millenia (2.3L/6/L4)	20	28	$661
Mazda MX-5 Miata (1.8L/4/L4)	23	29	$610
Mazda MX-5 Miata (1.8L/4/M5)	25	29	$587
Mazda Protegé (1.6L/4/M5)	29	34	$495
Mazda Protegé (1.6L/4/L4)	26	33	$528
Mazda Protegé (1.8L/4/L4)	24	29	$610
Mazda Protegé (1.8L/4/M5)	26	30	$566
M-Benz C230 Kompressor (2.3L/4/L5)	21	29	$634
M-Benz C280 (2.8L/6/L5)	21	27	$661
M-Benz C43 AMG (4.3L/8/L5)	18	23	$793
M-Benz CL500 (5L/8/L5)	15	22	$881
M-Benz CL600 (6L/12/L5)	13	19	$991
M-Benz CLK320 (3.2L/6/L5)	21	29	$634
M-Benz CLK320 cabriolet (3.2L/6/L5)	19	28	$661
M-Benz CLK430 (4.3L/8/L5)	18	25	$721
M-Benz E300 turbodiesel (3L/6/L5)	26	36	$511
M-Benz E320 (3.2L/6/L5)	21	30	$610
M-Benz E320 (3.2L/6/L5)	20	28	$661
M-Benz E320 4matic (3.2L/6/L5)	20	28	$661
M-Benz E320 4matic (3.2L/6/L5)	20	26	$689
M-Benz E430 (4.3L/8/L5)	19	26	$721
Mercury Cougar (2L/4/L4)	23	31	$587
Mercury Cougar (2.5L/6/M5)	19	28	$661
Mercury Cougar (2L/4/M5)	24	34	$547
Mercury Cougar (2.5L/6/L4)	20	29	$661
Mercury Grand Marquis (4.6L/8/L4)	17	24	$793
Mercury Mystique (2.5L/6/L4)	20	29	$661
Mercury Mystique (2L/4/M5)	24	34	$547
Mercury Mystique (2.5L/6/M5)	19	28	$661
Mercury Mystique (2L/4/L4)	23	31	$587
Mercury Sable (3L/6/L4)	20	28	$661
Mercury Sable (3L/6/L4)	18	26	$721
Mercury Sable Wgn. (3L/6/L4)	18	26	$721
Mercury Sable Wgn. (3L/6/L4)	19	27	$689
Mercury Tracer (2L/4/L4)	25	34	$528
Mercury Tracer (2L/4/M5)	28	37	$495
Merc. Villager FWD Wgn. (3.3L/6/L4)	17	24	$793
Mitsubishi Diamante (3.5L/6/L4)	18	24	$755
Mitsubishi Eclipse (2L/4/L4)	20	27	$661
Mitsubishi Eclipse (2L/4/L4)	21	30	$610
Mitsubishi Eclipse (2L/4/L4)	19	25	$721
Mitsubishi Eclipse (2L/4/M5)	23	31	$587
Mitsubishi Eclipse (2L/4/M5)	22	33	$566
Mitsubishi Eclipse (2L/4/M5)	21	28	$661
Mitsu. Eclipse Convert. (2L/4/M5)	23	31	$587
Mitsu. Eclipse Convert. (2.4L/4/L4)	21	28	$661
Mitsu. Eclipse Convert. (2.4L/4/M5)	22	30	$610
Mitsu. Eclipse Convert. (2L/4/L4)	20	27	$661
Mitsubishi Galant (2.4L/4/M5)	23	31	$587
Mitsubishi Galant (3L/6/L4)	20	27	$661
Mitsubishi Galant (2.4L/4/L4)	21	28	$661
Mitsubishi Mirage (1.5L/4/L4)	28	36	$495
Mitsubishi Mirage (1.8L/4/L4)	26	33	$528
Mitsubishi Mirage (1.5L/4/M5)	33	40	$440
Mitsubishi Mirage (1.8L/4/M5)	28	36	$495
Nissan Altima (2.4L/4/M5)	24	31	$566
Nissan Altima (2.4L/4/L4)	22	30	$610
Nissan Maxima (3L/6/M5)	22	27	$661
Nissan Maxima (3L/6/L4)	21	28	$661
Nissan Quest (3.3L/6/L4)	17	24	$793
Nissan Sentra (2L/4/M5)	23	31	$587
Nissan Sentra (1.6L/4/M5)	29	39	$466
Nissan Sentra (2L/4/L4)	23	30	$610
Nissan Sentra (1.6L/4/L4)	27	36	$495
Olds Alero (3.4L/6/L4)	20	28	$661
Olds Alero (2.4L/4/L4)	22	30	$610
Olds Aurora (4L/8/L4)	17	26	$721
Olds Cutlass (3.1L/6/L4)	20	29	$661
Olds Cutlass (2.4L/4/L4)	22	30	$610
Olds 88 (3.8L/6/L4)	19	29	$661
Olds 88 (3.8L/6/L4)	18	27	$721
Olds Intrigue (3.5L/6/L4)	19	27	$689
Olds Intrigue (3.8L/6/L4)	19	30	$661
Olds Silhouette FWD (3.4L/6/L4)	18	25	$721
Plymouth Breeze (2L/4/M5)	26	37	$495
Plymouth Breeze (2L/4/L4)	22	31	$610
Plymouth Breeze (2.4L/4/L4)	21	30	$610
Plymouth Voyager 2WD (3L/6/L4)	19	26	$721
Plymouth Voyager 2WD (3.3L/6/L4)	18	24	$755
Plymouth Voyager 2WD (3.8L/6/L4)	17	24	$793
Plymouth Voyager 2WD (2.4L/4/L3)	20	26	$689
Pontiac Bonneville (3.8L/6/L4)	18	27	$721
Pontiac Bonneville (3.8L/6/L4)	19	28	$661
Pontiac Firebird (5.7L/8/M6)	19	28	$661
Pontiac Firebird (3.8L/6/M5)	19	30	$661
Pontiac Firebird (5.7L/8/L4)	18	24	$755
Pontiac Firebird (3.8L/6/L4)	19	29	$661
Pontiac Grand Am (3.4L/6/L4)	20	28	$661
Pontiac Grand Am (2.4L/4/L4)	22	30	$610
Pontiac Grand Prix (3.8L/6/L4)	18	28	$689
Pontiac Grand Prix (3.8L/6/L4)	19	30	$661
Pontiac Grand Prix (3.1L/6/L4)	20	29	$661
Pontiac Montana FWD (3.4L/6/L4)	18	25	$721
Pontiac Sunfire (2.4L/4/M5)	23	33	$566
Pontiac Sunfire (2.2L/4/L3)	23	29	$610
Pontiac Sunfire (2.2L/4/L4)	23	31	$587
Pontiac Sunfire (2.4L/4/L4)	22	30	$610
Pontiac Sunfire (2.2L/4/M5)	24	34	$547
Saab 9-3 (2L/4/L4)	19	25	$721
Saab 9-3 (2L/4/M5)	20	27	$661
Saab 9-3 (2L/4/M5)	19	27	$689

Car (eng./# of cyl./trans.)	City	Hwy	Cost
Saab 9-3 Conv. (2L/4/M5)	19	27	$689
Saab 9-3 Conv. (2L/4/L4)	19	25	$721
Saab 9-3 Conv. (2L/4/M5)	20	27	$661
Saab 9-5 (3L/6/L4)	18	26	$721
Saab 9-5 (2.3L/4/M5)	21	30	$610
Saab 9-5 (2.3L/4/L4)	19	26	$721
Saturn SC (1.9L/4/M5)	27	38	$495
Saturn SC (1.9L/4/L4)	25	35	$528
Saturn SC (1.9L/4/L4)	27	37	$495
Saturn SC (1.9L/4/M5)	29	40	$466
Saturn SL (1.9L/4/M5)	29	40	$466
Saturn SL (1.9L/4/L4)	27	37	$495
Saturn SW (1.9L/4/M5)	28	28	$480
Saturn SW (1.9L/4/L4)	25	35	$528
Subaru Impreza AWD (2.2L/4/M5)	22	29	$610
Subaru Impreza AWD (2.5L/4/L4)	22	28	$634
Subaru Impreza AWD (2.2L/4/L4)	23	29	$610
Subaru Impreza AWD (2.5L/4/M5)	22	29	$610
Subaru Legacy AWD (2.2L/4/M5)	22	29	$610
Subaru Legacy AWD (2.5L/4/M5)	21	27	$661
Subaru Legacy AWD (2.5L/4/L4)	21	26	$661
Subaru Legacy AWD (2.2L/4/L4)	22	29	$610
Sub. Legacy Wgn. AWD (2.5L/4/M5)	21	27	$661
Sub. Legacy Wgn. AWD (2.2L/4/M5)	22	29	$610
Sub. Legacy Wgn. AWD (2.5L/4/L4)	21	26	$661
Sub. Legacy Wgn. AWD (2.2L/4/L4)	22	29	$610
Suzuki Esteem (1.6L/4/L4)	27	34	$528
Suzuki Esteem (1.6L/4/M5)	30	37	$466
Suzuki Swift (1.3L/4/M5)	39	43	$387
Suzuki Swift (1.3L/4/A3)	30	34	$495
Toyota Avalon (3L/6/L4)	21	29	$634
Toyota Camry (2.2L/4/L4)	23	30	$610
Toyota Camry (3L/6/M5)	21	28	$661
Toyota Camry (2.2L/4/M5)	23	32	$566
Toyota Camry (3L/6/L4)	20	28	$661
Toyota Celica (2.2L/4/M5)	22	28	$634
Toyota Celica (2.2L/4/L4)	22	28	$634
Toyota Celica Conv. (2.2L/4/L4)	23	30	$610
Toyota Celica Conv. (2.2L/4/M5)	22	28	$634
Toyota Corolla (1.8L/4/L3)	28	33	$528
Toyota Corolla (1.8L/4/M5)	31	38	$466
Toyota Corolla (1.8L/4/L4)	28	36	$495
Toyota Sienna (3L/6/L4)	18	24	$755
Toyota Solara (3L/6/M5)	21	28	$661
Toyota Solara (2.2L/4/L4)	23	30	$610
Toyota Solara (3L/6/L4)	20	28	$661
Toyota Solara (2.2L/4/M5)	23	32	$566

Car (eng./# of cyl./trans.)	City	Hwy	Cost
VW New Beetle (2L/4/L4)	22	28	$634
VW New Beetle (1.9L/4/M5)	42	49	$345
VW New Beetle (1.9L/4/L4)	34	45	$396
VW New Beetle (2L/4/M5)	24	31	$566
VW Golf (2L/4/M5)	24	31	$566
VW Golf (1.9L/4/L4)	34	45	$396
VW Golf (1.9L/4/M5)	42	49	$345
VW Golf (2L/4/L4)	22	28	$634
VW Jetta (1.9L/4/L4)	34	45	$396
VW Jetta (2.8L/6/L4)	19	26	$721
VW Jetta (2L/4/M5)	24	31	$566
VW Jetta (2.8L/6/M5)	19	28	$661
VW Jetta (1.9L/4/M5)	42	49	$345
VW Jetta (2L/4/L4)	22	28	$634
VW Passat (1.8L/4/M5)	23	32	$566
VW Passat (1.8L/4/L5)	21	31	$610
VW Passat (2.8L/6/L5)	18	29	$661
VW Passat (2.8L/6/M5)	20	29	$661
VW Passat Syncro (2.8L/6/L5)	17	26	$721
VW Passat Wgn. (1.8L/4/L5)	21	31	$610
VW Passat Wgn. (2.8L/6/L5)	18	29	$661
VW Passat Wgn. (2.8L/6/M5)	20	29	$661
VW Passat Wgn. (1.8L/4/M5)	23	32	$566
VW Passat Wgn. Syncro (2.8L/6/L5)	17	26	$721
Volvo C70 (2.3L/5/L4)	20	27	$661
Volvo C70 (2.4L/5/L4)	20	27	$661
Volvo C70 (2.3L/5/M5)	20	28	$661
Volvo C70 Conv. (2.3L/5/M5)	20	27	$661
Volvo C70 Conv. (2.4L/5/L4)	19	27	$689
Volvo C70 Conv. (2.3L/5/L4)	19	26	$721
Volvo S70 (2.4L/5/M5)	21	29	$634
Volvo S70 (2.3L/5/M5)	20	28	$661
Volvo S70 (2.3L/5/L4)	20	27	$661
Volvo S70 (2.4L/5/L4)	20	27	$661
Volvo S70 (2.4L/5/L4)	20	28	$661
Volvo S70 AWD (2.4L/5/L4)	18	25	$721
Volvo S70 AWD (2.3L/5/L4)	18	25	$721
Volvo S80 (2.8L/6/L4)	18	27	$721
Volvo S80 (2.9L/6/L4)	19	27	$689
Volvo V70 (2.3L/5/M5)	20	28	$661
Volvo V70 (2.4L/5/M5)	21	29	$634
Volvo V70 (2.4L/5/L4)	20	27	$661
Volvo V70 (2.4L/5/L4)	20	28	$661
Volvo V70 (2.3L/5/L4)	20	27	$661
Volvo V70 AWD (2.4L/5/L4)	18	25	$721
Volvo V70 AWD (2.3L/5/L4)	18	25	$721

MAINTENANCE

After you buy a car, maintenance costs will be a significant portion of your operating expenses. This chapter allows you to consider and compare some of these costs *before* deciding which car to purchase. These costs include preventive maintenance servicing—such as changing the oil and filters—as well as the cost of repairs after your warranty expires. On the following pages, we compared the costs of preventive maintenance and nine likely repairs for the 1999 models. Since the cost of a repair also depends on the shop and the mechanic, this chapter includes tips for finding a good shop, communicating effectively with a mechanic, and extending the life of your car.

Preventive maintenance is the periodic servicing, specified by the manufacturer, that keeps your car running properly. For example, regularly changing the oil and oil filter. Every owner's manual specifies a schedule of recommended servicing for at least the first 50,000 miles, and the tables on the following pages estimate the cost of following this preventive maintenance schedule.

If for some reason you do not have an owner's manual with the preventive maintenance schedule, contact the manufacturer to obtain one.

Note: Some dealers and repair shops create their own maintenance schedules which call for more frequent (and thus more expensive) servicing than the manufacturer's recommendations. If the servicing recommended by your dealer or repair shop doesn't match what the car maker recommends, make sure you understand and agree to the extra items.

The tables also list the costs for nine repairs that typically occur during the first 100,000 miles. There is no precise way to predict exactly when a repair will be needed. But if you keep a car for 75,000 to 100,000 miles, it is likely that you will experience most of these repairs at least once. The last column provides a relative indication of how expensive these nine repairs are for many cars. Repair cost is rated as *Very Good* if the total for nine repairs is in the bottom fifth of all the cars rated, and *Very Poor* if the total is in the top fifth.

Most repair shops use "flat-rate manuals" to estimate repair costs. These manuals list the approximate time required for repairing many items. Each automobile manufacturer publishes its own manual and there are several independent manuals as well. For many repairs, the time varies from one manual to another. Some repair shops even use different manuals for different repairs. To determine a repair bill, a shop multiplies the time listed in its manual by its hourly labor rate and then adds the cost of parts.

Our cost estimates are based on flat-rate manual repair times multiplied by a nationwide average labor rate of $50 per hour. All estimates also include the cost of replaced parts and related adjustments, which are based on 1997 figures.

Prices in the following tables may not predict the exact costs of these repairs. For example, the labor rate for your area may be more or less than the national average. However, the prices will provide you with a relative comparison of maintenance costs for various automobiles.

	PM Costs to 50,000 Miles	Water Pump	Alternator	Front Brake Pads	Starter	Fuel Injection	Fuel Pump	Struts/ Shocks	Timing Belt/Chain	Power Steering Pump	Relative Maint. Cost
Subcompact											
Chevrolet Metro	837	266	386	111	328	313	620	265	116	790	Vry. Pr.
Dodge/Plymouth Neon	747	248	326	129	230	182	306	142	213	281	Vry. Gd.
Ford Escort	703	185	315	107	300	98	130	173	170	160	Vry. Gd.
Honda Civic	942	193	353	100	374	154	230	182	130	390	Good
Hyundai Accent	378	200	294	78	293	106	200	159	173	524	Vry. Gd.
Kia Sephia	749	236	327	84	289	268	375	289	202	399	Average
Mazda Miata	840	237	373	92	202	290	406	227	172	636	Poor
Mazda Protegé	840	262	244	94	267	312	304	251	158	747	Poor
Mercury Tracer	703	175	279	104	264	78	187	258	135	175	Vry. Gd.
Mitsubishi Mirage	1111	225	275	121	177	159	390	204	117	633	Average
Nissan Sentra	771	177	456	94	307	186	153	204	396	328	Average
Saturn SC	937	139	207	96	182	114	246	166	275	246	Vry. Gd.
Saturn SL/SW	937	139	207	96	182	114	246	166	265	246	Vry. Gd.
Subaru Impreza	626	214	372	113	398	150	319	340	169	459	Average
Suzuki Esteem	837	242	795	115	338	287	482	430	188	626	Vry. Pr.
Suzuki Swift	837	266	308	115	270	259	610	341	186	661	Vry. Pr.
Volkswagen New Beetle	217	283	697	93	331	186	388	237	179	410	Poor
Compact											
Acura Integra	1165	274	408	100	340	160	432	286	185	590	Poor
BMW 3 Series	333	157	360	108	357	169	298	454	403	477	Poor
BMW Z3	333	157	357	116	359	249	269	485	391	481	Poor
Chevrolet Cavalier	747	144	220	99	137	139	575	233	298	372	Good
Chevrolet Prizm	907	192	471	118	401	190	265	365	178	631	Poor
Chrysler Sebring	730	230	248	140	348	181	260	155	230	351	Good
Dodge Avenger	730	230	248	140	323	140	260	175	210	506	Good
Ford Contour	703	269	424	93	402	72	230	184	203	211	Good
Honda Prelude	944	265	362	100	342	165	329	277	210	555	Poor
Hyundai Elantra	378	180	297	70	308	109	182	204	185	514	Vry. Gd.
Hyundai Tiburon	378	175	295	73	306	104	177	172	185	511	Vry. Gd.
Infiniti G20	759	199	406	108	270	166	204	229	656	494	Poor
Average	**739**	**228**	**374**	**113**	**305**	**186**	**339**	**279**	**291**	**435**	

	PM Costs to 50,000 Miles	Water Pump	Alternator	Front Brake Pads	Starter	Fuel Injection	Fuel Pump	Struts/ Shocks	Timing Belt/Chain	Power Steering Pump	Relative Maint. Cost
Compact (cont.)											
Mazda 626	840	216	256	101	243	243	385	190	166	314	Good
Mercury Mystique	715	269	423	93	402	72	230	176	203	211	Good
Mitsubishi Eclipse	747	268	391	118	291	146	256	161	217	306	Good
Mitsubishi Galant	1062	253	287	118	221	184	264	147	204	357	Vry. Gd.
Oldsmobile Alero	752	348	270	102	319	199	600	367	256	306	Poor
Pontiac Grand Am	752	386	236	99	231	147	600	287	244	285	Average
Pontiac Sunfire	752	144	220	99	137	150	590	233	298	368	Good
Subaru Legacy	606	219	201	113	272	150	319	297	389	359	Average
Toyota Celica	983	245	360	98	277	210	393	318	155	654	Poor
Toyota Corolla	907	222	427	95	339	193	283	331	181	625	Poor
Volkswagen Golf	217	238	468	117	373	163	379	189	94	245	Average
Volkswagen Jetta	217	238	468	117	373	163	379	184	94	245	Average
Intermediate											
Audi A4[1]	0	323	752	158	583	413	270	322	195	470	Vry. Pr.
Audi A8[1]	0	566	830	175	661	186	628	379	415	524	Vry. Pr.
Buick Century	759	127	205	104	248	211	355	261	414	244	Good
Buick Regal	759	169	219	109	212	193	396	259	382	247	Good
Cadillac Catera	581	278	756	155	433	276	298	276	257	590	Vry. Pr.
Chevrolet Camaro	759	173	287	106	263	156	599	497	239	391	Poor
Chrysler Cirrus	730	292	301	124	235	196	274	114	204	365	Good
Chrysler Concorde	730	280	199	129	245	190	276	244	230	278	Good
Dodge Intrepid	730	87	200	129	245	188	276	264	230	278	Vry. Gd.
Dodge Stratus	730	213	330	122	213	144	274	134	197	370	Vry. Gd.
Ford Mustang	772	193	413	107	341	136	229	181	339	314	Average
Ford Taurus	685	170	325	95	355	132	278	198	350	211	Good
Honda Accord	944	223	356	100	291	137	317	244	219	504	Average
Hyundai Sonata	378	255	307	85	168	109	205	175	275	598	Good
Mazda Millenia	838	306	782	126	252	362	459	365	292	910	Vry. Pr.
Mercedes-Benz C-Class	1059	323	947	109	454	183	227	236	196	512	Vry. Pr.
Mercury Sable	685	213	292	95	361	87	269	179	227	208	Vry. Gd.
Average	**739**	**228**	**374**	**113**	**305**	**186**	**339**	**279**	**291**	**435**	

[1]Audi preventative maintenance costs are covered under warranty for the first 50,000 miles or 36 months.

	PM Costs to 50,000 Miles	Water Pump	Alternator	Front Brake Pads	Starter	Fuel Injection	Fuel Pump	Struts/ Shocks	Timing Belt/Chain	Power Steering Pump	Relative Maint. Cost
Intermediate (cont.)											
Nissan Altima	747	112	331	104	250	197	196	291	795	260	Average
Nissan Maxima	778	244	470	106	328	245	288	544	590	512	Vry. Pr.
Oldsmobile Cutlass	759	182	180	94	181	192	382	310	332	381	Good
Oldsmobile Intrigue	759	137	181	110	249	126	388	242	262	164	Vry. Gd.
Plymouth Breeze	730	213	345	122	213	104	274	134	194	370	Vry. Gd.
Pontiac Firebird	759	152	264	106	254	162	599	258	239	391	Average
Pontiac Grand Prix	759	135	220	108	244	216	333	278	444	257	Good
Saab 9-3	668	209	505	137	296	168	321	539	644	673	Vry. Pr.
Saab 9-5	720	214	505	133	301	163	306	260	623	791	Vry. Pr.
Subaru Outback	606	219	201	113	272	150	319	297	389	359	Average
Toyota Avalon	983	254	461	98	383	248	286	328	192	575	Poor
Toyota Camry	983	267	450	106	372	243	283	316	170	602	Poor
Toyota Solara	983	267	450	106	372	243	283	316	170	602	Poor
Volkswagen Passat	222	257	630	136	413	180	346	238	159	372	Poor
Volvo S70	1170	245	544	116	289	149	323	217	158	495	Average
Volvo S80	1170	241	442	91	302	198	246	297	149	557	Average
Large											
Acura CL	1164	233	351	100	296	132	275	239	189	760	Average
Acura RL	1164	506	410	100	411	147	343	309	313	609	Vry. Pr.
Acura TL	1164	268	510	100	443	140	393	294	191	677	Vry. Pr.
Audi A6[1]	0	315	574	172	475	340	322	339	239	447	Vry. Pr.
BMW 5 Series	333	157	619	126	367	151	230	505	547	364	Vry. Pr.
Buick LeSabre	766	225	222	116	210	141	253	218	269	322	Vry. Gd.
Buick Park Avenue	766	223	221	114	207	139	321	188	285	345	Vry. Gd.
Buick Riviera	766	223	217	118	259	145	402	171	274	379	Good
Cadillac Deville	581	137	224	130	267	131	382	1120	746	337	Vry. Pr.
Cadillac Eldorado	581	141	201	118	330	131	384	1120	755	367	Vry. Pr.
Cadillac Seville	581	141	188	115	267	131	396	1120	575	337	Vry. Pr.
Chevrolet Lumina	766	130	219	105	244	192	409	214	442	257	Good
Chevrolet Malibu	759	281	218	104	250	147	490	494	244	254	Average
Average	**739**	**228**	**374**	**113**	**305**	**186**	**339**	**279**	**291**	**435**	

[1]Audi preventative maintenance costs are covered under warranty for the first 50,000 miles or 36 months.

Maintenance Costs

	PM Costs to 50,000 Miles	Water Pump	Alternator	Front Brake Pads	Starter	Fuel Injection	Fuel Pump	Struts	Timing Belt	Power Steering Pump	Relative Maint. Cost
Large (cont.)											
Chevrolet Monte Carlo	766	130	219	105	244	192	394	187	434	257	Good
Chrysler LHS	747	280	199	129	245	190	276	244	230	278	Good
Ford Crown Victoria	772	171	352	108	361	228	263	82	328	383	Average
Infiniti I30	759	244	470	106	328	245	288	544	590	512	Vry. Pr.
Infiniti Q45	759	126	510	113	426	314	332	431	955	463	Vry. Pr.
Lexus ES300	759	268	570	107	343	250	288	395	181	580	Poor
Lexus GS300/400	759	309	472	107	296	300	330	167	188	679	Poor
Lexus LS400	759	380	585	117	621	342	358	166	260	708	Vry. Pr.
Lexus SC300/400	759	266	505	107	293	313	305	286	183	679	Poor
Lincoln Continental	759	218	382	125	324	152	371	594	430	358	Poor
Lincoln Town Car	759	164	374	110	258	141	339	90	325	386	Good
Mercedes-Benz E-Class	1277	452	962	146	377	191	260	248	282	607	Vry. Pr.
Mercury Cougar	756	217	446	152	355	182	274	295	368	403	Poor
Mercury Grand Marquis	772	166	351	110	258	203	311	89	325	388	Good
Mitsubishi Diamante	1137	364	328	115	491	183	549	322	246	656	Vry. Pr.
Oldsmobile 88	752	225	226	116	210	141	254	238	267	387	Good
Oldsmobile Aurora	775	131	317	118	309	141	473	185	486	374	Average
Pontiac Bonneville	752	225	226	116	176	149	254	238	267	379	Vry. Gd.
Minivan											
Chevrolet Astro	707	225	228	109	264	223	421	110	234	402	Good
Chevrolet Venture	707	133	284	126	253	173	448	192	355	399	Average
Chrys. Town and Country	651	106	343	132	206	124	273	174	248	299	Vry. Gd.
Dodge Caravan	651	253	311	132	231	143	283	174	224	274	Vry. Gd.
Ford Windstar	629	311	420	105	342	150	303	206	544	248	Poor
GMC Safari	707	225	233	109	264	216	421	111	236	402	Good
Honda Odyssey	942	256	404	101	388	146	441	253	181	638	Poor
Isuzu Oasis	942	256	404	101	388	146	441	253	181	638	Poor
Mercury Villager	656	267	372	116	296	310	347	225	209	388	Average
Nissan Quest	656	224	335	128	208	356	258	228	212	428	Average
Oldsmobile Silhouette	707	133	284	126	253	166	448	192	365	359	Average
Average	**739**	**228**	**374**	**113**	**305**	**186**	**339**	**279**	**291**	**435**	

Minivan (cont.)	PM Costs to 50,000 Miles	Water Pump	Alternator	Front Brake Pads	Starter	Fuel Injection	Fuel Pump	Struts/ Shocks	Timing Belt/Chain	Power Steering Pump	Relative Maint. Cost
Plymouth Voyager	651	253	311	132	231	143	281	174	206	274	Vry. Gd.
Pontiac Montana	707	134	284	126	253	166	448	192	365	359	Average
Toyota Sienna	983	286	567	90	376	261	387	252	366	569	Vry. Pr.
Average	739	228	374	113	305	186	339	279	291	435	

TIP

Top Ten Things to Do on a Test Drive

The biggest mistake most of us make when buying a new car is not taking a good, long test drive. Plan on spending at least an hour to an hour and a half with the car, and include the following:

1. Take the car on a highway to review handling, acceleration, braking and wind noise.
2. Take the car on the bumpiest road you know.
3. Parallel park the car.
4. Pull the car in and out of your driveway and garage.
5. Sit in the passenger and back seats.
6. Put things in and out of the trunk or cargo space.
7. Look for blind spots.
8. Try the driver's seat in various positions.
9. Take a ride with other members of your family.
10. Make sure everyone tries on the seat belts.

Service Contracts

Each year, about 25 percent of new car buyers buy "service contracts." Averaging around $380 in price, a service contract is one of the most expensive options you can buy. In fact, service contracts are a major profit source for many dealers.

A service contract is not a warranty. It is more like an insurance plan that, in theory, covers repairs that are not covered by your warranty or that occur after the warranty runs out.

Service contracts are generally a very poor value. The companies who sell contracts are very sure that, on average, your repairs will cost considerably less than what you pay for the contract—if not, they wouldn't be in business.

Tip: One alternative to buying a service contract is to deposit the cost of the contract into a savings account. If the car needs a major repair not covered by your warranty, the money in your account will cover the cost. Most likely, you'll be building up your down payment for your next car!

If you believe that you really need a service contract, contact an insurance company, such as GEICO. You can save up to 50-percent by buying from an insurance company.

Here are some important questions to ask before buying a service contract:

How reputable is the company responsible for the contract? If the company offering the contract goes out of business, you will be out of luck. Recently, a number of independent service contract companies have gone under, so be very careful about who you buy from. Check with your Better Business Bureau or office of consumer affairs if you are not sure of a company's reputation. Service contracts from car and insurance companies are more likely to remain in effect than those from independent companies.

Exactly what does the contract cover and for how long? Service contracts vary considerably—different items are covered and different time limits are offered. This is true even among service contracts offered by the same company. For example, Ford's plans range from 4 years/36,000 miles maximum coverage to 6 years/100,000 miles maximum coverage, with other options for only powertrain coverage.

If you plan to resell your car in a few years, you won't want to purchase a long-running service contract. Some service contracts automatically cancel when you resell the car, while others require a hefty transfer fee before extending privileges to the new owner.

Some automakers offer a "menu" format which lets you pick the items you want covered in your service contract. Find out if the contract pays for preventive maintenance, towing, and rental car expenses. If not written into the contract, assume they are not covered.

Finally, think twice before purchasing travel services offered in the contract. Such amenities are offered by auto clubs, and you should compare prices before adding them into your contract cost.

How will the repair bills be paid? It is best to have the service contractor pay bills directly. Some contracts require you to pay the repair bill, and reimburse you later.

Where can the car be serviced? Can you take the car to any mechanic if you have trouble on the road? What if you move?

What other costs can be expected? Most service contracts will have a deductible expense. Compare deductibles on various plans. Also, some companies charge the deductible for each individual repair while other companies charge per visit, regardless of the number of repairs made.

Turbocharging

A turbocharger is an air pump that forces more air into the engine for combustion. Most turbo chargers consist of an air compressor driven by a small turbine wheel that is powered by the engine's exhaust. The turbine takes advantage of energy otherwise lost and forces increased efficiency from the engine. Turbochargers are often used to increase the power and sometimes the fuel efficiency of small engines. Engines equipped with turbochargers are more expensive than standard engines. The extra power may not be necessary when you consider the added expense and the fact that turbocharging adds to the complexity of the engine.

Tips for Dealing with a Mechanic

Call around. Don't choose a shop simply because it's nearby. Calling a few shops may turn up estimates cheaper by half.

Don't necessarily go for the lowest price. A good rule is to eliminate the highest and lowest estimates; the mechanic with the highest estimate is probably charging too much, and the lowest may be cutting too many corners.

Check the shop's reputation. Call your local consumer affairs agency and the Better Business Bureau. They don't have records on every shop, but if their reports on a shop aren't favorable, you can disqualify it.

Look for certification. Mechanics can be certified by the National Institute for Automotive Service Excellence, an industry-wide yardstick for competence. Certification is offered in eight areas of repair and shops with certified mechanics are allowed to advertise this fact. However, make sure the mechanic working on your car is certified for the repair.

Take a look around. A well-kept shop reflects pride in workmanship. A skilled and efficient mechanic would probably not work in a messy shop.

Don't sign a blank check. The service order you sign should have specific instructions or describe your vehicle's symptoms. Signing a vague work order could make you liable to pay for work you didn't want. Be sure you are called for final approval before the shop does extra work.

Show interest. Ask about the repair. A mechanic may become more helpful just knowing that you're interested. But don't act like an expert if you don't really understand what's wrong. Demonstrating your ignorance, on the other hand, may set you up to be taken by a dishonest mechanic, so strike a balance.

Express your satisfaction. If you're happy with the work, compliment the mechanic and ask for him or her the next time you come in. You will get to know each other and the mechanic will get to know your vehicle.

Develop a "sider." If you know a mechanic, ask about work on the side—evenings or weekends. The labor will be cheaper.

Test drive, then pay! Before you pay for a major repair, you should take the car for a test drive. The few extra minutes you spend checking out the repair could save you a trip back to the mechanic. If you find that the problem still exists, there will be no question that the repair wasn't properly completed. It is more difficult to prove the repair wasn't properly made after you've left the shop.

Repair Protection By Credit Card

TIP Paying your auto repair bills by credit card can provide a much-needed recourse if you are having problems with an auto mechanic. According to federal law, you have the right to withhold payment for sloppy or incorrect repairs. Of course, you may withhold no more than the amount of the repair in dispute.

In order to use this right, you must first try to work out the problem with the mechanic. Also, unless the credit card company owns the repair shop (this might be the case with gasoline credit cards used at gas stations), two other conditions must be met. First, the repair shop must be in your home state (or within 100 miles of your current address), and second, the cost of repairs must be over $50. Until the problem is settled or resolved in court, the credit card company cannot charge you interest or penalties on the amount in dispute.

If you decide to take action, send a letter to the credit card company and a copy to the repair shop, explaining the details of the problem and what you want as settlement. Send the letter by certified mail with a return receipt requested.

Sometimes the credit card company or repair shop will attempt to put a "bad mark" on your credit record if you use this tactic. Legally, you can't be reported as delinquent if you've given the credit card company notice of your dispute, but a creditor can report that you are disputing your bill, which goes in your record. However, you have the right to challenge any incorrect information and add your side of the story to your file.

For more information, write to the Federal Trade Commission, Credit Practices Division, 601 Pennsylvania Avenue, NW, Washington, DC 20580.

With the popularity of self-service gasoline stations, many of us overlook the simplest and most vital maintenance task of all: checking various items to prevent serious problems down the road. All it takes is about fifteen minutes a month to do the following checks. *Warning:* Many new vehicles have electric cooling fans that operate when the engine is off. Be sure to keep your hands away from the fan if the engine is warm.

Coolant: We'll start with the easiest fluid to check. Most vehicles have a plastic reservoir next to the radiator. This bottle will have "full hot" and "full cold" marks on it. If coolant is below "full cold" mark, add water to bring it up to that mark. (Anti-freeze should be used if you want extra protection in cold weather.) *Caution:* If vehicle is hot, do not open the radiator cap. The pressure and heat released can cause a severe burn.

Brakes: The most important safety item on the vehicle is the most ignored. A simple test will signal problems. (With power brakes, turn on engine to test.) Push the brake pedal down and hold it down. It should stop firmly and stay about halfway to the floor. If the stop is mushy or the pedal keeps moving to the floor, you should have your brakes checked. Checking the brake fluid on most vehicles is also easy. Your owner's manual tells you where to find the fluid reservoir, which indicates minimum and maximum fluid levels. If you add your own brake fluid, buy it in small cans and keep them tightly sealed. Brake fluid absorbs moisture, and excess moisture can damage your brake system. Have the brakes checked if you need to replace brake fluid regularly.

Oil: A few years ago, the phrase "fill it up and check the oil" was so common that it seemed like one word. Today, checking the oil often is the responsibility of the driver. To check your oil, first turn off the engine. Find the dipstick (look for a loop made of flat wire located on the side of the engine). If the engine has been running, be careful, because the dipstick and surrounding engine parts will be hot. Grab the loop, pull out the dipstick, clean it off, and reinsert it into the engine. Pull it out again and observe the oil level. "Full" and "add" are marked at the end of the stick. If the level is between "add" and "full," you are OK. If it is below "add," you should add enough oil until it reaches the "full" line. To add oil, remove the cap at the top of the engine. You may have to add more than one quart. Changing your oil regularly (every 3000-5000 miles based on your driving habits) is the single most important way to protect your engine. Many owner's manuals also contain directions for doing so. Change the oil filter whenever you change the oil.

Transmission Fluid: An automatic transmission is a complicated and expensive item. Checking your transmission fluid level is easy and can prevent a costly repair job. As in the oil check, you must first find the transmission fluid dipstick. Usually it is at the rear of the engine and looks like a smaller version of the oil dipstick. To get an accurate reading, the engine should be warmed up and running. If fluid is below the "add" line, pour in one pint at a time, but do not overfill the reservoir.

While you check the fluid, also note its color. It should be a bright, cherry red. If it is a darker, reddish brown, the fluid needs changing. If it is very dark, nearly black, and has a burnt smell (like varnish), your transmission may be damaged. You should take it to a specialist.

Automatic transmission fluid is available at most department stores; check your owner's manual for the correct type for your vehicle.

Power Steering: The power steering fluid reservoir is usually connected by a belt to the engine. To check it, unscrew the cap and look in the reservoir. There will be markings inside; some vehicles have a little dipstick built in to the cap.

Belts: You may have one or more belts connected to your engine. A loose belt in the engine can lead to electrical, cooling, or even air conditioning problems. To check, simply push down on the middle of each belt. It should feel tight. If you can push down more than half an inch, the belt needs tightening.

Battery: If your battery has caps on the top, lift off the caps and check that fluid comes up to the bottom of the filler neck. If it doesn't, add water (preferably distilled). If it is very cold outside, add water only if you are planning to drive the vehicle immediately. Otherwise the newly added water can freeze and damage your battery.

Also, look for corrosion around the battery connections. It can prevent electrical circuits from being completed, leading you to assume your perfectly good battery is "dead." If cables are corroded, remove and clean with fine sandpaper or steel wool. The inside of the connection and the battery posts should be shiny when you put the cables back on. *Caution:* Do not smoke or use any flame when checking the battery.

Tires: Improperly inflated tires are a major cause of premature tire failure. Check for proper inflation at least once a month. The most fuel-efficient inflation level can be found on the information label in your driver's side door well. The maximum pressure listed on the tire may not be appropriate for your car. Since many gas station pumps do not have gauges, and those that do are generally inaccurate, you should invest in your own tire gauge.

Air Filter: Probably the easiest item to maintain is your air filter. You can usually check the filter by just looking at it. If it appears dirty, change it—it's a simple task. If you are not sure how clean your filter is, try the following: Once the engine warms up, put the vehicle in park or neutral and, with the emergency brake on, let the vehicle idle. Open the filter lid and remove the filter. If the engine begins to run faster, change the filter.

Battery Safety

Almost all motorists have had to jump start a vehicle because of a dead battery. But that innocent-looking battery can cause some serious injuries.

Batteries produce hydrogen gas when they discharge or undergo heavy use (such as cranking the engine for a long period of time). A lit cigarette or a spark can cause this gas to explode. Whenever you work with the battery, always remove the negative (or ground) cable first and reconnect it last; it is usually marked with a minus sign. This precaution will greatly reduce the chance of causing a spark that could ignite any hydrogen gas present.

For a safe jump start:

1 Connect each end of the red cable to the positive (+) terminal on each battery.

2 Connect one end of the black cable to the negative (-) terminal of the *good* battery.

3 Connect the other end of the black cable to exposed metal away from the battery of the vehicle being started.

4 To avoid damaging electrical parts, make sure the engine is idling before disconnecting the cables.

Saving Gasoline

A cold-running engine dramatically reduces fuel economy. Most engines operate efficiently at 180 degrees, and an engine running at 125 degrees can waste one out of every ten gallons of gas. Your engine temperature is controlled by a thermostat valve. A faulty thermostat can be a major cause of poor fuel economy. If you feel that your vehicle should be getting better mileage, have your thermostat checked. They are inexpensive and easy to replace.

WARRANTIES

long with your new car comes a warranty, which is a promise from the manufacturer that the car will perform as it should. Most of us never read the warranty—until it is too late. In fact, because warranties are often difficult to read and understand, most of us don't really know what our warranties offer. This chapter will help you understand what to look for in a new car warranty, tip you off to secret warranties, and provide you with the best and worst among the 1999 warranties.

There are two types of warranties: one provided by the manufacturer and one implied by law.

Manufacturers' warranties are either "full" or "limited." The best warranty you can get is a full warranty because, by law, it must cover all aspects of the product's performance. Any other guarantee is called a limited warranty, which is what most car manufacturers offer. Limited warranties must be clearly marked as such, and you must be told exactly what is covered.

Warranties implied by law are warranties of merchantability and fitness. The "warranty of merchantability" ensures that your new car will be fit for the purpose for which it is used—that means safe, efficient, and trouble-free transportation. The "warranty of fitness" guarantees that if the dealer says a car can be used for a specific purpose, it will perform that purpose.

Many claims made by the salesperson are also considered warranties. They are called expressed warranties and you should have them put in writing if you consider them to be important. If the car does not live up to promises made to you in the showroom, you may have a case against the seller.

The manufacturer can restrict the amount of time the limited warranty is in effect. And in most states, the manufacturer can also limit the time that the warranty implied by law is in effect.

Through the warranty, the manufacturer is promising that the car's parts and design are free from defects, and that for a certain period the car will operate soundly provided it is used in a normal fashion. This period of time is usually measured in both months and miles— whichever comes first is the limit.

While the warranty is in effect, the manufacturer will perform, at no charge to the owner, repairs that are necessary because of defects in materials or in the way the car was manufactured.

The warranty does not cover parts that have to be replaced because of normal wear, such as filters, fuses, light bulbs, wiper blades, clutch linings, brake pads, or the addition of oil, fluids, coolants, and lubricants. Tires, batteries, and the emission control system are covered by separate warranties. Options, such as a stereo system, should have their own warranties as well. Service should be provided through the dealer. A separate rust (corrosion) warranty is also included.

The costs for the required maintenance listed in the owner's manual are not covered by the warranty. Problems resulting from misuse, negligence, changes you make in the car, accidents, or lack of required maintenance are also not covered.

Any implied warranties, including the warranties of merchantability and fitness, can at most be limited to the duration of the written warranty. Also, manufacturer warranties try to disclaim responsibility for other problems caused by repairs, such as the loss of time or use of your car, or any expenses they might cause. In at least 9 states, such limitations on your warranty rights are invalid.

In addition to the rights granted to you in the warranty, you may have other rights under your state laws.

To keep your warranty in effect, you must operate and maintain your car according to the instructions in your owner's manual. Remember, it is important to keep a record of all maintenance performed on your car.

To have your car repaired under the warranty, take it to an authorized dealer or service center. The work should be done in a reasonable amount of time during normal business hours.

Be careful not to confuse your warranty with a service contract. The *service contract* must be purchased separately while the warranty is yours at no extra cost when you buy the car. (See page 55 for more on service contracts.)

Corrosion Warranty: All manufacturers warrant against corrosion. The typical corrosion warranty lasts for six years or 100,000 miles, whichever comes first.

Some dealers offer extra rust protection at an additional cost. Before you purchase this option, compare the extra protection offered to the corrosion warranty already included in the price of the car—it probably already provides sufficient protection against rust.

Emission System Warranty: The emission system is warranted by federal law. Any repairs required during the first two years or 24,000 miles will be paid for by the manufacturer if an original engine part fails because of a defect in materials or workmanship, and the failure causes your car to exceed federal emissions standards. Major com-

ponents, such as an onboard computer emissions control unit, are covered for eight years or up to 80,000 miles.

Using leaded fuel in a car designed for unleaded fuel will void your emission system warranty and may prevent the car from passing your state's inspection. Because an increasing number of states are requiring an emissions test before a car can pass inspection, you may have to pay to fix the system if you used the wrong type of fuel. Repairs to emission systems are usually very expensive.

Dealer Options & Your Warranty

Make sure that "dealer-added" options will not void your warranty. For example, some consumers who have purchased cruise control as an option to be installed by the dealer have found that their warranty is void when they take the car in for engine repairs. Also, some manufacturers warn that dealer-supplied rustproofing will void your corrosion warranty. If you are in doubt, contact the manufacturer before you authorize the installation of dealer-supplied options. If the manufacturer says that adding the option will not void your warranty, get it in writing.

Getting Warranty Service

Ford dealers are finally offering better warranty service to their customers! Now, most Ford dealers will perform warranty work on all Ford vehicles, regardless of where the vehicle was purchased. Previously, only the selling dealer was required to perform repairs under warranty. Individual Ford dealers can still set their own policy, however, so it is best to call and ask before taking your vehicle in for warranty service. GM, Japanese, and European car dealers also provide this service to their customers, and Chrysler "recommends" that dealers follow this policy.

If dealers report a number of complaints about a certain part and the manufacturer determines that the problem is due to faulty design or assembly, the manufacturer may permit dealers to repair the problem at no charge to the customer even though the warranty is expired. In the past, this practice was often reserved for customers who made a big fuss. The availability of the free repair was never publicized, which is why we call these *secret* warranties.

Manufacturers deny the existence of secret warranties. They call these free repairs "policy adjustments" or "goodwill service." Whatever they are called, most consumers never hear about them.

Many secret warranties are disclosed in service bulletins that the manufacturers send to dealers. These bulletins outline free repair or reimbursement programs, as well as other problems and their possible causes and solutions.

Service bulletins from many manufacturers may be on file at the National Highway Traffic Safety Administration. For copies of the bulletins on file, send a letter with the make, model and year of the car, and the year you believe the service bulletin was issued, to the NHTSA's Technical Reference Library, Room 5108, NHTSA, Washington, DC 20590. If you write to the government, ask for "service bulletins" rather than "secret warranties."

If you find that a secret warranty is in effect and repairs are being made at no charge after the warranty has expired, contact the Center for Auto Safety, 2001 S Street, NW, Washington, DC 20009. They will publish the information so others can benefit.

Disclosure Laws: Spurred by the proliferation of secret warranties and the failure of the FTC to take action, California, Connecticut, Virginia, and Wisconsin have passed legislation that requires consumers to be notified of secret warranties on their cars. Several other states have introduced similar warranty bills.

Typically, the laws require the following: Direct notice to consumers within a specified time after the adoption of a warranty adjustment policy; notice of the disclosure law to new car buyers; reimbursement, within a number of years after payment, to owners who paid for covered repairs before they learned of the extended warranty service; and dealers must inform consumers who complain about a covered defect that it is eligible for repair under warranty.

New York's bill has another requirement—the establishment of a toll-free number for consumer questions, despite opposition from Ford, GM, Toyota, and other auto manufacturers.

If you live in a state with a secret warranty law already in effect, write your state attorney general's office (in care of your state capitol) for information. To encourage passage of such a bill, contact your state representative (in care of your state capitol).

Secret Warranties Made Public

Due to past secret warranty problems, three auto companies are required to make their service bulletins public.

Ford: Information on goodwill adjustments is available through Ford's "defect line" at 800-241-3673.
General Motors: Bulletins are available from the past three years for a charge and free indexes to bulletins are available through GM dealers or call 800-551-4123.
Volkswagen: An index of all service bulletins can be ordered by calling 800-544-8021.

Uncovering Secret Warranties

Every auto company makes mistakes building cars. When they do, they often issue technical service bulletins telling dealers how to fix the problem. Rarely do they publicize these fixes, many of which are offered for free, called secret warranties. The Center for Auto Safety has published a new book called *Little Secrets of the Auto Industry*, a consumer guide to secret warranties. This book explains how to find out about secret warranties, offers tips for going to small claims court and getting federal and state assistance, and lists information on state secret warranty laws. To order a copy, send $17.50 to: Center for Auto Safety, Pub. Dept., 2001 S Street, NW, Washington, DC 20009.

Comparing Warranties

Warranties are difficult to compare because they contain lots of fine print and confusing language. The following table will help you understand this year's new car warranties. Because the table does not contain all the details about each warranty, you should review the actual warranty to make sure you understand its fine points. Remember, you have the right to inspect a warranty before you buy—it's the law.

The table provides information on five areas covered by a typical warranty:

The **Basic Warranty** covers most parts of the car against manufacturer's defects. The tires, batteries, and items you may add to the car are covered under separate warranties. The table describes coverage in terms of months and miles; for example, 36/36,000 means the warranty is good for 36 months or 36,000 miles, whichever comes first. This is the most important part of your warranty.

The **Powertrain Warranty** usually lasts longer than the basic warranty. Because each manufacturer's definition of the powertrain is different, it is important to find out exactly what your warranty will cover. Powertrain coverage should include parts of the engine, transmission, and drivetrain. The warranty on some luxury cars will often cover some additional systems such as steering, suspension, and electrical systems.

The **Corrosion Warranty** usually applies only to actual holes due to rust. Read this section carefully, because many corrosion warranties *do not* apply to what the manufacturer may describe as cosmetic rust or bad paint.

The **Roadside Assistance** column indicates whether or not the warranty includes a program for helping with problems on the road. Typically, these programs cover such things as lock outs, jump starts, flat tires, running out of gas and towing. Most of these are offered for the length of the basic warranty. Some have special limitations or added features, which we have pointed out. Because each one is different, check yours out carefully.

The last column contains the **Warranty Rating Index,** which provides an overall assessment of this year's warranties. The higher the Index number, the better the warranty. The Index number incorporates the important features of each warranty. In developing the Index, we gave the most weight to the basic and powertrain components of the warranties. The corrosion warranty was weighted somewhat less, and the roadside assistance features received the least weight. We also considered special features such as whether you had to bring the car in for corrosion inspections, or if rental cars were offered when warranty repairs were being done.

After evaluating all the features of the new warranties, here are this year's best and worst ratings.

1999 Warranties: The Best and The Worst

The Best		The Worst	
Volkswagen Passat	1816	Suzuki	670
Audi	1591	Honda	834
Infiniti	1518	Chrysler	932
Volkswagen	1470	Dodge	932
Volvo	1411	Plymouth	932

The higher the index number, the better the warranty. See the table on the following pages for complete details.

Manufacturer	Basic Warranty	Powertrain Warranty	Corrosion Warranty	Roadside Assistance	Index	Warranty Rating
Acura	48/50,000	48/50,000	60/unlimited	48/50,000	1163	Average
Audi	36/50,000[1]	36/50,000	120/unlimited	36/50,000[2]	1591	Very Good
BMW	48/50,000[3]	48/50,000	72/unlimited	48/50,000[2]	1404	Good
Buick	36/36,000	36/36,000	72/100,000	36/36,000	956	Very Poor
Cadillac	48/50,000	48/50,000	72/100,000	Lifetime[5,6]	1255	Good
Chevrolet	36/36,000	36/36,000	72/100,000	36/36,000	956	Very Poor
Chrysler	36/36,000	36/36,000	60/100,000	36/36,000	932	Very Poor
Dodge	36/36,000	36/36,000	60/100,000	36/36,000	932	Very Poor
Ford	36/36,000	36/36,000	60/unlimited	36/36,000	942	Very Poor
Honda	36/36,000	36/36,000	60/unlimited	None	834	Very Poor
Hyundai	36/36,000	60/60,000	60/100,000	Unlimited[4]	1136	Average
Infiniti	48/60,000	72/70,000	84/unlimited	48/unlimited	1518	Very Good
Isuzu	36/50,000	60/60,000	72/100,000	60/60,000	1228	Good
Kia	36/36,000	60/60,000	60/100,000	36/36,000[2]	1126	Average
Lexus	48/50,000	72/72,000	72/unlimited	48/50,000	1367	Good
Lincoln	48/50,000[8]	48/50,000	60/unlimited	48/50,000	1163	Average
Mazda	36/50,000	36/50,000	60/unlimited	36/50,000[9]	1090	Poor
Mercedes-Benz	48/50,000	48/50,000	48/50,000	Lifetime	1107	Poor
Mercury	36/36,000	36/36,000	60/unlimited	36/36,000	942	Very Poor
Mitsubishi	36/36,000	60/60,000	84/100,000	36/36,000	1124	Average
Nissan	36/36,000	60/60,000	60/unlimited	36/36,000[7]	1050	Poor
Oldsmobile	36/36,000	36/36,000	72/100,000	36/36,000[2]	1006	Poor
Olds Aurora	48/50,000	48/50,000	72/100,000	48/50,000[2]	1227	Good
Plymouth	36/36,000	36/36,000	60/100,000	36/36,000	932	Very Poor
Pontiac	36/36,000	36/36,000	72/100,000	36/36,000	956	Very Poor

[1] Includes all service, repairs and parts to 36/50,000.
[2] Covers trip interruption expenses.
[3] Includes all service, repairs and parts to 36/36,000.
[4] Includes towing for accidents.
[5] <48/50,000=Free; >48/50,000=Small Charge.
[6] Covers trip interruption expenses up to 48/50,000 for a warranty failure.
[7] Limited roadside services.
[8] The basic warranty also includes car rental payments of a maximum of $30/day for 5 days (if car kept overnight for servicing).
[9] Millenia and MPV only.
[10] Suzuki Soft Tops have a 24/24,000 Basic Warranty on the soft top itself.
[11] Includes all service, repairs and parts to 24/24,000.

Manufacturer	Basic Warranty	Powertrain Warranty	Corrosion Warranty	Roadside Assistance	Index	Warranty Rating
Saab	48/50,000	48/50,000	72/unlimited	48/50,000[2]	1279	Good
Saturn	36/36,000	36/36,000	72/100,000	36/36,000[2]	1006	Poor
Subaru	36/36,000	60/60,000	60/unlimited	None	978	Poor
Suzuki[10]	36/36,000	36/36,000	36/unlimited	None	670	Very Poor
Toyota	36/36,000	60/60,000	60/unlimited	Optional	978	Poor
Volkswagen	24/24,000[11]	120/100,000	72/unlimited	24/24,000[2]	1470	Very Good
VW Passat	24/24,000[11]	120/100,000	144/unlimited	24/24,000[2]	1816	Very Good
Volvo	48/50,000	48/50,000	96/unlimited	48/50,000[2]	1411	Very Good

[1] Includes all service, repairs and parts to 36/50,000.
[2] Covers trip interruption expenses.
[3] Includes all service, repairs and parts to 36/36,000.
[4] Includes towing for accidents.
[5] <48/50,000=Free; >48/50,000=Small Charge.
[6] Covers trip interruption expenses up to 48/50,000 for a warranty failure.
[7] Limited roadside services.
[8] The basic warranty also includes car rental payments of a maximum of $30/day for 5 days (if car kept overnight for servicing).
[9] Millenia and MPV only.
[10] Suzuki Soft Tops have a 24/24,000 Basic Warranty on the soft top itself.
[11] Includes all service, repairs and parts to 24/24,000.

INSURANCE

Insurance is a big part of ownership expenses, yet it's often forgotten in the showroom. As you shop, remember that the car's design and accident history may affect your insurance rates. Some cars cost less to insure because experience has shown that they are damaged less, less expensive to fix after a collision, or stolen less.

This chapter provides you with the information you need to make a wise insurance purchase. We discuss the different types of insurance, offer special tips on reducing this cost, and include information on occupant injury, theft, and bumper ratings—all factors that can affect your insurance.

More and more consumers are saving hundreds of dollars by shopping around for insurance. In order to be a good comparison shopper, you need to know a few things about automobile insurance. First, there are six basic types of coverage:

Collision Insurance: This pays for the damage to your car after an accident.

Comprehensive Physical Damage Insurance: This pays for damages when your car is stolen or damaged by fire, floods, or other perils.

Property Damage Liability: This pays claims and defense costs if your car damages someone else's property.

Medical Payments Insurance: This pays for your car's occupants' medical expenses resulting from an accident.

Bodily Injury Liability: This provides money to pay claims against you and to pay for the cost of your legal defense if your car injures or kills someone.

Uninsured Motorists Protection: This pays for injuries caused by an uninsured or a hit-and-run driver.

A number of factors determine what these coverages will cost you. A car's design can affect both the chances and severity of an accident. A car with a well-designed bumper may escape damage altogether in a low-speed crash. Some cars are easier to repair than others or may have less expensive parts.

Cars with four doors tend to be damaged less than cars with two doors.

The reason one car may get a discount on insurance while another receives a surcharge also depends upon the way it is traditionally driven. Sports cars, for example, are usually surcharged due, in part, to the typical driving habits of their owners. Four-door sedans and station wagons generally merit discounts.

Insurance companies use this and other information to determine whether to offer a *discount* on insurance premiums for a particular car, or whether to levy a *surcharge*.

Not all companies offer discounts or surcharges, and many cars receive neither. Some companies offer a discount or impose a surcharge on collision premiums only. Others apply discounts and surcharges on both collision and comprehensive coverage. Discounts and surcharges usually range from 10 to 30 percent. Allstate offers discounts of up to 35 percent on certain cars. Remember that one company may offer a discount on a particular car while another may not.

Check with your insurance agent to find out whether your company has a rating program. The "ratings" pages at the end of the book indicate the expected insurance rates for each of the 1999 models.

No-Fault Insurance

One of the major expenses of vehicular accidents has been the cost of determining who is "at fault." With the traditional liability system, both parties hire lawyers, wait months or years for court decisions, and incur large legal costs. Aside from economic damages, or out of pocket costs, victims can also sue for non-economic, or pain and suffering damages. An award for pain and suffering can account for the gross disparity between awards in similar cases. This was the only method of coverage, until consumers, insurers, and state regulators realized that most of the insurance premium dollar was spent on legal fees and non-economic awards.

Attempting to reduce costs, many states have instituted "no-fault" policies. True no-fault applies to state laws that provide for the payment of policyholder benefits <u>and</u> restrict the right to sue.

The concept of no-fault is that each person's losses are covered by their personal insurance protection, regardless of who is at fault. Lawsuits are permitted only under certain conditions, known as a threshold. A verbal threshold allows additional legal action only if certain serious injuries occur. A monetary threshold sets a dollar amount that medical claims must reach before permitting a lawsuit.

No-Fault laws vary from state to state. These variations include the conditions of the right to sue, threshold standards, and the inclusion or exclusion of property damage. So be sure to consult your state to learn about the details of auto insurance coverage.

No-Fault States

Colorado	Massachusetts	New York
Florida	Michigan	North Dakota
Hawaii	Minnesota	Pennsylvania
Kansas	New Jersey	Utah
Kentucky		Puerto Rico

States Without No-Fault

Alabama	Louisiana	Oregon
Alaska	Maine	Rhode Island
Arizona	Maryland	South Carolina
Arkansas	Mississippi	South Dakota
California	Missouri	Tennessee
Connecticut	Montana	Texas
Delaware	Nebraska	Vermont
District of Columbia	Nevada	Virginia
Georgia	New Hampshire	Washington
Idaho	New Mexico	West Virginia
Illinois	North Carolina	Wisconsin
Indiana	Ohio	Wyoming
Iowa	Oklahoma	

Insurance Injury Statistics

The insurance industry regularly publishes information about the accident history of cars currently on the road. The most reliable source of this rating information is the Highway Loss Data Institute (HLDI). These ratings, which range from very good to very poor, are based on the frequency of medical claims under personal injury protection coverages. A few companies will charge you more to insure a car rated poor than for one rated good.

A car's accident history may not match its crash test performance. Such discrepancies arise because the accident history includes driver performance. A sports car, for example, may have good crash test results but a poor accident history because its owners tend to drive relatively recklessly.

If you want more information about the injury history, bumper performance, and theft rating of today's cars, write to HLDI, 1005 North Glebe Road, Arlington, VA 22201.

Reducing Insurance Costs

After you have shopped around and found the best deal by comparing the costs of different coverages, consider other factors that will affect your final insurance bill.

Your Annual Mileage: The more you drive, the more your vehicle will be "exposed" to a potential accident. The insurance cost for a car rarely used will be less than the cost for a frequently used car.

Where You Drive: If you regularly drive and park in the city, you will most likely pay more than if you drive in rural areas.

Youthful Drivers: Usually the highest premiums are paid by male drivers under the age of 25. Whether or not the under-25-year-old male is married also affects insurance rates. (Married males pay less.) As the driver gets older, rates are lowered.

In addition to shopping around, take advantage of certain discounts to reduce your insurance costs. Most insurance companies offer discounts of 5 to 30 percent on various parts of your insurance bill. The availability of discounts varies among companies and often depends on where you live. Many consumers do not benefit from these discounts simply because they don't ask about them.

To determine whether you are getting all the discounts that you're entitled to, ask your insurance company for a complete list of the discounts that it offers.

Here are some of the most common insurance discounts:

Driver Education/Defensive Driving Courses: Many insurance companies offer (and in some cases mandate) discounts to young people who have successfully completed a state-approved driver education course. Typically, this can mean a $40 reduction in the cost of coverage. Also, a discount of 5-15 percent is available in some states to those who complete a defensive driving course.

Good Student Discounts: Many insurance companies offer discounts of up to 25 percent on insurance to full-time high school or college students who are in the upper 20 percent of their class, on the dean's list, or have a B or better grade point average.

Good Driver Discounts: Many companies will offer discounts to drivers with an accident and violation-free record.

Mature Driver Credit: Drivers ages 50 and older may qualify for up to a 10 percent discount, or a lower price bracket.

Sole Female Driver: Some companies offer discounts of 10 percent for females, ages 30 to 64, who are the only driver in a household, citing favorable claims experience.

Non-Drinkers and Non-Smokers: A limited number of companies offer incentives ranging from 10-25 percent to those who abstain.

Farmer Discounts: Many companies offer farmers either a discount of 10-30 percent or a lower price bracket.

Car Pooling: Commuters sharing driving may qualify for discounts of 5-25 percent or a lower price bracket.

Insuring Driving Children: Children away at school don't drive the family car very often, so it's usually less expensive to insure them on the parents' policy rather than separately. If you do insure them separately, discounts of 10-40 percent or a lower price bracket are available.

Don't Speed

Besides endangering the lives of your passengers and other drivers, speeding tickets will increase your insurance premium. It only takes one speeding ticket to lose your "preferred" or "good driver" discount, which requires a clean driving record. Two or more speeding tickets or accidents can increase your premium by 40% to 200%. Some insurers may simply drop your coverage. According to the Insurance Institute for Highway Safety (IIHS), you are 17% more likely to be in an accident if you have just one speeding ticket. Insurance companies know this and will charge you for it.

Desirable Cars: Premiums are usually much higher for cars with high collision rates or that are the favorite target of thieves.

Passive Restraints/Anti-Lock Brake Credit: Many companies offer discounts (from 10 to 30 percent) for automatic belts and air bags. Some large companies are now offering a 5 percent discount to owners of vehicles with anti-lock brakes.

Anti-Theft Device Credits: Discounts of 5 to 15 percent are offered in some states for cars equipped with a hood lock and an alarm or a disabling device (active or passive) that prevents the car from being started.

Account Credit: Some companies offer discounts of up to 10 percent for insuring your home and auto with the same company.

Long-Term Policy Renewal: Although not available in all states, some companies offer price breaks of 5-20 percent to customers who renew a long-term policy.

First Accident Allowance: Some insurers offer a "first accident allowance," which guarantees that if a customer achieves five accident-free years, his or her rates won't go up after the first at-fault accident.

Deductibles: Opting for the largest reasonable deductible is the obvious first step in reducing premiums. Increasing your deductible to $500 from $200 could cut your collision premium about 20 percent. Raising the deductible to $1,000 from $200 could lower your premium about 45 percent. The discounts may vary by company.

Collision Coverage: The older the car, the less the need for collision insurance. Consider dropping collision insurance entirely on an older car. Regardless of how much coverage you carry, the insurance company will only pay up to the car's "book value." For example, if your car requires $1,000 in repairs, but its "book value" is only $500, the insurance company is required to pay only $500.

Uninsured Motorist Coverage/Optional Coverage: The necessity of both of these policies depends upon the extent of your health insurance coverage. In states where they are not required, consumers with applicable health insurance may not want uninsured motorist coverage. Also, those with substantial health insurance coverage may not want an optional medical payment policy.

Rental Cars: If you regularly rent cars, special coverage on your personal auto insurance can cover you while renting for far less than rental agencies offer.

Multi-Car Discount: Consumers insuring more than one car in the household with the same insurer can save up to 20 percent.

Tip: Expensive fender bender repairs can add up for both you and your insurance company. To reduce repairs, look for a car with bumpers that can withstand a 5-mph impact without damage. See page 70 for more information on bumpers.

Beep, Beep

As car instrument panels become more and more sophisticated, there is growing confusion about the location of horn buttons. There are no regulations requiring a standard location so manufacturers put them in various places around the steering wheel. On your test drive, make sure the horn button is easy to locate and use. When renting a car or driving an unfamiliar car, also be sure you know where the horn button is located. Proper use of a car horn can avoid serious accidents. Because of this, the Center for Auto Safety has been urging the government to standardize horn location since 1980. If you have experienced a problem due to a non-standard horn location, we urge you to contact the National Highway Traffic Safety Administration, Rulemaking Division, 400 7th St., SW, Washington, DC 20590 and the Center for Auto Safety, 2001 S Street, NW, Suite 410, Washington, DC 20009.

The risk of your vehicle being stolen is an important factor in the cost of your insurance. In fact, each year over 1.5 million vehicles are stolen. As a result, the market is flooded with expensive devices designed to prevent theft. Before you spend a lot of money on anti-theft devices, consider this: Of the vehicles stolen, nearly 80 percent were unlocked and 40 percent actually had the keys in the ignition. Most of these thefts are by amateurs. While the most important way to protect your vehicle is to keep it locked and remove the keys, this precaution will not protect you from the pros. If you live or travel in an area susceptible to auto thefts, or have a high-priced vehicle, here are some steps you can take to prevent theft.

Inexpensive Prevention:

☑ Replace door lock buttons with tapered tips. They make it difficult to hook the lock with a wire hanger. (But it will also keep you from breaking into your own vehicle!)

☑ Buy an alarm sticker (even if you don't have an alarm) for one of your windows.

☑ Buy an electric etching tool (about $15) and write your driver's license number in the lower corners of the windows and on unpainted metal items where it can be seen. Many police departments offer this service at no charge. They provide a sticker and enter the number into their records. The purpose of these identifying marks is to deter the professional thief who is planning to take the vehicle apart and sell the components. Since the parts can be traced, your vehicle becomes less attractive.

☑ Remove the distributor wire. This is a rather inconvenient, but effective, means of rendering your vehicle inoperable. If you are parking in a particularly suspect place, or leaving your vehicle for a long time, you may want to try this. On the top of the distributor, there is a short wire running to the coil. Removing the wire makes it impossible to start the vehicle.

A recently popular anti-theft device is a long rod that locks the steering wheel into place. It costs about $50 and requires a separate key to remove. Beware, however, that thieves now use a spray can of freon to freeze the lock, making it brittle enough to be smashed open with a hammer.

More Serious Measures:

☑ Cutting off the fuel to the engine will keep someone from driving very far with your vehicle. For around $125, you can have a fuel cutoff device installed that enables you to open or close the gasoline line to the engine. One drawback is that the thief will be able to drive a few blocks before running out of gas. If your vehicle is missing, you'll have to check your neighborhood first!

☑ Another way to deter a pro is to install a second ignition switch for about $150. To start your vehicle, you activate a hidden switch. The device is wired in such a complicated manner that a thief could spend hours trying to figure it out. Time is the thief's worst enemy, and the longer it takes to start your vehicle, the more likely the thief is to give up.

☑ The most common anti-theft devices on the market are alarms. These cost from $100 to $500 installed. Their complexity ranges from simply sounding your horn when someone opens your door to setting off elaborate sirens when someone merely approaches the vehicle. Alarms usually require a device such as a key or remote control to turn them on or off. Some people buy the switch, mount it on their vehicle, and hope that its presence will intimidate the thief.

The Highway Loss Data Institute regularly compiles statistics on motor vehicle thefts. In rating cars, they consider the frequency of theft and the loss resulting from the theft. The result is an index based on "relative average loss payments per insured vehicle year." The list below includes the most and least stolen cars among the 1999 models.

Auto Theft

Most Stolen		Least Stolen	
Lexus GS 300	1,002	Saturn SC 2dr.	13
Mercedes S class 4dr.	736	Subaru Impreza Wgn.	17
BMW 3 Series 2dr.	619	Buick LeSabre 4dr.	18
Lexus LS 400 4dr.	605	Chevrolet Lumina 4dr.	21
Lexus SC 300/400	584	Saturn SW	22
BMW 3 Series (conv.)	450	Ford Taurus Wgn.	23
Acura Integra 2 dr.	410	Pontiac Sunfire 4dr.	23
Acura Integra 4dr.	367	Oldsmobile 88 4dr.	25

Bumpers

The main purpose of the bumper is to protect your car in low-speed collisions. Despite this intention, most of us have been victims of a $200 to $400 repair bill resulting from a seemingly minor impact. Since most bumpers offered little or no damage protection in low-speed crashes, the federal government *used* to require that auto makers equip cars with bumpers capable of withstanding up to 5-mph crashes with no damage. Unfortunately, this is no longer the case.

In the early eighties, while under pressure from car companies, the government rolled back the requirement that bumpers protect cars in collisions up to 5-mph. Now, car companies only build bumpers to protect cars in 2.5-mph collisions—about the speed at which we walk. This rollback has cost consumers millions of dollars in increased insurance premiums and repair costs. While the rollback satisfied car companies, most car owners were unhappy.

To let consumers know that today's bumpers offer widely varying amounts of protection in 5-mph collisions, each year the Insurance Institute for Highway Safety tests bumpers to see how well they prevent damage. Thankfully, some automobile manufacturers are betting that consumers still want better bumpers on at least some of their models. For example, in a 5-mph front test, the Ford Contour suffered $1056 worth of damage while the Lincoln Continental took only $16 worth of damage.

These results are rather startling when you consider that the sole purpose of a bumper is to protect a car from damage in low-speed collisions. Only about one-third of the cars tested to date have bumpers which actually prevented damage in front and rear 5-mph collisions. As the Institute's figures show, there is no correlation between the price of the car and how well the bumper worked.

Unfortunately, we can't simply look at a bumper and determine how good it will be at doing its job—protecting a car from inevitable bumps. The solution to this problem is quite simple—simply require car makers to tell the consumer the highest speed at which their car could be crashed with no damage to the car. Three states—California, Hawaii, and New York—have passed laws requiring car companies to disclose in the showroom, in various formats, the expected performance of the bumper on the car. These laws are currently being challenged by the car companies and we won't see them implemented for some time.

Following are the results of the IIHS bumper crash tests, listed from the best to the worst performers. We have included some of the cars which we believe will have similiar bumpers in 1999. *Note:* If the bumpers have changed at all since the time it was tested, the result could be drastically different. This should, however, give you a good basis for comparison. When available, additional information is on each car's page.

Bumper Bashing—Damage Repair Costs in 5-mph Crash Tests

Car (Year)	Front Crash	Rear Crash	Total Cost
Best			
Merc. Sable/Ford Taurus (96-99)	$0	$0	$0
Subaru Forester (98-99)	$9	$0	$9
Volkswagen New Beetle (98-99)	$16	$0	$16
Lincoln Continental (98-99)	$0	$16	$16
Ford Windstar (95-99)	$0	$83	$83
Worst			
Isuzu Rodeo/Honda Passport (98-99)	$1142	$2341	$3483
Kia Sportage (95-99)	$670	$2674	$3344
Land Rover Discovery (95-99)	$771	$2145	$2916
Toyota 4Runner (90-99)	$849	$2026	$2875
Mitsubishi Montero (92-99)	$471	$2374	$2845

TIRES

For most of us, buying tires has become an infrequent task. The reason—most cars now come with radial tires, which last much longer than the bias and bias-belted tires of the past. However, when we do get around to buying tires, making an informed purchase is not easy. The tire has to perform more functions simultaneously than any other part of the car (steering, bearing the load, cushioning the ride, and stopping). And not only is the tire the hardest-working item on the car, but there are nearly 1,800 tire lines to choose from. With only a few major tire manufacturers selling all those tires, the difference in many tires may only be the brand name.

Because it is so difficult to compare tires, it is easy to understand why many consumers mistakenly use price and brand name to determine quality. One company's definition of "first line" or "premium" may be entirely different from another's. But there is help. The U.S. government now requires tires to be rated according to their safety and expected mileage.

A little-known system grades tires on their *treadwear*, *traction*, and *heat resistance*. The grades are printed on the sidewall and are also attached to the tire on a paper label. In addition, every dealer can provide you with the grades of the tires they sell.

Treadwear: The treadwear grade gives you an idea of the mileage you can expect from a tire. It is shown in numbers—300, 310, 320, 330, and so forth. A tire graded 400 should give you 33 percent more mileage than one graded 300. In order to *estimate* the expected actual mileage, multiply the treadwear grade by 200. Under average conditions a tire graded 300 should last 60,000 miles. Because driving habits vary considerably, use the treadwear as a *relative* basis of comparison rather than an absolute predictor of mileage. Tire wear is affected by regional differences in the level of abrasive material used in road surfaces.

Traction: Traction grades of A, B, and C describe the tire's ability to stop on wet surfaces. Tires graded A will stop on a wet road in a shorter distance than tires graded B or C. Tires rated C have poor traction. If you drive frequently on wet roads, buy a tire with a higher traction grade.

Heat Resistance: Heat resistance is also graded A, B, and C. This grading is important because hot-running tires can result in blowouts or tread separation. An A rating means the tire will run cooler than one rated B or C, and it is less likely to fail if driven over long distances at highway speeds. In addition, tires that run cooler tend to be more fuel efficient. If you do a lot of high speed driving, a high heat resistance grade is best.

Speed Ratings: All passenger car tires meet government standards up to 85 mph. Some tires are tested at higher speeds because certain cars require tires that perform at higher speeds. Consult your owner's manual for the right speed rating for your car. See the tire size code: (For example, P215/60 SR15). The 'S' indicates the tire is tested for speeds up to 112 mph. Other letters include: "T" for up to 118 mph; "H" for up to 130 mph; "V" for up to 149 mph; "Z" for over 149 mph.

The tables at the end of this section give you a list of the highest rated tires on the market. For a complete listing of all the tires on the market, you can call the Auto Safety Hotline toll free, at 800-424-9393 or 800-424-9153 (TTY). (In Washington, DC, the number is 202-366-7800.)

There are few consumer products on the market today as price competitive as tires. While this situation provides a buyer's market, it does require some price shopping.

The price of a tire is based on its size, and tires come in as many as nine sizes. For example, the list price of the same Goodyear Arriva tire can range from $74.20 to $134.35, depending on its size. Some manufacturers do not provide list prices, leaving the appropriate markup to the individual retailer. Even when list prices are provided, dealers rarely use them. Instead, they offer tires at what is called an "everyday low price," which can range from 10 to 25 percent below list.

The following tips can help you get the best buy.

1 Check to see which manufacturer makes the least expensive "off brand." Only twelve manufacturers produce the over 1,800 types of tires sold in the U.S. So you can save money and still get high quality.

2 Remember, generally the wider the tire, the higher the price.

3 Don't forget to inquire about balancing and mounting costs when comparing tire prices. In some stores, the extra charges for balancing, mounting and valve stems can add up to more than $25. Other stores may offer them as a customer service at little or no cost. That good buy in the newspaper may turn into a poor value when coupled with these extra costs. Also, compare warranties; they do vary from company to company.

4 Never pay list price for a tire. A good rule of thumb is to pay at least 30 to 40 percent off the suggested list price.

5 Use the treadwear grade the same way you would the "unit price" in a supermarket. It is the best way to ensure that you are getting the best tire value. The tire with the lowest cost per grade point is the best value. For example, if tire A costs $100 and has a treadwear grade of 300, and tire B costs $80 and has a treadwear grade of 200:

Tire A:
$100 ÷ 300 = $.33 per point

Tire B:
$80 ÷ 200 = $.40 per point

Since 33 cents is less than 40 cents, tire A is the better buy even though its initial cost is more.

New Tire Registration

You may be missing out on free or low-cost replacement tires or, worse, driving on potentially hazardous ones, if you don't fill out the tire registration form when you buy tires. The law once required all tire sellers to submit buyers' names automatically to the manufacturer, so the company could contact them if the tires were ever recalled. While this is still mandatory for tire dealers and distributors owned by tire manufacturers, it is not required of independent tire dealers. A recent government study found that 70 percent of independent tire dealers had not registered a single tire purchase. Ask for the tire registration card when you buy tires, and remember to fill it out and send it in. This information will allow the company to notify you if the tire is ever recalled.

Do Tires Affect Fuel Economy?

Yes, a tire's *rolling resistance* affects its fuel economy. In the past, fuel efficiency (low rolling resistance) was traded off with traction. Tires with good traction had lower fuel economy. Michelin has introduced a new rubber compound that doesn't sacrifice traction for fuel economy. In order to give consumers better information and to encourage the widespread use of this new compound, we have asked that the government change its heat resistance grade to a fuel efficiency rating.

Tire Grades
America's Top-Rated Tires

Brand Name	Model	Description	Grades			Expected Mileage		
			Trac.	Heat	Tred.	High	Medium	Low
Vogue	P225/	60R16 97S	A	B	660	198,000	132,000	99,000
Michelin	X One	All	A	B	620	186,000	124,000	93,000
Michelin	X Radial Plus	All	A	B	620	186,000	124,000	93,000
Vogue	P215/	65R15 95S	A	B	580	174,000	116,000	87,000
Michelin	XH4	All	A	B	580	174,000	116,000	87,000
Vogue	P205/	75R14 95S	A	B	580	174,000	116,000	87,000
Vogue	P215/	70R15 97S	A	B	580	174,000	116,000	87,000
Vogue	P225/	75R15 102S	A	B	580	174,000	116,000	87,000
Vogue	P235/	70R15 102S	A	B	580	174,000	116,000	87,000
Vogue	P205/	75R15 97S	A	B	580	174,000	116,000	87,000
Vogue	P205/	70R15 95S	A	B	580	174,000	116,000	87,000
Sigma	Supreme Touring SSR-75 SR	All Others	A	B	560	168,000	112,000	84,000
Dean	Touring Edition (SR)	All	A	B	560	168,000	112,000	84,000
Kelly	Aqua Tour	All	A	B	560	168,000	112,000	84,000
Multimile	Grand Am Touring ST	All	A	B	560	168,000	112,000	84,000
Sigma	Supreme Touring ST	All	A	B	560	168,000	112,000	84,000
Big-O	Legacy Tour Plus 60/65/70 SR	All	A	B	560	168,000	112,000	84,000
Lee	Ultra Touring GT	All	A	B	560	168,000	112,000	84,000
American	Gold 70 SR	P205+	A	B	560	168,000	112,000	84,000
Hercules	Mega Touring LXT SR	All	A	B	560	168,000	112,000	84,000
Goodrich	The Advantage Plus	Thru 205+	A	B	560	168,000	112,000	84,000
Falls	Mark VII (SR)	All	A	B	560	168,000	112,000	84,000
Starfire	Constellation	All	A	B	560	168,000	112,000	84,000
El Dorado	Legend	All	A	B	560	168,000	112,000	84,000
Cordovan	Grand Prix TRNG LXE	All Others	A	B	560	168,000	112,000	84,000
Cordovan	Grand Prix Touring STX	All	A	B	560	168,000	112,000	84,000
Cordovan	Grand Prix Touring ST	All	A	B	560	168,000	112,000	84,000
Concorde	Touring 9000	All	A	B	560	168,000	112,000	84,000
Co-Op	Golden Mark 60/65/70	All	A	B	560	168,000	112,000	84,000
Embassy	Diplomat	All	A	B	560	168,000	112,000	84,000
Winston	Signature (C)	All	A	B	560	168,000	112,000	84,000
Medalist	Primera	P205+	A	B	560	168,000	112,000	84,000
Duralon	Ultra 85	All	A	B	540	162,000	108,000	81,000
Medalist	Primera	195 Thru	A	B	540	162,000	108,000	81,000
Toyo	800+ 65	All	A	B	540	162,000	108,000	81,000
Hankook	Mileage Plus	All	A	B	540	162,000	108,000	81,000
Goodyear	Wingfoot HP	All Others	A	B	540	162,000	108,000	81,000
OHTSU	HS311	All	A	B	540	162,000	108,000	81,000
Goodyear	Infinitred	All Others	A	B	540	162,000	108,000	81,000
Goodrich	The Advantage Plus	P195	A	B	540	162,000	108,000	81,000
Toyo	800+ 70,75	15	A	B	540	162,000	108,000	81,000
Falken	FK315	All	A	B	540	162,000	108,000	81,000
Uniroyal	Tiger Paw Touring TR 70 SR	14	A	B	540	162,000	108,000	81,000
American	Gold 70 SR	Thru P195	A	B	540	162,000	108,000	81,000
Toyo	800+ 60	15 & 16	A	B	540	162,000	108,000	81,000
Vogue	P215/	75R15 100	A	B	540	162,000	108,000	81,000
Dunlop	Elite 65	15 & 16	A	B	540	162,000	108,000	81,000
Road King	Premium GT	All	A	B	540	162,000	108,000	81,000
Uniroyal	Tiger Paw Touring TR	15&16	A	B	540	162,000	108,000	81,000
Goodrich	The Advantage Plus 65 SR	All	A	B	520	156,000	104,000	78,000
Delta	Supreme 70/75	15	A	B	520	156,000	104,000	78,000
General	Ameri G4S	All	A	B	520	156,000	104,000	78,000
Dunlop	Elite 65	14	A	B	520	156,000	104,000	78,000
American	Gold Tour Plus 65 SR	All	A	B	520	156,000	104,000	78,000
Goodyear	Infinitred	13	A	B	520	156,000	104,000	78,000
Kleber	CP751,701	15	A	B	520	156,000	104,000	78,000
Toyo	800+ 75,70,60	14	A	B	520	156,000	104,000	78,000
Centennial	Interceptor	15 & 16	A	B	520	156,000	104,000	78,000
National	XT6000 70/75	15	A	B	520	156,000	104,000	78,000
Toyo	800+ 70	175/70R14	B	B	520	156,000	104,000	78,000

Brand Name	Model	Description	Grades			Expected Mileage		
			Trac.	Heat	Tred.	High	Medium	Low
Medalist	Primera 65 SR	All	A	B	520	156,000	104,000	78,000
Pirelli	P400 Aquamile	All	A	B	520	156,000	104,000	78,000
Remington	Touring	15 & 16	A	B	520	156,000	104,000	78,000
Riken	Classic MR-60	15	A	B	520	156,000	104,000	78,000
National	XT5000	15	A	B	520	156,000	104,000	78,000
Uniroyal	Tiger Paw AWP	14	A	B	500	150,000	100,000	75,000
Uniroyal	Tiger Paw AWP	All 15 Exc.	A	B	500	150,000	100,000	75,000
Michelin	X Radial	All	A	B	500	150,000	100,000	75,000
Remington	Touring	14	A	B	500	150,000	100,000	75,000
Delta	Chaparral A/T LT	15	A	B	500	150,000	100,000	75,000
Uniroyal	Tiger Paw AWP	P225/60R16	B	B	500	150,000	100,000	75,000
Regul	Trail Blazer LT	15	A	B	500	150,000	100,000	75,000
Uniroyal	Tiger Paw AWP	P235/75R15	B	B	500	150,000	100,000	75,000
Duralon	Vertex IV	All	A	B	500	150,000	100,000	75,000
Cordovan	Grand Prix TRNG LXE	75 SR	A	B	500	150,000	100,000	75,000
Road King	Regency Touring	All	A	B	500	150,000	100,000	75,000
Sigma	Supreme Touring SSR-75 SR	All	A	B	500	150,000	100,000	75,000
Centennial	Interceptor	14	A	B	500	150,000	100,000	75,000
Cavalier	Sport LT	15	A	B	500	150,000	100,000	75,000
Sumitomo	SC890 75	15	A	B	500	150,000	100,000	75,000
Atlas	Pinnacle TE 70/75	14 & 15	A	B	500	150,000	100,000	75,000
Atlas	Pinnacle TE 70	13	A	B	500	150,000	100,000	75,000
American	Prospector A/T LT	15	A	B	500	150,000	100,000	75,000
Dayton	Touring 70/75S	All	A	B	500	150,000	100,000	75,000
Peerless	Permasteel LE	All	A	B	500	150,000	100,000	75,000
Firestone	Affinity	All	A	B	500	150,000	100,000	75,000
Firestone	Affinity T-2	All	A	B	500	150,000	100,000	75,000
Toyo	800+ 75	235/75RL15	A	B	500	150,000	100,000	75,000
Gillette	Kodiak LE	All	A	B	500	150,000	100,000	75,000
Michelin	Rainforce MX4 (P-Metric)	All	A	B	500	150,000	100,000	75,000
Medalist	Sport Track Radial LT	15	A	B	500	150,000	100,000	75,000
National	Chaparral A/T LT	15	A	B	500	150,000	100,000	75,000
Multimile	Grand Am Touring LSS	75 (SR)	A	B	500	150,000	100,000	75,000
Concorde	Max 6000	All Except	A	B	480	144,000	96,000	72,000
Co-Op	Golden Mark 75	All	A	B	480	144,000	96,000	72,000
Winston	Classic 70 (C)	All	A	B	480	144,000	96,000	72,000
Kelly	Navigator 800S	All Others	A	B	480	144,000	96,000	72,000
Cavalier	SRX	All Others	A	B	480	144,000	96,000	72,000
Monarch	Ultra Trak A/S	All Others	A	B	480	144,000	96,000	72,000
Sears	Aquahandler	All Others	A	B	480	144,000	96,000	72,000
Lee	GT VI Steel Trak	All Others	A	B	480	144,000	96,000	72,000
Ultra-Tech	Touring A/S	All	A	B	480	144,000	96,000	72,000
Spartan	USA 1	All Others	A	B	480	144,000	96,000	72,000
Star	Imperial PSR	All Except	A	B	480	144,000	96,000	72,000
Kleber	CPR600S	All	A	B	480	144,000	96,000	72,000
Cooper	Grand Classic STE (SR)	All	A	A	480	144,000	96,000	72,000
El Dorado	Crusader II (SR)	All	A	B	480	144,000	96,000	72,000
Riken	Classic MR-GT	All Others	A	B	480	144,000	96,000	72,000
Hankook	K405	All	A	B	480	144,000	96,000	72,000
Hallmark	PWR4	All Others	A	B	480	144,000	96,000	72,000
Dean	Cheetah Tourng 70 GT	SR All	A	B	480	144,000	96,000	72,000
Pacemark	Premium A/S	All Except	A	B	480	144,000	96,000	72,000
Starfire	Spectrum LXR	All	A	B	480	144,000	96,000	72,000
Delta	Road Max	All Others	A	B	480	144,000	96,000	72,000
Dunlop	Elite 65	13	A	B	480	144,000	96,000	72,000
Republic	Weather King	All Except	A	B	480	144,000	96,000	72,000
Regul	Pacesetter IV Plus	15	A	B	480	144,000	96,000	72,000
Fisk	Fisk Classic	15	A	B	480	144,000	96,000	72,000
Falls	P794 SR/TR	All	A	B	480	144,000	96,000	72,000
Hercules	Ultra Plus	All	A	B	480	144,000	96,000	72,000

COMPLAINTS

Americans spend billions of dollars on motor vehicle repairs every year. While many of those repairs are satisfactory, there are times when getting your vehicle fixed can be a very difficult process. In fact, vehicle defects and repairs are the number one cause of consumer complaints in the U.S., according to the Federal Trade Commission.

This chapter is designed to help you resolve your complaint, whether it's for a new vehicle still under warranty or for one you've had for years. In addition, we offer a guide to arbitration, the names and addresses of consumer groups, federal agencies and the manufacturers themselves. Finally, we tell you how to take the important step of registering your complaint with the U.S. Department of Transportation.

No matter what your complaint, keep accurate records. Copies of the following items are indispensable in helping to resolve your problems:

☑ your service invoices

☑ bills you have paid

☑ letters you have written to the manufacturer or the repair facility owner

☑ written repair estimates from your independent mechanic.

Resolving Complaints: If you are having trouble, here are some basic steps to help you resolve your problem:

1 First, return your vehicle to the repair facility that did the work. Bring a written list of the problems and make sure that you keep a copy of the list. Give the repair facility a reasonable opportunity to examine your vehicle and attempt to fix it. Speak directly to the service manager (not to the service writer who wrote up your repair order), and ask him or her to test drive the vehicle with you so that you can point out the problem.

2 If that doesn't resolve the problem, take the vehicle to a diagnostic center for an independent examination. This may cost $45 to $60. Get a written statement defining the problem and outlining how it may be fixed. Give your repair shop a copy. If your vehicle is under warranty, do not allow any warranty repair by an independent mechanic; you may not be reimbursed by the manufacturer.

3 If your repair shop does not respond to the independent assessment, present your problem to a mediation panel. These panels hear both sides of the story and try to come to a resolution.

If the problem is with a new vehicle dealer, or if you feel that the manufacturer is responsible, you may be able to use one of the manufacturer's mediation programs discussed on pg. 78.

If the problem is solely with an independent dealer, a local Better Business Bureau (BBB) may be able to mediate your complaint. It may also offer an arbitration hearing. In any case, the BBB should enter your complaint into its files on that establishment.

When contacting any mediation program, determine how long the process takes, who makes the final decision, whether you are bound by that decision, and whether the program handles all problems or only warranty complaints.

4 If there are no mediation programs in your area, contact private consumer groups, local government agencies, or your local "action line"

newspaper columnist, newspaper editor, or radio or TV broadcaster. A phone call or letter from them may persuade a repair facility to take action. Send a copy of your letter to the repair shop.

5 One of your last resorts is to bring a law suit against the dealer, manufacturer, or repair facility in small claims court. The fee for filing such an action is usually small, and you generally act as your own attorney, saving attorney's fees. There is a monetary limit on the amount you can claim, which varies from state to state. Your local consumer affairs office, state attorney general's office, or the clerk of the court can tell you how to file such a suit.

6 Finally, talk with an attorney. It's best to select an attorney who is familiar with handling automotive problems. If you don't know of one, call the lawyer referral service listed in the telephone directory (or see box) and ask for the names of attorneys who deal with automobile problems. If you can't afford an attorney, contact the Legal Aid Society.

Warranty Complaints: If your vehicle is under warranty or you are having problems with a factory-authorized dealership, here are some special guidelines:

Have the warranty available to show the dealer. Make sure you call the problem to the dealer's attention before the end of the warranty period.

If you are still unsatisfied after giving the dealer a reasonable opportunity to fix your vehicle, contact the manufacturer's representative (also called the zone representa-

tive) in your area. This person can authorize the dealer to make repairs or take other steps to resolve the dispute. Your dealer will have your zone representative's name and telephone number. Explain the problem and ask for a meeting and a personal inspection of your vehicle.

If you can't get satisfaction from the zone representative, call or write the manufacturer's owner relations department. Your owner's manual contains this phone number and address. In each case, as you move up the chain, indicate the steps you have already taken.

Your next option is to present your problem to a complaint-handling panel or to the arbitration program in which the manufac-

turer of your vehicle participates. See page 78 for additional information.

If you complain of a problem during the warranty period, you have a right to have the problem fixed even after the warranty runs out. If your warranty has not been honored, you may be able to "revoke acceptance," which means that you return the vehicle to the dealer. If you are successful, you may be entitled to a replacement vehicle, or to a full refund of the purchase price and reimbursement of legal fees under the Magnuson-Moss Warranty Act. Or, if you are covered by one of the state Lemon Laws (see page 85), you may be able to return the vehicle and receive a refund or replacement from the manufacturer.

Legal Aid

If you need legal assistance with your repair problem, the Center for Auto Safety has a list of lawyers who specialize in helping consumers with auto repair problems. For the names of some attorneys in your area, send a stamped, self-addressed envelope to: Center for Auto Safety, 2001 S Street, NW, Washington, DC 20009-1160. Or, check their website at www.autosafety.org for a shorter list of lemon law attorneys.

In addition, the Center has published *The Lemon Book,* a detailed, 368-page guide to resolving automobile complaints. The book is available for $17.50 directly from the Center.

Attorneys Take Note: For information on litigation assistance provided by the Center for Auto Safety, including The Lemon Law Litigation Manual, please contact the Center for Auto Safety at the above address.

Auto Safety Hotline

One of the most valuable but often unused services of the government is the Auto Safety Hotline. By calling the Hotline to report safety problems, your particular concern or problem will become part of the National Highway Traffic Safety Administration's (NHTSA) complaint database. This complaint program is extraordinarily important to government decision makers who often take action based on this information. In addition, it provides consumer groups, like the Center for Auto Safety, with the evidence they need to force the government to act. Unless government engineers or safety advocates have evidence of a wide-scale problem, little can be done to get the manufacturers to correct the defect.

Few government services have the potential to do as much for the consumer as this complaint database, so we encourage you to voice your concerns to the government.

Your letter can be used as the basis of safety defect investigations and recall campaigns. When you file a complaint, be sure to indicate that your name and address can be made public. Without names and addresses, it is more difficult for consumer groups to uncover safety defects.

Hotline Complaints: When you call the Hotline to report a safety problem, you will be mailed a questionnaire asking for information that the agency's technical staff will need to evaluate the problem. This information also gives the government an indication of which vehicles are causing consumers the most problems.

You can also use this questionnaire to report defects in tires and child safety seats. In fact, we strongly encourage you to report problems with child safety seats. Now that they are required by law in all fifty states, we have noticed that numerous design and safety problems have surfaced. If the government knows about these problems, they will be more likely to take action so that modifications are made to these life-saving devices.

After you complete and return the questionnaire, the following things will happen:
1. A copy will go to NHTSA's safety defect investigators.
2. A copy will be sent to the manufacturer of the car or equipment, with a request for help in resolving the problem.
3. You will be notified that your questionnaire has been received.
4. Your problem will be recorded in the complaint database which we use to provide you with complaint ratings.

Hotline Services: Hotline operators can also provide information on recalls. If you want recall information on a particular automobile, simply tell the Hotline operator the make, model, and year of the car, or the type of equipment involved. You will receive any recall information that NHTSA has about that car or item. This information can be very important if you are not sure whether your car has ever been recalled. If you want a printed copy of the recall information, it will be mailed within twenty-four hours at no charge.

If you have other car-related problems, the Hotline operators can refer you to the appropriate federal, state, and local government agencies. If you need information about federal safety standards and regulations, you'll be referred to the appropriate experts.

You may call the Hotline day or night, seven days a week. If you call when no operators are available, a recorded message will ask you to leave your name and address and a description of the information you want. The appropriate materials will be mailed to you.

Complaints and Safety Information

Auto Safety Hotline
800-424-9393
(in Washington, DC: 202-366-0123)
TTY for hearing impaired:
800-424-9153
(in Washington, DC: 202-366-7800)

The toll-free Auto Safety Hotline can provide information on recalls, record information about safety problems, and refer you to the appropriate government experts on other vehicle related problems. You can even have recall information mailed to you within 24 hours of your call at no charge.

Arbitration

One method of resolving automobile repair problems is through arbitration. This procedure requires that both parties present their cases to an arbitrator or panel. You can seek repairs, reimbursement of expenses, or a refund or replacement for your car through arbitration. Keep in mind that this is not a court, and arbitrators are generally not required to apply the law, but to find a compromise. You should investigate both options before deciding which to pursue.

In theory, arbitration can be a free, effective means of resolving disputes. It is designed to be somewhat informal, relatively speedy, and you do not need a lawyer to present your case. Plus, you avoid the time and expense of going to court.

Almost all manufacturers now offer some form of arbitration, usually for problems that arise during the warranty period. Some companies sponsor their own and others subscribe to programs run by groups like the Better Business Bureau or the National Center for Dispute Settlement. Your owner's manual will identify which programs you can use. Also, contact your state attorney general to find out if your state offers a program.

How it works: Upon receiving your complaint, the arbitration program will attempt to mediate a resolution between you and the manufacturer or dealer. If you are not satisfied with the proposed solution, you have the right to have your case heard at an arbitration hearing.

In all cases, the customers present their cases in written form and are able to make an oral presentation. If an arbitration program is incorporated into your warranty, you may have to use that program before filing a legal claim. Federal law requires that arbitration programs incorporated into a warranty be nonbinding on the consumer. So, if you do not like the result, you can seek other remedies.

Arbitration programs have different eligibility requirements, so be sure you are eligible for the program you are considering.

Let the Federal Trade Commission, the Center for Auto Safety, Consumers for Auto Reliability and Safety (their addresses are on pages 82 and 83), and your state attorney general (c/o your state capitol) know of your experience with arbitration. It is particularly important to contact these offices if you have a complaint about how your case was handled.

Dispute Settlement Board: Sponsored by Ford, each case is considered by a four-person panel that includes one dealer. Oral presentations are permitted. Only cases involving warranty related issues are reviewed. For information, call 800-392-3673.

Chrysler Customer Arbitration Board: In 1997, the National Center for Dispute Settlement (NCDS) started handling cases in most states. The Customer Arbitration Board handles disputes in California. In both programs, written submissions must be made by each party. Customers who live in AR, KY, MN, OH, CA and in states where complaints are handled by NCDS have the right to request oral presentation. Both program's boards consist of a local consumer advocate, an independent, A.S.E. certified technical representative, and a representative from the general public. Both boards will only hear cases under warranty. For information, call 800-992-1997.

Better Business Bureau (BBB) Arbitration Programs (Auto Line): The BBB always tries to mediate a dispute before recommending arbitration. About 19% of the disputes it handles actually go to arbitration. The arbitrators are selected at random and an impartial technical expert can be present if requested. The consumer can object if conflict exists.

Arbitrators are volunteers from the local community and are not always automobile experts. This can both help and harm your case. As a result, it is important to be well prepared when participating in the BBB program. If you're not, the potential exists for the dealer or manufacturer to appear as the "expert" on automobiles. For more information, contact your local BBB or 800-955-5100.

Automobile Consumer Action Program: AUTOCAP was established by the National Automobile Dealers Association (NADA) to assist consumers in resolving auto sales or service disputes with dealers and manufacturers. The program is sponsored on a voluntary basis by state and local dealer associations. Currently, most AUTOCAPs do not operate under the FTC guidelines required for warranty cases. Sixty-five percent of the cases that AUTOCAP considers are resolved in preliminary mediation. Of those cases that go to arbitration, 45 percent are resolved in favor of the consumer, 22 percent are a compromise, and 33 percent are in favor of the company.

For more information and the name of your local panel, contact: AUTOCAP, 8400 Westpark Drive, McLean, Virginia 22102; 703-821-7144.

Ten Tips for Arbitration: Arbitration is designed to be easier and less intimidating than going to court. However, the process can still be nerve-racking, especially if you've never been through it before. Here are some tips to help make the process as simple and straightforward as possible.

1. Before deciding to go to arbitration, get a written description of how the program works and make sure you understand the details. If you have any questions, contact the local representatives of the program. Remember, the manufacturer or dealer probably has more experience with this process than you do.
2. Make sure the final decision is nonbinding on you. If the decision is binding, you give up your right to appeal or go to court.
3. Determine whether the program allows you to appear at the hearing. If not, make sure your written statement is completely accurate and contains all the appropriate receipts and documentation. If you think of something that you want considered after you have sent in your material, send it immediately and specifically request that the additional information be included.
4. Make sure the program follows the required procedures. If the arbitration program is incorporated into the car's warranty, for example, the panel must make a decision on your case within 40

days of receiving your complaint.
5. Contact the manufacturer's representative and request copies of any technical service bulletins that apply to your car. (See "Secret Warranties" on page 59 for a description of technical service bulletins and how to get them.) Service bulletins may help you prove that your car is defective.
6. Well before the hearing, ask the program representative to send you copies of all material submitted by the other party. You may want to respond to this information.
7. Make sure all your documents are in chronological order, and include a brief outline of the events. Submit copies of all material associated with your problem and a copy of your warranty.
8. Even though you may be very angry about the situation, try to present your case in a calm,

logical manner.
9. If you are asking for a refund or a replacement for your car in accordance with your state's Lemon Law, do not assume that the arbitrator is completely familiar with the law. Be prepared to explain how it entitles you to your request. Also, if given a refund or replacement, be prepared to be charged a usage fee reflecting the amount you used the vehicle.
10. In most programs, you have to reject the decision in order to go to court to pursue other action. If you accept the decision, you may limit your rights to pursue further action. You will, however, have additional claims if the manufacturer or dealer does not properly follow through on the decision or if your car breaks down again.

State-Run Arbitration

State-run arbitration programs are often more fair to consumers than national programs. The following states have set up programs (or guidelines) which are far better than their national counterparts. If you live in one of these areas, contact your attorney general's office (in care of your state capitol) for information. If your state is not listed below, you should still contact your state attorney general's office for advice on arbitration.

Connecticut	Massachusetts	New York
Florida	Montana	Texas
Georgia	New Hampshire	Vermont
Hawaii	New Jersey	Washington
Maine		

Complaint Index

Thanks to the efforts of the Center for Auto Safety, we are able to provide you with the vehicle complaints on file with the National Highway Traffic Safety Administration (NHTSA). Each year, thousands of Americans call the government to register complaints about their vehicles. The federal government collects this information but has never released it to the public.

The complaint index is the result of our analysis of these complaints. It is based on a ratio of the number of complaints for each vehicle to the sales of that vehicle. In order to predict the expected complaint performance of the 1999 models, we have examined the complaint history of that car's *series*. The term *series* refers to the fact that when a manufacturer introduces a new model, that vehicle remains essentially unchanged, on average, for 4-6 years. For example, the Pontiac Bonneville was introduced in 1992 and remains essentially the same car for 1999. As such, we have compiled the complaint experience for that series in order to give you some additional information to use in deciding which car to buy. For those vehicles just introduced in 1998 or 1999, we do not yet have enough data to develop a complaint index.

The following table presents the complaint indexes for the best and worst 1999 models. Higher index numbers mean the vehicle generated a greater number of complaints. Lower numbers indicate fewer complaints. After calculating the indexes, we compared the results among all 1999 vehicles.

1999 Complaint Ratings

The Best		The Worst	
Vehicle	**Index**	**Vehicle**	**Index**
Acura RL	86	Dodge Caravan	4988
Suzuki Swift	317	Chrysler T&C	4743
Lexus LS400	444	Chevrolet Venture	4568
Nissan Maxima	500	Mitsubishi Mirage	4201
Infiniti Q45	545	Mitsubishi Diamante	4045
Lexus ES300	614	Chrysler Sebring	3816
Honda Prelude	615	Chrysler Cirrus	3743
Mercedes-Benz C-Class	618	Oldsmobile Cutlass	3262
Infiniti I30	707	Mitsubishi Eclipse	2962
Nissan Sentra	732	Plymouth Voyager	2834
Mazda Millenia	756	Ford Windstar	2729
Mercedes-Benz E-Class	782	Hyundai Tiburon	2728
Toyota Celica	804	Oldsmobile Silhouette	2706
Chevrolet Lumina	818	Hyundai Elantra	2508
Acura Integra	819	Dodge Neon	2479
Toyota Avalon	870	Buick Park Avenue	2459
Honda Civic	874	Dodge Avenger	2405
Pontiac Sunfire	878	Pontiac Grand Prix	2345
Cadillac DeVille	881	Cadillac Catera	2218
Chevrolet Cavalier	894	Ford Crown Victoria	2024
Buick Regal	910	Hyundai Sonata	2005
Buick LeSabre	921	GMC Safari	1910
Lexus SC300/400	938	Mercury Tracer	1881
BMW Z3	1027	Pontiac Montana	1874

Every year automobile manufacturers spend millions of dollars making their voices heard in government decision making. For example, General Motors and Ford have large staffs in Detroit and Washington that work solely to influence government activity. But who looks out for the consumer?

For over twenty-five years, the nonprofit Center for Auto Safety (CAS) has told the consumer's story to government agencies, to Congress and to the courts. Its efforts focus on all consumers rather than only those with individual complaints.

CAS was established in 1970 by Ralph Nader and Consumers Union. As consumer concerns about auto safety issues expanded, so did the work of CAS. It became an independent group in 1972, and the original staff of two has grown to fourteen attorneys and researchers. CAS' activities include:

Initiating Safety Recalls: CAS analyzes over 50,000 consumer complaints each year. By following problems as they develop, CAS requests government investigations and recalls of defective vehicles. CAS was responsible for the Ford Pinto faulty gas tank recall, the Firestone 500 steel-belted radial tire recall, and the record recall of over 3 million Evenflo One Step child seats.

Representing the Consumer in Washington: CAS follows the activities of federal agencies and Congress to ensure that they carry out their responsibilities to the American taxpayer. CAS brings a consumer's point of view to vehicle safety policies and rule-making. Since 1970, CAS has submitted more than 500 petitions and comments on federal safety standards.

One major effort in this area has been the successful fight for adoption of automatic crash protection in passenger cars. These systems are a more effective and less intrusive alternative to crash protection than mandatory safety belt laws or belts that must be buckled in order to start the car.

In 1992, the Center for Auto Safety uncovered a fire defect that dwarfed the highly publicized flammability of the Ford Pinto. It had to do with the side-saddle gas tanks on full size 1973-87 GM pickups and 1988-90 crew cabs that tend to explode on impact. Over 1,600 people have been killed in fire crashes involving these trucks. After mounting a national campaign to warn consumers to steer clear of these GM fire hazards, the U.S. Department of Transportation (DOT) granted CAS' petition and conducted one of its biggest defect investigations in history. The result—GM was asked to recall its pickups. GM, sadly, denied this request.

Thanks to a petition originally filed by CAS, NHTSA adopted a new registration system to better enable manufacturer notification to parents with defective child seats. This will enable more parents to find out about potentially hazardous safety seats.

Exposing Secret Warranties: CAS played a prominent role in the disclosure of secret warranties, "policy adjustments," as they are called by manufacturers. These occur when an auto maker agrees to pay for repair of certain defects beyond the warranty period but refuses to notify consumers. (See "Secret Warranties" on page 61.)

Improving Rust Warranties: Rust and corrosion cost American car owners up to $14 billion annually. CAS has been successful in its efforts to get domestic and foreign auto companies to lengthen their all-important corrosion warranties.

Lemon Laws: CAS' work on Lemon Laws aided in the enactment of state laws which make it easier to return a defective new automobile and get money back.

Tire Ratings: After a suspension between 1982-84, consumers have reliable treadwear ratings to help them get the most miles for their dollar. CAS' lawsuit overturned DOT's revocation of this valuable new tire information program.

Initiating Legal Action: When CAS has exhausted other means of obtaining relief for consumer problems, it will initiate legal action. For example, in 1978 when the Department of Energy attempted to raise the price of gasoline 4 cents per gallon without notice or comment, CAS succeeded in stopping this illegal move through a lawsuit, thus saving consumers $2 billion for the six month period that the action was delayed.

A CAS lawsuit against the Environmental Protection Agency (EPA) in 1985 forced the EPA to recall polluting cars, rather than let companies promise to make cleaner cars in the future. As part of the settlement, GM (which was responsible for the polluting cars) funded a $7 million methanol bus demonstration program in New York City.

Publications: CAS has many publications on automobiles, motor homes, recreational vehicles, and fuel economy, and a number of free information packets. For each of the packets listed below, or for a complete description of CAS' publications, send a separate self-addressed, business-sized envelope with 55¢ postage to the address below. Unless otherwise noted, packets listed below cover all known major problems since 1985 for the models indicated and explain what to do about them. Requests should include make, model, and year of vehicle (with Vehicle Identification Number), as well as the problem you are experiencing. (Allow 2 weeks for delivery.)

Audi
BMW
Cadillac
Chrys. Paint/Water Leaks
Chrys. Ultradrive Trans.
Chrys. Aries Reliant/K-Cars
Chrys. Cirrus/Stratus/Neon/Breeze
Chrys. Dakota/Durango
Chrys. LHS/Intrepid/Concorde
Chrys. Minivan
Chrys. Ram Van/Truck
Chrys. Sebring/Avenger
Ford Aerostar
Ford Auto. Trans.: Taurus/Sable/
  Continental
Ford Bronco II/Explorer/Ranger
Ford Cr. Vic./Gr. Marquis/
  Thunderbird/Cougar/Lincolns
Ford Contour/Mystique
Ford Escort/Lynx/Tracer
Ford F-Series Trucks
Ford Taurus/Sable
Ford Tempo/Topaz
Ford Mustang/Probe
Ford Paint
GM All Geo's/LeMans/Sprint/Nova
GM Saturn
GM Auto. Trans.: FWD

GM Auto. Trans.: RWD
GM Beretta/Corsica
GM Cut. Supr./Gr. Prix/Lumina/
  Regal
GM Celebrity/6000/Century/Cut.
  Ciera & Cruiser
GM Camaro/Firebird
GM Achieva/Calais/Gr. Am/Sky-
  lark/Somerset Regal
GM Roadmaster/Caprice
GM Cavalier/Cimarron/Firenza/
  Skyhawk/Sunbird/Sunfire/J2000
GM 98/Electra & Park Ave.
GM 88/LeSabre/Bonneville
GM Power Steering FWD
GM C/K Pickup/Suburban/Tahoe/
  Yukon/Blazer/Jimmy
GM S-Series/Blazer/Jimmy/
  Sonoma
GM Big Vans/Astro/Safari/APVs
GM Pontiac Fiero
GM Paint
Honda/Acura
Hyundai
Jeep—all models
Infinti
Isuzu
Mazda Cars, Mazda Trucks
Mercedes
Mitsubishi
Nissan Cars, Nissan Vans/Trucks
Renault/Eagle
Saab

Subaru
Toyota
Volkswagen
Volvo

CAS Website: CAS has a website (www.autosafety.org) to provide information to consumers and to organize consumer campaigns against auto companies on safety defects. All of the above consumer packages are on CAS' website. Consumers with lemons and safety defects can file electronic complaints with CAS and get referred to lemon lawyers. The best consumer campaigns are on stalling Fords (1983-95 Fords with defective ignition modules that cause stalling on highways) and GM fire-bombs (1973-82 GM pickups with side saddle gas tanks that explode on impact).

Help CAS help you: CAS depends on public support. Annual consumer membership is $20. All contributions to this nonprofit organization are tax-deductible. Annual membership includes a quarterly newsletter called "LEMON TIMES." To join, send a check to: Center for Auto Safety, 2001 S Street, NW, Washington, DC 20009-1160.

Lemon Aid

TIP

The Center for Auto Safety has published *The Lemon Book,* a detailed, 368 page guide to resolving automobile complaints. Co-authored by Ralph Nader and CAS Executive Director, Clarence Ditlow, this handbook is designed to help car buyers avoid lemons and tells you what to do if you wind up with one. To obtain this valuable book, send $17.50 to the Center for Auto Safety, 2001 S St., NW, Washington, DC 20009-1160. CAS is a non-profit consumer group supported, in part, by the sales of its publications.

Here are the names of additional consumer groups which you may find helpful:

Advocates for Highway and Auto Safety

750 First Street, NE, Suite 901
Washington, DC 20002
(202) 408-1711/408-1699 fax
www.saferoads.org
Focus: An alliance of consumer, health and safety groups, and insurance companies.

Consumer Action San Francisco

717 Market St., Suite 310
San Francisco, CA 94103
(415) 777-9635
www.consumer-action.org
Focus: General problems of California residents.

Consumers for Auto Reliability and Safety

1500 W. El Camino Ave, #333
Sacramento, CA 95833-1945
(530) 759-9440
Focus: Auto safety, airbags, and lemon laws.

Consumers Education and Protective Association

6048 Ogontz Avenue
Philadelphia, PA 19141
(215) 424-1441
Focus: Pickets on behalf of members to resolve auto purchase and repair problems.

SafetyBelt Safe, U.S.A.

P.O. Box 553
Altadena, CA 91003
(800)745-SAFE or (310)222-6860
Focus: Provides excellent information and training on child safety seats and safety belt usage.

Several federal agencies conduct automobile-related programs. Listed below is each agency with a description of the type of work it performs as well as the address and phone number for its headquarters in Washington, DC. Useful web sites are also listed.

National Highway Traffic Safety Administration

400 7th Street, SW, NOA-40
Washington, DC 20590
(202) 366-9550
www.nhtsa.dot.gov

NHTSA issues safety and fuel economy standards for new motor vehicles; investigates safety defects and enforces recall of defective vehicles and equipment; conducts research and demonstration programs on vehicle safety, fuel economy, driver safety, and automobile inspection and repair; provides grants for state highway safety programs in areas such as police traffic services, driver education and licensing, emergency medical services, pedestrian safety, and alcohol abuse.

Environmental Protection Agency

401 M Street, SW
Washington, DC 20460
(202) 260-2090
www.epa.gov

EPA is responsible for the control and abatement of air, noise, and toxic substance pollution. This includes setting and enforcing air and noise emission standards for motor vehicles and measuring fuel economy in new vehicles (EPA Fuel Economy Guide).

Federal Trade Commission

PA Avenue & 6th Street, NW
Washington, DC 20580
(202) 326-2000
www.ftc.gov

FTC regulates advertising and credit practices, marketing abuses, and professional services and ensures that products are properly labeled (as in fuel economy ratings). The commission covers unfair or deceptive trade practices in motor vehicle sales and repairs, as well as in non-safety defects.

Federal Highway Administration

400 7th Street, SW,
Room 3401, HHS1
Washington, DC 20590
(202) 366-1153

FHA develops standards to ensure highways are constructed to reduce occurrence and severity of accidents.

Department of Justice

Consumer Litigation
Civil Division
1331 Pennsylvania Avenue
National Place Bldg., Suite 950N
Washington, DC 20004
(202) 514-6786

The Department of Justice enforces the federal law that requires manufacturers to label new automobiles and forbids removal or alteration of labels before delivery to consumers. Labels must contain the make, model, vehicle identification number, dealer's name, suggested base price, manufacturer option costs, and manufacturer's suggested retail price.

Automobile Manufacturers

Acura Automobile Division
Mr. Richard B. Thomas
Exec. V. P. and General Manager
1919 Torrance Blvd.
Torrance, CA 90501-2746
(310) 783-2000/(310) 783-3900 (fax)

BMW of North America, Inc.
Mr. Victor H. Doolan
President
300 Chestnut Ridge Road
Woodcliff Lake, NJ 07675
(201) 307-4000/(201) 307-4003 (fax)

Chrysler Corporation
Mr. Robert Eaton
Chairman and CEO
1000 Chrysler Drive
Auburn Hills, MI 48326-2766
(810) 512-9300

Ford Motor Company
Mr. Jac Nasser
Chairman
The American Road
Dearborn, MI 48121
(313) 322-3000/(313) 446-9475 (fax)

General Motors Corporation
Mr. John F. Smith, Jr.
CEO and Chairman
100 Renaissance Center
Detroit, MI 48202-1000
(313) 556-5000/(313) 556-5108 (fax)

American Honda Motor Co.
Mr. K. Amemiya
President and CEO
1919 Torrance Blvd.
Torrance, CA 90501-2746
(310) 783-2000/(310) 783-3900 (fax)

Hyundai Motor America
Mr. M.H. Juhn
President and CEO
10550 Talbert Avenue
Fountain Valley, CA 92728
(714) 965-3939/(714) 965-3816 (fax)

American Isuzu Motors Inc.
Mr. Yasayuki Sudo
President
2300 Pellissier Place
Whittier, CA 90601
(562) 699-0500/(562) 692-7135 (fax)

Kia Motors America, Inc.
Mr. W.K. Kim
President and CEO
P.O. Box 52410
Irvine, CA 92619-2410
(949) 470-7000/(949) 470-2809 (fax)

Land Rover of America
Mr. Charles R. Hughes
President
4371 Parliament Place, P.O. Box 1503
Lanham, MD 20706
(301) 731-9040/(301) 731-9054 (fax)

Lexus Division/Toyota Motor Sales, U.S.A., Inc.
Mr. Bryan Bergsteinsson
Group Vice President & GM
19001 S. Western Ave.
Torrance, CA 90509
(310) 328-2075/(310) 781-3290 (fax)

Mazda Motor of America, Inc.
Mr. Richard Beattle
President and CEO
7755 Irvine Center Dr.
Irvine, CA 92718
(714) 727-1990/(714) 727-6529 (fax)

Mercedes-Benz of N.A.
Mr. Michael Jackson
President
1 Mercedes Drive
Montvale, NJ 07645-0350
(201) 573-0600/(201) 573-0117 (fax)

Mitsubishi Motor Sales
Mr. Hiroshi Yajima
President and CEO
6400 Katella Ave.
Cypress, CA 90630-0064
(714) 372-6000/(714) 373-1019 (fax)

Nissan Motor Corp. U.S.A.
Mr. Minoru Nakamura
President and CEO
P.O. Box 191
Gardena, CA 90248-0191
(310) 532-3111/(310) 719-3343 (fax)

Saab Cars USA, Inc.
Mr. Joel Manby
President and CEO
4405-A International Drive
Norcross, GA 30093
(770) 279-0100/(770) 279-6499 (fax)

Subaru of America, Inc.
Mr. Yasuo Fujiki
Chairman and CEO
P.O. Box 6000
Cherry Hill, NJ 08034-6000
(609) 488-8500/(609) 488-0485 (fax)

American Suzuki Motor Corp.
Mr. Manabu Nakamura
President
3251 Imperial Hwy., P.O. Box 1100
Brea, CA 92822-1100
(714) 996-7040/(714) 524-2512 (fax)

Toyota Motor Sales, U.S.A., Inc.
Mr. Yoshio Ishizaka
President and CEO
19001 S. Western Avenue
Torrance, CA 90509
(310) 618-4000/(310) 618-7800 (fax)

Volkswagen of America, Inc.
Volkswagen Canada Inc.
Mr. Clive Warrilow
President
3800 Hamlin Road
Auburn Hills, MI 48326
(810) 340-5000/(810) 340-4643 (fax)

Volvo Cars of North America
Mr. Hans Olov Olsson
President and CEO
7 Volvo Drive
Rockleigh, NJ 07647
(201) 767-4710/(201) 784-4535 (fax)

Lemon Laws

Sometimes, despite our best efforts, we buy a vehicle that just doesn't work right. There may be little problem after little problem, or perhaps one big problem that never seems to be fixed. Because of the bad taste that such vehicles leave in the mouths of consumers who buy them, these vehicles are known as "lemons."

In the past, it's been difficult to obtain a refund or replacement if a vehicle was a lemon. The burden of proof was left to the consumer. Because it is hard to define exactly what constitutes a lemon, many lemon owners were unable to win a case against a manufacturer. However, as of 1993, all states have passed "Lemon Laws." Although

there are some important state-to-state variations, all of the laws have similarities: They establish a period of coverage, usually one year from delivery or the written warranty period, whichever is shorter; they may require some form of noncourt arbitration; and most importantly they define a lemon. In most states a lemon is a new car, truck, or van that has been taken back to the shop at least four times for the same repair, or is out of service for a total of 30 days during the covered period.

This time does not mean consecutive days. In some states the total time must be for the same repair; in others, it can be based on different repair problems.

Be sure to keep careful records of your repairs since some states now require only one of the three or four repairs to be within the specified time period.

Specific information about laws in your state can be obtained from your state attorney general's office (c/o your state capitol) or your local consumer protection office. The following table offers a general description of the Lemon Law in your state and what you need to do to set it in motion (*Notification/Trigger*). An **L** indicates that the law covers leased vehicles and we indicate where state-run arbitration programs are available. State-run programs are the best type of arbitration.

Alabama	**Qualification:** 3 unsuccessful repairs or 30 calendar days out of service within shorter of 24 months or 24,000 miles, provided 1 repair attempt or 1 day out of service is within shorter of 1 year or 12,000 miles. **Notification/Trigger:** Certified mail notice to manufacturer, who has 14 calendar days to make final repair.
Alaska	**Qualification:** 3 unsuccessful repairs or 30 business days out of service within shorter of 1 year or warranty. **Notification/Trigger:** Certified mail notice to manufacturer and dealer, or agent within 60 days after expiration of warranty or 1 year. Consumer must demand refund or replacement to be delivered within 60 days after mailing the notice. Final repair attempt within 30 days of receipt of notice.
Arizona	**Qualification:** 4 unsuccessful repairs or 30 calendar days out of service within shorter of 2 years or 24,000 miles. **Notification/Trigger:** Written notice to manufacturer and opportunity to repair.
Arkansas	**Qualification:** 3 unsuccessful repairs, or 1 unsuccessful repair of a problem likely to cause death or serious bodily injury within longer of 24 months or 24,000 miles. **Notification/Trigger:** Certified or registered mail notice to manufacturer. Manufacturer has 10 days to notify consumer of repair facility. Facility has 10 days to repair.
California	**Qualification:** 4 unsuccessful repairs or 30 calendar days out of service within shorter of 1 year or 12,000 miles. **Notification/Trigger:** Written notice to manufacturer and delivery of car to repair facility for repair attempt within 30 days. *State has certified guidelines for arbitration.* **L**
Colorado	**Qualification:** 4 unsuccessful repairs or 30 business days out of service within shorter of 1 year or warranty. **Notification/Trigger:** Prior certified mail notice for each defect occurrence and opportunity to repair.
Conn.	**Qualification:** 4 unsuccessful repairs or 30 calendar days out of service within shorter of 1 year or warranty. **Notification/Trigger:** Report to manufacturer, agent or dealer. Written notice to manufacturer only if required in owner's manual or warranty. *State-run arbitration program is available.* **L**

Delaware	**Qualification:** 4 unsuccessful repairs or 30 calendar days out of service within shorter of 1 year or warranty. **Notification/Trigger:** Written notice to manufacturer and opportunity to repair. L
D.C.	**Qualification:** 4 unsuccessful repairs or 30 calendar days out of service or 1 unsuccessful repair of a safety-related defect, within shorter of 2 years or 18,000 miles. **Notification/Trigger:** Report of each defect occurrence to manufacturer, agent or dealer. *District-run arbitration program is available.* Note: Enforcement by D.C. is suspended until October 1, 1999. L
Florida	**Qualification:** 3 unsuccessful repairs or 15 calendar days out of service within shorter of 12 months or 12,000 miles. **Notification/Trigger:** Written notice by certified or express mail to manufacturer who has 10 calendar days for final repair attempt after delivery to designated dealer. *State-run arbitration program is available.* L
Georgia*	**Qualification:** 3 unsuccessful repair attempts or 30 calendar days out of service within shorter of 24,000 miles or 24 months, with 1 repair or 15 days out of service within shorter of 1 year or 12,000 miles; or one unsuccessful repair of a serious safety defect in the braking or steering system within shorter of 1 year or 12,000 miles. **Notification/Trigger:** Certified mail notice return receipt requested. Manufacturer has 7 days to notify consumer of repair facility. Facility has 14 days to repair. *State-run arbitration program is available.* L
Hawaii	**Qualification:** 3 unsuccessful repairs, or 1 unsuccessful repair of a nonconformity likely to cause death or serious bodily injury, or out of service within shorter of 2 years or 24,000 miles. **Notification/Trigger:** Written notice to manufacturer and opportunity to repair. *State-run arbitration program is available.* L
Idaho	**Qualification:** 4 repair attempts or 30 business days out of service within shorter of 12 months or 12,000 miles. **Notification/Trigger:** Written notice to manufacturer or dealer.
Illinois*	**Qualification:** 4 unsuccessful repairs or 30 business days out of service within shorter of 1 year or 12,000 miles. **Notification/Trigger:** Written notice to manufacturer and opportunity to repair.
Indiana	**Qualification:** 4 unsuccessful repairs or 30 business days out of service within the shorter of 18 months or 18,000 miles. **Notification/Trigger:** Written notice to manufacturer only if required in warranty. L
Iowa	**Qualification:** 3 unsuccessful repairs, or 1 unsuccessful repair of a nonconformity likely to cause death or serious bodily injury, or 20 calendar days out of service within shorter of 2 years or 24,000 miles. **Notification/Trigger:** Written notice to manufacturer and final opportunity to repair within 10 calendar days of receipt of notice. *State has certified guidelines for arbitration.* L
Kansas	**Qualification:** 4 unsuccessful repairs of the same problem or 30 calendar days out of service or 10 total repairs of any problem within shorter of 1 year or warranty. **Notification/Trigger:** Actual notice to manufacturer.
Kentucky	**Qualification:** 4 unsuccessful repairs or 30 calendar days out of service within shorter of 1 year or 12,000 miles. **Notification/Trigger:** Written notice to manufacturer.
Louisiana	**Qualification:** 4 unsuccessful repairs or 30 calendar days out of service within shorter of 1 year or warranty. **Notification/Trigger:** Report to manufacturer or dealer. L
Maine	**Qualification:** 3 unsuccessful repairs (when at least 2 times the same agent attempted the repair) or 15 business days out of service within shorter of 2 years or 18,000 miles. **Notification/Trigger:** Written notice to manufacturer or dealer only if required in warranty or owner's manual. Manufacturer has 7 business days after receipt for final repair attempt. *State-run arbitration program is available.* L
Maryland	**Qualification:** 4 unsuccessful repairs, 30 calendar days out of service or 1 unsuccessful repair of braking or steering system within shorter of 15 months or 15,000 miles. **Notification/Trigger:** Certified mail notice, return receipt requested to manu. or factory branch and opportunity to repair within 30 calendar days of receipt of notice. L
Mass.	**Qualification:** 3 unsuccessful repairs or 15 business days out of service within shorter of 1 year or 15,000 miles. **Notification/Trigger:** Notice to manufacturer or dealer who has 7 business days to attempt a final repair. *State-run arbitration program is available.*

*Warning: Consumers who seek a refund or replacement under the lemon law may lose other important legal rights in regards to the dealer and manufacturer.

Michigan	**Qualification:** 4 unsuccessful repairs or 30 calendar days out of service within shorter of 1 year or warranty. **Notification/Trigger:** Certified mail notice, return receipt requested, to manufacturer who has 5 business days to repair after delivery.
Minn.	**Qualification:** 4 unsuccessful repairs or 30 business days out of service or 1 unsuccessful repair of total braking or steering loss likely to cause death or serious bodily injury within shorter of 2 years or warranty. **Notification/Trigger:** At least one written notice to manufacturer, agent or dealer and opportunity to repair. L
Miss.	**Qualification:** 3 unsuccessful repairs or 15 business days out of service within shorter of 1 year or warranty. **Notification/Trigger:** Written notice to manufacturer who has 10 business days to repair after delivery to designated dealer.
Missouri	**Qualification:** 4 unsuccessful repairs or 30 business days out of service within shorter of 1 year or warranty. **Notification/Trigger:** Written notice to manufacturer who has 10 calendar days to repair after delivery to designated dealer.
Montana	**Qualification:** 4 unsuccessful repairs or 30 business days out of service after notice within shorter of 2 years or 18,000 miles. **Notification/Trigger:** Written notice to manufacturer and opportunity to repair. *State-run arbitration program is available.*
Nebraska	**Qualification:** 4 unsuccessful repairs or 40 calendar days out of service within shorter of 1 year or warranty. **Notification/Trigger:** Certified mail notice to manufacturer and opportunity to repair.
Nevada	**Qualification:** 4 unsuccessful repairs or 30 calendar days out of service within shorter of 1 year or warranty. **Notification/Trigger:** Written notice to manufacturer.
N. H.	**Qualification:** 3 unsuccessful repairs by same dealer or 30 business days out of service within warranty. **Notification/Trigger:** Report to manufacturer, distributor, agent or dealer (on forms provided by manufacturer) and final opportunity to repair before arbitration. *State-run arbitration program is available.* L
N. J.	**Qualification:** 3 unsuccessful repairs or 20 calendar days out of service within shorter of 2 years or 18,000 miles. **Notification/Trigger:** Certified mail notice, written notice to manufacturer who has 15 days to repair. *State-run arbitration program is available.* L
N. M.	**Qualification:** 4 unsuccessful repairs or 30 business days within shorter of 1 year or warranty. **Notification/Trigger:** Written notice to manufacturer, agent or dealer and opportunity to repair.
N. Y.	**Qualification:** 4 unsuccessful repairs or 30 calendar days out of service within shorter of 2 years or 18,000 miles. **Notification/Trigger:** Certified notice to manufacturer, agent or dealer. *State-run arbitration program is available.* L
N. C.	**Qualification:** 4 unsuccessful repairs within the shorter of 24 months, 24,000 miles or warranty or 20 business days out of service during any 12 month period of the warranty. **Notification/Trigger:** Written notice to manufacturer and opportunity to repair within 15 calendar days of receipt only if required in warranty or owner's manual. L
N. D.	**Qualification:** 3 unsuccessful repairs or 30 business days out of service within shorter of 1 year or warranty. **Notification/Trigger:** Direct written notice and opportunity to repair to manufacturer. *(Manufacturer's informal arbitration process serves as a prerequisite to consumer refund of replacement.)* L
Ohio	**Qualification:** 3 unsuccessful repairs of same nonconformity, 30 calendar days out of service, 8 total repairs of any problem, or 1 unsuccessful repair of problem likely to cause death or serious bodily injury within shorter of 1 year or 18,000 miles. **Notification/Trigger:** Report to manufacturer, its agent or dealer.
Okla.	**Qualification:** 4 unsuccessful repairs or 45 calendar days out of service within shorter of 1 year or warranty. **Notification/Trigger:** Written notice to manufacturer and opportunity to repair.
Oregon	**Qualification:** 4 unsuccessful repairs or 30 business days out of service within shorter of 1 year or 12,000 miles. **Notification/Trigger:** Direct written notice to manufacturer and opportunity to repair. L

Penn.	**Qualification:** 3 unsuccessful repairs or 30 calendar days out of service within shorter of 1 year, 12,000 miles, or warranty. **Notification/Trigger:** Delivery to authorized service and repair facility. If delivery impossible, written notice to manufacturer or its repair facility obligates them to pay for delivery.
R. I.	**Qualification:** 4 unsuccessful repairs or 30 calendar days out of service within shorter of 1 year or 15,000 miles. **Notification/Trigger:** Report to dealer or manufacturer who has 7 days for final repair opportunity. *(Manufacturer's informal arbitration process serves as a prerequisite to consumer refund of replacement.)* L
S. C.	**Qualification:** 3 unsuccessful repairs or 30 calendar days out of service within shorter of 1 year or 12,000 miles. **Notification/Trigger:** Written notice to manufacturer by certified mail and opportunity to repair only if manufacturer informed consumer of such at time of sale. Manufacturer has 10 days to notify consumer of repair facility. Facility has 10 days to repair. *State-run arbitration program is available.* L
S. D.	**Qualification:** 4 unsuccessful repairs, at least 1 of which occurred during the shorter of 1 year or 12,000 miles, or 30 calendar days out of service during the shorter of 24 months or 24,000 miles. **Notification/Trigger:** Certified mail notice to manufacturer and final opportunity to repair. Manufacturer has 7 calendar days to notify consumer of repair facility. Facility has 14 days to repair. *(Manufacturer's informal arbitration process serves as a prerequisite to consumer refund or replacement.)*
Tenn.	**Qualification:** 4 unsuccessful repairs or 30 calendar days out of service within shorter of 1 year or warranty. **Notification/Trigger:** Certified mail notice to manufacturer and final opportunity to repair within 10 calendar days. L
Texas	**Qualification:** 4 unsuccessful repairs when 2 occurred within shorter of 1 year or 12,000 miles, and other 2 occur within shorter of 1 year or 12,000 miles from date of 2nd repair attempt; or 2 unsuccessful repairs of a serious safety defect when 1 occurred within shorter of 1 year or 12,000 miles and other occurred within shorter of 1 year or 12,000 miles from date of 1st repair; or 30 calendar days out of service within shorter of 2 years or 24,000 miles and at least 2 attempts were made within shorter of 1 year or 12,000 miles. **Notification/Trigger:** Written notice to manufacturer. *State-run arbitration program is available.* L
Utah	**Qualification:** 4 unsuccessful repairs or 30 business days out of service within shorter of 1 year or warranty. **Notification/Trigger:** Report to manufacturer, agent or dealer. L
Vermont	**Qualification:** 3 unsuccessful repairs when at least 1st repair was within warranty, or 30 calendar days within warranty. **Notification/Trigger:** Written notice to manufacturer (on provided forms) after 3rd repair attempt, or 30 days. Arbitration must be held within 45 days after notice, during which time manufacturer has 1 final repair. *State-run arbitration program is available.* L
Virginia	**Qualification:** 3 unsuccessful repairs, or 1 repair attempt of a serious safety defect, or 30 calendar days out of service within 18 months. **Notification/Trigger:** Written notice to manufacturer. If 3 unsuccessful repairs or 30 days already exhausted before notice, manufacturer has 1 more repair attempt not to exceed 15 days.
Wash.	**Qualification:** 4 unsuccessful repairs, 30 calendar days out of service (15 during warranty period), or 2 repairs of serious safety defects, first reported within shorter of the warranty or 24 months or 24,000 miles. One repair attempt and 15 of the 30 days must fall within manufacturer's express warranty of at least 1 year or 12,000 miles. **Notification/Trigger:** Written notice to manufacturer. *State-run arbitration program is available.* L *Note: Consumer should receive replacement or refund within 40 calendar days of request.*
W. V.	**Qualification:** 3 unsuccessful repairs or 30 calendar days out of service or 1 unsuccessful repair of problem likely to cause death or serious bodily injury within shorter of 1 year or warranty. **Notification/Trigger:** Prior written notice to manufacturer and at least one opportunity to repair.
Wisc.	**Qualification:** 4 unsuccessful repairs or 30 calendar days out of service within shorter of 1 year or warranty. **Notification/Trigger:** Report to manufacturer or dealer. L *Note: Consumer should receive replacement or refund within 30 calendar days after offer to return title.*
Wyoming	**Qualification:** 3 unsuccessful repairs or 30 business days out of service within 1 year. **Notification/Trigger:** Direct written notice to manufacturer and opportunity to repair.

SHOWROOM STRATEGIES

Buying a car means matching wits with a seasoned professional. But if you know what to expect, you'll have a much better chance of getting a really good deal! This chapter offers practical advice on buying a car, tips on getting the best price and financing, information on buying vs. leasing, and tips on avoiding lemons. We'll also take a peek at some options for the future that will increase driving safety.

For most of us, the auto showroom can be an intimidating environment. We're matching wits with professional negotiators over a very complex product. Being prepared is the best way to turn a potentially intimidating showroom experience into a profitable one. Here's some advice on handling what you'll find in the showroom.

Beware of silence. Silence is often used to intimidate, so be prepared for long periods of time when the salesperson is "talking with the manager." This tactic is designed to make you want to "just get the negotiation over with." Instead of becoming a victim, do something that indicates you are serious about looking elsewhere. Bring the classified section of the newspaper and begin circling other cars or review brochures from other manufacturers. By sending the message that you have other options, you increase your bargaining power and speed up the process.

Don't fall in love with a car. Never look too interested in any particular car. Advise family members who go with you against being too enthusiastic about any one car. *Tip:* Beat the dealers at their own game— bring along a friend who tells you that the price is "too much compared to the *other* deal."

Keep your wallet in your pocket. Don't leave a deposit, even if it's refundable. You'll feel pressure to rush your shopping, and you'll have to return and face the salesperson again before you are ready.

Shop at the end of the month. Salespeople anxious to meet sales goals are more willing to negotiate a lower price at this time.

Buy last year's model. The majority of new cars are the same as the previous year, with minor cosmetic changes. You can save considerably by buying in early fall when dealers are clearing space for "new" models. The important trade-off you make using this technique is that the car maker may have added air bags or anti-lock brakes to an otherwise unchanged vehicle.

Buying from stock. You can often get a better deal on a car that the dealer has on the lot. However, these cars usually have expensive options you may not want or need. Do not hesitate to ask the dealer to remove an option (and its accompanying charge) or sell you the car without charging for the option. The longer the car sits there, the more interest the dealer pays on the car, which increases the dealer's incentive to sell.

Ordering a car. Domestic cars can be ordered from the manufacturer. Simply offering a fixed amount over invoice may be attractive because it's a sure sale and the dealership has not invested in the car. All the salesperson has to do is take your order.

If you do order a car, make sure when it arrives that it includes only the options you requested. Don't fall for the trick where the dealer offers you unordered options at a "special price," because it was their mistake. If you didn't order the option, don't pay for it.

Don't trade in. Although it is more work, you can usually do better by selling your old car yourself than by trading it in. To determine what you'll gain by selling the car yourself, check the NADA "Blue Book" at your credit union or library. The difference between the trade-in price (what the dealer will give you) and the retail price (what you typically can sell it for) is your extra payment for selling the car yourself.

If you do decide to trade your car in at the dealership, *keep the buying and selling separate.* First, negotiate the best price for your new car, then find out how much the dealer will give you for your old car. Keeping the two deals separate ensures that you know what you're paying for your new car and simplifies the entire transaction.

Question everything the dealer writes down. Nothing is etched in stone. Because things are written down, we tend not to question them. This is wrong—always assume that anything written down is negotiable.

Test drive without the salesperson. When you test drive a car, go alone and take a good long test drive. If a dealership will not let you take a car without a salesperson, go to another dealership. Test driving without the distraction of a salesperson is a necessity when trying out a new car. See page 54 for tips on test driving.

Avoiding Lemons

One way to avoid the sour taste of a lemon after you've bought your car is to protect yourself *before* you sign on the dotted line. These tips will help you avoid problems down the road.

1 **Avoid new models.** Any new car in its very first year of production often turns out to have a lot of defects. Sometimes the manufacturer isn't able to remedy the defects until the second, third, or even fourth year of production. If the manufacturer has not worked out problems by the third model year, the car will likely be a lemon forever.

2 **Avoid the first cars off the line.** Most companies close down their assembly lines every year to make annual style changes. In addition to adding hundreds of dollars to the price of a new car, these changes can introduce new defects. It can take a few months to iron out these bugs. Ask the dealer when the vehicle you are interested in was manufactured, or look on the metal tag found on the inside of the driver-side door frame to find the date of manufacture.

3 **Avoid delicate options.** Delicate options have the highest frequency-of-repair records. Power seats, power windows, power antennas, and special roofs are nice conveniences—until they break down. Of all the items on the vehicles, they tend to be the most expensive to repair.

4 **Inspect the dealer's checklist.** Request a copy of the dealer's pre-delivery service and adjustment checklist (also called a "make-ready list") at the time your new vehicle is delivered. Write the request directly on the new vehicle order. This request informs the dealer that you are aware of the dealer's responsibility to check your new car for defects.

5 **Examine the car on delivery.** Most of us are very excited when it comes time to take the vehicle home. This is the time where a few minutes of careful inspection can save hours of aggravation later. Carefully look over the body for any damage, check for the spare tire and jack equipment, make sure all electrical items work, and make sure all the hubcaps and body molding are on. You may want to take a short test drive. Finally, make sure you have the owner's manual, warranty forms, and all the legal documents.

Getting the Best Price

One of the most difficult aspects of buying a new car is getting the best price. Most of us are at a disadvantage negotiating because we don't know how much the car actually cost the dealer. The difference between what the dealer paid and the sticker price represents the negotiable amount.

Until recently, the key to getting the best price was finding out the dealer cost. Many shoppers now ask to see the factory invoice, so some dealers promote their cars by offering to sell at only $49 or $99 over invoice. This sounds like a good deal, but these cars often have options you may not want and most invoice prices do not reveal the extra, hidden profit to the dealer.

Now that most savvy consumers know to check the so-called "dealer invoice," the industry has camouflaged this number. Special incentives, rebates, and kickbacks can account for $500 to $2,000 worth of extra profit to a dealer selling a car at "dealer invoice." The non-profit Center for the Study of Services recently discovered that in 37 percent of cases when dealers are forced to bid against each other for the sale, they offered the buyer a price below the "dealer invoice"—an unlikely event if the dealer was actually losing money. The bottom line is that "dealer invoice" doesn't mean anything anymore.

Because the rules have changed, we believe that most consumers are ill-advised to try and negotiate with a dealer. Introducing competition is the best way to get the lowest price on a new car. What this means is that you have to convince 3 or 4 dealers that you are, in fact, prepared to buy a car; that you have decided on the make, model, and features; and that your decision now rests solely on which dealer will give you the best price. You can try to do this by phone, but often dealers will not give you the best price, or will quote you a price over the phone that they will not honor later. Instead, you should try to do this in person. As anyone knows who has ventured into an auto showroom simply to get the best price, the process can be lengthy and arduous. Nevertheless, if you can convice the dealer that you are serious and are willing to take the time to go to a number of dealers, it will pay off. Otherwise, we suggest you use the CarBargains service listed on the next page.

If you find a big savings at a dealership far from your home, call a local dealer with the price. They may very well match it. If not, pick up the car from the distant dealer, knowing your trip has saved you hundreds of dollars. You can still bring it to your local dealer for warranty work and repairs. Here are some other showroom strategies:

Beware of misleading advertising. New car ads are meant to get you into the showroom. They usually promise low prices, big rebates, high trade-in, and spotless integrity—don't be deceived. Advertised prices are rarely the true selling price. They usually exclude transportation charges, service fees, or document fees. And always look out for the asterisk, both in advertisements and on invoices. It can be a signal that the advertiser has something to hide.

Don't talk price until you're ready to buy. On your first few trips to the showroom, simply look over the cars, decide what options you want, and do your test driving.

Shop the corporate twins. Page 18 contains a list of corporate twins—nearly identical cars that carry different name plates. Check the price and options of the twins of the car you like. A higher priced twin may have more options, so it may be a better deal than the lower priced car without the options you want.

Watch out for dealer preparation overcharges. Before paying the dealer to clean your car, make sure that preparation is not included in the basic price. The price sticker will state: "Manufacturer's suggested retail price of this model includes dealer preparation."

If you must negotiate... negotiate up from the "invoice" price rather than down from the sticker price. Simply make an offer close to or at the "invoice" price. If the sales person says that your offer is too low to make a profit, ask to see the factory invoice.

The 180-Degree Turn

If you try to negotiate a car purchase, remember that you have the most important weapon in the bargaining process: *the 180-degree turn*. Be prepared to walk away from a deal, even at the risk of losing the "very best deal" your salesperson has ever offered, and you will be in the best position to get a genuine "best deal." Remember: dealerships need you, the buyer, to survive.

Price Shopping Service

Even with the information that we provide you in this chapter of *The Car Book*, most of us will *not* be well prepared to negotiate a good price for the cars we are considering. In fact, as we indicated on the previous page, we don't believe that you can negotiate the best price with *a* dealer. The key to getting the best price is to get the dealers to compete with each other. This page describes a new and easy way to find the best price by actually getting the dealers to compete.

CarBargains is a service of the non-profit Center for the Study of Services, a Washington, DC, consumer group, set up to provide comparative price information for many products and services.

CarBargains will "shop" the dealerships in your area and obtain at least five price quotes for the make and model of the car that you want to buy. The dealers who submit quotes know that they are competing with other area dealerships and have agreed to honor the prices that they submit. It is important to note that CarBargains is not an auto broker or "car buying" service; they have no affiliation with dealers.

Here's how the service works:

1. You provide CarBargains with the make, model, and style of car you wish to buy (Ford Taurus GL, for example) by phone or mail.

2. Within two weeks, CarBargains will send you dealer quote sheets from at least 5 local dealers who have bid against one another to sell you that car. The offer is actually a commitment to a dollar amount above (or below) "factory invoice cost" for that model.

You will also receive a printout with the exact dealer cost for the car and each available option. Included in the information will be the name of the sales manager responsible for honoring the quote.

3. Use the factory invoice cost printout to add up the invoice cost for the base car and the options you want and then determine which dealer offers the best price using the dealer quote sheets. Contact the sales manager of that dealership and arrange to purchase the car.

If a car with the options you want is not available on the dealer's lot, you can have the dealer order the car from the factory or, in some cases, from another dealer at the agreed price.

When you receive your quotes, you will also get some suggestions on low-cost sources of financing and a valuation of your used car (trade-in).

The price for this service may seem expensive, but when you consider the savings that will result by having dealers bid against each other, as well as the time and effort of trying to get these bids yourself, we believe it's a great value. First of all, the dealers know they have a bona fide buyer (you've paid $165 for the service) and they know they are bidding against 5–7 of their competitors.

To obtain CarBargains' competitive price quotes, send a check for $165 to CarBargains, 733 15th St., NW, Suite 820CB, Washington, DC 20005. Include your complete mailing address, phone number (in case of questions), and the exact make, model, and year of the car you want to buy. You should receive your bids within 2-3 weeks. For faster service, call them at 800-475-7283. Or, visit their website at consumer.checkbook.org.

Auto Brokers

While CarBargains is a non-profit organization created to help you find the best price for the car you want to purchase, auto brokers are typically in the business to make money. As such, whatever price you end up paying for the car will include additional profit for the broker. While many brokers are legitimately trying to get their customers the best price, others have developed special relationships with certain dealers and may not do much shopping for you. As a consumer, it is difficult to tell which are which. If you use a broker, make sure the contract to purchase the car is with the dealer, not the broker. In addition, it is best to pay the broker *after* the service is rendered, not before. There have been cases where the auto broker makes certain promises, takes your money, and you never hear from him or her again. If CarBargains is not for you, then we suggest you consider using a buying service associated with your credit union or auto club, which can arrange for the purchase of a car at some fixed price over "dealer invoice."

Depreciation

Over the past 20 years, new vehicle depreciation costs have steadily increased. A recent study conducted by Runzheimer International shows that depreciation and interest now account for slightly over 50 percent of the costs of owning and operating a vehicle. This number is up from 41 percent in 1976. On the other hand, the relative cost of gasoline has dropped by half, from 35 percent to 17 percent of every dollar spent on the average car. Other costs, including insurance, maintenance, and tires, have remained at relatively steady shares of the automotive dollar.

The high cost of depreciation is largely due to skyrocketing new car prices. While there is no reliable method of predicting retained value, your best bet is to purchase a popular new car. Chances are that it will also be popular as a used car.

Most new cars are traded in within four years and are then available on the used car market. The priciest used cars may not necessarily be the highest quality. Supply and demand, as well as appearance, are extremely important factors in determining used car prices.

1994 Cars with the Best and Worst Resale Value

The following table indicates which of the 100 top-selling '94 cars held their value the best and which did not.

The Best				The Worst			
Model	1994 Price	1998 Price	Retained Value	Model	1994 Price	1998 Price	Retained Value
Volvo 850	$27,695	$19,500	70%	Ford Tempo	$10,375	$5,275	49%
Honda Civic	$12,950	$8,975	69%	Cadillac Deville	$32,990	$16,050	48%
Pontiac Sunbird/2000	$12,424	$8,500	68%	Buick Century	$16,105	$7,825	48%
Saturn SC1	$11,695	$7,950	68%	Olds Cutlass Ciera	$16,485	$7,825	47%
Geo Prizm	$10,730	$7,200	67%	Mer. Grand Marquis	$22,130	$10,425	47%
Chevy Camaro	$18,745	$12,550	67%	Cadillac Seville	$40,990	$18,850	46%
Ford Mustang	$17,270	$11,450	66%	Ford Taurus	$18,785	$8,475	45%
Pontiac Firebird	$19,895	$13,075	66%	Lincoln Town Car	$35,700	$15,975	45%
Lexus ES300	$30,600	$20,025	65%	Chrysler LHS/NY'er	$25,386	$10,850	43%
Volkswagen Golf/Jetta	$15,700	$10,250	65%	Ford Crown Victoria	$20,000	$8,300	41%

Prices based on the *N.A.D.A. Official Used Car Guide*, July 1998.

Financing

You've done your test drive, researched prices, studied crash tests, determined the options you want, and haggled to get the best price. Now you have to decide how to pay for the car.

If you have the cash, *pay for the car right away*. You avoid finance charges, you won't have a large debt haunting over you and the full value of the car is yours. You can then make the monthly payments to yourself to save up for your next car.

However, most of us cannot afford to pay cash for a car, which leaves two options: financing or leasing. While leasing *seems* more affordable, financing will actually cost you less. When you finance a car, you own it after you finish your payments. At the end of a lease, you have nothing. We don't recommend leasing, but if you want more information, see page 96.

Here are some tips when financing your car:

Shop around for interest rates. Most banks and credit unions will knock off at least a quarter of a percent for their customers. Have these quotes handy when you talk financing with the dealer.

The higher your down payment, the less you'll have to finance. This will not only reduce your overall interest charges, but often qualifies you for a lower interest rate. Down payments are typically 10-20% of the final price.

Avoid long car loans. The monthly payments are lower, but you'll pay far more in overall interest charges. For example, a two year, $15,000 loan at 9% will cost you $1,446.51 in interest; the same amount at five years will cost you $3,682.52 — over twice as much!

Check out manufacturer promotional rates — the 2.9-3.9% rates you see advertised. These low rates are usually only valid on 2-3 year loans.

Read everything you are asked to sign and ask questions about anything you don't fully understand.

Make sure that an extended warranty has *not* been added to the purchase price. Dealers will sometimes add this cost without informing the consumer. Extended warranties are generally a bad value. See the "Warranties" chapter for more information.

GAP Insurance: GAP insurance covers the difference between what you owe on a car and its actual value, should the car be "totaled" or stolen. If you finance or lease through a dealer, he or she will likely suggest you purchase GAP insurance, which can cost up to $500. If you think this situation is likely, then your financing plan is probably too long.

Whether you need GAP or not, be wary of how dealers try to sell GAP. Dealers may insist the only way to give you financing is if you purchase GAP insurance — this is untrue. When negotiating finance

---

Don't Be Tongue-Tied

Beware of high pressure phrases like "I've talked to the manager and this is really the best we can do...as it is, we're losing money on this deal." It is rare that this is true. Dealers are in the business to make money and most do very well. Don't tolerate a take it or leave it attitude. Simply repeat that you will only buy when you see the deal you want and that you don't appreciate the dealer pressuring you. Threaten to leave if the dealer continues to pressure you to buy today.

Don't let the dealer answer your questions with a question. For instance, if you ask, "Can I get air conditioning with this car?" And the salesperson answers, "If I get you air conditioning in this car, will you buy today?" This response tries to force you to decide to buy before you are ready. Ask the dealer to just answer your question and that you'll buy when you're ready. Remember, its the dealer's job to answer questions, not yours.

If you are having a difficult time getting what you want, ask the dealer: "Why won't you let me buy a car today?" Most salespeople will be thrown off by this phrase as they are often too busy trying to use it on you. If they respond in frustration, "OK, what do you want?" then you can say straightforward answers to simple questions.

Make sure you get a price, don't settle for: "If you're shopping price, go to the other dealers first and then come back." This technique insures that they don't have to truly negotiate. Your best response is: "I only plan to come back if your price is the lowest, so that's what I need today, your lowest price."

terms, be sure to ask if GAP insurance has been added to the cost, as the dealer may not tell you.

Credit Unions vs. Banks: Credit unions generally charge fewer and lower fees and offer better rates than banks. In addition, credit unions offer counseling services where consumers can find pricing information on cars or compare monthly payments for financing. You can join a credit union either through your employer, an organization or club, or if you have a relative who is part of a credit union.

Low Rate or Cash Back? Sometimes auto manufacturers offer a choice of below market financing or cash back. The following table will tell you if it is better to take the lower rate or the cash back rebate. For example, say you want to finance $18,000. Your credit union or bank offers you 8.5% for an auto loan and the dealer offers either a 6% loan or a $1,500 rebate. Which is better? Find your bank or credit union's rate (8.5%) and the dealer's low rate (6%) on the table. Find where the two intersect on the table and you will find the difference per thousand dollars between the two interest rates (47). When you multiply this number (47) by the number of thousands you're financing (18 for $18,000), you get $846. Since the dealer's $1,500 rebate is more than the breakeven $846, taking your bank's rate (8.5%) and the rebate is a better deal than the dealer's low rate (6%). If the answer had been more than $1,500, then the dealer's rate would have been the better deal. An asterisk (*) means that the bank or credit union's rate is the better deal.

Destination Charges

There once was a time when you could go directly to the factory and buy a car, saving yourself a few hundred dollars in destination and freight charges. Today, destination charges are a non-negotiable part of buying a new car, no matter where you purchase it. They are, however, an important factor when comparing prices. You'll find the destination charges on the price sticker attached to the vehicle. According to automakers, destination charges are the cost of shipping a vehicle from its "final assembly point" to the dealership. The cost of shipping other components for final assembly is sometimes also added.

But, the following table illustrates that there is little correlation between destination charges and where the cars are assembled:

Vehicle	Destination Charge	Assembly Country	Parts from N. America
BMW 318i	$570	U.S./Germany	5%
Ford Taurus	$550	U.S.	85%
Hyundai Elantra	$435	Korea	1%
Saturn SC	$440	U.S.	95%

Based on data from Automotive News 1997 Market Data Book.

Rebate vs. Low Rates (Four Year Loan)

Multiply the number that intersects your dealer's rate with the rate from your credit union or bank by the number of thousands you are financing. If the result is less than the rebate, take the rebate; if it is above the rebate, go for the dealer financing.

Bank/ C.U. Rate	Dealer Rate						
	2%	3%	4%	5%	6%	7%	8%
7.0	94	76	57	38	19	*	*
7.5	103	85	66	48	29	10	*
8.0	111	93	75	57	38	19	*
8.5	120	102	84	66	47	28	10
9.0	128	111	93	75	56	38	19
9.5	136	119	101	83	65	47	28

Based on data from *Everybody's Money*, a publication of the Credit Union National Association.

Leasing vs. Buying

As car prices continue to rise, many car buyers are being seduced by the heavily advertised low monthly lease payments. Don't be deceived—in general, leasing costs more than buying outright or financing. When you pay cash or finance a car, you own an asset; leasing leaves you with nothing except all the headaches and responsibilities of ownership with none of the benefits. In addition, leased cars are often not covered by lemon laws. When you lease you pay a monthly fee for a predetermined time in exchange for the use of a car. However, you also pay for maintenance, insurance and repairs as if you owned the car. Finally, when it comes time to turn in the car, it has to be in top shape—otherwise, you'll have to pay for repairs or body work.

If you are considering a lease, here are some leasing terms you need to know and some tips to get you through the process:

Capitalized Cost is the price of the car if you were to purchase it. Negotiate this as if you were buying the cars. **Capitalized Cost Reduction** is your down payment.

Know the make and model of the vehicle you want. Tell the agent exactly how you want the car equipped. You don't have to pay for options you don't request. Decide in advance how long you will keep the car.

Find out the price of the options on which the lease is based. Typically, they will be full retail price. Their cost can be negotiated (albeit with some difficultly) before you settle on the monthly payment.

Find out how much you are required to pay at delivery. Most leases require at least the first month's payment. Others have a security deposit, registration fees, or other "hidden" costs. When shopping around, make sure price quotes include security deposit and taxes—sales tax, monthly use tax, or gross receipt tax. Ask how the length of the lease affects your monthly cost.

Find out the annual mileage limit. Don't accept a contract with a lower limit than you need. Most standard contracts allow 15,000 to 18,000 miles per year. If you go under the allowance one year, you can go over it the next. Watch out for **Excess Mileage fees**. If you go over, you'll get charged per mile.

Avoid "capitalized cost reduction" or "equity leases." Here the lessor offers to lower the monthly payment by asking you for more money up front — in other words, a down payment.

Ask about early termination. Between 30 and 40 percent of two year leases are terminated early, and 40–60 percent of four-year leases terminate early—this means expensive early termination fees. If you terminate the lease before it is up, what are the financial penalties? Typically, they are very high, so watch out. Ask the dealer *exactly* what you would owe at the end of each year if you wanted out of the lease. Remember, if your car is stolen, the lease will typically be terminated. While your insurance should cover the value of the car, you still may owe additional amounts per your lease contract.

Avoid maintenance contracts. Getting work done privately is cheaper in the long run—and don't forget, this is a new car with a standard warranty.

Arrange for your own insurance. By shopping around, you can generally find less expensive insurance than what's offered by the lessor.

Ask how quickly you can expect delivery. If your agent can't deliver in a reasonable time, maybe he or she can't meet the price quoted.

Retain your option to buy the car at the end of the lease at a predetermined price. The price should equal the residual value; if it is more, then the lessor is trying to make an additional profit. Regardless of how the end-of-lease value is determined, if you want the car make an offer based on the current "Blue

---

Leasewise

Why haggle when you can let someone else do it for you? *Leasewise*, a new service from the Center for the Study of Services, makes dealers bid for your lease. First, they get leasing bids from dealers on the vehicles you're interest in. Next, you'll receive a detailed report with all the bids, the dealer and invoice cost of the vehicle, and a complete explanation of the various bids. Then, you can lease from the lowest bidder or use the report as leverage with another dealer. The service costs $290. For more information, call 800-475-7283, or visit consumer.checkbook.org.

Book" value of the car at the end of the lease.

Residual Value is the value of your car at the end of the lease.

Find out how the lease price was figured. Lease prices are generally based on the manufacturer's suggested retail price, less the predetermined residual value. The best values are cars with a high expected residual value. To protect themselves, lessors tend to underestimate residual value, but you can do little about this estimate.

Make sure options like a sunroof or stereo are added to the Capitalized Cost. When you purchase dealer-added options, be sure they add the full cost of the option to the Capitalized Cost so that you only pay for the depreciated value of the option, not the full cost.

Send away for Driving A Bargain. This handy brochure from the Consumer Federation of America is guaranteed to keep the cost of leasing down. Send a self-addressed stamped envelope to: Driving a Bargain, Box 12099, Washington, DC 20005.

Here's what First National Lease Systems' Automotive Lease Guide estimates the residual values for a few 1999 cars will be after four years:

Cadillac DeVille	38%
Dodge Caravan SE	40%
Ford Taurus LX	32%
Honda Accord DX sdn.	51%
Infiniti Q45	42%
Lexus LS400	49%
Mazda Miata	47%
Mercury Tracer GS sdn.	34%
Nissan Quest XE	43%
Plymouth Neon sdn.	35%
Toyota Camry LE sdn.	51%

Financing vs. Leasing

The following table compares the typical costs of leasing vs. buying the same car over a three and six years. Your actual costs may vary, but you can use this format to compare the cars you are considering. Our example assumes the residual value to be about 54% after three years and 36% after six years.

3 Years	Lease	Finance
MSRP	$22,000.00	$22,000.00
Purchase Cost of Car	$20,000.00	$20,000.00
Down Payment		$2,000.00
Monthly Payment	$359.49	$364.98
Total Payments	$12,941.64	$13,139.11[1]
Amount left on loan		$7,758.62
Less value of vehicle		$11,017.90
Overall Cost, first 3 years	$12,941.64	$11,879.83
6 Years		
MSRP	$22,000.00	$22,000.00
Cost of Car	$40,000.00[2]	$20,000.00
Down Payment		$2,000.00
Monthly Payment	$359.49	$364.98
Total Payment	$25,883.28	$21,898.51[3]
Less value of vehicle		$8,000.00
Overall Cost, 6 years	$25,883.28	$15,898.51

[1]First 3 years of 5 year loan with 8% annual percentage rate.
[2]Two 3-year leases.
[3]5 year loan with 8% annual percentage rate, no monthly payments in 6th year.

Options: The Future of Safety

Many car manufacturers claim that cars are safe enough today since airbags, anti-lock brakes and traction control are becoming standard features. The fact is there's lots more that can be done. We continue to pay high prices in personal injury and insurance premiums for accidents that could be less serious if manufacturers would market more advanced safety features.

While these features may increase the car costs, those increases would be minor in relation to the dramatic reduction in the risk of injuries in crashes. Unfortunately, car makers are slow to offer us new technology. Following are a few options that will dramatically increase driving safety—if manufacturers choose to offer them.

Radar Brakes: Using radar to detect approaching objects, a warning sounds for the need to brake. It could perhaps be used to automatically apply the brakes when a driver falls asleep, and would be invaluable when parallel parking.

Side Airbags: The newest automatic crash protection technology has found its way into a handful of 1999 models, and one day may become the standard. These airbags come out of doors and out of the back of the front seat to protect the driver and passenger in crashes from all directions as well as rollovers.

Air Pads: Air pads are double layers of plastic with multiple compartments which look like ordinary trim in the uninflated condition. When the crash sensors for the airbags detect a crash, the air pads inflate out a few inches over all hard surfaces, such as the area over the windshield.

Glass-Plastic Glazing: This adds a layer of thin, strong, transparent plastic on the inside surface of all windows. When the glass breaks, the plastic layer holds the pieces of glass away from the occupants and provides a "safety net" to reduce the chance of ejection.

Pressure Sensitive Brake Lights: These lights illuminate with varying intensity based on the pressure applied to the brakes and the speed in which it's applied. Slowing for a stop sign triggers a slow progression from dim to bright, full pressure on the brake pedal would issue a bright beacon.

Navigation Computer: With the use of global-positioning satellites, these on-board computers would eliminate the need for road maps. They could provide instructions on how to get to particular locations, such as hospitals, airports, restaurants and hotels, as well as warn of traffic and construction delays. GM, Volvo and Acura have begun experimenting with these systems in their cars. Using much the same technology, Lincoln's RESCU (Remote Emergency Satellite Cellular Unit) will send a distress signal for help to either a tow truck or an ambulance, depending on which signal you send.

Smart Airbags: Several auto makers are devloping smart airbag systems which will differentiate between an adult, a child, a rear-facing child seat or an empty seat, using various heat, ultrasonic sound wave and infrared sensors. Not only will they save lives, smart airbags will prevent the passenger side airbag from deploying when the passenger seat is empty—saving thousands in repair costs.

Black Box Monitor: This device would detect whether the driver is driving drunk or irresponsibly. By monitoring the car's behavior and noting irregular actions, it will shut the car down.

Intelligent Brakes: These brakes sense and compensate for over- or under-steering.

Crash Recorder: This would record airbag performance in the event of an accident. (Introduced in 1995 Saturns.)

Toyota's Drowsy Driving Warning Sytem: By monitoring the steering and pulse of the driver, this innovation checks the driver to verify alertness. Once it detects drowsiness, the system will warn the driver with lights and sound to wake up, then shake the seat, and finally automatically stop the car.

Self-Dimming Mirrors: A gel-like material placed between two glass sheets darkens and lightens to reduce the headlight glare from mirrors while driving at night.

Inflatable Curtain: Volvo is developing an inflatable curtain, which deploys like an airbag, to provide increased protection against head injuries during side impact collisions. The curtain covers the sides of the car's interior, cushioning the heads of all the occupants.

RATINGS

This chapter provides an overview of the most important features of the new 1999 cars. In this section of *The Car Book,* you can see on each "car page" all the ingredients you need to make a smart choice. In addition to some descriptive text and a photo, the page contains six important information boxes:

THE DESCRIPTION

The vast majority of information in *The Car Book* is purely objective—we research and present the facts so that you can make an informed choice among the models that fit your taste and pocketbook. For the fourth year we are adding, among other new features, some background details. Specifically, for every car we include some general information to help you round out the hard facts. Much of the information in this section is subjective and you may not share our opinion. Nevertheless, like the photo which gives you a general idea of what the car looks like, the description will give you a snapshot of some of the features we think are worth noting and which may not show up in the statistics.

GENERAL INFORMATION

This is additional information you may want to consider when buying a new car.

Where made: Here we tell you where the car was assembled and where its parts were manufactured. If more than one country is listed, the first is where the majority of parts originate or where the vehicle was assembled.

Year of Production: We generally recommend against buying a car during its first model year of production. Each year the model is made, the production process is usually improved and there are fewer minor design defects. Therefore, the longer a car has been made, the less likely you are to be plagued with manufacturing and design defects. On the other hand, the newer a car is, the more likely it is to have the latest in engineering.

Parking Index: Using the car's length, wheelbase and turning circle, we have calculated how easy it will be to maneuver this car in tight spots. This rating of *very easy* to *very hard* is an indicator of how much difficulty you may have parking.

Bumpers: Here we indicate the damage-resistance of the car's bumpers. *Weak* bumpers meet only the basic government requirements at 2.5-mph. *Strong* bumpers are just as damage-resistant at 5-mph. This information may not be available for some minivans.

Theft Rating: This rating is given by the Insurance Institute for Highway Safety. It predicts the likelihood of the car being stolen or broken into based on its past history. If no information appears, it means that the car is too new to have a rating.

Corporate Twins: Often a car company will make numerous models on the same platform. This is a list of this car's twins.

Green Rating: This rating is based on data from the American Council for an Energy Efficient Economy. It incorporates the fuel economy and the emissions of a vehicle to derive an environmental impact rating.

PRICES

This box contains sample price information. When available, we list the base and the most luxurious version of the car. The difference is often substantial. Usually the more expensive versions have fancy trim, larger engines and lots of automatic equipment. The least expensive versions usually have manual transmission and few extra features. In addition, some manufacturers try to sell popular options as part of a package.

This information provides an idea of the price range and the expected dealer markup. Be prepared for higher retail prices when you get to the showroom. Manufacturers like to load their cars with factory options, and dealers like to add their own items such as fabric protection and paint sealant. Remember, prices and dealer costs can change during the year. Use these figures for general reference and comparisons, not as a precise indication of exactly how much the car you are interested in will cost. See page 92 for a new buying service designed to ensure that you get the very best price.

RATINGS

These are ratings in eight important categories, as well as an overall comparative rating. We have adopted the Olympic rating system with "10" being the best.

Comparative Rating: This is the "bottom line." Using a combination of all of the ratings, this tells how this car stacks up against the other '98's on a scale of 1 to 10. Due to the importance of crash tests, cars with no crash test results as of our publication date cannot be given an overall rating. More recent results may be available from the Auto Safety Hotline at 800-424-9393.

Crash Test Performance: This rating compares the 1999 models against all crash test results to date. We give the best performers a 10 and the worst a 1. Remember to compare crash test results relative to other cars in the same size class. For details, see the "safety" chapter.

Safety Features: This is an evaluation of how much extra safety is built into the car. We give credit for airbags, ABS, daytime running lights, belt height adjustors and pretensioners, and built-in child safety seats. For details, see the "safety" chapter.

Fuel Economy: Here we compare the EPA mileage ratings of each car. The gas misers get a 10 and the guzzlers get a 1. For more information, see the "fuel economy" chapter.

PM Cost: Each manufacturer suggests a preventive maintenance schedule designed to keep the car in good shape and to protect your rights under the warranty. Those with the lowest PM costs get a 10 and the highest a 1. See the "maintenance" chapter for the actual costs and more information.

Repair Cost: It is virtually impossible to predict exactly what any new car will cost you in repairs. As such, we take nine typical repairs that you are likely to experience *after* your warranty expires and compare those costs among this year's models. Those with the lowest cost get a 10 and the highest a 1. For details, see the "maintenance" chapter.

Warranty: This is an overall assessment of the car's warranty when compared to all 1999 warranties. We give the highest rated warranties a 10 and the lowest a 1. See the "warranty" chapter for details.

Complaints: This is where you'll find how your car stacks up against hundreds of others on the road, based on the U.S. government complaint data. If the car has not been around long enough to have developed a complaint history, it is given a 5. The least complained about cars get a 10 and the most problematic, a 1. See the "complaints" chapter for details.

Insurance Cost: Insurance companies have rated most of the cars on the road to determine how they plan to charge for insurance. Here, you'll find whether you can expect a discount or a surcharge for what we expect to be the most popular model. If the car is likely to receive neither, we label it *regular*. Those receiving a discount get a 10, any cars with a surcharge get a 1; any with neither get a 5.

SAFETY

For most of us, safety is a critical consideration in buying a new car. This box will tell you, at a glance, whether or not the car has the safety features you care about.

Frontal Crash Test: Here's where we tell you if the frontal crash test was either *very good, good, average, poor,* or *very poor.*

Side Crash Test: We've also included the car's performance in side crash tests. Here we indicate whether the side crash test was *very good, good, average, poor,* or *very poor.*

Airbag: Here's where you'll find out which occupants benefit from this invaluable safety feature, including side airbags, and who is left unprotected.

Anti-lock Brakes: Find out if this model has the two- or four-wheel anti-lock brakes, and whether you'll have to pay extra for it.

Daytime Running Lights: Daytime runnings lights reduce your chances of being in a crash by up to 40 percent by increasing the visibility of your vehicle. Here we indicate whether daytime running lights are *standard, optional* or *none.*

Belt Adjustors: People often don't wear safety belts because they are uncomfortable. In fact, a belt's effectiveness is due, in part, to how well it fits your body. In order to make sure shoulder belts fit properly (squarely across the front of your chest) some manufacturers have installed height adjustable seat belt adjusters. Availability is indicated for either the front and back seat occupants, just the front seat occupants, or neither.

Built-in Child Safety Seats: Some manufacturers are offering "built-in" child safety seats which reduces the chances that your child rides unprotected.

Pretensioners: This valuable safety feature improves the seat belt's effectiveness at protecting occupants in a crash. During the collision, the seat belt not only locks, but automatically retracts to keep passengers from further harm. Availability is indicated for both front occupants, unless otherwise noted.

SPECIFICATIONS

Here are the "nuts and bolts." In this box we have listed seven key specifications which enable you to evaluate how best that car meets your particular needs. We provide the information for what we expect to be the most popular model.

Fuel Economy: This is the EPA-rated fuel economy for city and highway driving measured in miles per gallon. Most models have a number of fuel economy ratings because of different engine and transmission options. For more individual ratings, see the "fuel economy" chapter. Electric vehicles are rated in miles per kilowatt hour.

Driving Range: Given the car's expected fuel economy and gas tank size, this gives an idea of how far you can go on a full tank.

Seating: This figure represents the maximum number of seating positions equipped with safety belts. When more than one number is listed (for example, 5/6/7) it means that different models have different seat configurations.

Length: This is the overall length of the car from bumper to bumper.

Head/Leg Room: This tells how roomy the front seat is.

Interior Space: This tells how roomy the car is. For minivans, see cargo space.

Cargo Space: This gives you the cubic feet available for cargo. For minivans, it is the back of the two front seats to the rear of the vehicle. In cars, it's the trunk space.

COMPETITION

Here we tell you how the car stacks up with its competition. Use this information to compare the overall rating of similar cars and broaden your choice of new car possibilities. This may help you select a more economical or better performing car than the one you were originally considering. We've added page references so you can easily check out the competition. This list is only a guideline, not an all-inclusive list of every possible alternative.

For 1999, the Acura CL offers either a 2.3-liter, 4-cylinder standard engine, which produces 150 hp, or the optional 3.0-liter V-6 which provides more power at the cost of fuel economy.

Standard safety features include ABS, and driver and front passenger front airbags. Also standard are rear headrests, cruise control, power moonroof, leather interior, front side window defoggers, keyless entry, and an anti-theft alarm. The 3.0CL offers heated door mirrors, heated seats and a smooth ride.

The Ratings

	POOR			GOOD
COMPARATIVE RATING*				
FRONTAL CRASH TEST				
SAFETY FEATURES				
FUEL ECONOMY				
PM COST				
REPAIR COST				
WARRANTY				
COMPLAINTS				
INSURANCE COST				

Safety

FRONTAL CRASH TEST	No government results
SIDE CRASH TEST	No government results
AIRBAGS	Dual
ANTI-LOCK BRAKES	4-Wheel
DAY. RUNNING LIGHTS	None
BELT ADJUSTORS	None
BUILT-IN CHILD SEAT	None
PRETENSIONERS	Standard

General Information

WHERE MADE	U.S.
YEAR OF PRODUCTION	Third
PARKING INDEX	Hard
BUMPERS	Strong
THEFT RATING	High
TWINS	
GREEN RATING	Poor

Specifications

FUEL ECONOMY (cty/hwy)	24/31	Average
DRIVING RANGE (miles)	473	Long
SEATING	5	
LENGTH (in.)	190	
HEAD/LEG ROOM (in.)	37.4/42.9	Cramped
INTERIOR SPACE (cu. ft.)	84.7	Vry. Cramped
CARGO SPACE (cu. ft.)	12	Small

Specifications may vary.

Prices

Model	Retail	Mkup
2.3 CL Coupe Manual	22,310	10%
2.3 CL ECT Automatic	23,110	10%

Competition

	POOR			GOOD	Pg.
Acura CL					102
Chev. Monte Carlo					127
Chrysler Sebring					134
Dodge Avenger					136

*Due to the importance of crash tests, cars with no results as of publication date cannot be given an overall rating.

Acura Integra

There are three versions of this Honda Civic-based hatchback. The standard engine, a 1.8-liter, on the base RS and mid-level LS delivers over 140 hp, more than enough for this fairly light car. The GS-R gets a 170-hp VTEC version of the 1.8-liter and doesn't lose a bit in fuel economy.

The 5-speed is responsive and the handling ranks among the best for small cars. The Integra emphasizes sportiness rather than luxury. Front seats, driver's controls, and instruments are fine, but the rear seat is definitely not for adults on long trips. This year ABS is standard on all Integras.

The Ratings

	POOR			GOOD
COMPARATIVE RATING		■		
FRONTAL CRASH TEST			■	
SAFETY FEATURES			■	
FUEL ECONOMY			■	
PM COST	■			
REPAIR COST		■		
WARRANTY			■	
COMPLAINTS				■
INSURANCE COST	■			

Safety

FRONTAL CRASH TEST	Average
SIDE CRASH TEST	No government results
AIRBAGS	Dual
ANTI-LOCK BRAKES	4-Wheel
DAY. RUNNING LIGHTS	None
BELT ADJUSTORS	Std. (Sdn.), None (Cpe.)
BUILT-IN CHILD SEAT	None
PRETENSIONERS	None

General Information

WHERE MADE	Japan
YEAR OF PRODUCTION	Sixth
PARKING INDEX	Very Easy
BUMPERS	Strong
THEFT RATING	Very High
TWINS	
GREEN RATING	Average

Specifications

FUEL ECONOMY (cty/hwy)	25/32	Good
DRIVING RANGE (miles)	376	Very Short
SEATING	5	
LENGTH (in.)	172.4	
HEAD/LEG ROOM (in.)	38.6/42.7	Average
INTERIOR SPACE (cu. ft.)	77.1	Vry. Cramped
CARGO SPACE (cu. ft.)	13.3	Small

Specifications may vary.

Prices

Model	Retail	Mkup
RS 3dr Manual	16,200	11%
LS 3 dr Manual	19,200	11%
LS Sedan Manual	20,000	11%
GS Sedan Manual	21,400	11%

Competition

	POOR			GOOD	Pg.
Acura Integra		■			**103**
Chevrolet Cavalier		■			123
Honda Civic		■			150
Mitsubishi Eclipse	■				182

Acura RL

Of all Acura models, the RL is the most luxurious. It is built on the same wheelbase and track width as the Legend, however, major improvements have been made in ride and comfort. The RL has a 3.5 liter 24 valve V6 engine, standard ABS brakes, and front and side airbags for both front occupants.

In terms of luxury, you'll find: leather interior, heated front seats, front and rear headrests, automatic climate control, heated door mirrors, front side window defoggers, remote keyless entry, an alarm system, and a moonroof.

The Ratings

	POOR → GOOD
COMPARATIVE RATING*	(no rating)
FRONTAL CRASH TEST	(no rating)
SAFETY FEATURES	7
FUEL ECONOMY	2
PM COST	1
REPAIR COST	2
WARRANTY	6
COMPLAINTS	9
INSURANCE COST	9

Safety

FRONTAL CRASH TEST	No government results
SIDE CRASH TEST	No government results
AIRBAGS	Dual & Side
ANTI-LOCK BRAKES	4-Wheel
DAY. RUNNING LIGHTS	None
BELT ADJUSTORS	Standard
BUILT-IN CHILD SEAT	None
PRETENSIONERS	None

General Information

WHERE MADE	Japan
YEAR OF PRODUCTION	Fourth
PARKING INDEX	Average
BUMPERS	Strong
THEFT RATING	
TWINS	
GREEN RATING	Poor

Specifications

FUEL ECONOMY (cty/hwy)	18/24	Very Poor
DRIVING RANGE (miles)	378	Very Short
SEATING	5	
LENGTH (in.)	195.1	
HEAD/LEG ROOM (in.)	38.8/42.1	Cramped
INTERIOR SPACE (cu. ft.)	96.5	Average
CARGO SPACE (cu. ft.)	14	Average

Specifications may vary.

Prices

Model	Retail	Mkup
Sedan	41,200	13%

Competition

	POOR → GOOD	Pg.
Acura RL	(no rating)	104
Audi A8	7	108
Buick Park Avenue	3	114
Cadillac Seville	5	120

*Due to the importance of crash tests, cars with no results as of publication date cannot be given an overall rating.

Acura TL

The TL stands for Touring Luxury - and Acura is hoping to attract Lexus ES300 buyers. The TL comes standard with dual airbags and 4-wheel ABS; traction control is a great option.

This year you'll only find the 3.2 model, as the TL no longer has a 2.5 liter engine. While this gives the TL more power, it reduces its fuel economy scores. Its speed-sensitive power steering is responsive and light. There are few options to choose from. The TL has Acura's usual leather interior, automatic climate control, side window defoggers, and an anti-theft system, so be prepared for a high base price. The TL has a conservative look and the spacious interior and smooth ride are what you would expect from a luxury car.

The Ratings

	POOR ... GOOD
COMPARATIVE RATING*	(no rating)
FRONTAL CRASH TEST	(no rating)
SAFETY FEATURES	▮ (high)
FUEL ECONOMY	▮ (low)
PM COST	▮ (poor)
REPAIR COST	▮ (poor)
WARRANTY	▮ (high)
COMPLAINTS	▮ (mid)
INSURANCE COST	▮ (mid)

Safety

FRONTAL CRASH TEST	No government results
SIDE CRASH TEST	No government results
AIRBAGS	Dual
ANTI-LOCK BRAKES	4-Wheel
DAY. RUNNING LIGHTS	None
BELT ADJUSTORS	Standard
BUILT-IN CHILD SEAT	None
PRETENSIONERS	None

General Information

WHERE MADE	Japan
YEAR OF PRODUCTION	First
PARKING INDEX	Average
BUMPERS	Strong
THEFT RATING	Very High
TWINS	
GREEN RATING	Poor

Specifications

FUEL ECONOMY (cty/hwy)	19/27	Poor
DRIVING RANGE (miles)	396	Short
SEATING	5	
LENGTH (in.)	192.9	
HEAD/LEG ROOM (in.)	39.9/42.4	Roomy
INTERIOR SPACE (cu. ft.)	96.5	Average
CARGO SPACE (cu. ft.)	14.3	Average

Specifications may vary.

Prices

Model	Retail	Mkup
2.5 Sedan	30,700	11%
3.2 Sedan	33,150	11%

Competition

	POOR ... GOOD	Pg.
Acura TL	(no rating)	**105**
Infiniti I30	▮ (good)	159
Lexus ES300	▮ (good)	163
Merc.-Benz C-Class	▮ (mid)	173

*Due to the importance of crash tests, cars with no results as of publication date cannot be given an overall rating.

Audi A4

With the addition of the 1.8T Avant, A4's line-up is a 1.8 liter four cylinder or a 2.8 liter V6 engine for either a sedan or a sport wagon (Avant). The A4 is available with either front-wheel drive or all-wheel drive, called Quattro, which improves overall handling and traction on slick roads. Next generation front airbags, as well as seat mounted front side airbags are both standard and contribute to the A4's admirable crash test ratings. New colors have been added for the '99 model, as well as lockable head rests, remote locking, a first aid kit, and a larger right side mirror for better visibility. A system that complies with the California Transitional Low Emissions standards is optional. Audi covers the preventive maintenance costs for the first 50,000 miles.

The Ratings

	POOR ←→ GOOD
COMPARATIVE RATING	Good
FRONTAL CRASH TEST	Good
SAFETY FEATURES	Above Average
FUEL ECONOMY	Below Average
PM COST	Above Average
REPAIR COST	Poor
WARRANTY	Good
COMPLAINTS	Above Average
INSURANCE COST	Average

Safety

FRONTAL CRASH TEST	Very Good
SIDE CRASH TEST	No government results
AIRBAGS	Dual & Side (New Design)
ANTI-LOCK BRAKES	4-Wheel
DAY. RUNNING LIGHTS	None
BELT ADJUSTORS	Standard
BUILT-IN CHILD SEAT	None
PRETENSIONERS	Standard

General Information

WHERE MADE	Germany
YEAR OF PRODUCTION	Fourth
PARKING INDEX	Easy
BUMPERS	Strong
THEFT RATING	
TWINS	
GREEN RATING	Poor

Specifications

FUEL ECONOMY (cty/hwy)	23/32	Average
DRIVING RANGE (miles)	451	Long
SEATING	5	
LENGTH (in.)	178	
HEAD/LEG ROOM (in.)	38.1/41.3	Vry. Cramped
INTERIOR SPACE (cu. ft.)	87.7	Cramped
CARGO SPACE (cu. ft.)	14	Average

Specifications may vary.

Prices

Model	Retail	Mkup
1.8T Sedan FWD	23,790	12%
2.8 Sedan FWD	28,390	12%
Avant Wagon FWD	30,465	12%
Avant Quattro Wagon AWD	31,040	12%

Competition

	POOR ←→ GOOD	Pg.
Audi A4	Good	106
Lexus ES300	Good	163
Oldsmobile Aurora	Average	191
Volvo S70	Good	222

Audi A6

In June of '98 Audi added the A6 Avant wagon to its collection, powered by the standard 2.8 liter 5 valve V6 engine. The 5-speed transmission allows the vehicle to switch between engine and driver controlled shifting. Front seat passengers are protected by next generation front airbags, and seat mounted side airbags. New is a larger right outside mirror, lockable headrests for front passengers, a first aid kit, and new exterior colors. Rear side airbags are optional as is adherence to California Transitional Low Emissions standards. The suspension is improved and there is an all-wheel drive option. Audi covers the preventive maintenance costs for the first 50,000 miles and their warranty is the best in the industry. Unfortunately, no frontal or side crash tests are available.

The Ratings

	POOR ⟶ GOOD
COMPARATIVE RATING*	(no rating)
FRONTAL CRASH TEST	(no rating)
SAFETY FEATURES	▮ (high)
FUEL ECONOMY	▮ (low)
PM COST	▮ (very high)
REPAIR COST	▮ (very low)
WARRANTY	▮ (very high)
COMPLAINTS	▮ (mid)
INSURANCE COST	▮ (very high)

Safety

FRONTAL CRASH TEST	No government results
SIDE CRASH TEST	No government results
AIRBAGS	Dual & Side (New Design)
ANTI-LOCK BRAKES	4-Wheel
DAY. RUNNING LIGHTS	None
BELT ADJUSTORS	Standard
BUILT-IN CHILD SEAT	None
PRETENSIONERS	Standard

General Information

WHERE MADE	Germany
YEAR OF PRODUCTION	Second
PARKING INDEX	Average
BUMPERS	Strong
THEFT RATING	
TWINS	
GREEN RATING	Poor

Specifications

FUEL ECONOMY (cty/hwy)	17/27	Poor
DRIVING RANGE (miles)	407	Short
SEATING	5	
LENGTH (in.)	192	
HEAD/LEG ROOM (in.)	39.3/41.3	Cramped
INTERIOR SPACE (cu. ft.)	108.3	Vry. Roomy
CARGO SPACE (cu. ft.)	17.2	Very Large

Specifications may vary.

Prices

Model	Retail	Mkup
Sedan	33,750	12%
Avant Wagon 4WD	36,600	12%

Competition

	POOR ⟶ GOOD	Pg.
Audi A6	(no rating)	107
Infiniti I30	▮	159
Mazda Millenia	▮	171
Volvo S70	▮	222

*Due to the importance of crash tests, cars with no results as of publication date cannot be given an overall rating.

Audi A8

Audi's three-year-old luxury flagship comes with lots of extras. Its unique aluminum frame is 40% lighter than steel frames. Nevertheless, it performed excellently in government crash tests proving that light weight doesn't have to mean a sacrifice in safety. Passengers are protected by front and side airbags for all occupants. The A8 is available with a front drive 3.7 liter V8 engine or an all-wheel drive 4.2 quattro. The standard transmission is a 5 speed automatic Tiptronic allowing drivers either automatic or driver controlled shifting without a clutch. The anti-slip system improves steering control by automatically channeling power to the wheel with the most traction. The A8 also offers wiring for a hands-free telephone and heated seats.

The Ratings

	POOR — GOOD
COMPARATIVE RATING	■ (high)
FRONTAL CRASH TEST	■ (high)
SAFETY FEATURES	■ (high)
FUEL ECONOMY	■ (low)
PM COST	■ (mid)
REPAIR COST	■ (very low)
WARRANTY	■ (mid)
COMPLAINTS	■ (low-mid)
INSURANCE COST	■ (low-mid)

Safety

FRONTAL CRASH TEST	Very Good
SIDE CRASH TEST	No government results
AIRBAGS	Dual & Side (New Design)
ANTI-LOCK BRAKES	4-Wheel
DAY. RUNNING LIGHTS	None
BELT ADJUSTORS	Standard
BUILT-IN CHILD SEAT	None
PRETENSIONERS	Standard

General Information

WHERE MADE	Germany
YEAR OF PRODUCTION	Third
PARKING INDEX	Hard
BUMPERS	Strong
THEFT RATING	
TWINS	
GREEN RATING	Very Poor

Specifications

FUEL ECONOMY (cty/hwy)	17/26	Very Poor
DRIVING RANGE (miles)	521	Very Long
SEATING	5	
LENGTH (in.)	198.2	
HEAD/LEG ROOM (in.)	38.9/41.3	Cramped
INTERIOR SPACE (cu. ft.)	99.8	Roomy
CARGO SPACE (cu. ft.)	17.6	Very Large

Specifications may vary.

Prices

Model	Retail	Mkup
3.7 Sedan	57,400	14%
4.2 Quattro Sedan	65,000	14%

Competition

	POOR — GOOD	Pg.
Audi A8	■ (high)	**108**
Cadillac DeVille	■ (high)	118
Cadillac Seville	■ (mid)	120
Oldsmobile Aurora	■ (low-mid)	191

New for the 3 Series are the 323i and the 328i sedans. The coupe and the convertible remain unchanged this year. Great safety features this year include standard front side airbags for even the base model 318ti and standard adjustable rear head rests. Dual airbags and 4-wheel ABS are standard as well.

The 1.8-liter engine on the base level 318 is strong enough. The 2.5-liter on the 323 is better, but less fuel efficient. Front seats offer excellent comfort on long trips; however, the back seat is a squeeze for adults. Controls are excellent. Depending upon engine choice, you can decide between meeting TLEV or LEV emission standards. Look for side crash tests this year.

The Ratings

	POOR → GOOD
COMPARATIVE RATING*	(no rating)
FRONTAL CRASH TEST	(no rating)
SAFETY FEATURES	Good
FUEL ECONOMY	Below average
PM COST	Good
REPAIR COST	Poor
WARRANTY	Above average
COMPLAINTS	Below average
INSURANCE COST	Below average

Safety

FRONTAL CRASH TEST	No government results
SIDE CRASH TEST	No government results
AIRBAGS	Dual & Side (New Design)
ANTI-LOCK BRAKES	4-Wheel
DAY. RUNNING LIGHTS	None
BELT ADJUSTORS	Standard
BUILT-IN CHILD SEAT	None
PRETENSIONERS	Standard

General Information

WHERE MADE	Germany
YEAR OF PRODUCTION	First
PARKING INDEX	Easy
BUMPERS	Strong
THEFT RATING	Very High
TWINS	
GREEN RATING	Average

Specifications

FUEL ECONOMY (cty/hwy)	23/32	Average
DRIVING RANGE (miles)	457	Long
SEATING	5	
LENGTH (in.)	176	
HEAD/LEG ROOM (in.)	38.4/41.4	Vry. Cramped
INTERIOR SPACE (cu. ft.)	90.7	Cramped
CARGO SPACE (cu. ft.)	10.7	Very Small

Specifications may vary.

Prices

Model	Retail	Mkup
318ti Coupe 3dr	23,300	9%
323is Coupe	28,700	12%
323iC Convertible Coupe	34,700	12%
328is Coupe	33,200	12%

Competition

	POOR → GOOD	Pg.
BMW 3 Series	(no rating)	109
Audi A4	Good	106
Lexus ES300	Good	163
Merc.-Benz C-Class	Average	173

*Due to the importance of crash tests, cars with no results as of publication date cannot be given an overall rating.

BMW 5 Series

Since the recent redesign, the 5 Series is roomier, more luxurious and loaded with airbags. It comes with dual airbags, side airbags up front, and a side airbag that inflates next to passengers' heads for protection during a rollover. If six standard airbags aren't enough, you can get two more optional side airbags for rear passengers. 4-wheel ABS and traction control are also standard.

The 528 comes with a powerful 2.8-liter, inline 6 engine. A whopping 4.4-liter V8 engine is available on the 540 with a six speed transmission. A stiffer suspension and 17 inch tires highlight a sport package for the 5 Series sedans. While expensive to maintain (not to mention purchase!), BMW gets high marks for safety.

The Ratings

	POOR ← → GOOD
COMPARATIVE RATING*	(no rating)
FRONTAL CRASH TEST	(no rating)
SAFETY FEATURES	Good
FUEL ECONOMY	Poor
PM COST	Good
REPAIR COST	Poor
WARRANTY	Good
COMPLAINTS	Average
INSURANCE COST	Poor-Average

Safety

FRONTAL CRASH TEST	No government results
SIDE CRASH TEST	No government results
AIRBAGS	Dual & Side
ANTI-LOCK BRAKES	4-Wheel
DAY. RUNNING LIGHTS	None
BELT ADJUSTORS	Standard
BUILT-IN CHILD SEAT	None
PRETENSIONERS	Standard

General Information

WHERE MADE	Germany
YEAR OF PRODUCTION	Third
PARKING INDEX	Average
BUMPERS	Weak
THEFT RATING	
TWINS	
GREEN RATING	Poor

Specifications

FUEL ECONOMY (cty/hwy)	20/29	Poor
DRIVING RANGE (miles)	453	Long
SEATING	4	
LENGTH (in.)	188	
HEAD/LEG ROOM (in.)	38.7/41.7	Cramped
INTERIOR SPACE (cu. ft.)	92.5	Cramped
CARGO SPACE (cu. ft.)	11.1	Very Small

Specifications may vary.

Prices

Model	Retail	Mkup
528i Sedan	38,900	11%
540iA	50,500	12%
540i	53,300	12%
528iT	38,900	11%

Competition

	POOR ← → GOOD	Pg.
BMW 5 Series	(no rating)	110
Audi A8	Good	108
Cadillac DeVille	Good	118
Oldsmobile Aurora	Average	191

*Due to the importance of crash tests, cars with no results as of publication date cannot be given an overall rating.

The Z3, the convertible roadster based on the 3 Series platform, has no changes for 1999. Standard safety features include dual airbags, seat belt pretensioners, traction control, and 4-wheel ABS.

For engines, you can get a 1.90-liter, 4-cylinder engine with 138 hp, but most will want the bigger 2.80-liter, 6-cylinder engine which offers 189 hp. An M roadster version of the Z3 comes with 17 inch wheels and a 3.2-liter, 240 hp engine. The interior offers bins for small luggage, but don't expect to bring much along with you. Noise levels are tolerable and controls easy to use. With its long-nosed, short-tailed appearance, the Z3 is the 90's version of the traditional sports car.

The Ratings

	POOR — GOOD
COMPARATIVE RATING*	(no rating)
FRONTAL CRASH TEST	(no rating)
SAFETY FEATURES	●●●●●●●○○
FUEL ECONOMY	●●○○○○○○○
PM COST	●●●●●●●●●
REPAIR COST	●●○○○○○○○
WARRANTY	●●●●●●●○○
COMPLAINTS	●●●●●●●○○
INSURANCE COST	●●●●●●●●●

Safety

FRONTAL CRASH TEST	No government results
SIDE CRASH TEST	No government results
AIRBAGS	Dual & Side
ANTI-LOCK BRAKES	4-Wheel
DAY. RUNNING LIGHTS	None
BELT ADJUSTORS	Standard
BUILT-IN CHILD SEAT	None
PRETENSIONERS	Standard

General Information

WHERE MADE	Germany/U.S.
YEAR OF PRODUCTION	Fourth
PARKING INDEX	Very Easy
BUMPERS	Weak
THEFT RATING	
TWINS	
GREEN RATING	Average

Specifications

FUEL ECONOMY (cty/hwy)	19/26	Poor
DRIVING RANGE (miles)	304	Very Short
SEATING	2	
LENGTH (in.)	158.5	
HEAD/LEG ROOM (in.)	37.6/41.8	Vry. Cramped
INTERIOR SPACE (cu. ft.)	47	Vry. Cramped
CARGO SPACE (cu. ft.)	5	Very Small

Specifications may vary.

Prices

Model	Retail	Mkup
2.3 2-seater Roadster Coupe	29,950	11%
2.8 2-seater Roadster Coupe	36,200	12%
M 2-seater Roadster Coupe	42,700	12%
2.8 2-seater Coupe	36,200	12%

Competition

	POOR — GOOD	Pg.
BMW Z3	(no rating)	111
Chrysler Sebring	●●○○○○○○○	134
Ford Mustang	●●●○○○○○○	144
Mitsubishi Eclipse	●●○○○○○○○	182

*Due to the importance of crash tests, cars with no results as of publication date cannot be given an overall rating.

Buick Century

Highlighting the changes for the '99 Buick Century are traction control, ABS, a tire inflation monitor, and automatic dimming outside rear-view mirrors—all standard this year. In addition, improved suspension gives the Century a smoother ride. The OnStar communications system is optional. This voice activated cell phone can be used to get directions, or help in an emergency. Advanced steering technology adapts steering resistance to travel speed. Steering is more rigid at higher speeds, to provide greater control of the vehicle, and easier at lower speeds to promote maneuverability. The engine is a 3.1-liter V6 with 160 hp. There are two trim levels: Custom and Limited. A great option for parents is the built-in child seat. Ride and handling are improved by a new rear suspension.

The Ratings

	POOR ··· GOOD
COMPARATIVE RATING	▣ (above average)
FRONTAL CRASH TEST	▣ (above average)
SAFETY FEATURES	▣ (good)
FUEL ECONOMY	▣ (poor)
PM COST	▣ (above average)
REPAIR COST	▣ (good)
WARRANTY	▣ (poor)
COMPLAINTS	▣ (above average)
INSURANCE COST	▣ (good)

Safety

FRONTAL CRASH TEST	Good
SIDE CRASH TEST	Average
AIRBAGS	Dual (New Design)
ANTI-LOCK BRAKES	4-Wheel
DAY. RUNNING LIGHTS	Standard
BELT ADJUSTORS	Standard
BUILT-IN CHILD SEAT	Optional
PRETENSIONERS	None

General Information

WHERE MADE	Canada/U.S.
YEAR OF PRODUCTION	Third
PARKING INDEX	Average
BUMPERS	Strong
THEFT RATING	
TWINS	Regal, Gr. Prix
GREEN RATING	Poor

Specifications

FUEL ECONOMY (cty/hwy)	20/29	Poor
DRIVING RANGE (miles)	429	Average
SEATING	6	
LENGTH (in.)	194.6	
HEAD/LEG ROOM (in.)	39.4/42.4	Roomy
INTERIOR SPACE (cu. ft.)	118.5	Very Roomy
CARGO SPACE (cu. ft.)	16.7	Large

Specifications may vary.

Prices

Model	Retail	Mkup
Custom Sedan	18,415	6%
Limited Sedan	19,775	6%

Competition

	POOR ··· GOOD	Pg.
Buick Century	▣	**112**
Ford Contour	▣	141
Honda Accord	▣	149
Pontiac Grand Prix	▣	200

Buick LeSabre

Buick offers only one engine with the LeSabre, a 3.8 liter V6 engine that can deliver up to 30 mpg on the highway. Like its twin, the Oldsmobile 88, the LeSabre emphasizes a soft ride. For crisper handling, order LeSabre's Gran Touring package. Interior room is spacious, especially in back. This year the Buick offers GM's OnStar communications system which, in addition to contacting emergency and navigational services, also signals when airbags deploy, and can be used as a tracking device in the event of theft. Finally, the few changes this year include the use of Buick's de-powered airbags.

The Ratings

	POOR → GOOD
COMPARATIVE RATING	████ (high)
FRONTAL CRASH TEST	(above average)
SAFETY FEATURES	(above average)
FUEL ECONOMY	(below average)
PM COST	(average)
REPAIR COST	(good)
WARRANTY	(poor)
COMPLAINTS	(good)
INSURANCE COST	(average)

Safety

FRONTAL CRASH TEST	Good
SIDE CRASH TEST	Poor
AIRBAGS	Dual (New Design)
ANTI-LOCK BRAKES	4-Wheel
DAY. RUNNING LIGHTS	Standard
BELT ADJUSTORS	Standard
BUILT-IN CHILD SEAT	None
PRETENSIONERS	None

General Information

WHERE MADE	Canada/U.S.
YEAR OF PRODUCTION	Eighth
PARKING INDEX	Very Hard
BUMPERS	Strong
THEFT RATING	Very Low
TWINS	Olds 88, Pont. Bonneville
GREEN RATING	Poor

Specifications

FUEL ECONOMY (cty/hwy)	19/30	Poor
DRIVING RANGE (miles)	441	Long
SEATING	6	
LENGTH (in.)	200.8	
HEAD/LEG ROOM (in.)	38.8/42.6	Average
INTERIOR SPACE (cu. ft.)	125.5	Very Roomy
CARGO SPACE (cu. ft.)	17	Very Large

Specifications may vary.

Prices

Model	Retail	Mkup
Custom Sedan	22,465	8%
Limited Sedan	25,790	9%

Competition

	POOR → GOOD	Pg.
Buick LeSabre		**113**
Ford Cr. Victoria		142
Oldsmobile 88		189
Toyota Avalon		212

Buick Park Avenue

Buick previously redesigned half of its six car lineup including the Park Avenue. Their goal was to provide a smooth ride without sacrificing comfort and handling. Changes for '99 include new tail lamps, new exterior colors and a new sound system. But more importantly Buick has added de-powered airbags for front seat occupants. The Park Avenue even automatically unlocks the doors within 15 seconds of airbag deployment. There are two engine choices available for the Park Avenue, both are 3.8 liter V-6's. The standard engine delivers a respectable 19/28 mpg while the turbo charged version sacrifices fuel economy slightly, delivering 18/27 mpg. Standard features include keyless entry and delayed locking.

The Ratings

	POOR GOOD
COMPARATIVE RATING	▮ (3rd)
FRONTAL CRASH TEST	▮ (4th)
SAFETY FEATURES	▮ (7th)
FUEL ECONOMY	▮ (3rd)
PM COST	
REPAIR COST	▮ (8th)
WARRANTY	▮ (1st)
COMPLAINTS	▮ (2nd)
INSURANCE COST	▮ (8th)

Safety

FRONTAL CRASH TEST	Average
SIDE CRASH TEST	No government results
AIRBAGS	Dual (New Design)
ANTI-LOCK BRAKES	4-Wheel
DAY. RUNNING LIGHTS	Standard
BELT ADJUSTORS	Standard
BUILT-IN CHILD SEAT	None
PRETENSIONERS	None

General Information

WHERE MADE	Canada/U.S.
YEAR OF PRODUCTION	Third
PARKING INDEX	Hard
BUMPERS	Strong
THEFT RATING	
TWINS	Riviera, Seville, Aurora
GREEN RATING	Poor

Specifications

FUEL ECONOMY (cty/hwy)	19/28	Poor
DRIVING RANGE (miles)	435	Average
SEATING	6	
LENGTH (in.)	206.8	
HEAD/LEG ROOM (in.)	39.8/42.4	Roomy
INTERIOR SPACE (cu. ft.)	131.2	Very Roomy
CARGO SPACE (cu. ft.)	19.1	Very Large

Specifications may vary.

Prices

Model	Retail	Mkup
Base Sedan	30,675	9%
Uultra Sedan	35,550	9%

Competition

	POOR GOOD	Pg.
Buick Park Avenue	▮	**114**
Audi A8	▮	108
Cadillac DeVille	▮	118
Toyota Avalon	▮	212

Buick Regal

The Regal comes in two trim levels: LS and GS. The LS gets a 3.80-liter, V6 engine, while the GS comes with a 240 hp, supercharged version of the V6. This year both engines have been altered to perform better in cold weather. With a slightly longer wheelbase then earlier models, there is a bit more interior room and trunk space. Buick engineers designed the Regal to be the smoothest and quietest running sedan they make.

An all-new Regal was introduced for the 1997 model year. Changes for this year include improved steering, and better suspension on the LS, improved ABS for both versions, standard tire inflation monitor, and reduced-force front airbags. Optional OnStar and Buick's advanced steering system continue as standard features.

The Ratings

	POOR — GOOD
COMPARATIVE RATING	
FRONTAL CRASH TEST	
SAFETY FEATURES	
FUEL ECONOMY	
PM COST	
REPAIR COST	
WARRANTY	
COMPLAINTS	
INSURANCE COST	

Safety

FRONTAL CRASH TEST	Good
SIDE CRASH TEST	Average
AIRBAGS	Dual (New Design)
ANTI-LOCK BRAKES	4-Wheel
DAY. RUNNING LIGHTS	Standard
BELT ADJUSTORS	Standard
BUILT-IN CHILD SEAT	None
PRETENSIONERS	None

General Information

WHERE MADE	Canada/U.S.
YEAR OF PRODUCTION	Third
PARKING INDEX	Average
BUMPERS	Strong
THEFT RATING	
TWINS	Century, Gr. Prix
GREEN RATING	Poor

Specifications

FUEL ECONOMY (cty/hwy)	19/30	Poor
DRIVING RANGE (miles)	429	Average
SEATING	5	
LENGTH (in.)	196.2	
HEAD/LEG ROOM (in.)	39.4/42.4	Roomy
INTERIOR SPACE (cu. ft.)	118.5	Very Roomy
CARGO SPACE (cu. ft.)	16.7	Large

Specifications may vary.

Prices

Model	Retail	Mkup
LS Sedan	21,045	8%
GS Sedan	23,790	9%

Competition

	POOR — GOOD	Pg.
Buick Regal		**115**
Ford Contour		141
Hyundai Sonata		156
Toyota Camry		213

Buick Riviera

The Riviera, Buick's sleek luxury sports coupe, is designed to grab your eye with its unique style. Its twins include the Park Avenue, Cadillac Seville, and Olds Aurora—all big, American cars. This year the Riviera gets Buick's de-powered airbags for the front occupants.

At over 17 feet and almost two tons, the Riviera is big, especially for a coupe. The new, and only, engine is a supercharged, 3.80-liter V8 engine that produces 240 hp. The seats are very comfortable with ample interior room and interior noise is very low. The Riviera continues to offer advanced steering and suspension for better highway steering, and options such as lumbar support and heated seats, OnStar, and a passenger side outside mirror that pivots when the car is in reverse.

The Ratings

	POOR GOOD
COMPARATIVE RATING	▓ (below midpoint)
FRONTAL CRASH TEST	▓ (below midpoint)
SAFETY FEATURES	▓ (above midpoint)
FUEL ECONOMY	▓ (low)
PM COST	▓ (mid)
REPAIR COST	▓ (mid-high)
WARRANTY	▓ (poor)
COMPLAINTS	▓ (mid-high)
INSURANCE COST	▓ (good)

Safety

FRONTAL CRASH TEST	Average
SIDE CRASH TEST	No government results
AIRBAGS	Dual (New Design)
ANTI-LOCK BRAKES	4-Wheel
DAY. RUNNING LIGHTS	Standard
BELT ADJUSTORS	Standard
BUILT-IN CHILD SEAT	None
PRETENSIONERS	None

General Information

WHERE MADE	Canada/U.S.
YEAR OF PRODUCTION	Fifth
PARKING INDEX	Hard
BUMPERS	Strong
THEFT RATING	Very Low
TWINS	Pk. Ave., Seville, Aurora
GREEN RATING	Poor

Specifications

FUEL ECONOMY (cty/hwy)	18/27	Poor
DRIVING RANGE (miles)	416	Short
SEATING	5	
LENGTH (in.)	207.2	
HEAD/LEG ROOM (in.)	38.2/42.6	Cramped
INTERIOR SPACE (cu. ft.)	116.9	Very Roomy
CARGO SPACE (cu. ft.)	17.4	Very Large

Specifications may vary.

Prices

Model	Retail	Mkup
Coupe	32,500	9%

Competition

	POOR GOOD	Pg.
Buick Riviera	▓ (below mid)	**116**
Lexus ES300	▓ (good)	163
Merc.-Benz C-Class	▓ (mid-high)	173
Volvo S70	▓ (good)	222

Cadillac Catera

There are few changes for the Catera this year. It still offers a 3.0 liter V6 engine, and interior comfort and ride are what you have come to expect from a Cadillac—excellent with little noise. As with many of this year's models, a traction control system automatically prevents slipping by giving more power to the wheels with the best traction. The 1999 Catera is the first Cadillac to meet California's Low Emissions Vehicle standards, a trend that the manufacturer will hopefully continue with its other models. Standard features include dual airbags and 4-wheel ABS, and a shoulder-lap belt for the center passenger in the rear. As a competitor with other luxury models, the Catera offers standard leather seats, an anti-theft system for the radio, and three memory settings for the driver's seat and rear view mirrors.

The Ratings

	POOR	GOOD
COMPARATIVE RATING*		
FRONTAL CRASH TEST		
SAFETY FEATURES		
FUEL ECONOMY		
PM COST		
REPAIR COST		
WARRANTY		
COMPLAINTS		
INSURANCE COST		

Safety

FRONTAL CRASH TEST	No government results
SIDE CRASH TEST	No government results
AIRBAGS	Dual
ANTI-LOCK BRAKES	4-Wheel
DAY. RUNNING LIGHTS	Standard
BELT ADJUSTORS	Standard
BUILT-IN CHILD SEAT	None
PRETENSIONERS	Standard

General Information

WHERE MADE	Germany
YEAR OF PRODUCTION	Third
PARKING INDEX	Easy
BUMPERS	Weak
THEFT RATING	
TWINS	
GREEN RATING	Very Poor

Specifications

FUEL ECONOMY (cty/hwy)	18/24	Very Poor
DRIVING RANGE (miles)	336	Very Short
SEATING	5	
LENGTH (in.)	194	
HEAD/LEG ROOM (in.)	38.7/42.2	Cramped
INTERIOR SPACE (cu. ft.)	98.2	Roomy
CARGO SPACE (cu. ft.)	14.5	Average

Specifications may vary.

Prices

Model	Retail	Mkup
Sedan w/Cloth Trim	29,995	4%

Competition

	POOR	GOOD	Pg.
Cadillac Catera			**117**
Audi A4			106
Lexus ES300			163
Oldsmobile 88			189

*Due to the importance of crash tests, cars with no results as of publication date cannot be given an overall rating.

Cadillac DeVille

The DeVille comes in three versions: DeVille Concours, DeVille, and DeVille d'Elegance. Cadillac's Northstar V8 engine (4.6 liter, 300 hp) provides plenty of power. An advanced traction system, road texture detection, ABS, and front and side airbags for the front occupants are all standard. All models have Magnasteer, a speed-sensitive steering system that alters steering effort at different vehicle speeds. Steering at lower speeds requires less effort. For 1999, extras include: new exterior and interior colors and massaging lumbar seats for the Concours and d'Elegance. An optional radio allows listeners to program traffic and weather reports over other running programs, including CDs and cassettes. The DeVille performs excellently in both side and frontal crash tests.

The Ratings

	POOR GOOD
COMPARATIVE RATING	■ (9th)
FRONTAL CRASH TEST	■ (8th)
SAFETY FEATURES	■ (7th)
FUEL ECONOMY	■ (2nd)
PM COST	■ (8th)
REPAIR COST	■ (1st)
WARRANTY	■ (5th)
COMPLAINTS	■ (7th)
INSURANCE COST	■ (10th)

Safety

FRONTAL CRASH TEST	Very Good
SIDE CRASH TEST	Very Good
AIRBAGS	Dual & Side
ANTI-LOCK BRAKES	4-Wheel
DAY. RUNNING LIGHTS	Standard
BELT ADJUSTORS	Standard
BUILT-IN CHILD SEAT	None
PRETENSIONERS	None

General Information

WHERE MADE	U.S.
YEAR OF PRODUCTION	Seventh
PARKING INDEX	Very Hard
BUMPERS	Weak
THEFT RATING	Low
TWINS	
GREEN RATING	Very Poor

Specifications

FUEL ECONOMY (cty/hwy)	17/26	Very Poor
DRIVING RANGE (miles)	430	Average
SEATING	6	
LENGTH (in.)	209.8	
HEAD/LEG ROOM (in.)	38.5/42.6	Average
INTERIOR SPACE (cu. ft.)	116.8	Very Roomy
CARGO SPACE (cu. ft.)	20	Very Large

Specifications may vary.

Prices

Model	Retail	Mkup
Base Sedan	37,695	8%
d'elegance Sedan	41,295	8%
Concours Sedan	42,295	8%

Competition

	POOR GOOD	Pg.
Cadillac DeVille	■	118
Audi A8	■	108
Buick LeSabre	■	113
Oldsmobile Aurora	■	191

Cadillac Eldorado

Performance and comfort are what Cadillac aims for in both the base level Eldorado and the upscale Touring Coupe. The Eldorado comes standard with 4-wheel ABS, daytime running lamps, traction control, road texture detection, Cadillac's Magnasteer system, and dual airbags. The OnStar communications system is an option for both models. As with other large Cadillacs, the signature Northstar V8 comes standard with the base model Eldorado.

The Touring Coupe comes with a more powerful, 300 hp engine and offers Cadillac's massaging lumbar seats. Both of these sacrifice fuel economy for performance. The front seat is comfortable and roomy, but the rear seat is cramped and inaccessible. The Eldorado is plagued by a high theft rate, expensive repair costs, and unavailable crash test results.

The Ratings

	POOR — GOOD
COMPARATIVE RATING*	
FRONTAL CRASH TEST	
SAFETY FEATURES	▪ (mid)
FUEL ECONOMY	▪ (low)
PM COST	▪ (high)
REPAIR COST	▪ (low)
WARRANTY	▪ (mid-high)
COMPLAINTS	▪ (low-mid)
INSURANCE COST	▪ (high)

Safety

FRONTAL CRASH TEST	No government results
SIDE CRASH TEST	No government results
AIRBAGS	Dual
ANTI-LOCK BRAKES	4-Wheel
DAY. RUNNING LIGHTS	Standard
BELT ADJUSTORS	None
BUILT-IN CHILD SEAT	None
PRETENSIONERS	None

General Information

WHERE MADE	U.S.
YEAR OF PRODUCTION	Eighth
PARKING INDEX	Hard
BUMPERS	Weak
THEFT RATING	High
TWINS	
GREEN RATING	Very Poor

Specifications

FUEL ECONOMY (cty/hwy)	17/26	Very Poor
DRIVING RANGE (miles)	430	Average
SEATING	5	
LENGTH (in.)	200.6	
HEAD/LEG ROOM (in.)	37.8/42.6	Cramped
INTERIOR SPACE (cu. ft.)	99.56	Roomy
CARGO SPACE (cu. ft.)	15.3	Average

Specifications may vary.

Prices

Model	Retail	Mkup
Base Touring Coupe	38,495	8%
Touring Coupe	42,695	8%

Competition

	POOR — GOOD	Pg.
Cadillac Eldorado		119
Buick Riviera	▪ (low-mid)	116
Oldsmobile Aurora	▪ (mid)	191
Volvo S70	▪ (high)	222

*Due to the importance of crash tests, cars with no results as of publication date cannot be given an overall rating.

Cadillac Seville

In September of 1998 this Cadillac was the first launched into the European market. Not much has changed from last year's model. Cadillac's massaging seats are now standard, and side airbags have been added as a standard safety feature along with dual airbags, traction control, and 4-wheel ABS. Optional are the OnStar communications system, heated seats, and an adaptive seat that adjusts to the body and position of the occupant.

The SLS trim level comes with a 4.6-liter, V8 engine with 275 hp. The STS comes with a more powerful V8. Ride and handling are good and there is ample interior room. Trunk space and fuel tank are both sizeable.

The Ratings

	POOR — GOOD
COMPARATIVE RATING	▓ (mid)
FRONTAL CRASH TEST	▓ (mid-low)
SAFETY FEATURES	▓ (good)
FUEL ECONOMY	▓ (poor)
PM COST	▓ (good)
REPAIR COST	▓ (poor)
WARRANTY	▓ (good)
COMPLAINTS	▓ (mid-low)
INSURANCE COST	▓ (good)

Safety

FRONTAL CRASH TEST	Average
SIDE CRASH TEST	No government results
AIRBAGS	Dual & Side
ANTI-LOCK BRAKES	4-Wheel
DAY. RUNNING LIGHTS	Standard
BELT ADJUSTORS	Standard
BUILT-IN CHILD SEAT	None
PRETENSIONERS	Standard

General Information

WHERE MADE	U.S.
YEAR OF PRODUCTION	Second
PARKING INDEX	Very Hard
BUMPERS	Weak
THEFT RATING	Average
TWINS	Riviera, Pk. Ave., Aurora
GREEN RATING	Very Poor

Specifications

FUEL ECONOMY (cty/hwy)	17/26	Very Poor
DRIVING RANGE (miles)	398	Short
SEATING	5	
LENGTH (in.)	201	
HEAD/LEG ROOM (in.)	38.2/42.5	Cramped
INTERIOR SPACE (cu. ft.)	104.18	Roomy
CARGO SPACE (cu. ft.)	15.7	Large

Specifications may vary.

Prices

Model	Retail	Mkup
SLS Sedan	42,495	8%
STS Sedan	48,995	12%

Competition

	POOR — GOOD	Pg.
Cadillac Seville	▓ (mid)	**120**
Audi A8	▓ (good)	108
Buick Park Avenue	▓ (low)	114
Oldsmobile Aurora	▓ (low-mid)	191

The automatic transmission on the Astro has been updated this year, though it still has the same standard 4.3-liter, V6 workhorse engine. Like its twin, the Safari, the Astro is a basic van used primarily for hauling and towing. It offers one of the largest cargo and towing capacities in the van market. Standard features include dual airbags, 4-wheel ABS and daytime running lamps. A built-in child safety seat is optional and highly recommended. The new all-wheel drive system automatically sets in when the rear wheels begin to slip in two-wheel drive mode. Fuel economy is fairly dismal, as well. You can choose between rear-wheel drive or all-wheel drive. If you are looking to carry cargo, this is a good bet. But, if you are looking for a people-mover, the Astro is easily outclassed by its younger minivan competitors.

The Ratings

	POOR — GOOD
COMPARATIVE RATING	
FRONTAL CRASH TEST	
SAFETY FEATURES	
FUEL ECONOMY	
PM COST	
REPAIR COST	
WARRANTY	
COMPLAINTS	
INSURANCE COST	

Safety

FRONTAL CRASH TEST	Poor
SIDE CRASH TEST	No government results
AIRBAGS	Dual (New Design)
ANTI-LOCK BRAKES	4-Wheel
DAY. RUNNING LIGHTS	Standard
BELT ADJUSTORS	Standard
BUILT-IN CHILD SEAT	Optional
PRETENSIONERS	None

General Information

WHERE MADE	U.S.
YEAR OF PRODUCTION	Fifteenth
PARKING INDEX	Average
BUMPERS	Strong
THEFT RATING	Average
TWINS	GMC Safari
GREEN RATING	Very Poor

Specifications

FUEL ECONOMY (cty/hwy)	16/21	Very Poor
DRIVING RANGE (miles)	463	Long
SEATING	7-8	
LENGTH (in.)	189.8	
HEAD/LEG ROOM (in.)	39.2/41.6	Cramped
INTERIOR SPACE (cu. ft.)		
CARGO SPACE (cu. ft.)	170.4	Very Large

Specifications may vary.

Prices

Model	Retail	Mkup
Cargo Van, 111" WB, RWD	19,340	9%
Passenger Van, 2wd, 111 WB"	20,174	9%

Competition

	POOR — GOOD	Pg.
Chevrolet Astro		**121**
Dodge Caravan		137
Ford Windstar		146
Plymouth Voyager		196

For 1999, the Camaro gets a larger fuel tank, traction control, and an oil monitor that notifies the driver when the oil needs to be changed. 4-wheel ABS is standard on all models. The sport appearance package gets you bigger wheels and extensions for the front fascia and rear spoiler.

If you are looking for a car with lots of power, the Camaro is a good choice. The standard engine is a 3.8-liter V6 with 200 hp. If you need even more power, the Z28 models have a 5.7-liter V8 that is slightly less economical. The standard manual transmission is more fuel efficient than the optional automatic. The Camaro is roomy up front, but the rear seat is almost too small for even young children.

The Ratings

	POOR — GOOD
COMPARATIVE RATING	▮ (low)
FRONTAL CRASH TEST	▮ (high)
SAFETY FEATURES	▮ (high)
FUEL ECONOMY	▮ (low-mid)
PM COST	▮ (mid)
REPAIR COST	▮ (low-mid)
WARRANTY	▮ (low)
COMPLAINTS	▮ (mid)
INSURANCE COST	▮ (low)

Safety

FRONTAL CRASH TEST	Very Good
SIDE CRASH TEST	Good
AIRBAGS	Dual (New Design)
ANTI-LOCK BRAKES	4-Wheel
DAY. RUNNING LIGHTS	Standard
BELT ADJUSTORS	Standard
BUILT-IN CHILD SEAT	None
PRETENSIONERS	None

General Information

WHERE MADE	Canada
YEAR OF PRODUCTION	Seventh
PARKING INDEX	Hard
BUMPERS	Strong
THEFT RATING	Average
TWINS	Pontiac Firebird
GREEN RATING	Poor

Specifications

FUEL ECONOMY (cty/hwy)	19/30	Poor
DRIVING RANGE (miles)	412	Short
SEATING	4	
LENGTH (in.)	193.2	
HEAD/LEG ROOM (in.)	37.2/43	Cramped
INTERIOR SPACE (cu. ft.)	81.9	Vry. Cramped
CARGO SPACE (cu. ft.)	12.9	Small

Specifications may vary.

Prices

Model	Retail	Mkup
Base Coupe	16,625	8%
Z28 Coupe	20,470	9%
Base Convertible	22,125	8%
Z28 Convertible	27,450	8%

Competition

	POOR — GOOD	Pg.
Chevrolet Camaro	▮ (low)	122
Acura Integra	▮ (mid)	103
Ford Mustang	▮ (mid)	144
Mitsubishi Eclipse	▮ (low)	182

Chevrolet Cavalier

This year the Cavalier has the option of two fuel sources: gasoline or compressed natural gas (CNG), which meets California's Transitional Low Emission Vehicle standards. Also new this year are de-powered airbags. Standard safety features include 4-wheel ABS and daytime running lamps. Traction control is optional. While the Cavalier has good frontal crash test scores, the coupe performed poorly on side crash tests.

The models to choose from include a base coupe and sedan, RS coupe, LS sedan, plus the Z24 coupe and convertible. The standard 2.2-liter engine delivers good power; a more powerful 2.4-liter engine is optional on the base sedan and coupe, standard on the LS and Z24 models. Ride is good on smooth roads, but highway driving can be noisy.

The Ratings

	POOR → GOOD
COMPARATIVE RATING	▣ (mid)
FRONTAL CRASH TEST	▣ (good side)
SAFETY FEATURES	▣ (good side)
FUEL ECONOMY	▣ (good side)
PM COST	▣ (mid)
REPAIR COST	▣ (good side)
WARRANTY	▣ (poor side)
COMPLAINTS	▣ (good side)
INSURANCE COST	▣ (poor side)

Safety

FRONTAL CRASH TEST	Good
SIDE CRASH TEST	2dr very poor/ 4dr poor
AIRBAGS	Dual (New Design)
ANTI-LOCK BRAKES	4-Wheel
DAY. RUNNING LIGHTS	Standard
BELT ADJUSTORS	Standard
BUILT-IN CHILD SEAT	None
PRETENSIONERS	None

General Information

WHERE MADE	U.S./Mexico
YEAR OF PRODUCTION	Fifth
PARKING INDEX	Easy
BUMPERS	Strong
THEFT RATING	Low
TWINS	Pontiac Sunfire
GREEN RATING	Average

Specifications

FUEL ECONOMY (cty/hwy)	24/34	Good
DRIVING RANGE (miles)	435	Average
SEATING	5	
LENGTH (in.)	180.7	
HEAD/LEG ROOM (in.)	37.6/41.9	Vry. Cramped
INTERIOR SPACE (cu. ft.)	87.1	Cramped
CARGO SPACE (cu. ft.)	13.2	Small

Specifications may vary.

Prices

Model	Retail	Mkup
Base Coupe	11,710	6%
RS Coupe	12,970	6%
Base Sedan	11,810	6%
LS Sedan	14,250	6%

Competition

	POOR → GOOD	Pg.
Chevrolet Cavalier	▣ (mid)	**123**
Dodge/Plym. Neon	▣ (poor side)	139
Ford Escort	▣ (mid)	143
Honda Civic	▣ (mid)	150

Little has changed for 1999. The OnStar 24-hour roadside assistance system operated from the car's cellular phone is still optional on the Lumina, but new dual de-powered airbags are standard. 4-wheel ABS is still only optional on the base sedan and standard on all other models. Chevy also improved their daytime running lights to increase their longevity.

The standard 3.1-liter provides adequate power, and a more powerful 3.8-liter, V6 engine is available for the LTZ. The LTZ package also comes with an improved sport suspension. Ride is good and controls are logically designed. Optional child safety seats are a great safety feature. Though a steady seller for Chevrolet, the Lumina's overall score is hurt by a large number of complaints.

The Ratings

	POOR — GOOD
COMPARATIVE RATING	▮ (near good)
FRONTAL CRASH TEST	▮ (near good)
SAFETY FEATURES	▮ (above mid)
FUEL ECONOMY	▮ (below mid)
PM COST	▮ (below mid)
REPAIR COST	▮ (above mid)
WARRANTY	▮ (poor)
COMPLAINTS	▮ (above mid)
INSURANCE COST	▮ (good)

Safety

FRONTAL CRASH TEST	Very Good
SIDE CRASH TEST	Good
AIRBAGS	Dual (New Design)
ANTI-LOCK BRAKES	4-Wheel (opt)
DAY. RUNNING LIGHTS	Standard
BELT ADJUSTORS	Standard
BUILT-IN CHILD SEAT	Optional
PRETENSIONERS	None

General Information

WHERE MADE	Canada
YEAR OF PRODUCTION	Fifth
PARKING INDEX	Average
BUMPERS	Strong
THEFT RATING	Very Low
TWINS	Chevrolet Monte Carlo
GREEN RATING	Poor

Specifications

FUEL ECONOMY (cty/hwy)	20/29	Poor
DRIVING RANGE (miles)	407	Short
SEATING	6	
LENGTH (in.)	200.9	
HEAD/LEG ROOM (in.)	38.4/42.4	Cramped
INTERIOR SPACE (cu. ft.)	100.5	Roomy
CARGO SPACE (cu. ft.)	15.5	Average

Specifications may vary.

Prices

Model	Retail	Mkup
Base Sedan	17,395	8%
LS Sedan	19,395	8%
LTZ Sedan	19,745	8%

Competition

	POOR — GOOD	Pg.
Chevrolet Lumina	▮	**124**
Ford Taurus	▮	145
Subaru Legacy	▮	208
Toyota Camry	▮	213

Chevrolet Malibu

Chevrolet has equipped this car with its powerful 2.4-liter, 4-cylinder engine which can deliver 150 hp. Optional on the base and standard on the LS is a 3.1-liter, V6 engine. You'll find good interior room, nice handling and owner-friendly features such as 100,000 mile coolant and platinum-tip spark plugs. The Malibu performed well on frontal crash tests, but did not fare as well on side crash tests.

The Malibu is Chevy's challenge to the best-selling Taurus, Camry and Accord trio. You can choose between the base model or the fancier LS; both come standard with dual de-powered airbags, 4-wheel ABS and daytime running lamps. On the LS, leather seats are one of the list of options along with power seats for the driver.

The Ratings

	POOR — GOOD
COMPARATIVE RATING	▮ (4 of 10)
FRONTAL CRASH TEST	▮ (8 of 10)
SAFETY FEATURES	▮ (7 of 10)
FUEL ECONOMY	▮ (5 of 10)
PM COST	▮ (6 of 10)
REPAIR COST	▮ (2 of 10)
WARRANTY	▮ (2 of 10)
COMPLAINTS	▮ (4 of 10)
INSURANCE COST	▮ (9 of 10)

Safety

FRONTAL CRASH TEST	Good
SIDE CRASH TEST	Poor
AIRBAGS	Dual (New Design)
ANTI-LOCK BRAKES	4-Wheel
DAY. RUNNING LIGHTS	Standard
BELT ADJUSTORS	Standard
BUILT-IN CHILD SEAT	None
PRETENSIONERS	None

General Information

WHERE MADE	U.S.
YEAR OF PRODUCTION	Third
PARKING INDEX	Easy
BUMPERS	Strong
THEFT RATING	Very Low
TWINS	Oldsmobile Cutlass
GREEN RATING	Average

Specifications

FUEL ECONOMY (cty/hwy)	22/30	Average
DRIVING RANGE (miles)	390	Short
SEATING	5	
LENGTH (in.)	190.4	
HEAD/LEG ROOM (in.)	39.4/42.2	Average
INTERIOR SPACE (cu. ft.)	98.6	Roomy
CARGO SPACE (cu. ft.)	16.4	Large

Specifications may vary.

Prices

Model	Retail	Mkup
Base Sedan	15,670	9%
LS Sedan	18,620	9%

Competition

	POOR — GOOD	Pg.
Chevrolet Malibu	▮ (4 of 10)	**125**
Ford Taurus	▮ (7 of 10)	145
Honda Accord	▮ (6 of 10)	149
Nissan Altima	▮ (1 of 10)	185

Chevrolet Metro

Very few changes are made to the Metro this year. A new paint job and Chevrolet's de-powered airbags are the most noteable. 4-wheel ABS is optional; daytime running lamps and dual airbags are standard.

A coupe is the only base model available; the LSi models come in coupe and sedan. The base coupe's 1.0-liter engine puts out a puny 55 hp, but is one of the leaders in fuel efficiency with an astonishing 41/47 mpg. The 1.3-liter engine, standard on the LSi models, now uses multiport fuel injection, raising hp from 70 to 79. Interior space is cramped and trunk space is skimpy. With a price tag under $10,000, the Metro is as basic as transportation gets.

The Ratings

	POOR → GOOD
COMPARATIVE RATING	▮ (poor)
FRONTAL CRASH TEST	▮ (good)
SAFETY FEATURES	▮ (above avg)
FUEL ECONOMY	▮ (very good)
PM COST	▮ (below avg)
REPAIR COST	▮ (poor)
WARRANTY	▮ (poor)
COMPLAINTS	▮ (good)
INSURANCE COST	▮ (poor)

Safety

FRONTAL CRASH TEST	Good
SIDE CRASH TEST	No government results
AIRBAGS	Dual (New Design)
ANTI-LOCK BRAKES	4-Wheel (opt)
DAY. RUNNING LIGHTS	Standard
BELT ADJUSTORS	None
BUILT-IN CHILD SEAT	None
PRETENSIONERS	None

General Information

WHERE MADE	Canada
YEAR OF PRODUCTION	Fifth
PARKING INDEX	Very Easy
BUMPERS	Weak
THEFT RATING	
TWINS	Suzuki Swift
GREEN RATING	Good

Specifications

FUEL ECONOMY (cty/hwy)	41/47	Very Good
DRIVING RANGE (miles)	453	Long
SEATING	4	
LENGTH (in.)	149.4	
HEAD/LEG ROOM (in.)	39.1/42.5	Average
INTERIOR SPACE (cu. ft.)	85.8	Vry. Cramped
CARGO SPACE (cu. ft.)	8.4	Very Small

Specifications may vary.

Prices

Model	Retail	Mkup
Base Hatchback 3dr	8,755	6%
Lsi Hatchback 3dr	9,555	7%
LSI Sedan	10,155	7%

Competition

	POOR → GOOD	Pg.
Chevrolet Metro	▮	**126**
Ford Escort	▮	143
Hyundai Accent	▮	154
Kia Sephia	▮	162

Chevrolet Monte Carlo

Like the most of Chevrolet's line this year, few changes are made beyond a new exterior paint choice and de-powered airbags. The optional Onstar roadside assistance system is available and the Monte Carlo comes with two trim levels, an LS or Z34. Dual airbags, 4-wheel ABS and daytime running lamps are both standard.

The standard engine is a 3.1-liter V6 that produces 160 hp. The Z34 has a 3.8-liter V6 that delivers more power with no decrease in fuel economy. A high performance suspension also comes with the Z34. Other features include 100,000 mile spark plugs and 150,000 mile coolant. Essentially a two-door version of the popular Lumina, the Monte Carlo offers many options, so choose carefully.

The Ratings

	POOR — GOOD
COMPARATIVE RATING	
FRONTAL CRASH TEST	
SAFETY FEATURES	
FUEL ECONOMY	
PM COST	
REPAIR COST	
WARRANTY	
COMPLAINTS	
INSURANCE COST	

Safety

FRONTAL CRASH TEST	Very Good
SIDE CRASH TEST	Good
AIRBAGS	Dual (New Design)
ANTI-LOCK BRAKES	4-Wheel
DAY. RUNNING LIGHTS	Standard
BELT ADJUSTORS	Standard
BUILT-IN CHILD SEAT	None
PRETENSIONERS	None

General Information

WHERE MADE	Canada
YEAR OF PRODUCTION	Fifth
PARKING INDEX	Average
BUMPERS	Strong
THEFT RATING	Low
TWINS	Chevrolet Lumina
GREEN RATING	Poor

Specifications

FUEL ECONOMY (cty/hwy)	20/29	Poor
DRIVING RANGE (miles)	407	Short
SEATING	6	
LENGTH (in.)	200.7	
HEAD/LEG ROOM (in.)	37.9/42.4	Cramped
INTERIOR SPACE (cu. ft.)	96.1	Average
CARGO SPACE (cu. ft.)	15.5	Average

Specifications may vary.

Prices

Model	Retail	Mkup
LS Coupe	17,945	8%
Z34 Coupe	20,295	8%

Competition

	POOR — GOOD	Pg.
Chev. Monte Carlo		**127**
Chrysler Sebring		134
Dodge Avenger		136
Nissan Maxima		186

After the major changes last year, this year's Prizm gets new de-powered airbags to enhance its safety options. Available in a base and up-level LSi model, this sedan gets high marks for safety. In addition to the new airbags: daytime running lamps and rear shoulder belts. Safety options include 4-wheel ABS and side airbags, which are a must.

The 1.8-liter, dual overhead cam engine makes the Prizm more powerful than when it was a Geo product. Inside, the seats are comfortable and firm, but the rear is a bit tight. Built on the same assembly line as the Toyota Corolla, the Prizm cost much less than its more popular twin, yet offers top quality craftsmanship along with highly sought-after safety features like side airbags for a low price.

The Ratings

	POOR — GOOD
COMPARATIVE RATING	▮ (low-middle)
FRONTAL CRASH TEST	▮ (good)
SAFETY FEATURES	▮ (good)
FUEL ECONOMY	▮ (good)
PM COST	▮ (middle)
REPAIR COST	▮ (low)
WARRANTY	▮ (low)
COMPLAINTS	▮ (middle)
INSURANCE COST	▮ (poor)

Safety

FRONTAL CRASH TEST	Good
SIDE CRASH TEST	Good
AIRBAGS	Dual (New Design)/opt. side
ANTI-LOCK BRAKES	4-Wheel (opt)
DAY. RUNNING LIGHTS	Standard
BELT ADJUSTORS	Standard
BUILT-IN CHILD SEAT	Optional
PRETENSIONERS	Standard

General Information

WHERE MADE	U.S.
YEAR OF PRODUCTION	Second
PARKING INDEX	Very Easy
BUMPERS	Strong
THEFT RATING	
TWINS	Toyota Corolla
GREEN RATING	Average

Specifications

FUEL ECONOMY (cty/hwy)	31/37	Very Good
DRIVING RANGE (miles)	449	Long
SEATING	5	
LENGTH (in.)	174.3	
HEAD/LEG ROOM (in.)	39.3/42.5	Roomy
INTERIOR SPACE (cu. ft.)	88.0	Cramped
CARGO SPACE (cu. ft.)	12.1	Small

Specifications may vary.

Prices

Model	Retail	Mkup
Base Sedan	12,143	5%
Lsi Sedan	14,714	8%

Competition

	POOR — GOOD	Pg.
Chevrolet Prizm	▮	**128**
Honda Civic	▮	150
Hyundai Accent	▮	154
Nissan Sentra	▮	188

Chevrolet Venture

A few perks have been added for the 1999s: leather seating options, rear window defogger, and heated outside mirrors are among the list. Like the Caravan, the Venture has sliding doors on both sides. You'll also find standard dual airbags, 4-wheel ABS and daytime running lamps. Side airbags are optional and recommended.

There is only one engine choice, a 3.4-liter V6. The interior is spacious, allowing this minivan to carry some of the largest loads in the industry. You have a choice between standard or extended length versions and the options list is quite long. Seating for seven is comfortable and removal of the seats is relatively easy. The Venture performed well in recent crash tests which should make it a viable alternative to the Chrysler minivans.

The Ratings

	POOR — GOOD
COMPARATIVE RATING	
FRONTAL CRASH TEST	
SAFETY FEATURES	
FUEL ECONOMY	
PM COST	
REPAIR COST	
WARRANTY	
COMPLAINTS	
INSURANCE COST	

Safety

FRONTAL CRASH TEST	Good
SIDE CRASH TEST	No government results
AIRBAGS	Dual & Side (New Design)
ANTI-LOCK BRAKES	4-Wheel
DAY. RUNNING LIGHTS	Standard
BELT ADJUSTORS	Standard
BUILT-IN CHILD SEAT	Optional
PRETENSIONERS	Standard

General Information

WHERE MADE	U.S.
YEAR OF PRODUCTION	Third
PARKING INDEX	Average
BUMPERS	Strong
THEFT RATING	
TWINS	Silhouette, Montana
GREEN RATING	Very Poor

Specifications

FUEL ECONOMY (cty/hwy)	18/25	Very Poor
DRIVING RANGE (miles)	430	Average
SEATING	7-8	
LENGTH (in.)	186.9	
HEAD/LEG ROOM (in.)	39.9/39.9	Vry. Cramped
INTERIOR SPACE (cu. ft.)		
CARGO SPACE (cu. ft.)	126.6	Very Large

Specifications may vary.

Prices

Model	Retail	Mkup
Reg. WB 3dr. Pass	20,249	9%
Pass., Reg. WB, Sedan	21,429	9%
Pass., Ext. WB 3dr.	21,769	9%
Pass., Ext., WB Sedan	22,359	9%

Competition

	POOR — GOOD	Pg.
Chevrolet Venture		**129**
Dodge Caravan		137
Ford Windstar		146
Plymouth Voyager		196

Named after the 300 series from decades ago, the 300M is Chrysler's new flagship. First available in the spring of 1998, it is now in 30 international markets, with slightly different features. The 300M is powered by an all new aluminum 3.5 liter V6 with 253 hp engine. ABS and low speed traction control are standard. Front driver and passenger airbags are de-powered, but, surprisingly, side airbags are not present.

Leather interior, heated front seats, a theft-deterrent system, fog lamps, TLEV emission controls, heated rear view mirrors, and a CD player all make the list of standard features.

The Ratings

	POOR — GOOD
COMPARATIVE RATING*	(blank)
FRONTAL CRASH TEST	(blank)
SAFETY FEATURES	▨
FUEL ECONOMY	▨
PM COST	▨
REPAIR COST	(blank)
WARRANTY	▨
COMPLAINTS	▨
INSURANCE COST	▨

Safety

FRONTAL CRASH TEST	No government results
SIDE CRASH TEST	No government results
AIRBAGS	Dual (New Design)
ANTI-LOCK BRAKES	4-Wheel
DAY. RUNNING LIGHTS	None
BELT ADJUSTORS	Standard
BUILT-IN CHILD SEAT	None
PRETENSIONERS	None

General Information

WHERE MADE	Canada
YEAR OF PRODUCTION	First
PARKING INDEX	Average
BUMPERS	
THEFT RATING	
TWINS	
GREEN RATING	Very Poor

Specifications

FUEL ECONOMY (cty/hwy)	18/27	Poor
DRIVING RANGE (miles)	387	Very Short
SEATING	5	
LENGTH (in.)	197.8	
HEAD/LEG ROOM (in.)	38/43.5	Average
INTERIOR SPACE (cu. ft.)	105.1	Very Roomy
CARGO SPACE (cu. ft.)	16.8	Large

Specifications may vary.

Prices

Model	Retail	Mkup
Sedan	28,300	8%

Competition

	POOR — GOOD	Pg.
Chrysler 300M	(blank)	130
Cadillac DeVille	▨	118
Oldsmobile Aurora	▨	191
Volvo S70	▨	222

*Due to the importance of crash tests, cars with no results as of publication date cannot be given an overall rating.

Chrysler Cirrus

The Cirrus is the top trim level of its two siblings, the Stratus and Breeze. For 1999, the Cirrus gets a quieter interior space, an optional anti-theft system, and improved suspension. The LXi, now the only model, comes fully loaded with lots of standard features including leather seats and power everything. Dual airbags and ABS are also standard.

The Cirrus comes with a 2.5-liter V6 engine, the only engine available. Chrysler's innovative cab-forward design increases interior room, similar to their bigger LH cousins. Additionally, the Cirrus has a high number of complaints and the warranty isn't much better, either.

The Ratings

	POOR	GOOD
COMPARATIVE RATING		
FRONTAL CRASH TEST		
SAFETY FEATURES		
FUEL ECONOMY		
PM COST		
REPAIR COST		
WARRANTY		
COMPLAINTS		
INSURANCE COST		

Safety

FRONTAL CRASH TEST	Average
SIDE CRASH TEST	Average
AIRBAGS	Dual (New Design)
ANTI-LOCK BRAKES	4-Wheel
DAY. RUNNING LIGHTS	None
BELT ADJUSTORS	Standard
BUILT-IN CHILD SEAT	None
PRETENSIONERS	None

General Information

WHERE MADE	U.S.
YEAR OF PRODUCTION	Fifth
PARKING INDEX	Average
BUMPERS	Weak
THEFT RATING	Average
TWINS	Stratus, Breeze
GREEN RATING	Poor

Specifications

FUEL ECONOMY (cty/hwy)	19/27	Poor
DRIVING RANGE (miles)	368	Very Short
SEATING	5	
LENGTH (in.)	187	
HEAD/LEG ROOM (in.)	38.1/42.3	Cramped
INTERIOR SPACE (cu. ft.)	95.9	Average
CARGO SPACE (cu. ft.)	15.7	Large

Specifications may vary.

Prices

Model	Retail	Mkup
LXi Sedan	19,460	9%

Competition

	POOR	GOOD	Pg.
Chrysler Cirrus			131
Buick LeSabre			113
Mercury Sable			178
Toyota Camry			213

Chrysler Concorde

The Concorde has two trim levels available. The LX gets a 2.7-liter, V6 engine that puts out 200 hp. The LXi comes with a larger 3.2-liter, V6 with 20 more hp than the base engine. Both engines are all aluminum with good performance and fuel economy. With the 1999's you have the option of meeting California's Transitional Low Emission Vehicle standards. Dual airbags are standard but you still have to pay extra for ABS.

Head and leg room is ample and there's even more room in this year's trunk.

The Ratings

	POOR				GOOD
COMPARATIVE RATING*					
FRONTAL CRASH TEST					
SAFETY FEATURES			■		
FUEL ECONOMY			■		
PM COST				■	
REPAIR COST				■	
WARRANTY	■				
COMPLAINTS			■		
INSURANCE COST					■

Safety

FRONTAL CRASH TEST	No government results
SIDE CRASH TEST	No government results
AIRBAGS	Dual (New Design)
ANTI-LOCK BRAKES	4-Wheel (opt)
DAY. RUNNING LIGHTS	None
BELT ADJUSTORS	Standard
BUILT-IN CHILD SEAT	None
PRETENSIONERS	None

General Information

WHERE MADE	Canada
YEAR OF PRODUCTION	Second
PARKING INDEX	Hard
BUMPERS	Strong
THEFT RATING	Low
TWINS	Dodge Intrepid
GREEN RATING	Poor

Specifications

FUEL ECONOMY (cty/hwy)	21/30	Average
DRIVING RANGE (miles)	434	Average
SEATING	5	
LENGTH (in.)	209.1	
HEAD/LEG ROOM (in.)	38.3/42.1	Cramped
INTERIOR SPACE (cu. ft.)	107.6	Very Roomy
CARGO SPACE (cu. ft.)	18.7	Very Large

Specifications may vary.

Prices

Model	Retail	Mkup
LX Sedan	21,510	8%

Competition

	POOR				GOOD	Pg.
Chrysler Concorde						132
Buick Park Avenue		■				114
Ford Crown Victoria				■		142
Toyota Avalon					■	212

*Due to the importance of crash tests, cars with no results as of publication date cannot be given an overall rating.

Chrysler LHS

Introduced in May of 1998 as a 1999 model, the LHS offers a 3.5 liter aluminum V6 engine. De-powered airbags for front occupants, and an anti-theft system are standard. This year the LHS has an all new, stiffer structure.

Most anything you'll want comes standard on the outgoing LHS including ABS. The only options are a sunroof and a CD-player. The 3.5-liter V6 is powerful and should deliver average gas mileage for such a large car. Thanks to the touring suspension that comes standard, the handling is as precise as any other car this size. Like the LH sedans, the LHS has excellent interior space due to the cab-forward design. Controls are nicely placed and passengers will ride in comfort with plenty of room in the back seat.

The Ratings

	POOR GOOD
COMPARATIVE RATING*	
FRONTAL CRASH TEST	
SAFETY FEATURES	
FUEL ECONOMY	
PM COST	
REPAIR COST	
WARRANTY	
COMPLAINTS	
INSURANCE COST	

Safety

FRONTAL CRASH TEST	No government results
SIDE CRASH TEST	No government results
AIRBAGS	Dual (New Design)
ANTI-LOCK BRAKES	4-Wheel
DAY. RUNNING LIGHTS	None
BELT ADJUSTORS	Standard
BUILT-IN CHILD SEAT	None
PRETENSIONERS	None

General Information

WHERE MADE	Canada
YEAR OF PRODUCTION	First
PARKING INDEX	Hard
BUMPERS	
THEFT RATING	Average
TWINS	
GREEN RATING	Very Poor

Specifications

FUEL ECONOMY (cty/hwy)	18/27	Poor
DRIVING RANGE (miles)	383	Very Short
SEATING	5	
LENGTH (in.)	207.7	
HEAD/LEG ROOM (in.)	38.3/42.2	Cramped
INTERIOR SPACE (cu. ft.)	107.3	Very Roomy
CARGO SPACE (cu. ft.)	18.7	Very Large

Specifications may vary.

Prices

Model	Retail	Mkup
Sedan	28,400	8%

Competition

	POOR GOOD	Pg.
Chrysler LHS		133
Buick LeSabre		113
Chevrolet Lumina		124
Ford Crown Victoria		142

*Due to the importance of crash tests, cars with no results as of publication date cannot be given an overall rating.

The standard 2-liter, 4-cylinder engine on the LX trim level will probably not satisfy the drivers Chrysler is hoping to reach; the optional 2.5-liter V6 on the uplevel LXi is slightly more peppy. Interior room is better than most competitors, though rear-seat occupants will find minimal comfort. Beware: the convertible Sebring JT is not the same car as the hardtop Sebring. The convertible is based on the Cirrus.

No changes have been made for 1999 other than a few new color choices and Chrysler's de-powered airbags. This aggressive looking coupe competes well with other sports coupes. Dual airbags are standard, but you'll have to pay extra for ABS.

The Ratings

	POOR GOOD
COMPARATIVE RATING	▮ (low)
FRONTAL CRASH TEST	▮ (high)
SAFETY FEATURES	▮ (mid-high)
FUEL ECONOMY	▮ (mid)
PM COST	▮ (mid-high)
REPAIR COST	▮ (mid-high)
WARRANTY	▮ (low)
COMPLAINTS	▮ (very low)
INSURANCE COST	▮ (very low)

Safety

FRONTAL CRASH TEST	Very Good
SIDE CRASH TEST	No government results
AIRBAGS	Dual (New Design)
ANTI-LOCK BRAKES	4-Wheel (opt)
DAY. RUNNING LIGHTS	None
BELT ADJUSTORS	Standard
BUILT-IN CHILD SEAT	None
PRETENSIONERS	None

General Information

WHERE MADE	U.S.
YEAR OF PRODUCTION	Fifth
PARKING INDEX	Hard
BUMPERS	Strong
THEFT RATING	High
TWINS	Avenger
GREEN RATING	Average

Specifications

FUEL ECONOMY (cty/hwy)	22/31	Average
DRIVING RANGE (miles)	421	Average
SEATING	5	
LENGTH (in.)	190.9	
HEAD/LEG ROOM (in.)	39.1/43.3	Roomy
INTERIOR SPACE (cu. ft.)	90.7	Cramped
CARGO SPACE (cu. ft.)	13.1	Small

Specifications may vary.

Prices

Model	Retail	Mkup
LX Coupe	17,125	8%
LXI Coupe	21,225	9%
JX Convertible Coupe	23,870	9%
JXI Convertible Coupe	26,185	9%

Competition

	POOR GOOD	Pg.
Chrysler Sebring	▮ (low)	134
Acura Integra	▮ (mid)	103
Buick Riviera	▮ (mid)	116
Chev. Monte Carlo	▮ (mid)	127

Four versions of the Town and Country are available this year: SX, LX, LXi and the Limited. A luxury minivan, it offers leather and suede interior, heated power seats, and lots of power equipment. Dual airbags and ABS are standard; optional built-in child seats are a must for any parents, but not available with leather seats. The Town and Country offers a 3.3-liter V6 to go with the standard automatic overdrive, but its gas mileage is among the lowest for minivans. You may want to opt for the new optional 3.8-liter V6 that comes with all-wheel drive, and meets Low Emission Vehicle standards. If you want a firmer suspension, check out the trailer-towing package. The ride is comfortable on smooth roads. A high number of complaints overshadows an otherwise popular minivan.

The Ratings

	POOR ← → GOOD
COMPARATIVE RATING	(poor end)
FRONTAL CRASH TEST	(middle)
SAFETY FEATURES	(middle-good)
FUEL ECONOMY	(poor end)
PM COST	(good)
REPAIR COST	(good end)
WARRANTY	(poor)
COMPLAINTS	(poor end)
INSURANCE COST	(good end)

Safety

FRONTAL CRASH TEST	Good
SIDE CRASH TEST	No government results
AIRBAGS	Dual (New Design)
ANTI-LOCK BRAKES	4-Wheel
DAY. RUNNING LIGHTS	None
BELT ADJUSTORS	Standard
BUILT-IN CHILD SEAT	Optional
PRETENSIONERS	None

General Information

WHERE MADE	U.S.
YEAR OF PRODUCTION	Fourth
PARKING INDEX	Average
BUMPERS	Strong
THEFT RATING	Average
TWINS	Gr. Caravan, Gr. Voyager
GREEN RATING	Very Poor

Specifications

FUEL ECONOMY (cty/hwy)	18/24	Very Poor
DRIVING RANGE (miles)	420	Average
SEATING	7	
LENGTH (in.)	186.4	
HEAD/LEG ROOM (in.)	39.8/40.6	Cramped
INTERIOR SPACE (cu. ft.)		
CARGO SPACE (cu. ft.)	124.9	Very Large

Specifications may vary.

Prices

Model	Retail	Mkup
LX AWD	30,735	10%
LXI AWD	34,275	10%
LXI FWD	31,610	10%
Limited FWD	33,665	10%

Competition

	POOR ← → GOOD	Pg.
Chrysler T&C	(poor end)	135
Dodge Caravan	(poor end)	137
Ford Windstar	(middle-good)	146
Plymouth Voyager	(poor end)	196

Dodge Avenger

The twin of the Chrysler Sebring, is a stylish coupe first introduced in 1995. For 1999 it gets de-powered airbags in the front seats, and a two new colors: plum and shark blue. The sporty Avenger has a new sport package that comes with bigger wheels and a spoiler. Dual airbags are standard, but you'll have to pay extra for ABS.

The standard 2-liter, 4-cylinder engine on the base and ES models is barely adequate. Most buyers will probably want the optional 2.5-liter V6 which is more powerful but fuel economy will suffer. Interior room is better than most competitors, and rear-seat occupants will find lots of comfort. While an excellent performer in frontal crash tests, the Avenger suffers from a high number of complaints.

The Ratings

	POOR — GOOD
COMPARATIVE RATING	▪ (below mid)
FRONTAL CRASH TEST	▪ (far right)
SAFETY FEATURES	▪ (upper mid)
FUEL ECONOMY	▪ (mid)
PM COST	▪ (upper mid)
REPAIR COST	▪ (upper mid)
WARRANTY	▪ (left)
COMPLAINTS	▪ (low-left)
INSURANCE COST	▪ (far left)

Safety

FRONTAL CRASH TEST	Very Good
SIDE CRASH TEST	No government results
AIRBAGS	Dual (New Design)
ANTI-LOCK BRAKES	4-Wheel (opt)
DAY. RUNNING LIGHTS	None
BELT ADJUSTORS	Standard
BUILT-IN CHILD SEAT	None
PRETENSIONERS	None

General Information

WHERE MADE	U.S.
YEAR OF PRODUCTION	Fifth
PARKING INDEX	Hard
BUMPERS	Strong
THEFT RATING	Average
TWINS	Sebring
GREEN RATING	Poor

Specifications

FUEL ECONOMY (cty/hwy)	22/32	Average
DRIVING RANGE (miles)	429	Average
SEATING	5	
LENGTH (in.)	190.2	
HEAD/LEG ROOM (in.)	39.1/43.3	Roomy
INTERIOR SPACE (cu. ft.)	90.7	Cramped
CARGO SPACE (cu. ft.)	13.1	Small

Specifications may vary.

Prices

Model	Retail	Mkup
Base Coupe	15,370	8%
ES Coupe	17,645	8%

Competition

	POOR — GOOD	Pg.
Dodge Avenger	▪ (mid)	**136**
Acura Integra	▪ (mid)	103
Buick Riviera	▪ (low-left)	116
Chev. Monte Carlo	▪ (mid)	127

Dodge Caravan

New for the top selling minivan in America is the ES model, a more luxurious version of the minivan. This Caravan remains the standard by which all other minivans are compared to.

The standard 4-cylinder engine is really not adequate. Go for one of the three V6 engines to get more power with only a small sacrifice in fuel efficiency. Both the 2.4 liter I4 and the 3.8 liter V6 meet Low Emission Vehicle standards. Order the heavy duty suspension or "sport handling group" for improved cornering. The longer wheelbase and length of the Grand Caravan translates into more cargo room. The built-in child restraints are a great option. Comfort is good for seven and the seats are easy to remove. However, be cautious as the Caravan has a poor complaint rating.

The Ratings

	POOR ··· GOOD
COMPARATIVE RATING	▪
FRONTAL CRASH TEST	▪
SAFETY FEATURES	▪
FUEL ECONOMY	▪
PM COST	▪
REPAIR COST	▪
WARRANTY	▪
COMPLAINTS	▪
INSURANCE COST	▪

Safety

FRONTAL CRASH TEST	Good
SIDE CRASH TEST	No government results
AIRBAGS	Dual (New Design)
ANTI-LOCK BRAKES	4-Wheel (opt)
DAY. RUNNING LIGHTS	None
BELT ADJUSTORS	Standard
BUILT-IN CHILD SEAT	Optional
PRETENSIONERS	None

General Information

WHERE MADE	U.S./Canada
YEAR OF PRODUCTION	Fourth
PARKING INDEX	Average
BUMPERS	Strong
THEFT RATING	Average
TWINS	Plymouth Voyager
GREEN RATING	Average

Specifications

FUEL ECONOMY (cty/hwy)	20/26	Poor
DRIVING RANGE (miles)	460	Long
SEATING	7	
LENGTH (in.)	186.3	
HEAD/LEG ROOM (in.)	39.8/40.6	Cramped
INTERIOR SPACE (cu. ft.)		
CARGO SPACE (cu. ft.)	126.7	Very Large

Specifications may vary.

Prices

Model	Retail	Mkup
Base	17,905	9%
SE 112"wb	21,780	10%
Grand Caravan	21,040	9%
Grand Caravan SE	22,775	9%

Competition

	POOR ··· GOOD	Pg.
Dodge Caravan	▪	137
Chrysler T&C	▪	135
Ford Windstar	▪	146
Plymouth Voyager	▪	196

Dodge Intrepid

After last year's big changes, this year's model is virtually unchanged. A new theft deterrent system, optional leather seats, and optional adherence to Transitional Low Emission Vehicle Standards are all part of the offering this year. Dual airbags are standard but you still have to pay extra for ABS.

Two trim levels are available. The base gets a 2.7-liter, V6 engine. The ES trim level comes with a larger 3.2-liter, V6 with 20 more hp than the base engine. Both engines are all aluminum with improved performance and better fuel economy than previous engines. Also, the ES engine comes with the Autostick, a stick/automatic combo, which is growing in popularity. Head and leg room and trunk space are ample.

The Ratings

	POOR — GOOD
COMPARATIVE RATING *	(no rating)
FRONTAL CRASH TEST	(no rating)
SAFETY FEATURES	▮
FUEL ECONOMY	▮
PM COST	▮
REPAIR COST	▮
WARRANTY	▮
COMPLAINTS	▮
INSURANCE COST	▮

Safety

FRONTAL CRASH TEST	No government results
SIDE CRASH TEST	No government results
AIRBAGS	Dual (New Design)
ANTI-LOCK BRAKES	4-Wheel (opt)
DAY. RUNNING LIGHTS	None
BELT ADJUSTORS	Standard
BUILT-IN CHILD SEAT	None
PRETENSIONERS	None

General Information

WHERE MADE	Canada
YEAR OF PRODUCTION	Second
PARKING INDEX	Hard
BUMPERS	Strong
THEFT RATING	Low
TWINS	Chrysler Concorde
GREEN RATING	Poor

Specifications

FUEL ECONOMY (cty/hwy)	21/30	Average
DRIVING RANGE (miles)	434	Average
SEATING	5	
LENGTH (in.)	203.7	
HEAD/LEG ROOM (in.)	38.3/42.2	Cramped
INTERIOR SPACE (cu. ft.)	104.5	Roomy
CARGO SPACE (cu. ft.)	18.4	Very Large

Specifications may vary.

Prices

Model	Retail	Mkup
Base Sedan	19,890	8%
ES Sedan	22,640	9%

Competition

	POOR — GOOD	Pg.
Dodge Intrepid	(no rating)	**138**
Buick LeSabre	▮	113
Chevrolet Lumina	▮	124
Toyota Avalon	▮	212

*Due to the importance of crash tests, cars with no results as of publication date cannot be given an overall rating.

Dodge/Plymouth Neon

The Neon benefits from its cab-forward design, which provides excellent interior space for a small car. Dual de-powered airbags are standard and new for '99; ABS is optional.

The single-cam version of the 2-liter engine provides adequate power, but the dual-cam version has even more zing. Not only is it longer than its competitors, the Neon is also taller, resulting in more head room. Choose the sedan with options, or get the "sport" coupe package with dual cams and a firmer suspension.

The Ratings

	POOR	GOOD
COMPARATIVE RATING	▮	
FRONTAL CRASH TEST		▮
SAFETY FEATURES		▮
FUEL ECONOMY		▮
PM COST		▮
REPAIR COST		▮
WARRANTY	▮	
COMPLAINTS	▮	
INSURANCE COST	▮	

Safety

FRONTAL CRASH TEST	Good
SIDE CRASH TEST	No government results
AIRBAGS	Dual
ANTI-LOCK BRAKES	4-Wheel (opt)
DAY. RUNNING LIGHTS	None
BELT ADJUSTORS	Standard
BUILT-IN CHILD SEAT	None
PRETENSIONERS	None

General Information

WHERE MADE	U.S./Mexico
YEAR OF PRODUCTION	Fifth
PARKING INDEX	Easy
BUMPERS	Strong
THEFT RATING	Average
TWINS	
GREEN RATING	Good

Specifications

FUEL ECONOMY (cty/hwy)	28/39	Very Good
DRIVING RANGE (miles)	419	Average
SEATING	5	
LENGTH (in.)	171.8	
HEAD/LEG ROOM (in.)	39.6/42.5	Roomy
INTERIOR SPACE (cu. ft.)	91.2	Cramped
CARGO SPACE (cu. ft.)	11.8	Very Small

Specifications may vary.

Prices

Model	Retail	Mkup
Coupe	11,225	5%
Highline Coupe	11,520	8%
Sedan	11,425	6%
Highline Sedan	11,720	8%

Competition

	POOR	GOOD	Pg.
Dodge/Plym. Neon	▮		139
Chevrolet Cavalier		▮	123
Ford Escort	▮		143
Honda Civic	▮		150

Dodge Stratus

Intermediate

Besides new colors and aluminum cast wheels, other changes for 1999 include minor improvements to the suspension, reduced interior noise, and an anti-theft system.

The base model and ES trim level come standard with the 2.0-liter engine with a manual transmission. There is an optional 2.5-liter V6 engine with the AutoStick, a combination stick and automatic, and look into the 2.4 liter engine – it meets Low Emission Vehicle standards. The cab-forward design gives passengers ample interior space. The Stratus scored well in terms of maintenance costs, but a low complaint rating and a poor warranty prevent it from being a top pick.

The Ratings

	POOR GOOD
COMPARATIVE RATING	
FRONTAL CRASH TEST	
SAFETY FEATURES	
FUEL ECONOMY	
PM COST	
REPAIR COST	
WARRANTY	
COMPLAINTS	
INSURANCE COST	

Safety

FRONTAL CRASH TEST	Average
SIDE CRASH TEST	Average
AIRBAGS	Dual (New Design)
ANTI-LOCK BRAKES	4-Wheel (opt)
DAY. RUNNING LIGHTS	None
BELT ADJUSTORS	Standard
BUILT-IN CHILD SEAT	None
PRETENSIONERS	None

General Information

WHERE MADE	U.S.
YEAR OF PRODUCTION	Fifth
PARKING INDEX	Easy
BUMPERS	Weak
THEFT RATING	Average
TWINS	Cirrus, Breeze
GREEN RATING	Average

Specifications

FUEL ECONOMY (cty/hwy)	26/37	Good
DRIVING RANGE (miles)	504	Very Long
SEATING	5	
LENGTH (in.)	186	
HEAD/LEG ROOM (in.)	38.1/42.3	Cramped
INTERIOR SPACE (cu. ft.)	95.5	Average
CARGO SPACE (cu. ft.)	15.7	Large

Specifications may vary.

Prices

Model	Retail	Mkup
Base Sedan	15,140	8%
ES Sedan	18,960	9%

Competition

	POOR GOOD	Pg.
Dodge Stratus		**140**
Buick LeSabre		113
Ford Taurus		145
Oldsmobile Cutlass		192

140

Ford Contour

Called the Mondeo in Europe, the Contour, along with its twin the Mercury Mystique, are the U.S. versions of Ford's "world car,". For 1999, Ford gave it a larger fuel tank, and dropped the child safety seat. No other major changes occurred. Dual airbags are standard, but you'll have to pay extra for ABS.

The spare base GL trim level was dropped, so you can choose between the LX, which comes with more features standard, or the sportier SE. The LX's 2.0-liter engine is adequate, but you may want the SE's much more powerful 2.5-liter V6 that is very quiet and peppy. The Contour performed well on frontal crash tests, excellently on side. A weak warranty hurts an otherwise good car.

The Ratings

	POOR — GOOD
COMPARATIVE RATING	
FRONTAL CRASH TEST	
SAFETY FEATURES	
FUEL ECONOMY	
PM COST	
REPAIR COST	
WARRANTY	
COMPLAINTS	
INSURANCE COST	

Safety

FRONTAL CRASH TEST	Very Good
SIDE CRASH TEST	Very Good
AIRBAGS	Dual (New Design)
ANTI-LOCK BRAKES	4-Wheel (opt)
DAY. RUNNING LIGHTS	None
BELT ADJUSTORS	Standard
BUILT-IN CHILD SEAT	None
PRETENSIONERS	None

General Information

WHERE MADE	U.S./Mexico
YEAR OF PRODUCTION	Fifth
PARKING INDEX	Easy
BUMPERS	Strong
THEFT RATING	Low
TWINS	Mercury Mystique
GREEN RATING	Average

Specifications

FUEL ECONOMY (cty/hwy)	24/34	Good
DRIVING RANGE (miles)	435	Average
SEATING	5	
LENGTH (in.)	184.6	
HEAD/LEG ROOM (in.)	39/42.4	Average
INTERIOR SPACE (cu. ft.)	90.2	Cramped
CARGO SPACE (cu. ft.)	13.9	Average

Specifications may vary.

Prices

Model	Retail	Mkup
LX Sedan	14,460	6%
SE Sedan	15,955	9%
SVT Sedan	22,665	9%

Competition

	POOR — GOOD	Pg.
Ford Contour		**141**
Buick Century		112
Hyundai Sonata		156
Pontiac Grand Prix		200

Ford Crown Victoria

At last, this year the Crown Victoria gets ABS as a standard feature. Also available is Ford's natural gas version of this car which meets Ultra Low Emission Vehicle standards. In spite of its size, it is one of the most environmentally friendly vehicles on the road. After last year's improvements the exterior of the Crown Victoria is more contemporary and the suspension, tires and brakes were improved. Dual airbags are standard, and de-powered. Traction control is also optional. The 4.6-liter V8 is powerful. The base-level model comes with plenty of equipment, but to get more options, you have to move up to the LX. A handling and performance package increases engine hp by 20. An anti-theft system is standard and the car performed excellently on both frontal and side government crash tests.

The Ratings

	POOR ... GOOD
COMPARATIVE RATING	
FRONTAL CRASH TEST	
SAFETY FEATURES	
FUEL ECONOMY	
PM COST	
REPAIR COST	
WARRANTY	
COMPLAINTS	
INSURANCE COST	

Safety

FRONTAL CRASH TEST	Very Good
SIDE CRASH TEST	Very Good
AIRBAGS	Dual (New Design)
ANTI-LOCK BRAKES	4-Wheel
DAY. RUNNING LIGHTS	None
BELT ADJUSTORS	Standard
BUILT-IN CHILD SEAT	None
PRETENSIONERS	None

General Information

WHERE MADE	Canada
YEAR OF PRODUCTION	Eighth
PARKING INDEX	Very Hard
BUMPERS	Strong
THEFT RATING	Low
TWINS	Town Car, Gr. Marquis
GREEN RATING	Average

Specifications

FUEL ECONOMY (cty/hwy)	17/24	Very Poor
DRIVING RANGE (miles)	390	Very Short
SEATING	6	
LENGTH (in.)	212	
HEAD/LEG ROOM (in.)	39.4/42.5	Roomy
INTERIOR SPACE (cu. ft.)	111.4	Very Roomy
CARGO SPACE (cu. ft.)	20.6	Very Large

Specifications may vary.

Prices

Model	Retail	Mkup
Base Sedan	21,905	7%
LX Sedan	23,925	7%

Competition

	POOR ... GOOD	Pg.
Ford Cr. Victoria		**142**
Buick Park Avenue		114
Chevrolet Lumina		124
Nissan Maxima		186

Ford Escort

Not many changes for the Escort this year aside from new colors, and the elimination of the child safety seat. The new ZX2 coupe comes in a base 'Cool' version and a well-equipped 'Hot' version. The sedan and wagon, available in a base LX or uplevel SE, carryover unchanged. Dual airbags are standard, ABS is optional.

The sedan and wagon come standard with a 2-liter, 110 hp engine that is much improved from previous versions. The ZX2 gets a peppier Zetec 2-liter, 130 hp engine. The trunk is roomy, especially with the fold down rear seat. Seating for four is good, tight for three in the back. Merely an average performer on frontal and side crash tests, the Escort is hindered by a weak warranty and high insurance costs.

The Ratings

	POOR GOOD
COMPARATIVE RATING	▓ (3/10)
FRONTAL CRASH TEST	▓ (5/10)
SAFETY FEATURES	▓ (6/10)
FUEL ECONOMY	▓ (8/10)
PM COST	▓ (7/10)
REPAIR COST	▓ (10/10)
WARRANTY	▓ (2/10)
COMPLAINTS	▓ (6/10)
INSURANCE COST	▓ (1/10)

Safety

FRONTAL CRASH TEST	Average
SIDE CRASH TEST	Average
AIRBAGS	Dual (New Design)
ANTI-LOCK BRAKES	4-Wheel (opt)
DAY. RUNNING LIGHTS	None
BELT ADJUSTORS	Standard
BUILT-IN CHILD SEAT	None
PRETENSIONERS	None

General Information

WHERE MADE	Canada
YEAR OF PRODUCTION	Second
PARKING INDEX	Very Easy
BUMPERS	Strong
THEFT RATING	Average
TWINS	Mercury Tracer
GREEN RATING	Average

Specifications

FUEL ECONOMY (cty/hwy)	28/37	Good
DRIVING RANGE (miles)	416	Short
SEATING	5	
LENGTH (in.)	170.4	
HEAD/LEG ROOM (in.)	39/42.5	Average
INTERIOR SPACE (cu. ft.)	87.2	Cramped
CARGO SPACE (cu. ft.)	12.8	Small

Specifications may vary.

Prices

Model	Retail	Mkup
LX Sedan	11,455	6%
SE Sedan	12,935	7%
SE Wagon	14,135	7%
MZX2 Coupe Cool	11,610	6%

Competition

	POOR GOOD	Pg.
Ford Escort	▓ (3/10)	**143**
Chevrolet Cavalier	▓ (3/10)	123
Dodge/Plym. Neon	▓ (2/10)	139
Honda Civic	▓ (3/10)	150

Ford Mustang

The 1999 Mustang gets a slightly new design, new powertrain and better handling. The new engines are more powerful: the 3.8 liter V6 engine now has 190 hp, the 4.6 liter V8 has 260 hp. And take a good look at that 3.8 liter – it meets Low Emission Vehicle requirements. A traction control system helps to prevent wheel spin, and chassis improvements reduce noise and vibration.

Coupes and convertibles are available in base, sporty GT or limited-production Cobra models. All models have dual airbags, but ABS, standard on the other models, will cost extra on base Mustangs. The Mustang has a high theft rate, which is no surprise—it is a highly desirable sports car.

The Ratings

	POOR	GOOD
COMPARATIVE RATING	▪ (4)	
FRONTAL CRASH TEST		▪ (10)
SAFETY FEATURES		▪ (6)
FUEL ECONOMY	▪ (4)	
PM COST	▪ (4)	
REPAIR COST		▪ (7)
WARRANTY	▪ (2)	
COMPLAINTS		▪ (7)
INSURANCE COST	▪ (1)	

Safety

FRONTAL CRASH TEST	Very Good
SIDE CRASH TEST	Average
AIRBAGS	Dual
ANTI-LOCK BRAKES	4-Wheel (opt)
DAY. RUNNING LIGHTS	None
BELT ADJUSTORS	None
BUILT-IN CHILD SEAT	None
PRETENSIONERS	None

General Information

WHERE MADE	U.S./Canada
YEAR OF PRODUCTION	Sixth
PARKING INDEX	Easy
BUMPERS	Strong
THEFT RATING	High
TWINS	
GREEN RATING	Poor

Specifications

FUEL ECONOMY (cty/hwy)	20/29	Poor
DRIVING RANGE (miles)	385	Very Short
SEATING	4	
LENGTH (in.)	183.2	
HEAD/LEG ROOM (in.)	38.1/42.6	Cramped
INTERIOR SPACE (cu. ft.)	93.9	Average
CARGO SPACE (cu. ft.)	10.9	Very Small

Specifications may vary.

Prices

Model	Retail	Mkup
Base Coupe	16,150	8%
GT Coupe	20,150	9%
Base Coupe Convertible	20,650	9%
GT Convertible Coupe	24,150	9%

Competition

	POOR	GOOD	Pg.
Ford Mustang	▪ (4)		144
Acura Integra		▪ (6)	103
Chevrolet Camaro	▪ (3)		122
Pontiac Firebird	▪ (3)		198

Ford Taurus

For 1999, the Taurus gets a few cosmetic changes (new wheels, new consoles) and not much else. This year's model is very spacious inside and oval-shaped headlights and dash give it a fresh, unique look. All come standard with dual airbags, but ABS is optional.

A standard 3-liter V6 engine should provide ample power, although you can opt for the same sized engine with more horses. The SHO comes with many features that are optional on the base models as well as a 3.4-liter V8 which will really make the car move. The Taurus remains a fine choice, despite tough competitors like the best-selling Toyota Camry or the newly redesigned Honda Accord.

The Ratings

	POOR	GOOD
COMPARATIVE RATING		
FRONTAL CRASH TEST		
SAFETY FEATURES		
FUEL ECONOMY		
PM COST		
REPAIR COST		
WARRANTY		
COMPLAINTS		
INSURANCE COST		

Safety

FRONTAL CRASH TEST	Very Good
SIDE CRASH TEST	Good
AIRBAGS	Dual (New Design)
ANTI-LOCK BRAKES	4-Wheel (opt)
DAY. RUNNING LIGHTS	None
BELT ADJUSTORS	Standard
BUILT-IN CHILD SEAT	Optional(Wagon)
PRETENSIONERS	None

General Information

WHERE MADE	U.S./Canada
YEAR OF PRODUCTION	Fourth
PARKING INDEX	Average
BUMPERS	Strong
THEFT RATING	Low
TWINS	Mercury Sable
GREEN RATING	Poor

Specifications

FUEL ECONOMY (cty/hwy)	20/28	Poor
DRIVING RANGE (miles)	384	Very Short
SEATING	5	
LENGTH (in.)	197.5	
HEAD/LEG ROOM (in.)	39.2/42.2	Average
INTERIOR SPACE (cu. ft.)	101.5	Roomy
CARGO SPACE (cu. ft.)	15.8	Large

Specifications may vary.

Prices

Model	Retail	Mkup
LX Sedan	17,445	8%
SE Sedan	18,445	9%
SHO Sedan	29,000	10%
SE Wagon	19,445	9%

Competition

	POOR	GOOD	Pg.
Ford Taurus			**145**
Buick LeSabre			113
Subaru Legacy			208
Toyota Camry			213

The Windstar finally gets a fourth, sliding door, bringing it up to speed with other minivans in its class. The Windstar runs on either a 3.0 liter or a 3.8 liter V6. The 3.0 meets Low Emission Vehicle standards, the 3.8 meets Ultra Low Emission Vehicle standard for a surprisingly clean run.

For safety, Ford offers head and chest side impact airbags this year. The Windstar offers great optional built-in child restraints; dual airbags and 4-wheel ABS are both standard. The interior is very roomy. The Windstar continues to perform phenomenally on frontal government crash tests, but a high number of complaints casts doubt on its reliability.

The Ratings

	POOR — GOOD
COMPARATIVE RATING	▩ (below middle)
FRONTAL CRASH TEST	▩ (near good)
SAFETY FEATURES	▩ (good side)
FUEL ECONOMY	▩ (poor)
PM COST	▩ (good side)
REPAIR COST	▩ (below middle)
WARRANTY	▩ (poor)
COMPLAINTS	▩ (poor)
INSURANCE COST	▩ (good side)

Safety

FRONTAL CRASH TEST	Very Good
SIDE CRASH TEST	No government results
AIRBAGS	Dual (New Design)
ANTI-LOCK BRAKES	4-Wheel
DAY. RUNNING LIGHTS	None
BELT ADJUSTORS	Standard
BUILT-IN CHILD SEAT	Optional
PRETENSIONERS	None

General Information

WHERE MADE	U.S./Canada
YEAR OF PRODUCTION	Fifth
PARKING INDEX	Very Hard
BUMPERS	Strong
THEFT RATING	Very Low
TWINS	
GREEN RATING	Very Poor

Specifications

FUEL ECONOMY (cty/hwy)	17/23	Very Poor
DRIVING RANGE (miles)	520	Very Long
SEATING	7	
LENGTH (in.)	200.9	
HEAD/LEG ROOM (in.)	39.3/40.7	Vry. Cramped
INTERIOR SPACE (cu. ft.)		
CARGO SPACE (cu. ft.)	145.7	Very Large

Specifications may vary.

Prices

Model	Retail	Mkup
3.0L Wagon 3dr	20,220	7%
LX Wagon 3dr	23,660	10%
SE Wagon	27,495	10%
SEL Wagon	30,415	10%

Competition

	POOR — GOOD	Pg.
Ford Windstar	▩ (below middle)	146
Chrysler T&C	▩ (poor)	135
Dodge Caravan	▩ (poor)	137
Plymouth Voyager	▩ (poor)	196

GM EV1

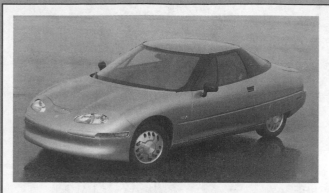

Marketed through Saturn, the EV1 is leading the way for zero emission vehicles. The EV1 is an actual car, not a glorified golf cart, and comes standard with dual airbags, traction control, ABS, daytime running lights and self-sealing tires with a tire pressure monitoring system. You'll find the EV1 available for lease in southern California and Arizona.

The EV1 runs on lead-acid batteries, which take up to 8 hours to recharge for a driving range of 70-90 miles. Acceleration is good but drains the juice faster. The typical engine purr is replaced by a high pitched whining during acceleration. Best for people with short commutes or quick trips, the EV1 continues to be a great start to a promising technology.

The Ratings

	POOR	GOOD
COMPARATIVE RATING		
FRONTAL CRASH TEST	■	
SAFETY FEATURES		■
FUEL ECONOMY		
PM COST		
REPAIR COST		
WARRANTY	■	
COMPLAINTS	■	
INSURANCE COST		

Safety

FRONTAL CRASH TEST	Poor
SIDE CRASH TEST	No government results
AIRBAGS	Dual
ANTI-LOCK BRAKES	4-Wheel
DAY. RUNNING LIGHTS	Standard
BELT ADJUSTORS	Standard
BUILT-IN CHILD SEAT	None
PRETENSIONERS	None

General Information

WHERE MADE	U.S.
YEAR OF PRODUCTION	Third
PARKING INDEX	Very Easy
BUMPERS	Weak
THEFT RATING	
TWINS	
GREEN RATING	Very Good

Specifications

FUEL ECONOMY (cty/hwy)	3.3/4.0[1]	
DRIVING RANGE (miles)	50-90	Very Short
SEATING	2	
LENGTH (in.)	169.7	
HEAD/LEG ROOM (in.)	37.6/42.6	Cramped
INTERIOR SPACE (cu. ft.)	50.4	Vry. Cramped
CARGO SPACE (cu. ft.)	9.7	Very Small

Specifications may vary.

Prices

Model	Retail	Mkup
EV1	33,995	
Monthly lease payments range		
from $399 to $549		

Competition

	POOR	GOOD	Pg.
GM EV1			**147**
Chevrolet Metro	■		126
Ford Escort		■	143
Hyundai Accent	■		154

[1]Values given in miles per kilowatt hour.

This year the Safari gets a few color changes inside and out, and the optional OnStar system. Like its twin, the Astro, the Safari is a basic van used primarily for hauling and towing. It offers one of the largest cargo and towing capacities in the van market. Standard features include dual airbags, 4-wheel ABS and daytime running lamps. A child safety seat is optional and highly recommended.

The standard 4.3-liter, V6 engine with automatic transmission provides plenty of power, enough to tow 5,500 pounds, but sloppy handling. Fuel economy is fairly dismal, as well. You can choose between rear-wheel drive or all-wheel drive. The seats are comfortable enough, but make sure there is enough leg room.

The Ratings

	POOR — GOOD
COMPARATIVE RATING	▮
FRONTAL CRASH TEST	▮
SAFETY FEATURES	▮
FUEL ECONOMY	▮
PM COST	▮
REPAIR COST	▮
WARRANTY	▮
COMPLAINTS	▮
INSURANCE COST	▮

Safety

FRONTAL CRASH TEST	Poor
SIDE CRASH TEST	No government results
AIRBAGS	Dual
ANTI-LOCK BRAKES	4-Wheel
DAY. RUNNING LIGHTS	Standard
BELT ADJUSTORS	Standard
BUILT-IN CHILD SEAT	Optional(2)
PRETENSIONERS	None

General Information

WHERE MADE	U.S.
YEAR OF PRODUCTION	Fifteenth
PARKING INDEX	Hard
BUMPERS	Strong
THEFT RATING	Average
TWINS	Chevrolet Astro
GREEN RATING	Very Poor

Specifications

FUEL ECONOMY (cty/hwy)	16/21	Very Poor
DRIVING RANGE (miles)	463	Long
SEATING	8	
LENGTH (in.)	189.8	
HEAD/LEG ROOM (in.)	39.2/41.6	Cramped
INTERIOR SPACE (cu. ft.)		
CARGO SPACE (cu. ft.)	170.4	Very Large

Specifications may vary.

Prices

Model	Retail	Mkup
Cargo Van SL 2wd, 111"wb	19,404	10%
Cargo Van, SL awd, 111" wb	21,804	10%
Passenger Van 2wd, 111" wb	20,238	9%
Passenger Van awd 111"wb	22,538	9%

Competition

	POOR — GOOD	Pg.
GMC Safari	▮	148
Chevrolet Astro	▮	121
Ford Windstar	▮	146
Pontiac Montana	▮	201

Honda Accord

All-new last year, the 1999 Accord is a carry-over from '98. Its latest makeover was its most dramatic in its 22 year history. At that time, changes were made to structure, engine, suspension, interior, and exterior. The Accord now has more interior room and trunk space, a smoother transmission, and a more distinctively styled coupe. More importantly, the base model's price remains unchanged, there are minor increases for mid-levels, and the top trim level *decreased* in price by about $900. Dual airbags are standard, ABS is optional.

The new standard engine on the base DX is a 2.3-liter engine which cranks out 135 hp. The LX and EX get the peppier version of the same engine with 150 hp. But, many will want the optional VTEC V6 engine.

The Ratings

	POOR — GOOD
COMPARATIVE RATING	▮ (middle)
FRONTAL CRASH TEST	▮ (good)
SAFETY FEATURES	▮ (mid)
FUEL ECONOMY	▮ (good)
PM COST	▮ (poor-mid)
REPAIR COST	▮ (mid)
WARRANTY	▮ (poor)
COMPLAINTS	▮ (mid)
INSURANCE COST	▮ (good)

Safety

FRONTAL CRASH TEST	Good (2dr & 4dr)
SIDE CRASH TEST	Good
AIRBAGS	Dual
ANTI-LOCK BRAKES	4-Wheel (opt)
DAY. RUNNING LIGHTS	None
BELT ADJUSTORS	Standard
BUILT-IN CHILD SEAT	None
PRETENSIONERS	None

General Information

WHERE MADE	U.S.
YEAR OF PRODUCTION	Second
PARKING INDEX	Easy
BUMPERS	Strong
THEFT RATING	Very High
TWINS	
GREEN RATING	Average

Specifications

FUEL ECONOMY (cty/hwy)	25/31	Good
DRIVING RANGE (miles)	479	Very Long
SEATING	5	
LENGTH (in.)	186.8	
HEAD/LEG ROOM (in.)	39.7/42.6	Roomy
INTERIOR SPACE (cu. ft.)	92.7	Cramped
CARGO SPACE (cu. ft.)	13.6	Average

Specifications may vary.

Prices

Model	Retail	Mkup
DX Sedan Manual	15,100	12%
LX Coupe Manual	18,290	12%
LX Coupe V6	21,550	12%
LX Sedan V6	21,550	12%

Competition

	POOR — GOOD	Pg.
Honda Accord	▮ (mid)	**149**
Chevrolet Malibu	▮ (poor-mid)	125
Ford Taurus	▮ (good)	145
Toyota Camry	▮ (mid)	213

The Ratings

	POOR	GOOD
COMPARATIVE RATING	■	
FRONTAL CRASH TEST		■
SAFETY FEATURES		■
FUEL ECONOMY		■
PM COST	■	
REPAIR COST		■
WARRANTY	■	
COMPLAINTS		■
INSURANCE COST	■	

This year Civics get new bumpers, but not much else. As before, you can buy a coupe with trim levels DX, HX, and EX; a sedan with trim levels DX, LX and EX; or a hatchback with trim levels, CX or DX. Dual airbags are standard and ABS is standard on the EX sedan, but remains optional on all other models.

The base engine is a 1.6-liter 4-cylinder which delivers 106 hp, and you can upgrade to more powerful engines with 115 or 127 hp on higher trim levels. Also available is a 1.6 liter, 4 cylinder compressed natural gas engine that meets ULEV standards. The ride is characterized by responsive handling and a smooth suspension. The Civic performed excellently in frontal crash tests, but only average in side. Against competitors like Cavalier, Escort and Neon, the Civic does very well.

Safety

FRONTAL CRASH TEST	2dr. Vry. Gd./4dr. Good
SIDE CRASH TEST	Average
AIRBAGS	Dual
ANTI-LOCK BRAKES	4-Wheel (opt)
DAY. RUNNING LIGHTS	None
BELT ADJUSTORS	Standard
BUILT-IN CHILD SEAT	None
PRETENSIONERS	None

General Information

WHERE MADE	U.S./Canada/Japan
YEAR OF PRODUCTION	Fourth
PARKING INDEX	Very Easy
BUMPERS	Strong
THEFT RATING	Average
TWINS	
GREEN RATING	Very Good

Specifications

FUEL ECONOMY (cty/hwy)	32/37	Very Good
DRIVING RANGE (miles)	411	Short
SEATING	5	
LENGTH (in.)	175.1	
HEAD/LEG ROOM (in.)	38.8/42.7	Average
INTERIOR SPACE (cu. ft.)	85.2	Vry. Cramped
CARGO SPACE (cu. ft.)	11.9	Very Small

Specifications may vary.

Prices

Model	Retail	Mkup
CX Hatchback Coupe Manual	10,650	6%
DX Coupe Manual	12,580	10%
DX Sedan Manual	12,735	10%
LX Sedan Manual	14,750	12%

Competition

	POOR	GOOD	Pg.
Honda Civic	■		150
Chevrolet Cavalier		■	123
Dodge/Plym. Neon	■		139
Ford Escort		■	143

Honda EV Plus

Along with GM's EV1, Honda's EV Plus is making strides in greening the U.S. market. Available only for lease, the EV Plus is being marketed through a few dealers in Los Angeles and Sacramento, CA. It comes with power everything and a keyless entry and security system. Dual airbags and ABS are standard.

The nickel-metal hydride batteries will allow you an estimated 100 miles before recharging. And recharging will take about 8 hours. Seating is generous with room for four. The interior is more attractively designed than the sparse EV1. One nice feature is the climate control system, which you can turn on and off by remote before you get in. Like the EV1, the EV Plus is another promising look at a futuristic technology.

The Ratings

	POOR				GOOD	
COMPARATIVE RATING*						
FRONTAL CRASH TEST						
SAFETY FEATURES		■				
FUEL ECONOMY						
PM COST						
REPAIR COST						
WARRANTY	■					
COMPLAINTS						
INSURANCE COST						

Safety

FRONTAL CRASH TEST	No government results
SIDE CRASH TEST	No government results
AIRBAGS	Dual
ANTI-LOCK BRAKES	4-Wheel
DAY. RUNNING LIGHTS	None
BELT ADJUSTORS	None
BUILT-IN CHILD SEAT	None
PRETENSIONERS	None

General Information

WHERE MADE	Japan
YEAR OF PRODUCTION	Second
PARKING INDEX	Very Easy
BUMPERS	
THEFT RATING	
TWINS	
GREEN RATING	Very Good

Specifications

FUEL ECONOMY (cty/hwy)	2.0/2.0[1]	
DRIVING RANGE (miles)		
SEATING	4	
LENGTH (in.)	159.3	
HEAD/LEG ROOM (in.)	39.6/41.9 Average	
INTERIOR SPACE (cu. ft.)	90	Cramped
CARGO SPACE (cu. ft.)	12	Small

Specifications may vary.

Prices

Model	Retail	Mkup
Only available for lease.	53,999	
Monthly payment is about $499.		

Competition

	POOR			GOOD		Pg.
Honda EV Plus						151
Chevrolet Metro		■				126
Ford Escort			■			143
GM EV1						147

*Due to the importance of crash tests, cars with no results as of publication date cannot be given an overall rating.
[1]Values given in miles per kilowatt hour.

This year the Odyssey gets a major overhaul. The wheelbase has been extended and it has two sliding doors (these are power doors on the EX). Dual airbags and ABS are standard. Traction control is available on the EX. Interior size has grown—this is no longer a tiny minivan.

The Odyssey gets a new 3.5 liter, 210 hp engine for 1999. That's one giant upgrade from years past, and the most powerful engine in its class. With these upgrades Honda is looking challenge Chrysler's minivan line, and with its new features, has a good chance at beating the competition.

The Ratings

	POOR	GOOD
COMPARATIVE RATING*		
FRONTAL CRASH TEST		
SAFETY FEATURES		
FUEL ECONOMY		
PM COST		
REPAIR COST		
WARRANTY		
COMPLAINTS		
INSURANCE COST		

Safety

FRONTAL CRASH TEST	No government results
SIDE CRASH TEST	No government results
AIRBAGS	Dual
ANTI-LOCK BRAKES	4-Wheel
DAY. RUNNING LIGHTS	None
BELT ADJUSTORS	Standard
BUILT-IN CHILD SEAT	None
PRETENSIONERS	None

General Information

WHERE MADE	Japan
YEAR OF PRODUCTION	First
PARKING INDEX	Hard
BUMPERS	Strong
THEFT RATING	Low
TWINS	
GREEN RATING	Poor

Specifications

FUEL ECONOMY (cty/hwy)	18/26	Poor
DRIVING RANGE (miles)	440	Average
SEATING	7	
LENGTH (in.)	201.2	
HEAD/LEG ROOM (in.)	41.2/41	Roomy
INTERIOR SPACE (cu. ft.)		
CARGO SPACE (cu. ft.)	163.3	Very Large

Specifications may vary.

Prices

Model	Retail	Mkup
LX 7 Pass. 5 dr	23,810	12%
LX 6 Pass. 5dr	24,220	12%
EX 6 Pass. 5dr	25,800	12%

Competition

	POOR	GOOD	Pg.
Honda Odyssey			**152**
Chrysler T&C			135
Dodge Caravan			137
Plymouth Voyager			196

*Due to the importance of crash tests, cars with no results as of publication date cannot be given an overall rating.

Honda Prelude

This year the Prelude gets a slightly stronger engine with the addition of 5 horses to bring it to 200 hp. The standard engine for both the base model and the SH is a 2.2-liter 4-cylinder engine, which is plenty to power this compact car. A mix between luxury and performance, the Prelude was redesigned two years ago, and has not changed much since. The redesign included more interior room, upgrades to the engines, and new exterior styling. Dual airbags are standard and ABS is optional.

The ride is firm, yet comfortable and provide the driver and passengers with the feel of a sports car. Controls are conventional and a larger trunk will make road trips easier. Test driving the Prelude is a must for sports car enthusiasts. The government still has not crash tested the Prelude and is not scheduled to do so this year.

The Ratings

	POOR — GOOD
COMPARATIVE RATING*	(blank)
FRONTAL CRASH TEST	(blank)
SAFETY FEATURES	▓ (7th)
FUEL ECONOMY	▓ (4th)
PM COST	▓ (3rd)
REPAIR COST	▓ (5th)
WARRANTY	▓ (2nd)
COMPLAINTS	▓ (9th)
INSURANCE COST	▓ (2nd)

Safety

FRONTAL CRASH TEST	No government results
SIDE CRASH TEST	No government results
AIRBAGS	Dual
ANTI-LOCK BRAKES	4-Wheel
DAY. RUNNING LIGHTS	None
BELT ADJUSTORS	Standard
BUILT-IN CHILD SEAT	None
PRETENSIONERS	None

General Information

WHERE MADE	Japan
YEAR OF PRODUCTION	Second
PARKING INDEX	Easy
BUMPERS	Strong
THEFT RATING	
TWINS	
GREEN RATING	Poor

Specifications

FUEL ECONOMY (cty/hwy)	22/27	Poor
DRIVING RANGE (miles)	390	Very Short
SEATING	4	
LENGTH (in.)	178	
HEAD/LEG ROOM (in.)	37.9/43	Cramped
INTERIOR SPACE (cu. ft.)	78.4	Vry. Cramped
CARGO SPACE (cu. ft.)	8.7	Very Small

Specifications may vary.

Prices

Model	Retail	Mkup
Base Coupe Manual	23,300	11%
Base Coupe Automatic	24,300	11%
Type SH Coupe Manual	25,800	11%

Competition

	POOR — GOOD	Pg.
Honda Prelude	(blank)	**153**
Acura Integra	▓ (5th)	103
Chevrolet Camaro	▓ (3rd)	122
Mitsubishi Eclipse	▓ (2nd)	182

*Due to the importance of crash tests, cars with no results as of publication date cannot be given an overall rating.

Hyundai Accent

There are no changes for the Accent this year. It's available in three trim levels: Accent L three door, GS three door hatchback, and GL four door sedan. ABS is optional only on the GS and GL. Dual airbags are standard on all models, as are side window defoggers, and seat belt height adjusters,

The 1.5-liter 4-cylinder engine that comes on all Accents is adequate for this light car and is fuel efficient. Although front seat occupants will be comfortable, passengers in the rear will feel cramped; choose the 4-door for more room. The Accent is not quite as fuel efficient or roomy as the Geo Metro and Suzuki Swift. The Accent is a decent subcompact which offers a little bit of everything.

The Ratings

	POOR ... GOOD
COMPARATIVE RATING	(rated poor side)
FRONTAL CRASH TEST	(rated mid-good)
SAFETY FEATURES	(rated middle)
FUEL ECONOMY	(rated good)
PM COST	(rated very good)
REPAIR COST	(rated very good)
WARRANTY	(rated middle)
COMPLAINTS	(rated poor-mid)
INSURANCE COST	(rated very poor)

Safety

FRONTAL CRASH TEST	Average
SIDE CRASH TEST	No government results
AIRBAGS	Dual
ANTI-LOCK BRAKES	4-Wheel (opt)
DAY. RUNNING LIGHTS	None
BELT ADJUSTORS	Standard
BUILT-IN CHILD SEAT	None
PRETENSIONERS	None

General Information

WHERE MADE	Korea
YEAR OF PRODUCTION	Fifth
PARKING INDEX	Very Easy
BUMPERS	Strong
THEFT RATING	Average
TWINS	
GREEN RATING	Average

Specifications

FUEL ECONOMY (cty/hwy)	28/37	Good
DRIVING RANGE (miles)	387	Very Short
SEATING	5	
LENGTH (in.)	162.1	
HEAD/LEG ROOM (in.)	38.7/42.6	Average
INTERIOR SPACE (cu. ft.)	71.9	Vry. Cramped
CARGO SPACE (cu. ft.)	10.7	Very Small

Specifications may vary.

Prices

Model	Retail	Mkup
Hatchback L 3dr Manual	9,099	5%
Hatchback GS 3dr Manual	9,899	7%
GL Sedan Manual	10,299	7%
GL Sedan Automatic	11,054	7%

Competition

	POOR ... GOOD	Pg.
Hyundai Accent	(rated poor side)	**154**
Chevrolet Metro	(rated poor-mid)	126
Ford Escort	(rated middle)	143
Kia Sephia	(rated poor side)	162

This year, the Elantra gets a new look, restyled from front to rear including a new grille, bumpers, and hood. The new 2.0 liter engine gives 140 hp, and it's the same engine from the Tiburon. You will find standard dual airbags. Unfortunately, ABS is only an option on the GLS, and not available on the base model.

The new engine is a 2.0-liter 4 cylinder, more powerful than the previous engine. The front seats are comfortable, but adults will feel cramped in the back. Ride and comfort are good in this small car and, with refined insulation, it should be relatively quiet. Available in both a sedan and wagon, the Elantra comes with plenty options to choose from. Of course, low prices are what you expect from Hyundai and the Elantra is no exception.

The Ratings

	POOR ··· GOOD
COMPARATIVE RATING*	(no rating)
FRONTAL CRASH TEST	(no rating)
SAFETY FEATURES	▮ (mid)
FUEL ECONOMY	▮ (mid-good)
PM COST	▮ (good)
REPAIR COST	▮ (good)
WARRANTY	▮ (below mid)
COMPLAINTS	▮ (poor)
INSURANCE COST	▮ (poor)

Safety

FRONTAL CRASH TEST	No government results
SIDE CRASH TEST	No government results
AIRBAGS	Dual
ANTI-LOCK BRAKES	4-Wheel (opt)
DAY. RUNNING LIGHTS	None
BELT ADJUSTORS	Standard
BUILT-IN CHILD SEAT	None
PRETENSIONERS	Standard

General Information

WHERE MADE	Korea
YEAR OF PRODUCTION	Fourth
PARKING INDEX	Very Easy
BUMPERS	Strong
THEFT RATING	
TWINS	
GREEN RATING	Average

Specifications

FUEL ECONOMY (cty/hwy)	24/33	Good
DRIVING RANGE (miles)	413	Short
SEATING	5	
LENGTH (in.)	174	
HEAD/LEG ROOM (in.)	38.6/43.2	Roomy
INTERIOR SPACE (cu. ft.)	93	Average
CARGO SPACE (cu. ft.)	11.4	Very Small

Specifications may vary.

Prices

Model	Retail	Mkup
Sedan Manual	11,499	8%
Sedan Automatic	12,299	8%
Wagon Manual	12,399	8%
Wagon Automatic	13,199	8%

Competition

	POOR ··· GOOD	Pg.
Hyundai Elantra	(no rating)	155
Chevrolet Cavalier	▮ (mid)	123
Dodge/Plym. Neon	▮ (below mid)	139
Subaru Impreza	▮ (mid)	207

*Due to the importance of crash tests, cars with no results as of publication date cannot be given an overall rating.

Hyundai Sonata

This year the Sonata has a new body, new engines, new transmissions, and new suspension. You can chose from a 2.4 liter 4 cylinder engine, or an aluminum 2.5 liter V6. The new engines, thicker glass, and a redesigned cabin all contribute to a quieter ride in the Sonata.

The all new Sonata is also much safer than models from past years. Side and front airbags are standard, with a front seat passenger detection system for both. If a small child or infant is in the seat, the bag will not deploy. Front belt pretensioners, and adjustable rear headrests are also standard.

The Ratings

	POOR GOOD
COMPARATIVE RATING	
FRONTAL CRASH TEST	
SAFETY FEATURES	
FUEL ECONOMY	
PM COST	
REPAIR COST	
WARRANTY	
COMPLAINTS	
INSURANCE COST	

Safety

FRONTAL CRASH TEST	Average
SIDE CRASH TEST	Very Poor
AIRBAGS	Dual & Side
ANTI-LOCK BRAKES	4-Wheel (opt)
DAY. RUNNING LIGHTS	None
BELT ADJUSTORS	Standard
BUILT-IN CHILD SEAT	None
PRETENSIONERS	Standard

General Information

WHERE MADE	Korea
YEAR OF PRODUCTION	First
PARKING INDEX	Easy
BUMPERS	Strong
THEFT RATING	Average
TWINS	
GREEN RATING	Poor

Specifications

FUEL ECONOMY (cty/hwy)	21/30	Average
DRIVING RANGE (miles)	439	Average
SEATING	5	
LENGTH (in.)	185	
HEAD/LEG ROOM (in.)	38.5/43.3	Roomy
INTERIOR SPACE (cu. ft.)	101.3	Roomy
CARGO SPACE (cu. ft.)	13.2	Small

Specifications may vary.

Prices

Model	Retail	Mkup
Sedan Manual	14,749	9%
Sedan Automatic	15,549	8%
GL Sedan	16,349	10%
GL V6	17,349	10%

Competition

	POOR GOOD	Pg.
Hyundai Sonata		156
Buick Regal		115
Ford Contour		141
Pontiac Grand Prix		200

Hyundai Tiburon

Hyundai's sportiest car continues in 1999 with no changes. The Tiburon closely resembles the exterior styling of the Toyota Celica and the interior designs of the Mitsubishi Eclipse and Ford Probe. This is no surprise since the Tiburon is Hyundai's challenge to these more established coupes like the Celica. Dual airbags and 4-wheel ABS are standard features.

Powering this all-new coupe is a 2.0-liter 4 cylinder engine that produces 140 horsepower. Surprising for a Hyundai, the suspension was tuned by engineers at Porsche. Expect the ride to be good on smooth roads; get onto something bumpy and you won't have much fun. The controls are well placed and easy to read. Pricewise, the Tiburon is an attractive alternative to competitors.

The Ratings

	POOR → GOOD
COMPARATIVE RATING*	(no rating)
FRONTAL CRASH TEST	(no rating)
SAFETY FEATURES	▮ (low)
FUEL ECONOMY	▮ (mid)
PM COST	▮ (high/good)
REPAIR COST	▮ (high/good)
WARRANTY	▮ (mid)
COMPLAINTS	▮ (low)
INSURANCE COST	▮ (mid)

Safety

FRONTAL CRASH TEST	No government results
SIDE CRASH TEST	No government results
AIRBAGS	Dual
ANTI-LOCK BRAKES	4-Wheel (opt)
DAY. RUNNING LIGHTS	None
BELT ADJUSTORS	Standard
BUILT-IN CHILD SEAT	None
PRETENSIONERS	None

General Information

WHERE MADE	Korea
YEAR OF PRODUCTION	Third
PARKING INDEX	Very Easy
BUMPERS	Strong
THEFT RATING	
TWINS	
GREEN RATING	Average

Specifications

FUEL ECONOMY (cty/hwy)	22/31	Average
DRIVING RANGE (miles)	384	Very Short
SEATING	5	
LENGTH (in.)	170.9	
HEAD/LEG ROOM (in.)	38/43.1	Average
INTERIOR SPACE (cu. ft.)	80	Vry. Cramped
CARGO SPACE (cu. ft.)	12.8	Small

Specifications may vary.

Prices

Model	Retail	Mkup
Hatchback Coupe Manual	13,599	9%
Hatchback Coupe Automatic	14,399	9%
MFX Hatchback Coupe Manual	14,899	11%
MFX Hatchback Coupe Auto.	15,699	11%

Competition

	POOR → GOOD	Pg.
Hyundai Tiburon	(no rating)	**157**
Acura Integra	▮ (mid)	103
Ford Mustang	▮ (mid-low)	144
Chevrolet Camaro	▮ (low)	122

*Due to the importance of crash tests, cars with no results as of publication date cannot be given an overall rating.

Infiniti G20

All new for this year, Infiniti brings back the G20 that ran from 91 through 96. An all aluminum 140 hp 2.0 liter 4 cylinder engine powers both the base and a touring model known as the G20t. A multi-link suspension system and advanced steering give the G20 great handling. You choose between a 4-speed automatic and a 5-speed manual transmission.

Dual and side airbags come standard for front occupants. ABS is also a standard feature. The G20t gives you a limited slip differential, fog lights, automatic temperature control. This new model has yet to be crash tested.

The Ratings

	POOR → GOOD
COMPARATIVE RATING*	(no rating)
FRONTAL CRASH TEST	(no rating)
SAFETY FEATURES	8/10
FUEL ECONOMY	6/10
PM COST	7/10
REPAIR COST	3/10
WARRANTY	9/10
COMPLAINTS	4/10
INSURANCE COST	4/10

Safety

FRONTAL CRASH TEST	No government results
SIDE CRASH TEST	No government results
AIRBAGS	Dual & Side
ANTI-LOCK BRAKES	4-Wheel
DAY. RUNNING LIGHTS	None
BELT ADJUSTORS	Standard
BUILT-IN CHILD SEAT	None
PRETENSIONERS	Standard

General Information

WHERE MADE	Japan
YEAR OF PRODUCTION	First
PARKING INDEX	Easy
BUMPERS	
THEFT RATING	
TWINS	
GREEN RATING	Poor

Specifications

FUEL ECONOMY (cty/hwy)	23/31	Average
DRIVING RANGE (miles)	429	Average
SEATING	5	
LENGTH (in.)	177.5	
HEAD/LEG ROOM (in.)	40/41.5	Average
INTERIOR SPACE (cu. ft.)	91	Cramped
CARGO SPACE (cu. ft.)	13.5	Small

Specifications may vary.

Prices

Model	Retail	Mkup
Standard Sedan Manual	20,995	9%
Standard Sedan Automatic	21,795	9%
Touring Sedan Manual	22,495	10%
Touring Sedan Automatic	23,295	10%

Competition

	POOR → GOOD	Pg.
Infiniti G20	(no rating)	**158**
Audi A4	9/10	106
Oldsmobile Intrigue	3/10	193
Toyota Avalon	7/10	212

*Due to the importance of crash tests, cars with no results as of publication date cannot be given an overall rating.

Infiniti I30

Essentially an upscale Nissan Maxima, the I30 has minor changes for 1999. A traction control system is a new option that enhances driver control. Dual and side airbags, as well as 4-wheel ABS are standard.

Like the Maxima, the I30 is powered by a 3.0-liter V6 engine, which is powerful enough to please most people. Fuel economy for this heavy car will be slightly lower than the Maxima, but still competitive with other mid-sized luxury cars. With a very rigid body shell, driver and passengers will move in comfort; the controls and gauges are easy to read and use. If you can live without the name-plate, consider a fully-loaded Maxima and save a couple thousand dollars.

The Ratings

	POOR — GOOD
COMPARATIVE RATING	
FRONTAL CRASH TEST	
SAFETY FEATURES	
FUEL ECONOMY	
PM COST	
REPAIR COST	
WARRANTY	
COMPLAINTS	
INSURANCE COST	

Safety

FRONTAL CRASH TEST	Good
SIDE CRASH TEST	Good
AIRBAGS	Dual & Side
ANTI-LOCK BRAKES	4-Wheel
DAY. RUNNING LIGHTS	None
BELT ADJUSTORS	Standard
BUILT-IN CHILD SEAT	None
PRETENSIONERS	Standard

General Information

WHERE MADE	Japan
YEAR OF PRODUCTION	Fourth
PARKING INDEX	Easy
BUMPERS	Strong
THEFT RATING	High
TWINS	Nissan Maxima
GREEN RATING	Poor

Specifications

FUEL ECONOMY (cty/hwy)	21/26	Poor
DRIVING RANGE (miles)	435	Average
SEATING	5	
LENGTH (in.)	189.6	
HEAD/LEG ROOM (in.)	40.1/43.9	Very Roomy
INTERIOR SPACE (cu. ft.)	99.6	Roomy
CARGO SPACE (cu. ft.)	14.1	Average

Specifications may vary.

Prices

Model	Retail	Mkup
Standard Sedan Automatic	28,900	10%
Touring Sedan Manual	31,200	11%
Touring Sedan Automatic	32,200	11%

Competition

	POOR — GOOD	Pg.
Infiniti I30		159
Audi A4		106
Buick Park Avenue		114
Lexus ES300		163

Infiniti's flagship sedan, the Q45, debuted in 1989 with a very aggressive ad campaign and an equally aggressively styled car. Since then, the Q45 has evolved into a quiet, luxury sedan. After a revision in '98, the Q45 enters this year with little change. New headlight styling and a new grille are the most noticeable changes. Performance is still its strong point. Dual airbags, 4-wheel ABS, pretensioners, and side airbags lead the list of safety features.

At nearly 3,900 pounds, Infiniti needed to find an engine powerful enough to move the Q45, so they chose a 4.1 liter V8 which produces over 260 horsepower. Plushness and comfort are what you would expect from the top of the luxury line and ride will be as smooth as silk, and not bouncy or floaty like other large cars.

The Ratings

	POOR — GOOD
COMPARATIVE RATING*	
FRONTAL CRASH TEST	
SAFETY FEATURES	▮ (6)
FUEL ECONOMY	▮ (2)
PM COST	▮ (6)
REPAIR COST	▮ (1)
WARRANTY	▮ (8)
COMPLAINTS	▮ (7)
INSURANCE COST	▮ (7)

Safety

FRONTAL CRASH TEST	No government results
SIDE CRASH TEST	No government results
AIRBAGS	Dual & Side
ANTI-LOCK BRAKES	4-Wheel
DAY. RUNNING LIGHTS	None
BELT ADJUSTORS	Standard
BUILT-IN CHILD SEAT	None
PRETENSIONERS	Standard

General Information

WHERE MADE	Japan
YEAR OF PRODUCTION	Third
PARKING INDEX	Average
BUMPERS	Strong
THEFT RATING	
TWINS	
GREEN RATING	Very Poor

Specifications

FUEL ECONOMY (cty/hwy)	17/24	Very Poor
DRIVING RANGE (miles)	439	Average
SEATING	5	
LENGTH (in.)	199.6	
HEAD/LEG ROOM (in.)	37.6/43.6	Average
INTERIOR SPACE (cu. ft.)	97.4	Average
CARGO SPACE (cu. ft.)	12.6	Small

Specifications may vary.

Prices**

Model	Retail	Mkup
Luxury Performance Sedan	47,900	10%
Q45t Luxury Performance Sdn.	49,900	10%

Competition

	POOR — GOOD	Pg.
Infiniti Q45		160
Cadillac DeVille	▮ (7)	118
Lexus ES300	▮ (8)	163
Merc.-Benz C-Class	▮ (6)	173

*Due to the importance of crash tests, cars with no results as of publication date cannot be given an overall rating.

Isuzu Oasis

The Oasis, is unchanged for 1999 and designed to be more like a car than a minivan. With a wide stance and low ground clearance, the Oasis drives much like a car and also has conventional doors instead of a sliding door like the rest of its minivan competition. Dual airbags and ABS are standard.

The power comes from a 2.3-liter 4-cylinder engine. The middle seat in the Oasis does not come out and the rear seat cleverly folds into the floor, but not quite flush, making the loading surface uneven. A low number of complaints makes the Oasis a good choice, if you're looking for something smaller than the typical minivan.

The Ratings

	POOR	GOOD
COMPARATIVE RATING*		
FRONTAL CRASH TEST		
SAFETY FEATURES		
FUEL ECONOMY		
PM COST		
REPAIR COST		
WARRANTY		
COMPLAINTS		
INSURANCE COST		

Safety

FRONTAL CRASH TEST	No government results
SIDE CRASH TEST	No government results
AIRBAGS	Dual
ANTI-LOCK BRAKES	4-Wheel
DAY. RUNNING LIGHTS	None
BELT ADJUSTORS	Standard
BUILT-IN CHILD SEAT	None
PRETENSIONERS	None

General Information

WHERE MADE	Japan
YEAR OF PRODUCTION	Fourth
PARKING INDEX	Average
BUMPERS	Strong
THEFT RATING	
TWINS	
GREEN RATING	Poor

Specifications

FUEL ECONOMY (cty/hwy)	21/26	Poor
DRIVING RANGE (miles)	404	Short
SEATING	7	
LENGTH (in.)	187.2	
HEAD/LEG ROOM (in.)	40.1/40.7	Cramped
INTERIOR SPACE (cu. ft.)		
CARGO SPACE (cu. ft.)	93.5	Very Large

Specifications may vary.

Prices

Model	Retail	Mkup
S 5dr	23,532	12%
LS 5dr	25,802	12%

Competition

	POOR	GOOD	Pg.
Isuzu Oasis			**161**
Chevrolet Venture			129
Dodge Caravan			137
Ford Windstar			146

*Due to the importance of crash tests, cars with no results as of publication date cannot be given an overall rating.

Kia Sephia

This year Kia rides on the changes from '98's major update to the Sephia. Slightly longer, and more roomier inside, the Sephia also got a new 1.8 liter 4 cylinder engine, with 125 hp. Dual airbags are standard and ABS is optional.

The Sephia comes in several trim levels: RS, LS, and GS but is available only as a sedan, unlike its competitors. The styling is similar to the old Mazda 323, which is no surprise as Mazda is a part-owner of Kia. The Sephia's low price tag and good crash test results could make it a major player in the small sedan market.

The Ratings

	POOR	GOOD
COMPARATIVE RATING	■	
FRONTAL CRASH TEST		■
SAFETY FEATURES		■
FUEL ECONOMY		■
PM COST		■
REPAIR COST		■
WARRANTY		■
COMPLAINTS		■
INSURANCE COST	■	

Safety

FRONTAL CRASH TEST	Good
SIDE CRASH TEST	No government results
AIRBAGS	Dual
ANTI-LOCK BRAKES	4-Wheel (opt)
DAY. RUNNING LIGHTS	None
BELT ADJUSTORS	Standard
BUILT-IN CHILD SEAT	None
PRETENSIONERS	None

General Information

WHERE MADE	Korea/Japan
YEAR OF PRODUCTION	Second
PARKING INDEX	Very Easy
BUMPERS	Strong
THEFT RATING	Average
TWINS	
GREEN RATING	Average

Specifications

FUEL ECONOMY (cty/hwy)	24/31	Average
DRIVING RANGE (miles)	349	Very Short
SEATING	5	
LENGTH (in.)	171.7	
HEAD/LEG ROOM (in.)	38.2/42.9	Average
INTERIOR SPACE (cu. ft.)	93	Average
CARGO SPACE (cu. ft.)	11	Very Small

Specifications may vary.

Prices

Model	Retail	Mkup
Sedan Manual	9,995	10%
Sedan Automatic	10,970	10%

Competition

	POOR	GOOD	Pg.
Kia Sephia	■		**162**
Chevrolet Cavalier		■	123
Ford Escort		■	143
Honda Civic		■	150

Lexus ES300

The Lexus ES300 enters 1999 with a few high tech modifications. A new drivetrain, electronic traction control, and skid control systems are among the list. Dual airbags and 4-wheel ABS are standard. Last year the ES300 added standard side airbags to its automatic crash protection features.

The new standard engine for the ES300, is a 3.0 liter V6 which produces 210 horsepower, slightly more powerful than the previous engine. Noise and vibration are kept to a minimum and handling is responsive. The ES300 is a solid, affordable luxury sedan, but if you can live without the nameplate, a fully-loaded Camry will be just as good and costs less, too.

The Ratings

	POOR			GOOD
COMPARATIVE RATING				
FRONTAL CRASH TEST				
SAFETY FEATURES				
FUEL ECONOMY				
PM COST				
REPAIR COST				
WARRANTY				
COMPLAINTS				
INSURANCE COST				

Safety

FRONTAL CRASH TEST	Good
SIDE CRASH TEST	Very Good
AIRBAGS	Dual & Side
ANTI-LOCK BRAKES	4-Wheel
DAY. RUNNING LIGHTS	Standard
BELT ADJUSTORS	Standard
BUILT-IN CHILD SEAT	None
PRETENSIONERS	Standard

General Information

WHERE MADE	Japan
YEAR OF PRODUCTION	Third
PARKING INDEX	Easy
BUMPERS	Strong
THEFT RATING	High
TWINS	Toyota Camry
GREEN RATING	Poor

Specifications

FUEL ECONOMY (cty/hwy)	19/26	Poor
DRIVING RANGE (miles)	416	Short
SEATING	5	
LENGTH (in.)	190.2	
HEAD/LEG ROOM (in.)	38/43.5	Average
INTERIOR SPACE (cu. ft.)	92.1	Cramped
CARGO SPACE (cu. ft.)	13.0	Small

Specifications may vary.

Prices

Model	Retail	Mkup
Luxury Sport Sedan	30,790	13%

Competition

	POOR	GOOD	Pg.
Lexus ES300			**163**
Buick Riviera			116
Cadillac DeVille			118
Infiniti I30			159

Fully revised for 1998, Lexus is hoping the GS sedans will become the new definitive luxury sports cars. Hoping to take on the BMW 5 Series and Mercedes-Benz E-Class, the GS sedans have been improved with bigger engines, a better suspension, and a more aggressive exterior design. Dual airbags, side airbags, pretensioners, traction control and 4-wheel ABS are all standard.

The GS300 gets a 3.0-liter engine that cranks out 225 hp. Most sports car enthusiasts will want to bigger 4.0-liter V8 engine on the GS400. An increased wheelbase allows for more interior room and a bigger trunk. On the GS sedans, 13 onboard computers are linked through a local-area network that lets you customize electronic features like interior lights.

The Ratings

	POOR ··· GOOD
COMPARATIVE RATING*	(blank)
FRONTAL CRASH TEST	(blank)
SAFETY FEATURES	■ (9th box)
FUEL ECONOMY	■ (2nd box)
PM COST	■ (7th box)
REPAIR COST	■ (6th box)
WARRANTY	■ (8th box)
COMPLAINTS	■ (4th box)
INSURANCE COST	■ (9th box)

Safety

FRONTAL CRASH TEST	No government results
SIDE CRASH TEST	No government results
AIRBAGS	Dual & Side (New Design)
ANTI-LOCK BRAKES	4-Wheel
DAY. RUNNING LIGHTS	Standard
BELT ADJUSTORS	Standard
BUILT-IN CHILD SEAT	None
PRETENSIONERS	Standard

General Information

WHERE MADE	Japan
YEAR OF PRODUCTION	Second
PARKING INDEX	Average
BUMPERS	Strong
THEFT RATING	Very High
TWINS	
GREEN RATING	Poor

Specifications

FUEL ECONOMY (cty/hwy)	20/25	Poor
DRIVING RANGE (miles)	446	Long
SEATING	5	
LENGTH (in.)	189.2	
HEAD/LEG ROOM (in.)	39/44.5	Very Roomy
INTERIOR SPACE (cu. ft.)	100	Roomy
CARGO SPACE (cu. ft.)	14.8	Average

Specifications may vary.

Prices

Model	Retail	Mkup
GS 300	36,900	13%
GS 400	44,950	14%

Competition

	POOR ··· GOOD	Pg.
Lexus GS300/400	(blank)	164
Cadillac DeVille	■ (8th box)	118
Merc.-Benz C-Class	■ (8th box)	173
Toyota Avalon	■ (8th box)	212

*Due to the importance of crash tests, cars with no results as of publication date cannot be given an overall rating.

Lexus LS400

For 1999, Lexus' flagship sedan receives few changes. Daytime running lights, interior trim changes, and new exterior colors are the small upgrades. The LS400 engine now has what Lexus calls VVTi, Variable Valve Timing, intelligent. This system provides better performance while improving fuel economy and reducing overall emissions outputs. The engine meets Transmission Low Emission Vehicle standards. Dual and side airbags and 4-wheel ABS is standard.

You'll find a very smooth ride and an extremely roomy rear seat. But, trunk space is rather small when compared to other large cars. An anti-theft system is standard and a computer navigation system is an option.

The Ratings

	POOR → GOOD
COMPARATIVE RATING*	(no rating)
FRONTAL CRASH TEST	(no rating)
SAFETY FEATURES	Good
FUEL ECONOMY	Poor
PM COST	Above average
REPAIR COST	Poor
WARRANTY	Good
COMPLAINTS	Good
INSURANCE COST	Good

Safety

FRONTAL CRASH TEST	No government results
SIDE CRASH TEST	No government results
AIRBAGS	Dual & Side
ANTI-LOCK BRAKES	4-Wheel
DAY. RUNNING LIGHTS	Standard
BELT ADJUSTORS	Standard
BUILT-IN CHILD SEAT	None
PRETENSIONERS	Standard

General Information

WHERE MADE	Japan
YEAR OF PRODUCTION	Fifth
PARKING INDEX	Easy
BUMPERS	Weak
THEFT RATING	Very High
TWINS	
GREEN RATING	Poor

Specifications

FUEL ECONOMY (cty/hwy)	18/25	Very Poor
DRIVING RANGE (miles)	484	Very Long
SEATING	5	
LENGTH (in.)	196.7	
HEAD/LEG ROOM (in.)	38.9/43.7	Roomy
INTERIOR SPACE (cu. ft.)	102	Roomy
CARGO SPACE (cu. ft.)	13.9	Average

Specifications may vary.

Prices

Model	Retail	Mkup
Luxury Sedan	53,200	15%

Competition

	POOR → GOOD	Pg.
Lexus LS400		**165**
Audi A8	Good	108
Cadillac Seville	Average	120
Oldsmobile Aurora	Below average	191

*Due to the importance of crash tests, cars with no results as of publication date cannot be given an overall rating.

Lexus SC300/400

These two luxury coupes differ only in standard engines and luxury appointments; many items standard on the more expensive SC400 will cost extra on the SC300. The SC300 has a plenty powerful 3-liter 6-cylinder engine. For about $7,500 more, you can step up to the SC400, with the 4-liter V8, which comes from the big Lexus LS400 and the all-new GS400. Be sure to get traction control. Handling is excellent, and ride is comfortably firm.

The front seats are very comfortable for average sized people, but check them out before you buy. The back seat is for kids only, and the trunk is skimpy. The instrument panel and controls are well designed. All SC models have dual airbags and ABS. Inexplicably, side airbags aren't even an option for this class of car. Daytime running lamps have been added this year.

The Ratings

	POOR — GOOD
COMPARATIVE RATING*	(no rating)
FRONTAL CRASH TEST	(no rating)
SAFETY FEATURES	▮ (high)
FUEL ECONOMY	▮ (low)
PM COST	▮ (mid-high)
REPAIR COST	▮ (low-mid)
WARRANTY	▮ (high)
COMPLAINTS	▮ (mid-high)
INSURANCE COST	▮ (lowest)

Safety

FRONTAL CRASH TEST	No government results
SIDE CRASH TEST	No government results
AIRBAGS	Dual
ANTI-LOCK BRAKES	4-Wheel
DAY. RUNNING LIGHTS	Standard
BELT ADJUSTORS	Standard
BUILT-IN CHILD SEAT	None
PRETENSIONERS	Standard

General Information

WHERE MADE	Japan
YEAR OF PRODUCTION	Eighth
PARKING INDEX	Easy
BUMPERS	Strong
THEFT RATING	Very High
TWINS	
GREEN RATING	Poor

Specifications

FUEL ECONOMY (cty/hwy)	19/24	Very Poor
DRIVING RANGE (miles)	443	Long
SEATING	4	
LENGTH (in.)	192.5	
HEAD/LEG ROOM (in.)	38.3/44.1	Roomy
INTERIOR SPACE (cu. ft.)	75.4	Vry. Cramped
CARGO SPACE (cu. ft.)	9.3	Very Small

Specifications may vary.

Prices

Model	Retail	Mkup
SC 300	41,100	13%
SC 400	53,000	14%

Competition

	POOR — GOOD	Pg.
Lexus SC300/400	(no rating)	166
Cadillac DeVille	▮ (good)	118
Toyota Avalon	▮ (good)	212
Volvo S70	▮ (good)	222

*Due to the importance of crash tests, cars with no results as of publication date cannot be given an overall rating.

Lincoln Continental

After a major design change last year, the Continental remains essentially the same for 1999. Side airbags have been added as a standard safety feature. The 4.6 liter V8 engine gets 15 more horses, bringing its engine to 275. The changes in '98 brought a more aerodynamic exterior, rounding the front and rear ends. Dual airbags and 4-wheel ABS are standard.

There is plenty of interior space and the Continental's mufflers were upgraded to be quieter. As for the ride, you can get an optional suspension system that lets you select from three different ride settings. Inside, you can get front and rear bench seats for up to six people, but most buyers opt for the two single bucket seats up front.

The Ratings

	POOR — GOOD
COMPARATIVE RATING*	(no rating)
FRONTAL CRASH TEST	(no rating)
SAFETY FEATURES	▮ (high)
FUEL ECONOMY	▮ (low)
PM COST	▮ (mid-high)
REPAIR COST	▮ (low-mid)
WARRANTY	▮ (mid)
COMPLAINTS	▮ (mid-high)
INSURANCE COST	▮ (high)

Safety

FRONTAL CRASH TEST	No government results
SIDE CRASH TEST	No government results
AIRBAGS	Dual & Side
ANTI-LOCK BRAKES	4-Wheel
DAY. RUNNING LIGHTS	None
BELT ADJUSTORS	Standard
BUILT-IN CHILD SEAT	None
PRETENSIONERS	None

General Information

WHERE MADE	U.S./Canada
YEAR OF PRODUCTION	Second
PARKING INDEX	Very Hard
BUMPERS	Strong
THEFT RATING	Average
TWINS	
GREEN RATING	Very Poor

Specifications

FUEL ECONOMY (cty/hwy)	17/25	Very Poor
DRIVING RANGE (miles)	420	Average
SEATING	6	
LENGTH (in.)	208.5	
HEAD/LEG ROOM (in.)	39.2/41.9	Average
INTERIOR SPACE (cu. ft.)	102	Roomy
CARGO SPACE (cu. ft.)	18.4	Very Large

Specifications may vary.

Prices

Model	Retail	Mkup
Sedan	38,325	9%

Competition

	POOR — GOOD	Pg.
Lincoln Continental	(no rating)	167
Audi A8	▮ (high)	108
Cadillac DeVille	▮ (high)	118
Toyota Avalon	▮ (mid-high)	212

*Due to the importance of crash tests, cars with no results as of publication date cannot be given an overall rating.

Still improving upon the changes made last year, for 1999 the Town Car gets standard side and de-powered dual airbags, a keyless entry system, rear window defroster, and traction assistance. 4-wheel ABS is standard. The new aerodynamic look may be hard for traditional Town Car lovers to take.

The engine is a 4.6-liter V8 found on previous versions of the Town Car. It produces 200 hp and is more than adequate to powering this over 4,000 lbs, six passenger sedan. The interior space was decreased but you won't notice it. The trunk space also decreased, as well, but the Town Car still remains America's travelling living room.

The Ratings

	POOR → GOOD
COMPARATIVE RATING*	(no rating)
FRONTAL CRASH TEST	(no rating)
SAFETY FEATURES	good
FUEL ECONOMY	poor
PM COST	good
REPAIR COST	poor
WARRANTY	good
COMPLAINTS	average
INSURANCE COST	good

Safety

FRONTAL CRASH TEST	No government results
SIDE CRASH TEST	No government results
AIRBAGS	Dual & Side (New Design)
ANTI-LOCK BRAKES	4-Wheel
DAY. RUNNING LIGHTS	None
BELT ADJUSTORS	Standard
BUILT-IN CHILD SEAT	None
PRETENSIONERS	None

General Information

WHERE MADE	Canada
YEAR OF PRODUCTION	Second
PARKING INDEX	Very Hard
BUMPERS	Strong
THEFT RATING	High
TWINS	Cr. Victoria, Gr. Marquis
GREEN RATING	Poor

Specifications

FUEL ECONOMY (cty/hwy)	17/24	Very Poor
DRIVING RANGE (miles)	390	Very Short
SEATING	6	
LENGTH (in.)	215.3	
HEAD/LEG ROOM (in.)	39.2/42.6	Roomy
INTERIOR SPACE (cu. ft.)	112.3	Very Roomy
CARGO SPACE (cu. ft.)	20.6	Very Large

Specifications may vary.

Prices

Model	Retail	Mkup
Executive	38,325	9%
Signature	40,325	9%
Cartier	42,825	9%

Competition

	POOR → GOOD	Pg.
Lincoln Town Car	(no rating)	**168**
Audi A8	good	108
Cadillac DeVille	good	118
Toyota Avalon	good	212

*Due to the importance of crash tests, cars with no results as of publication date cannot be given an overall rating.

Mazda 626

After some major changes last year, the Mazda 626 is the same for '99. The 626 is Mazda's alternative to the Accord. Over the past few years, it has done fairly well against stiff competition. Dual airbags are now standard, but you'll still pay extra for ABS. Look for crash tests later this year.

The base 2.0-liter, 4-cylinder engine is adequate and reasonably economical. For more power, consider the 2.5-liter V6, available on the LX and ES. However, the bigger V6 does require premium gas and gets worse mileage. Room, comfort and trunk space are good for four. With more room up front and a smaller price tag, the 626 competes fairly well against the more popular competition.

The Ratings

	POOR → GOOD
COMPARATIVE RATING*	(no rating)
FRONTAL CRASH TEST	(no rating)
SAFETY FEATURES	■ at position 4
FUEL ECONOMY	■ at position 8
PM COST	■ at position 3
REPAIR COST	■ at position 7
WARRANTY	■ at position 3
COMPLAINTS	■ at position 4
INSURANCE COST	■ at position 1

Safety

FRONTAL CRASH TEST	No government results
SIDE CRASH TEST	Average
AIRBAGS	Dual
ANTI-LOCK BRAKES	4-Wheel (opt)
DAY. RUNNING LIGHTS	None
BELT ADJUSTORS	Standard
BUILT-IN CHILD SEAT	None
PRETENSIONERS	None

General Information

WHERE MADE	Japan
YEAR OF PRODUCTION	Second
PARKING INDEX	Easy
BUMPERS	Strong
THEFT RATING	Average
TWINS	
GREEN RATING	Average

Specifications

FUEL ECONOMY (cty/hwy)	26/33	Good
DRIVING RANGE (miles)	469	Long
SEATING	5	
LENGTH (in.)	184.4	
HEAD/LEG ROOM (in.)	39.2/43.5	Very Roomy
INTERIOR SPACE (cu. ft.)	97.2	Average
CARGO SPACE (cu. ft.)	13.8	Average

Specifications may vary.

Prices

Model	Retail	Mkup
DX	15,550	10%
LX	17,650	10%
LX-V6	20,665	10%
ES-V6	23,240	10%

Competition

	POOR → GOOD	Pg.
Mazda 626	(no rating)	**169**
Buick Century	■ at position 7	112
Nissan Altima	■ at position 1	185
Oldsmobile Cutlass	■ at position 4	192

*Due to the importance of crash tests, cars with no results as of publication date cannot be given an overall rating.

Mazda Miata

This year look for an all-new Miata in showrooms. The new bodywork gives the Miata a more modern look. Because a new image was unavailable at press time, the '98 model is shown. Dual airbags are standard.

The 1.8-liter, 4-cylinder powering this small car gets a boost of a few horsepower, bringing it to 170. This should provide enough acceleration for most drivers. Brakes are good, even better with ABS. Controls and displays are sensibly designed. Fuel economy is just average and could be much better with only 2,200 pounds to haul. You won't get a soft, quiet ride, a spacious interior, or much of a trunk in a Miata, but you aren't buying it for any of those reasons either. You do get crisp, responsive handling, a peppy engine, and a car that will turn heads with the top down.

The Ratings

	POOR — GOOD
COMPARATIVE RATING *	(blank)
FRONTAL CRASH TEST	(blank)
SAFETY FEATURES	■ (6th)
FUEL ECONOMY	■ (7th)
PM COST	■ (4th)
REPAIR COST	■ (4th)
WARRANTY	■ (5th)
COMPLAINTS	■ (6th)
INSURANCE COST	■ (4th)

Safety

FRONTAL CRASH TEST	No government results
SIDE CRASH TEST	No government results
AIRBAGS	Dual
ANTI-LOCK BRAKES	4-Wheel (opt)
DAY. RUNNING LIGHTS	None
BELT ADJUSTORS	None
BUILT-IN CHILD SEAT	None
PRETENSIONERS	None

General Information

WHERE MADE	Japan
YEAR OF PRODUCTION	First
PARKING INDEX	Very Easy
BUMPERS	
THEFT RATING	Average
TWINS	
GREEN RATING	Average

Specifications

FUEL ECONOMY (cty/hwy)	25/29	Average
DRIVING RANGE (miles)	343	Very Short
SEATING	2	
LENGTH (in.)	155.3	
HEAD/LEG ROOM (in.)	37.1/42.7	Cramped
INTERIOR SPACE (cu. ft.)		
CARGO SPACE (cu. ft.)	3.6	Very Small

Specifications may vary.

Prices

Model	Retail	Mkup
Convertible 2dr	19,770	9%

Competition

	POOR — GOOD	Pg.
Mazda Miata	(blank)	**170**
Acura Integra	■	103
Ford Mustang	■	144
Mitsubishi Eclipse	■	182

Mazda Millenia

For 1999, the Millenia gets restyled in hopes that it will be a winner in the competitive intermediate market. Dual airbags and ABS are standard.

The standard 2.5-liter V6 found on the base model is more than adequate; however, the Millenia S comes with the more powerful and responsive supercharged 2.3-liter V6. The base engine runs on regular fuel, while the S version requires premium fuel, which will increase your operating costs. This front wheel drive sedan is small, though it still should be quite comfortable for 4 passengers, 5 in a pinch. A well designed car with good crash test scores, the Millenia deserves a close look in spite of its high maintenance costs.

The Ratings

	POOR ⟶ GOOD
COMPARATIVE RATING	▮ (7/10)
FRONTAL CRASH TEST	▮ (10/10)
SAFETY FEATURES	▮ (7/10)
FUEL ECONOMY	▮ (4/10)
PM COST	▮ (5/10)
REPAIR COST	▮ (1/10)
WARRANTY	▮ (5/10)
COMPLAINTS	▮ (8/10)
INSURANCE COST	▮ (4/10)

Safety

FRONTAL CRASH TEST	Very Good
SIDE CRASH TEST	No government results
AIRBAGS	Dual
ANTI-LOCK BRAKES	4-Wheel
DAY. RUNNING LIGHTS	None
BELT ADJUSTORS	Standard
BUILT-IN CHILD SEAT	None
PRETENSIONERS	None

General Information

WHERE MADE	Japan
YEAR OF PRODUCTION	Fifth
PARKING INDEX	Average
BUMPERS	Weak
THEFT RATING	High
TWINS	
GREEN RATING	Poor

Specifications

FUEL ECONOMY (cty/hwy)	20/28	Poor
DRIVING RANGE (miles)	432	Average
SEATING	5	
LENGTH (in.)	189.8	
HEAD/LEG ROOM (in.)	39.3/43.3	Roomy
INTERIOR SPACE (cu. ft.)	93.8	Average
CARGO SPACE (cu. ft.)	13.3	Small

Specifications may vary.

Prices

Model	Retail	Mkup
Cloth	28,995	12%
S	36,595	14%

Competition

	POOR ⟶ GOOD	Pg.
Mazda Millenia	▮ (7/10)	**171**
Lexus ES300	▮ (10/10)	163
Merc.-Benz C-Class	▮ (7/10)	173
Oldsmobile Aurora	▮ (4/10)	191

Mazda Protegé

You'll find a handful of changes on the 1999 Protegé, a sedan which offers more room inside than you might expect from a subcompact car. The Protegé was the replacement for the 323 and its larger size has produced a better riding car. Dual airbags are standard, and ABS can be found on higher models.

The Protegé comes in three trim levels. DX and LX models come standard with a 1.5-liter 4-cylinder engine that is relatively weak, although quite fuel efficient. The fancier ES comes with a 1.8-liter engine—more powerful, but less fuel efficient. The Protegé faces tough competition in a crowded subcompact market with the Civic and Sentra. Look for crash test results later this year.

The Ratings

	POOR ··· GOOD
COMPARATIVE RATING*	(no rating)
FRONTAL CRASH TEST	(no rating)
SAFETY FEATURES	■ (below average)
FUEL ECONOMY	■ (good)
PM COST	■ (below average)
REPAIR COST	■ (below average)
WARRANTY	■ (below average)
COMPLAINTS	■ (average)
INSURANCE COST	■ (below average)

Safety

FRONTAL CRASH TEST	No government results
SIDE CRASH TEST	No government results
AIRBAGS	Dual
ANTI-LOCK BRAKES	4-Wheel (opt)
DAY. RUNNING LIGHTS	None
BELT ADJUSTORS	Standard
BUILT-IN CHILD SEAT	None
PRETENSIONERS	None

General Information

WHERE MADE	Japan
YEAR OF PRODUCTION	First
PARKING INDEX	Very Easy
BUMPERS	
THEFT RATING	Average
TWINS	
GREEN RATING	Average

Specifications

FUEL ECONOMY (cty/hwy)	29/34	Good
DRIVING RANGE (miles)	457	Long
SEATING	5	
LENGTH (in.)	174.8	
HEAD/LEG ROOM (in.)	39.2/42.2	Average
INTERIOR SPACE (cu. ft.)	95.5	Average
CARGO SPACE (cu. ft.)	13.1	Small

Specifications may vary.

Prices

Model	Retail	Mkup
DX	12,145	6%
LX	13,545	8%
ES	15,295	9%

Competition

	POOR ··· GOOD	Pg.
Mazda Protegé	(no rating)	**172**
Chevrolet Cavalier	■ (below average)	123
Ford Escort	■ (below average)	143
Honda Civic	■ (below average)	150

Mercedes-Benz C-Class

For 1999, Mercedes has given more muscle to its C-Class, by adding a new engine with more horsepower to both the C230 and the C43. Traction control is standard, which automatically aids driving on slippery surfaces. Mercedes Electronic Stability Program, a high tech feature that prevents spins or slides, is standard in the C43 and optional on the C280. Dual airbags, side airbags and ABS are standard. The C-class is available with a 2.3-liter 4-cylinder supercharged engine (C230), a 2.8-liter 6-cylinder engine (C280), or a new 4.3-liter V8 engine (C43). Notable features include a unique brake system which shortens braking distances and a special child seat system that detects a special child seat and deactivate the passenger-side airbag.

The Ratings

	POOR GOOD
COMPARATIVE RATING	▓ (good side)
FRONTAL CRASH TEST	▓ (good side)
SAFETY FEATURES	▓ (good side)
FUEL ECONOMY	▓ (middle)
PM COST	▓ (poor side)
REPAIR COST	▓ (poor side)
WARRANTY	▓ (poor side)
COMPLAINTS	▓ (good end)
INSURANCE COST	▓ (good side)

Safety

FRONTAL CRASH TEST	Good
SIDE CRASH TEST	No government results
AIRBAGS	Dual & Side
ANTI-LOCK BRAKES	4-Wheel
DAY. RUNNING LIGHTS	None
BELT ADJUSTORS	Standard
BUILT-IN CHILD SEAT	None
PRETENSIONERS	Standard

General Information

WHERE MADE	Germany
YEAR OF PRODUCTION	Sixth
PARKING INDEX	Easy
BUMPERS	Weak
THEFT RATING	Average
TWINS	
GREEN RATING	Poor

Specifications

FUEL ECONOMY (cty/hwy)	21/27	Poor
DRIVING RANGE (miles)	394	Short
SEATING	5	
LENGTH (in.)	177.4	
HEAD/LEG ROOM (in.)	37.2/41.5	Vry. Cramped
INTERIOR SPACE (cu. ft.)	88	Cramped
CARGO SPACE (cu. ft.)	12.9	Small

Specifications may vary.

Prices

Model	Retail	Mkup
C230	31,200	13%
C280	35,600	13%
C43	53,000	13%

Competition

	POOR GOOD	Pg.
Merc.-Benz C-Class	▓ (good side)	**173**
Audi A4	▓ (good side)	106
Lexus ES300	▓ (good side)	163
Oldsmobile Aurora	▓ (middle)	191

Mercedes-Benz E-Class

Large

For 1999, Mercedes offers a full curtain side airbag system. Working with the already installed side, and front airbags this intricate automatic crash protection system is a standard feature. The E-Class has a distinctive styling with oval headlamps and a molded hood. Dual airbags, side airbags and ABS are standard.

With Mercedes' new nomenclature, the E stands for the mid-level size, and the numbers stand for the engine size. Available engines include a 3-liter diesel (E300), a new 3.2-liter V6 (E320), and a new 4.3-liter V8 (E430). The transmission is a five speed automatic. Notable features include a unique brake system which shortens braking distances and a special child seat system that will detect a special child seat and deactivate the passenger-side airbag.

The Ratings

	POOR → GOOD
COMPARATIVE RATING *	(no rating)
FRONTAL CRASH TEST	(no rating)
SAFETY FEATURES	good
FUEL ECONOMY	below average
PM COST	poor
REPAIR COST	poor
WARRANTY	poor-below average
COMPLAINTS	good
INSURANCE COST	good

Safety

FRONTAL CRASH TEST	No government results
SIDE CRASH TEST	No government results
AIRBAGS	Dual & Side
ANTI-LOCK BRAKES	4-Wheel
DAY. RUNNING LIGHTS	None
BELT ADJUSTORS	Standard
BUILT-IN CHILD SEAT	None
PRETENSIONERS	Standard

General Information

WHERE MADE	Germany
YEAR OF PRODUCTION	Fourth
PARKING INDEX	Average
BUMPERS	Weak
THEFT RATING	High
TWINS	
GREEN RATING	Poor

Specifications

FUEL ECONOMY (cty/hwy)	21/30	Average
DRIVING RANGE (miles)	538	Very Long
SEATING	5	
LENGTH (in.)	189.4	
HEAD/LEG ROOM (in.)	37.6/41.3	Vry. Cramped
INTERIOR SPACE (cu. ft.)	95	Average
CARGO SPACE (cu. ft.)	15.3	Average

Specifications may vary.

Prices

Model	Retail	Mkup
E320 2wd	46,200	13%
E320 AWD	48,990	13%
E430	51,300	13%
E320 Wagon 2wd	47,200	13%

Competition

	POOR → GOOD	Pg.
Merc.-Benz E-Class	(no rating)	**174**
Audi A8	good	108
Oldsmobile Aurora	average	191
Toyota Avalon	good	212

*Due to the importance of crash tests, cars with no results as of publication date cannot be given an overall rating.

Mercury Cougar

All new this year, the Mercury Cougar is the sporty option on the Mercury Mystique platform. Powering the car is a 2.0 liter 4 cylinder engine, or a 2.5 liter V-6, from which Mercury developed the names of the two Cougar series: I4 and V-6. The I4 comes with only a 5 speed automatic transmission, while the V-6 offers a 4 speed automatic as well.

The Cougar offers front de-powered airbags for the front occupants, and the option of side airbags as well. ABS is optional for both models, and traction assistance is also an extra for the V-6.

The Ratings

	POOR				GOOD
COMPARATIVE RATING*					
FRONTAL CRASH TEST					
SAFETY FEATURES			■		
FUEL ECONOMY				■	
PM COST			■		
REPAIR COST		■			
WARRANTY	■				
COMPLAINTS			■		
INSURANCE COST			■		

Safety

FRONTAL CRASH TEST	No government results
SIDE CRASH TEST	No government results
AIRBAGS	Dual (New Design) & Side (opt.)
ANTI-LOCK BRAKES	4-Wheel (opt)
DAY. RUNNING LIGHTS	None
BELT ADJUSTORS	Standard
BUILT-IN CHILD SEAT	None
PRETENSIONERS	None

General Information

WHERE MADE	U.S.
YEAR OF PRODUCTION	First
PARKING INDEX	Easy
BUMPERS	
THEFT RATING	Average
TWINS	
GREEN RATING	Poor

Specifications

FUEL ECONOMY (cty/hwy)	24/34	Good
DRIVING RANGE (miles)	450	Long
SEATING	4	
LENGTH (in.)	185	
HEAD/LEG ROOM (in.)	37.8/42.5	Cramped
INTERIOR SPACE (cu. ft.)	84.2	Vry. Cramped
CARGO SPACE (cu. ft.)	14.5	Average

Specifications may vary.

Prices

Model	Retail	Mkup
I4 Coupe	16,195	9%
V6 Coupe	16,695	9%

Competition

	POOR			GOOD	Pg.
Mercury Cougar					175
Buick Riviera		■			116
Chrysler Sebring		■			134
Mitsubishi Eclipse	■				182

*Due to the importance of crash tests, cars with no results as of publication date cannot be given an overall rating.

Mercury Grand Marquis

Large

The Marquis was all new last year, so there are very few changes in the '99 model. The new suspension, brakes, and bigger tires all give this Mercury a fluid, smooth ride. ABS is still a separate option, as is a traction control system. Dual airbags are standard, and de-powered.

The 4.6-liter V8 is responsive and powerful, but has predictably poor gas mileage for a car this size. While the Grand Marquis isn't quite as difficult to handle as some other big sedans, it will benefit from the improvements to the suspension. There's plenty of room for six and their luggage. The Grand Marquis performed excellently on the government front and side crash tests.

The Ratings

	POOR ··· GOOD
COMPARATIVE RATING	
FRONTAL CRASH TEST	
SAFETY FEATURES	
FUEL ECONOMY	
PM COST	
REPAIR COST	
WARRANTY	
COMPLAINTS	
INSURANCE COST	

Safety

FRONTAL CRASH TEST	Very Good
SIDE CRASH TEST	Very Good
AIRBAGS	Dual (New Design)
ANTI-LOCK BRAKES	4-Wheel (opt)
DAY. RUNNING LIGHTS	None
BELT ADJUSTORS	Standard
BUILT-IN CHILD SEAT	None
PRETENSIONERS	None

General Information

WHERE MADE	Canada
YEAR OF PRODUCTION	Eighth
PARKING INDEX	Very Hard
BUMPERS	Strong
THEFT RATING	Average
TWINS	
GREEN RATING	Poor

Specifications

FUEL ECONOMY (cty/hwy)	17/24	Very Poor
DRIVING RANGE (miles)	390	Very Short
SEATING	6	
LENGTH (in.)	212	
HEAD/LEG ROOM (in.)	39.4/42.5	Roomy
INTERIOR SPACE (cu. ft.)	109.3	Very Roomy
CARGO SPACE (cu. ft.)	20.6	Very Large

Specifications may vary.

Prices

Model	Retail	Mkup
GS Sedan	22,220	7%
LS Sedan	24,120	7%

Competition

	POOR ··· GOOD	Pg.
Merc. Gr. Marquis		**176**
Buick Park Avenue		114
Oldsmobile 88		189
Toyota Avalon		212

Mercury Mystique

For 1999, the Mystique comes with few changes. However, redesigned seating gives extra leg room to rear passengers, the brake system has improved, and the front suspension is better. Teamed with its twin, the Ford Contour, the Mystique is attractive because of its ride and solid mid-size car features. De-powered dual airbags are standard, but you'll have to pay extra for ABS and traction control.

The Mystique is about 6 inches longer than its predecessor, the Topaz, and front seat passengers are the biggest beneficiaries of the extra room. Both the base GS and the up-level LS come standard with a 2-liter engine that is only adequate. A more powerful 2.5-liter V6 with a tighter suspension system is optional.

The Ratings

	POOR ⟶ GOOD
COMPARATIVE RATING	▮ (mid)
FRONTAL CRASH TEST	▮ (high)
SAFETY FEATURES	▮ (mid)
FUEL ECONOMY	▮ (mid)
PM COST	▮ (mid)
REPAIR COST	▮ (high)
WARRANTY	▮ (low)
COMPLAINTS	▮ (low-mid)
INSURANCE COST	▮ (low-mid)

Safety

FRONTAL CRASH TEST	Very Good
SIDE CRASH TEST	Very Good
AIRBAGS	Dual (New Design)
ANTI-LOCK BRAKES	4-Wheel (opt)
DAY. RUNNING LIGHTS	None
BELT ADJUSTORS	Standard
BUILT-IN CHILD SEAT	Optional
PRETENSIONERS	None

General Information

WHERE MADE	U.S./Canada/Mexico
YEAR OF PRODUCTION	Fifth
PARKING INDEX	Average
BUMPERS	Strong
THEFT RATING	Very Low
TWINS	Ford Contour
GREEN RATING	Average

Specifications

FUEL ECONOMY (cty/hwy)	24/34	Good
DRIVING RANGE (miles)	435	Average
SEATING	5	
LENGTH (in.)	184.8	
HEAD/LEG ROOM (in.)	39/42.4	Average
INTERIOR SPACE (cu. ft.)	90.2	Cramped
CARGO SPACE (cu. ft.)	13.9	Average

Specifications may vary.

Prices

Model	Retail	Mkup
GS	16,390	9%
LS	17,745	9%

Competition

	POOR ⟶ GOOD	Pg.
Mercury Mystique	▮ (mid)	**177**
Buick Century	▮ (mid-high)	112
Hyundai Sonata	▮ (low)	156
Pontiac Grand Prix	▮ (mid)	200

Mercury Sable

Intermediate

This year the Sable adds a GS wagon model to the line up. Unlike its twin, the Taurus, the Sable does not sell nearly as well, but it is geared towards the upscale buyer—the luxury line of the Taurus. It has many more standard features. De-powered dual airbags are standard and ABS is optional.

Like its headlights, the interior takes the shape of an ovoid providing easy-to-use controls and dash. The standard engine, a 3-liter V6, is quite powerful and delivers decent gas mileage. For more power and slightly better gas mileage, you can select the bigger version of the same engine. A stiff structure improves handling over the past Sables. There is plenty of room for 4 adults and you can even squeeze in 5 or 6 if needed. The optional child seat on the wagon is a must for parents.

The Ratings

	POOR → GOOD
COMPARATIVE RATING	Good
FRONTAL CRASH TEST	Good
SAFETY FEATURES	Average
FUEL ECONOMY	Poor
PM COST	Good
REPAIR COST	Good
WARRANTY	Poor
COMPLAINTS	Average
INSURANCE COST	Average

Safety

FRONTAL CRASH TEST	Very Good
SIDE CRASH TEST	Good
AIRBAGS	Dual (New Design)
ANTI-LOCK BRAKES	4-Wheel (opt)
DAY. RUNNING LIGHTS	None
BELT ADJUSTORS	Standard
BUILT-IN CHILD SEAT	Optional (Wagon)
PRETENSIONERS	None

General Information

WHERE MADE	U.S./Canada
YEAR OF PRODUCTION	Fourth
PARKING INDEX	Hard
BUMPERS	Strong
THEFT RATING	Low
TWINS	Ford Taurus
GREEN RATING	Poor

Specifications

FUEL ECONOMY (cty/hwy)	20/28	Poor
DRIVING RANGE (miles)	384	Very Short
SEATING	5	
LENGTH (in.)	199.7	
HEAD/LEG ROOM (in.)	39.4/42.2	Average
INTERIOR SPACE (cu. ft.)	101.8	Roomy
CARGO SPACE (cu. ft.)	16	Large

Specifications may vary.

Prices

Model	Retail	Mkup
GS Sedan	18,445	9%
LS Sedan	19,545	9%
LS Wagon	20,645	9%

Competition

	POOR → GOOD	Pg.
Mercury Sable	Good	178
Buick LeSabre	Good	113
Nissan Maxima	Average	186
Toyota Camry	Average	213

Mercury Tracer

The Ratings

	POOR ... GOOD
COMPARATIVE RATING	▩ (2)
FRONTAL CRASH TEST	▩ (4)
SAFETY FEATURES	▩ (6)
FUEL ECONOMY	▩ (7)
PM COST	▩ (5)
REPAIR COST	▩ (9)
WARRANTY	▩ (2)
COMPLAINTS	▩ (3)
INSURANCE COST	▩ (1)

No changes for the Tracer this year, aside from leather seating, interior trunk release, and remote entry with an anti-theft system. Like other Mercurys, the Tracer is aimed at a more upscale car buyer than its Ford twin, the Escort. The Tracer comes with standard de-powered dual airbags, however, and ABS is only optional.

The 2.0-liter, 4-cylinder engine has been refined and should produce quick accelerations and smooth shifts. As is expected in a small car, fuel economy should be good. Ride is comfortable, but don't expect a bump free drive. Noise levels are good under average acceleration, anything more than average and you may have to turn up the radio. The Tracer is an upscale sedan for a low price.

Safety

FRONTAL CRASH TEST	Average
SIDE CRASH TEST	Average
AIRBAGS	Dual (New Design)
ANTI-LOCK BRAKES	4-Wheel (opt)
DAY. RUNNING LIGHTS	None
BELT ADJUSTORS	Standard
BUILT-IN CHILD SEAT	Optional
PRETENSIONERS	None

General Information

WHERE MADE	U.S./Canada/Mexico
YEAR OF PRODUCTION	Third
PARKING INDEX	Very Easy
BUMPERS	Strong
THEFT RATING	
TWINS	Ford Escort
GREEN RATING	Average

Specifications

FUEL ECONOMY (cty/hwy)	28/37	Good
DRIVING RANGE (miles)	416	Short
SEATING	5	
LENGTH (in.)	174.7	
HEAD/LEG ROOM (in.)	39/42.5	Average
INTERIOR SPACE (cu. ft.)	87.2	Cramped
CARGO SPACE (cu. ft.)	12.8	Small

Specifications may vary.

Prices

Model	Retail	Mkup
GS Sedan	11,530	6%
LS Sedan	13,070	7%
LS Wagon	14,275	7%

Competition

	POOR ... GOOD	Pg.
Mercury Tracer	▩ (2)	**179**
Honda Civic	▩ (4)	150
Nissan Sentra	▩ (8)	188
Subaru Impreza	▩ (4)	207

Developed jointly with Nissan and built in Ohio, the Villager is available in three trim levels: base GS, luxury LS, and sport-luxury Nautica. The Villager's resemblance to the Dodge Caravan is no coincidence, Villager designers know who they need to beat. This year, Villager adds a standard driver side sliding door and increases interior space. ABS and dual airbags are standard.

The 3.0-liter V6, with automatic overdrive, is acceptably responsive. Go for the towing package if you'll be hauling anything at all. The ride is a bit soft, very much like a regular passenger car's, with standard suspension. Handling is competent, but can be firmed up with the optional handling package. The middle and rear seats are easy to remove to increase cargo space.

The Ratings

	POOR	GOOD
COMPARATIVE RATING*		
FRONTAL CRASH TEST		
SAFETY FEATURES		(high)
FUEL ECONOMY	(low)	
PM COST		(high)
REPAIR COST	(mid)	
WARRANTY	(low)	
COMPLAINTS	(mid)	
INSURANCE COST	(mid)	

Safety

FRONTAL CRASH TEST	No government results
SIDE CRASH TEST	No government results
AIRBAGS	Dual (New Design)
ANTI-LOCK BRAKES	4-Wheel (opt)
DAY. RUNNING LIGHTS	None
BELT ADJUSTORS	Standard
BUILT-IN CHILD SEAT	Optional(2)
PRETENSIONERS	Standard

General Information

WHERE MADE	U.S./Canada/Japan
YEAR OF PRODUCTION	First
PARKING INDEX	Hard
BUMPERS	
THEFT RATING	Low
TWINS	Nissan Quest
GREEN RATING	Very Poor

Specifications

FUEL ECONOMY (cty/hwy)	17/24	Very Poor
DRIVING RANGE (miles)	410	Short
SEATING	7	
LENGTH (in.)	194.7	
HEAD/LEG ROOM (in.)	39.7/39.9	Vry. Cramped
INTERIOR SPACE (cu. ft.)		
CARGO SPACE (cu. ft.)	135.6	Very Large

Specifications may vary.

Prices

Model	Retail	Mkup
Base Wagon	22,415	10%
Estate Wagon	25,015	10%
Sport Wagon	25,015	10%

Competition

	POOR	GOOD	Pg.
Mercury Villager			180
Chevrolet Venture	(mid)		129
Dodge Caravan	(low)		137
Ford Windstar	(mid)		146

*Due to the importance of crash tests, cars with no results as of publication date cannot be given an overall rating.

This year the Mitsubishi offers the Diamante in only one trim level replacing the ES and the LS of previous years. In the '99 models you'll find a keyless entry system and new color selections.

Powering this new Diamante is a refined 3.5-liter V6 engine, which is good enough for this mid-size sedan. As with past Diamante's, the ride should be smooth and comfortable. Great safety features include an optional fold-down child safety seat and a standard 3-point seatbelt for the middle back seat. The new Cold Weather package offers traction control and heated front seats. Adherence to California's Low Emission Vehicle standards is optional.

The Ratings

	POOR	GOOD
COMPARATIVE RATING*		
FRONTAL CRASH TEST		
SAFETY FEATURES		
FUEL ECONOMY		
PM COST		
REPAIR COST		
WARRANTY		
COMPLAINTS		
INSURANCE COST		

Safety

FRONTAL CRASH TEST	No government results
SIDE CRASH TEST	No government results
AIRBAGS	Dual
ANTI-LOCK BRAKES	4-Wheel
DAY. RUNNING LIGHTS	None
BELT ADJUSTORS	Standard
BUILT-IN CHILD SEAT	Optional
PRETENSIONERS	Standard

General Information

WHERE MADE	Australia/Japan
YEAR OF PRODUCTION	Third
PARKING INDEX	Average
BUMPERS	Strong
THEFT RATING	
TWINS	
GREEN RATING	Poor

Specifications

FUEL ECONOMY (cty/hwy)	18/24	Very Poor
DRIVING RANGE (miles)	399	Short
SEATING	5	
LENGTH (in.)	194.1	
HEAD/LEG ROOM (in.)	39.4/43.6	Very Roomy
INTERIOR SPACE (cu. ft.)	100.9	Roomy
CARGO SPACE (cu. ft.)	14.2	Average

Specifications may vary.

Prices

Model	Retail	Mkup
ES	27,650	14%
LS	33,050	15%

Competition

	POOR	GOOD	Pg.
Mitsu. Diamante			**181**
Chevrolet Lumina			124
Ford Crown Victoria			142
Nissan Maxima			186

*Due to the importance of crash tests, cars with no results as of publication date cannot be given an overall rating.

There are few changes for this year's Eclipse: sunroof, and a security system with keyless entry are standard for the GS-T; and ABS and limited slip rear differential are standard on the GSX. Dual airbags are standard, as is ABS.

The RS is the stripped-down base model and the GS has a few more options. Both of those models get the standard 2-liter engine, which may not be powerful enough for sports enthusiasts. The up-level GS-T and GSX both get a turbo version that pumps out 50% more power, and the GSX comes with all-wheel drive. The Eclipse does have a back seat, but it's not really meant for adults. A high number of complaints hurt the Eclipse, despite a good crash test performance.

The Ratings

(Scale: POOR → GOOD)

COMPARATIVE RATING	Poor
FRONTAL CRASH TEST	Good
SAFETY FEATURES	Above average
FUEL ECONOMY	Average
PM COST	Average
REPAIR COST	Good
WARRANTY	Below average
COMPLAINTS	Poor
INSURANCE COST	Poor

Safety

FRONTAL CRASH TEST	Good
SIDE CRASH TEST	No government results
AIRBAGS	Dual
ANTI-LOCK BRAKES	4-Wheel
DAY. RUNNING LIGHTS	None
BELT ADJUSTORS	Standard
BUILT-IN CHILD SEAT	None
PRETENSIONERS	None

General Information

WHERE MADE	U.S./Canada/Japan
YEAR OF PRODUCTION	Fifth
PARKING INDEX	Easy
BUMPERS	Strong
THEFT RATING	High
TWINS	
GREEN RATING	Average

Specifications

FUEL ECONOMY (cty/hwy)	22/33	Average
DRIVING RANGE (miles)	437	Average
SEATING	4	
LENGTH (in.)	172.4	
HEAD/LEG ROOM (in.)	37.9/43.3	Average
INTERIOR SPACE (cu. ft.)	79.1	Vry. Cramped
CARGO SPACE (cu. ft.)	16.6	Large

Specifications may vary.

Prices

Model	Retail	Mkup
RS Manual	15,750	10%
GS Manual	17,910	10%
GS-T Turbo Manual	23,210	10%
GSX Turbo 4WD Manual	26,550	11%

Competition

(Scale: POOR → GOOD)

	Rating	Pg.
Mitsubishi Eclipse	Poor	182
Acura Integra	Good	103
Chevrolet Camaro	Below average	122
Ford Mustang	Average	144

One of the few all new vehicles this year the Galant comes in four trim levels. The DE comes with a 2.4 liter 4 cylinder engine, with either manual or automatic transmission. The LS and GTZ have a 3.0 liter V6 and an automatic transmission. The ES comes with either of these engines. Front airbags are standard on all models, for both driver and passenger. The LS and GTZ offer front side airbags. ABS is not available on the DE, costs extra with the ES 4 cylinder, and is standard on the ES V6, LS and GTZ. Rear head rests are available on the ES, LS and GTZ.

The Ratings

	POOR — GOOD
COMPARATIVE RATING*	(no rating)
FRONTAL CRASH TEST	(no rating)
SAFETY FEATURES	▉ (mid)
FUEL ECONOMY	▉ (mid-high)
PM COST	▉ (low)
REPAIR COST	▉ (high)
WARRANTY	▉ (mid)
COMPLAINTS	▉ (mid)
INSURANCE COST	▉ (mid)

Safety

FRONTAL CRASH TEST	No government results
SIDE CRASH TEST	No government results
AIRBAGS	Dual & Side (optional)
ANTI-LOCK BRAKES	4-Wheel
DAY. RUNNING LIGHTS	None
BELT ADJUSTORS	Standard
BUILT-IN CHILD SEAT	None
PRETENSIONERS	Standard

General Information

WHERE MADE	U.S./Canada/Japan
YEAR OF PRODUCTION	First
PARKING INDEX	Easy
BUMPERS	
THEFT RATING	High
TWINS	
GREEN RATING	Average

Specifications

FUEL ECONOMY (cty/hwy)	23/31	Average
DRIVING RANGE (miles)	440	Long
SEATING	5	
LENGTH (in.)	187.8	
HEAD/LEG ROOM (in.)	39.9/43.5	Very Roomy
INTERIOR SPACE (cu. ft.)	97.6	Average
CARGO SPACE (cu. ft.)	12.5	Small

Specifications may vary.

Prices

Model	Retail	Mkup
DE	16,990	9%
ES	17,990	10%
ES-V6	19,990	10%
LS	24,250	11%

Competition

	POOR — GOOD	Pg.
Mitsubishi Galant	(no rating)	**183**
Ford Escort	▉ (low)	143
Honda Civic	▉ (low)	150
Subaru Impreza	▉ (mid-low)	207

*Due to the importance of crash tests, cars with no results as of publication date cannot be given an overall rating.

Mitsubishi Mirage

Subcompact

Just some cosmetic changes for the Mirage this year: tail lamps, new seat fabric and exterior colors. You can choose from either a sedan or coupe model with two trim levels. All Mirages have dual airbags, but ABS is optional.

The 1.5-liter 4-cylinder engine that comes with the base model Mirage DE is not very powerful, though you'll be pleased with its fuel economy. The 1.8-liter engine on the LS coupes and sedans is much more powerful, but gas mileage suffers dramatically. Choose the 1.5 liter, 4 cylinder engine with manual transmission and California Low Emission Vehicle standards and you'll be getting one of this year's greenest vehicles. The Mirage handles crisply, and the interior is fairly comfortable for four people. Ride is decent.

The Ratings

	POOR ... GOOD
COMPARATIVE RATING*	(no rating)
FRONTAL CRASH TEST	(no rating)
SAFETY FEATURES	▮ (mid)
FUEL ECONOMY	▮ (high/good)
PM COST	▮ (low/poor)
REPAIR COST	▮ (mid-high)
WARRANTY	▮ (mid)
COMPLAINTS	▮ (low/poor)
INSURANCE COST	▮ (low/poor)

Safety

FRONTAL CRASH TEST	No government results
SIDE CRASH TEST	No government results
AIRBAGS	Dual
ANTI-LOCK BRAKES	4-Wheel
DAY. RUNNING LIGHTS	None
BELT ADJUSTORS	Standard
BUILT-IN CHILD SEAT	None
PRETENSIONERS	None

General Information

WHERE MADE	Japan
YEAR OF PRODUCTION	Third
PARKING INDEX	Very Easy
BUMPERS	Strong
THEFT RATING	
TWINS	
GREEN RATING	Good

Specifications

FUEL ECONOMY (cty/hwy)	33/40	Very Good
DRIVING RANGE (miles)	482	Very Long
SEATING	5	
LENGTH (in.)	168.1	
HEAD/LEG ROOM (in.)	38.6/43	Average
INTERIOR SPACE (cu. ft.)	85.6	Vry. Cramped
CARGO SPACE (cu. ft.)	11.5	Very Small

Specifications may vary.

Prices

Model	Retail	Mkup
DE Coupe Manual	11,150	8%
DE Sedan Automatic	13,140	9%
LS Coupe Manual	14,600	9%
LS Sedan Automatic	14,090	9%

Competition

	POOR ... GOOD	Pg.
Mitsubishi Mirage	(no rating)	184
Chevrolet Cavalier	▮ (mid)	123
Mercury Tracer	▮ (low)	179
Saturn SL/SW	▮ (mid-high)	206

*Due to the importance of crash tests, cars with no results as of publication date cannot be given an overall rating.

Nissan Altima

After the all-new model was released last year, there are only a few changes for this year's Altima. These include new windshield wipers, an improved stereo system, and new wheels on GLE models. Road noise was decreased with new insulation in '98. Standard dual airbags have been de-powered, ABS is still optional.

A revised 2.4-liter, 4-cylinder engine powers the new Altima, providing 150 hp. Four trim levels are available with a variety of new options packages. Be sure to look over the options list carefully. A remote keyless entry and security system is standard on the SE and GLE models. Poor performance on government crash tests gives the Altima a low overall score.

The Ratings

	POOR	GOOD
COMPARATIVE RATING	■	
FRONTAL CRASH TEST		
SAFETY FEATURES		
FUEL ECONOMY		
PM COST		
REPAIR COST		
WARRANTY		
COMPLAINTS		
INSURANCE COST	■	

Safety

FRONTAL CRASH TEST	Poor
SIDE CRASH TEST	Average
AIRBAGS	Dual (New Design)
ANTI-LOCK BRAKES	4-Wheel (opt)
DAY. RUNNING LIGHTS	None
BELT ADJUSTORS	Standard
BUILT-IN CHILD SEAT	None
PRETENSIONERS	Standard

General Information

WHERE MADE	U.S.
YEAR OF PRODUCTION	Second
PARKING INDEX	Easy
BUMPERS	Strong
THEFT RATING	High
TWINS	
GREEN RATING	Average

Specifications

FUEL ECONOMY (cty/hwy)	24/31	Average
DRIVING RANGE (miles)	437	Average
SEATING	5	
LENGTH (in.)	183.5	
HEAD/LEG ROOM (in.)	39.4/42	Average
INTERIOR SPACE (cu. ft.)	94	Average
CARGO SPACE (cu. ft.)	13.8	Average

Specifications may vary.

Prices

Model	Retail	Mkup
XE Sedan Manual	14,990	4%
GXE Manual	17,190	8%
SE Manual	18,490	9%
GLE Automatic	19,990	9%

Competition

	POOR	GOOD	Pg.
Nissan Altima	■		185
Buick LeSabre			113
Oldsmobile Cutlass			192
Toyota Camry			213

Nissan's flagship, the Maxima, gets no major changes for 1999. The big changes will be next year. Dual airbags are standard, and you'll have to pay extra for ABS and traction control. Side airbags are a option and optimal.

The 3-liter V6 is powerful and quite fuel efficient. The GXE and GLE trim levels come standard with an automatic transmission, while the SE comes with a five speed manual. The large wheelbase increases interior room, making the front seats quite comfortable and improving the ride. But handling is mediocre. The rear seats will be comfortable for most adults. You'll have the typical Nissan variety of trim levels and option packages, so shop carefully.

The Ratings

	POOR ← → GOOD
COMPARATIVE RATING	▪ (middle)
FRONTAL CRASH TEST	▪ (good side)
SAFETY FEATURES	▪ (good side)
FUEL ECONOMY	▪ (left-center)
PM COST	▪ (center)
REPAIR COST	▪ (poor end)
WARRANTY	▪ (left-center)
COMPLAINTS	▪ (good end)
INSURANCE COST	▪ (poor end)

Safety

FRONTAL CRASH TEST	Good
SIDE CRASH TEST	Good
AIRBAGS	Dual & Side(opt.) (New Design)
ANTI-LOCK BRAKES	4-Wheel (opt)
DAY. RUNNING LIGHTS	None
BELT ADJUSTORS	Standard
BUILT-IN CHILD SEAT	None
PRETENSIONERS	Standard

General Information

WHERE MADE	Japan
YEAR OF PRODUCTION	Fifth
PARKING INDEX	Easy
BUMPERS	Strong
THEFT RATING	Very High
TWINS	Infiniti I30
GREEN RATING	Poor

Specifications

FUEL ECONOMY (cty/hwy)	22/27	Poor
DRIVING RANGE (miles)	453	Long
SEATING	5	
LENGTH (in.)	189.4	
HEAD/LEG ROOM (in.)	40.1/43.9	Very Roomy
INTERIOR SPACE (cu. ft.)	99.6	Roomy
CARGO SPACE (cu. ft.)	14.5	Average

Specifications may vary.

Prices

Model	Retail	Mkup
GXE Manual	21,499	9%
SE Manual	23,499	10%
SE Automatic	24,499	10%
GLE Automatic	26,899	10%

Competition

	POOR ← → GOOD	Pg.
Nissan Maxima	▪ (center)	**186**
Chevrolet Lumina	▪ (good side)	124
Ford Taurus	▪ (good side)	145
Toyota Camry	▪ (center)	213

All-new for this year, the Quest gets a new exterior, a roomier interior, and the popular driver side sliding door. Dual airbags are standard and de-powered for '99. 4-wheel ABS is now standard on all models.

The new engine is a 3.3 liter V6, with 170 hp, acceleration and power are good with poor fuel economy. You'll find the ride and handling are good by minivan standards. On the interior, seating is comfortable and the Quest offers integrated child safety seats which are great options for parents. With Nissan's flexible seating system, you should be able to arrange the seating to suit most any purpose. The middle and rear seats are easy to remove to increase cargo space.

The Ratings

	POOR	GOOD
COMPARATIVE RATING*		
FRONTAL CRASH TEST		
SAFETY FEATURES		
FUEL ECONOMY		
PM COST		
REPAIR COST		
WARRANTY		
COMPLAINTS		
INSURANCE COST		

Safety

FRONTAL CRASH TEST	No government results
SIDE CRASH TEST	No government results
AIRBAGS	Dual (New Design)
ANTI-LOCK BRAKES	4-Wheel
DAY. RUNNING LIGHTS	None
BELT ADJUSTORS	Standard
BUILT-IN CHILD SEAT	Optional
PRETENSIONERS	Standard

General Information

WHERE MADE	U.S.
YEAR OF PRODUCTION	First
PARKING INDEX	Hard
BUMPERS	
THEFT RATING	Average
TWINS	Mercury Villager
GREEN RATING	Very Poor

Specifications

FUEL ECONOMY (cty/hwy)	17/24	Very Poor
DRIVING RANGE (miles)	410	Short
SEATING	7	
LENGTH (in.)	194.8	
HEAD/LEG ROOM (in.)	39.7/39.9	Vry. Cramped
INTERIOR SPACE (cu. ft.)		
CARGO SPACE (cu. ft.)	135.6	Very Large

Specifications may vary.

Prices

Model	Retail	Mkup
XE 7 pass	23,099	11%
GXE 7 pass	26,049	11%

Competition

	POOR	GOOD	Pg.
Nissan Quest			**187**
Chevrolet Venture			129
Ford Windstar			146
Plymouth Voyager			196

*Due to the importance of crash tests, cars with no results as of publication date cannot be given an overall rating.

A facelift for the '99 Sentra gives it new headlights, and grille. You have five trim levels to choose from: base, XE, GXE, GLE and the new sporty SE. Dual airbags are standard, optional ABS is available only on the GXE, SE, and GLE models.

The 1.6-liter, 4-cylinder engine, standard on all the trim levels except SE, is only adequate, but gets good gas mileage. The SE gets a 2.0-liter, 140 hp engine that provides more power. The Sentra handles and rides better than its predecessors and is good, basic transportation. With decent crash test results and an up-to-date look, the Sentra is a good choice and worth a test drive.

The Ratings

	POOR GOOD
COMPARATIVE RATING	
FRONTAL CRASH TEST	
SAFETY FEATURES	
FUEL ECONOMY	
PM COST	
REPAIR COST	
WARRANTY	
COMPLAINTS	
INSURANCE COST	

Safety

FRONTAL CRASH TEST	Average
SIDE CRASH TEST	Average
AIRBAGS	Dual (New Design)
ANTI-LOCK BRAKES	4-Wheel (opt)
DAY. RUNNING LIGHTS	None
BELT ADJUSTORS	Standard
BUILT-IN CHILD SEAT	None
PRETENSIONERS	Standard

General Information

WHERE MADE	U.S./Mexico
YEAR OF PRODUCTION	Fifth
PARKING INDEX	Very Easy
BUMPERS	Strong
THEFT RATING	Average
TWINS	
GREEN RATING	Average

Specifications

FUEL ECONOMY (cty/hwy)	29/39	Very Good
DRIVING RANGE (miles)	449	Long
SEATING	5	
LENGTH (in.)	171	
HEAD/LEG ROOM (in.)	39.1/42.3	Average
INTERIOR SPACE (cu. ft.)	87.2	Cramped
CARGO SPACE (cu. ft.)	10.7	Very Small

Specifications may vary.

Prices

Model	Retail	Mkup
Base Manual	11,499	5%
XE Manual	13,699	7%
GXE Manual	14,899	9%
SE Manual	16,749	9%

Competition

	POOR GOOD	Pg.
Nissan Sentra		**188**
Chevrolet Cavalier		123
Honda Civic		150
Saturn SL/SW		206

Oldsmobile 88

For 1999, the Oldsmobile 88 remains unchanged and will be phased out next year. The 88, which shares a platform with the Buick LeSabre and Pontiac Bonneville, used to come in three trim levels, but now only has two: the base and LS. The LSS trim level has become its own line (but don't be fooled, it's still based on the 88). Dual airbags and ABS are standard.

The 88's 3.8-liter V6, connected to an automatic overdrive, delivers plenty of smooth power. You only have one engine choice, as in years past, and the suspension favors a too-soft ride at the expense of handling. The optional touring suspension and speed-sensitive steering dramatically improve performance. The LSS is slightly smaller and aimed at the import car buyer. The 88, with its good crash tests, is worth considering.

The Ratings

	POOR → GOOD
COMPARATIVE RATING	▮ (good side)
FRONTAL CRASH TEST	▮ (good side)
SAFETY FEATURES	▮ (good side)
FUEL ECONOMY	▮ (poor side)
PM COST	▮ (middle)
REPAIR COST	▮ (good side)
WARRANTY	▮ (poor side)
COMPLAINTS	▮ (good side)
INSURANCE COST	▮ (good side)

Safety

FRONTAL CRASH TEST	Good
SIDE CRASH TEST	Poor
AIRBAGS	Dual (New Design)
ANTI-LOCK BRAKES	4-Wheel
DAY. RUNNING LIGHTS	Standard
BELT ADJUSTORS	Standard
BUILT-IN CHILD SEAT	None
PRETENSIONERS	None

General Information

WHERE MADE	U.S.
YEAR OF PRODUCTION	Eighth
PARKING INDEX	Very Hard
BUMPERS	Strong
THEFT RATING	Very Low
TWINS	LeSabre, Bonneville
GREEN RATING	Poor

Specifications

FUEL ECONOMY (cty/hwy)	19/29	Poor
DRIVING RANGE (miles)	432	Average
SEATING	5-6	
LENGTH (in.)	200.4	
HEAD/LEG ROOM (in.)	38.7/42.5	Average
INTERIOR SPACE (cu. ft.)	106	Very Roomy
CARGO SPACE (cu. ft.)	18	Very Large

Specifications may vary.

Prices

Model	Retail	Mkup
Base	22,795	8%
LS	24,195	8%

Competition

	POOR → GOOD	Pg.
Oldsmobile 88	▮	**189**
Buick LeSabre	▮	113
Mercury Gr. Marquis	▮	176
Pontiac Bonneville	▮	197

Oldsmobile Alero

The all new Alero is Oldsmobile's answer to the Honda Accord. The Alero comes in three trim levels. The GX and the standard GL run on a 2.4 liter 4 cylinder engine, and the GLS uses a 3.4 liter V6. All have a 4-speed automatic transmission.

Safety features standard on all models include de-powered airbags for front occupants, ABS and traction control. Also available for all models are rear window defoggers, a theft deterrent system, and daytime running lamps. The more luxurious GLS offers leather interior, a CD player, remote keyless entry, and front fog lights as standard features.

The Ratings

	POOR — GOOD
COMPARATIVE RATING*	
FRONTAL CRASH TEST	
SAFETY FEATURES	▮
FUEL ECONOMY	▮
PM COST	▮
REPAIR COST	▮
WARRANTY	▮
COMPLAINTS	▮
INSURANCE COST	▮

Safety

FRONTAL CRASH TEST	No government results
SIDE CRASH TEST	No government results
AIRBAGS	Dual (New Design)
ANTI-LOCK BRAKES	4-Wheel
DAY. RUNNING LIGHTS	Standard
BELT ADJUSTORS	Standard
BUILT-IN CHILD SEAT	None
PRETENSIONERS	None

General Information

WHERE MADE	U.S.
YEAR OF PRODUCTION	First
PARKING INDEX	Easy
BUMPERS	Strong
THEFT RATING	
TWINS	
GREEN RATING	Poor

Specifications

FUEL ECONOMY (cty/hwy)	22/30	Average
DRIVING RANGE (miles)	390	Short
SEATING	5	
LENGTH (in.)	186.7	
HEAD/LEG ROOM (in.)	38.2/42.1	Cramped
INTERIOR SPACE (cu. ft.)	92.6	Cramped
CARGO SPACE (cu. ft.)	14.6	Average

Specifications may vary.

Prices

Model	Retail	Mkup
GX Coupe	16,325	6%
GL Coupe	18,655	8%
GX Sedan	16,325	6%
GL Sedan	18,220	9%

Competition

	POOR — GOOD	Pg.
Oldsmobile Alero		190
Chrysler Sebring	▮	134
Dodge Avenger	▮	136
Honda Accord	▮	149

*Due to the importance of crash tests, cars with no results as of publication date cannot be given an overall rating.

Oldsmobile Aurora

First introduced in 1995, the Aurora enters 1999 with only the addition of a few exterior color choices. This is Oldsmobile's first attempt at updating the styling of their aging cars. The Onstar roadside assistance system is an option. Dual airbags, ABS, traction control, and speed-variable power steering are standard.

The Aurora benefits from a rigid structure and rides well for a car its size. However, it does tend to wallow in turns, which is typical of large cars. The 4-liter V8 is more powerful than most any of its competitors, and its fuel economy, though not notable, holds its own with the competition. Room for five is fine, though not quite as generous as some of the larger domestics.

The Ratings

	POOR — GOOD
COMPARATIVE RATING	
FRONTAL CRASH TEST	
SAFETY FEATURES	
FUEL ECONOMY	
PM COST	
REPAIR COST	
WARRANTY	
COMPLAINTS	
INSURANCE COST	

Safety

FRONTAL CRASH TEST	Average
SIDE CRASH TEST	No government results
AIRBAGS	Dual (New Design)
ANTI-LOCK BRAKES	4-Wheel
DAY. RUNNING LIGHTS	Standard
BELT ADJUSTORS	Standard
BUILT-IN CHILD SEAT	None
PRETENSIONERS	None

General Information

WHERE MADE	U.S./Canada
YEAR OF PRODUCTION	Fifth
PARKING INDEX	Very Hard
BUMPERS	Strong
THEFT RATING	Very Low
TWINS	Pk. Ave., Riviera, Seville
GREEN RATING	Very Poor

Specifications

FUEL ECONOMY (cty/hwy)	17/26	Very Poor
DRIVING RANGE (miles)	430	Average
SEATING	5	
LENGTH (in.)	205.4	
HEAD/LEG ROOM (in.)	38.4/42.6	Average
INTERIOR SPACE (cu. ft.)	102	Roomy
CARGO SPACE (cu. ft.)	16.1	Large

Specifications may vary.

Prices

Model	Retail	Mkup
Sedan	36,160	9%

Competition

	POOR — GOOD	Pg.
Oldsmobile Aurora		**191**
Audi A4		106
Buick Riviera		116
Infiniti I30		159

Oldsmobile Cutlass

In '87, Oldsmobile introduced the new Cutlass in an effort to attract younger buyers with sleeker lines and an improved interior. Outside, the 1999 Cutlass remains unchanged, though you'll see it in two new colors this year: bronze mist and dark cherry. Dual airbags are standard, ABS is optional.

Powering the new Cutlass will be an improved 3.1 liter V6 engine which should provide good, smooth power. A refined suspension should make the ride more enjoyable. Because of an increased wheelbase, passengers will have more head and leg room, making the interior very comfortable. The government's crash test this past year yielded good results, but a poor complaint score brings down the car's overall rating.

The Ratings

	POOR / GOOD
COMPARATIVE RATING	▮ (middle)
FRONTAL CRASH TEST	▮ (good)
SAFETY FEATURES	▮ (good)
FUEL ECONOMY	▮ (middle)
PM COST	▮ (middle)
REPAIR COST	▮ (good)
WARRANTY	▮ (poor)
COMPLAINTS	▮ (poor)
INSURANCE COST	▮ (good)

Safety

FRONTAL CRASH TEST	Good
SIDE CRASH TEST	Poor
AIRBAGS	Dual (New Design)
ANTI-LOCK BRAKES	4-Wheel
DAY. RUNNING LIGHTS	Standard
BELT ADJUSTORS	Standard
BUILT-IN CHILD SEAT	None
PRETENSIONERS	None

General Information

WHERE MADE	U.S.
YEAR OF PRODUCTION	Third
PARKING INDEX	Easy
BUMPERS	Strong
THEFT RATING	Average
TWINS	Chevrolet Malibu
GREEN RATING	Average

Specifications

FUEL ECONOMY (cty/hwy)	22/30	Average
DRIVING RANGE (miles)	395	Short
SEATING	5	
LENGTH (in.)	192	
HEAD/LEG ROOM (in.)	39.4/42.1	Average
INTERIOR SPACE (cu. ft.)	98	Average
CARGO SPACE (cu. ft.)	17	Very Large

Specifications may vary.

Prices

Model	Retail	Mkup
GL	17,800	8%
GLS	19,425	8%

Competition

	POOR / GOOD	Pg.
Olds Cutlass	▮ (middle)	192
Buick Regal	▮ (good)	115
Mercury Sable	▮ (good)	178
Toyota Camry	▮ (middle)	213

Oldsmobile Intrigue

With the Oldsmobile Intrigue, Olds wants to win over import buyers who like the Toyota Camry, Honda Accord and Nissan Maxima. A replacement for the geriatric Cutlass Supreme, the Intrigue looks vaguely like the Oldsmobile Aurora, but shares a platform with the Buick Regal and Pontiac Grand Prix. Dual airbags, 4-wheel ABS and traction control all come standard.

You'll find a 3.8-liter V6 engine under the hood, which provides adequate power. New for '99 is a 3.5 liter twin cam V6, only slightly more powerful. Interior space is good, and trunk space is ample. Consider the autobahn package which includes bigger tires, better steering and a higher performance brake system.

The Ratings

(POOR → GOOD)

COMPARATIVE RATING	Poor
FRONTAL CRASH TEST	Below Average
SAFETY FEATURES	Above Average
FUEL ECONOMY	Below Average
PM COST	Average
REPAIR COST	Good
WARRANTY	Poor
COMPLAINTS	Average
INSURANCE COST	Average

Safety

FRONTAL CRASH TEST	Average
SIDE CRASH TEST	Very Poor
AIRBAGS	Dual (New Design)
ANTI-LOCK BRAKES	4-Wheel
DAY. RUNNING LIGHTS	Standard
BELT ADJUSTORS	Standard
BUILT-IN CHILD SEAT	None
PRETENSIONERS	None

General Information

WHERE MADE	U.S./Canada
YEAR OF PRODUCTION	Second
PARKING INDEX	Average
BUMPERS	Strong
THEFT RATING	
TWINS	
GREEN RATING	Poor

Specifications

FUEL ECONOMY (cty/hwy)	19/27	Poor
DRIVING RANGE (miles)	391	Short
SEATING	5	
LENGTH (in.)	195.9	
HEAD/LEG ROOM (in.)	39.3/42.4	Average
INTERIOR SPACE (cu. ft.)	101	Roomy
CARGO SPACE (cu. ft.)	16.7	Large

Specifications may vary.

Prices

Model	Retail	Mkup
Base	20,890	8%
GL	22,290	9%
GLS	24,110	8%

Competition

(POOR → GOOD)

	Rating	Pg.
Olds Intrigue	Poor	193
Chevrolet Lumina	Good	124
Ford Taurus	Above Average	145
Toyota Camry	Below Average	213

The newest gadget for this minivan is a video system on the new Premier Edition, offering TV screens, a video player, CD player, and head phones. But aside from traveling entertainment, the Silhouette gets heated outside mirrors, an improved anti-theft system, and a more powerful engine. Dual airbags were de-powered on the '98s. Side airbags, and ABS are standard.

There are four models available: the GL, GS, and GLS, and the Premier. Each comes with an increasingly higher level of standard equipment. The engine is a 3.4 liter V6 which should provide good acceleration. There are many different seating arrangements and plenty of cup holders. A handy option is the power assist right-side sliding door. The new Silhouette should compete well.

The Ratings

	POOR → GOOD
COMPARATIVE RATING	▮ (below middle)
FRONTAL CRASH TEST	▮ (good side)
SAFETY FEATURES	▮ (good side)
FUEL ECONOMY	▮ (poor side)
PM COST	▮ (good side)
REPAIR COST	▮ (middle)
WARRANTY	▮ (poor side)
COMPLAINTS	▮ (poor side)
INSURANCE COST	▮ (good side)

Safety

FRONTAL CRASH TEST	Good
SIDE CRASH TEST	No government results
AIRBAGS	Dual & Side (New Design)
ANTI-LOCK BRAKES	4-Wheel
DAY. RUNNING LIGHTS	Standard
BELT ADJUSTORS	Standard
BUILT-IN CHILD SEAT	Optional(2)
PRETENSIONERS	Standard

General Information

WHERE MADE	U.S./Canada
YEAR OF PRODUCTION	Third
PARKING INDEX	Average
BUMPERS	Weak
THEFT RATING	
TWINS	Venture, Montana
GREEN RATING	Very Poor

Specifications

FUEL ECONOMY (cty/hwy)	18/25	Very Poor
DRIVING RANGE (miles)	430	Average
SEATING	7-8	
LENGTH (in.)	187.4	
HEAD/LEG ROOM (in.)	39.9/39.9	Vry. Cramped
INTERIOR SPACE (cu. ft.)		
CARGO SPACE (cu. ft.)	133.0	Very Large

Specifications may vary.

Prices

Model	Retail	Mkup
GS	24,430	9%
GL	24,065	9%
GLS	27,320	10%
Premiere Edition	30,605	9%

Competition

	POOR → GOOD	Pg.
Olds Silhouette	▮ (below middle)	194
Chrysler T&C	▮ (poor side)	135
Dodge Caravan	▮ (poor side)	137
Ford Windstar	▮ (middle)	146

Plymouth Breeze

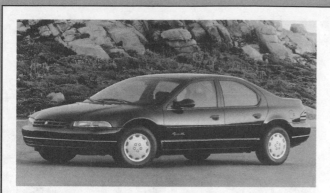

No changes this year for the Breeze, or its close twins, the Chrysler Cirrus and Dodge Stratus. Essentially a base model to its more upscale twins, the Breeze continues its Espresso package which includes wheel covers, accent colors on the front and rear end and a premium audio system. Dual airbags and 4-wheel ABS are standard.

Only one model is available and it comes standard with the 2.0-liter engine with a manual transmission. A 2.4-liter engine is optional and provides more power. The cab-forward design gives the passenger ample interior space. The Breeze only received average crash tests results, but a low price keeps it competitive.

The Ratings

	POOR GOOD
COMPARATIVE RATING	▮ (middle)
FRONTAL CRASH TEST	▮ (middle)
SAFETY FEATURES	▮ (middle)
FUEL ECONOMY	▮ (good)
PM COST	▮ (good)
REPAIR COST	▮ (good)
WARRANTY	▮ (poor)
COMPLAINTS	▮ (good)
INSURANCE COST	▮ (middle)

Safety

FRONTAL CRASH TEST	Average
SIDE CRASH TEST	Average
AIRBAGS	Dual (New Design)
ANTI-LOCK BRAKES	4-Wheel (opt)
DAY. RUNNING LIGHTS	None
BELT ADJUSTORS	Standard
BUILT-IN CHILD SEAT	None
PRETENSIONERS	None

General Information

WHERE MADE	U.S.
YEAR OF PRODUCTION	Fourth
PARKING INDEX	Easy
BUMPERS	Weak
THEFT RATING	Low
TWINS	Cirrus, Stratus
GREEN RATING	Average

Specifications

FUEL ECONOMY (cty/hwy)	26/37	Good
DRIVING RANGE (miles)	504	Very Long
SEATING	5	
LENGTH (in.)	186.7	
HEAD/LEG ROOM (in.)	38.1/42.3	Cramped
INTERIOR SPACE (cu. ft.)	67.2	Vry. Cramped
CARGO SPACE (cu. ft.)	15.7	Large

Specifications may vary.

Prices

Model	Retail	Mkup
Sedan	14,975	8%

Competition

	POOR GOOD	Pg.
Plymouth Breeze	▮ (middle)	**195**
Buick Regal	▮ (good)	115
Ford Contour	▮ (middle)	141
Subaru Legacy	▮ (good)	208

Plymouth Voyager

The Voyager is leading the pack in sales in a highly competitive minivan market. Safety features include standard de-powered dual airbags and a structure that meets '99 government side impact standards for trucks, vans and 4x4s. ABS is standard on the Grand Voyager, but you have to pay extra on the base models. You get to choose between four engines: an inadequate 2.5-liter 4-cylinder, an adequate 3-liter V6, a 3.3-liter V6 flex fuel option that runs on ethanol or gasoline, and a 3.3 liter gasoline V6. Since Grand Voyagers have a longer wheelbase and a body with more room, the 3.3-liter is worth the extra money. Handling improves with the heavy duty suspension, and the ride remains good. Of the three Chrysler minivans, the Voyager is the most affordable.

The Ratings

	POOR — GOOD
COMPARATIVE RATING	▪ (poor)
FRONTAL CRASH TEST	▪ (mid)
SAFETY FEATURES	▪ (mid)
FUEL ECONOMY	▪ (poor-mid)
PM COST	▪ (good)
REPAIR COST	▪ (good)
WARRANTY	▪ (poor)
COMPLAINTS	▪ (poor)
INSURANCE COST	▪ (very good)

Safety

FRONTAL CRASH TEST	Good
SIDE CRASH TEST	No government results
AIRBAGS	Dual (New Design)
ANTI-LOCK BRAKES	4-Wheel (opt)
DAY. RUNNING LIGHTS	None
BELT ADJUSTORS	Standard
BUILT-IN CHILD SEAT	Optional
PRETENSIONERS	None

General Information

WHERE MADE	U.S./Canada
YEAR OF PRODUCTION	Fourth
PARKING INDEX	Average
BUMPERS	Strong
THEFT RATING	Low
TWINS	Dodge Caravan
GREEN RATING	Very Poor

Specifications

FUEL ECONOMY (cty/hwy)	20/26	Poor
DRIVING RANGE (miles)	460	Long
SEATING	7	
LENGTH (in.)	186.3	
HEAD/LEG ROOM (in.)	39.8/40.6	Cramped
INTERIOR SPACE (cu. ft.)		
CARGO SPACE (cu. ft.)	126.7	Very Large

Specifications may vary.

Prices

Model	Retail	Mkup
Voyager	17,905	9%
Voyager SE	21,780	10%
Grand Voyager	21,040	9%
Grand Voyager SE	22,775	10%

Competition

	POOR — GOOD	Pg.
Plymouth Voyager	▪ (poor)	196
Chevrolet Venture	▪ (mid)	129
Dodge Caravan	▪ (poor-mid)	137
Ford Windstar	▪ (mid)	146

Pontiac Bonneville

A handful of new colors are the only change for this year's Bonneville. The base model is the SE, the SSE is more refined. The SLE is a sporty package available on the SE. Traction control is available on the SSE, and a super-charged engine is offered on both the SE and SSE. Dual airbags and ABS are standard; day-time running lamps are a great standard safety feature. ou can easily spend over $25,000 for a Bonneville, so shop wisely. Stick to the base SE with the performance and handling package. The base 3.8-liter V6 is powerful enough; the optional, supercharged V6 adds only a little more power and more repair complexity. Interior room and trunk space is good; the driver's visibility could be better. The Bonneville is a viable alternative to the Japanese luxury sports sedans.

The Ratings

	POOR GOOD
COMPARATIVE RATING	■ (good side)
FRONTAL CRASH TEST	■
SAFETY FEATURES	■
FUEL ECONOMY	■ (poor side)
PM COST	■
REPAIR COST	■
WARRANTY	■ (poor side)
COMPLAINTS	■
INSURANCE COST	■

Safety

FRONTAL CRASH TEST	Good
SIDE CRASH TEST	Poor
AIRBAGS	Dual (New Design)
ANTI-LOCK BRAKES	4-Wheel
DAY. RUNNING LIGHTS	Standard
BELT ADJUSTORS	Standard
BUILT-IN CHILD SEAT	None
PRETENSIONERS	None

General Information

WHERE MADE	U.S.
YEAR OF PRODUCTION	Eighth
PARKING INDEX	Hard
BUMPERS	Strong
THEFT RATING	Very Low
TWINS	LeSabre, 88
GREEN RATING	Poor

Specifications

FUEL ECONOMY (cty/hwy)	19/28	Poor
DRIVING RANGE (miles)	423	Average
SEATING	5	
LENGTH (in.)	200.5	
HEAD/LEG ROOM (in.)	39.2/42.6	Roomy
INTERIOR SPACE (cu. ft.)	108.8	Very Roomy
CARGO SPACE (cu. ft.)	18	Very Large

Specifications may vary.

Prices

Model	Retail	Mkup
SE	22,545	8%
SSE	29,545	8%

Competition

	POOR GOOD	Pg.
Pontiac Bonneville	■	**197**
Buick LeSabre	■	113
Infiniti I30	■	159
Lexus ES300	■	163

Pontiac Firebird

The twin of the Camaro, the Firebird has been a mainstay in the American sports car market for years. For 1999, the Firebird gets electronic traction control, a bigger fuel tank, an oil life monitor, and some new paint colors. Earlier this year the Firebird got great results in the government crash tests. Dual airbags and 4-wheel ABS are standard on all models.

The standard 3.8 liter V6 should offer good power and acceleration. The Trans Am comes standard with a 5.7-Liter V8 that is more powerful and only slightly less economical than the standard engine. Both the V6 and the V8 have a new limited slip rear differential that sends power to the wheel with the best traction in the event of wheel slippage The ride is firm and the handling is good. Room inside is good for the driver and front seat passenger.

The Ratings

	POOR	GOOD
COMPARATIVE RATING		
FRONTAL CRASH TEST		
SAFETY FEATURES		
FUEL ECONOMY		
PM COST		
REPAIR COST		
WARRANTY		
COMPLAINTS		
INSURANCE COST		

Safety

FRONTAL CRASH TEST	Very Good
SIDE CRASH TEST	Good
AIRBAGS	Dual
ANTI-LOCK BRAKES	4-Wheel
DAY. RUNNING LIGHTS	Standard
BELT ADJUSTORS	None
BUILT-IN CHILD SEAT	None
PRETENSIONERS	None

General Information

WHERE MADE	Canada
YEAR OF PRODUCTION	Seventh
PARKING INDEX	Average
BUMPERS	Strong
THEFT RATING	Average
TWINS	Chevrolet Camaro
GREEN RATING	Poor

Specifications

FUEL ECONOMY (cty/hwy)	19/30	Poor
DRIVING RANGE (miles)	412	Short
SEATING	4	
LENGTH (in.)	193.3	
HEAD/LEG ROOM (in.)	37.2/43	Cramped
INTERIOR SPACE (cu. ft.)	84	Vry. Cramped
CARGO SPACE (cu. ft.)	12.9	Small

Specifications may vary.

Prices

Model	Retail	Mkup
Firebird	18,015	8%
Formula	22,865	8%
Trans Am	25,975	8%
Convertible	24,305	8%

Competition

	POOR	GOOD	Pg.
Pontiac Firebird			198
Chevrolet Camaro			122
Ford Mustang			144
Mitsubishi Eclipse			182

One of the few all new models for 1999, the Grand Am has a long list of changes. A wider wheelbase and track width give the Grand Am a more solid appearance. A stronger, 170 horsepower 3.4 liter V6 engine is standard on the SE2 and GT models. The standard 2.4-liter Twin Cam engine for the SE and SE1 makes the Grand Am fun to drive, though fuel economy is poor. Also for '99 is a new cockpit design, redesigned bucket seats, four wheel fully independent suspension, enhanced traction system, fog lamps, and standard ABS. Dual airbags and daytime running lamps are standard and you can find height adjustable safety belts, which should improve comfort and safety. Armed with de-powered airbags for both front occupants, the Grand Am is set to be tested in the government's crash test this year.

The Ratings

	POOR — GOOD
COMPARATIVE RATING*	(no rating)
FRONTAL CRASH TEST	(no rating)
SAFETY FEATURES	▮
FUEL ECONOMY	▮
PM COST	▮
REPAIR COST	▮
WARRANTY	▮
COMPLAINTS	▮
INSURANCE COST	▮

Safety

FRONTAL CRASH TEST	No government results
SIDE CRASH TEST	No government results
AIRBAGS	Dual (New Design)
ANTI-LOCK BRAKES	4-Wheel
DAY. RUNNING LIGHTS	Standard
BELT ADJUSTORS	Standard (Sedan)
BUILT-IN CHILD SEAT	None
PRETENSIONERS	None

General Information

WHERE MADE	U.S.
YEAR OF PRODUCTION	First
PARKING INDEX	Average
BUMPERS	
THEFT RATING	Low
TWINS	
GREEN RATING	Average

Specifications

FUEL ECONOMY (cty/hwy)	22/30	Average
DRIVING RANGE (miles)	395	Short
SEATING	5	
LENGTH (in.)	186.3	
HEAD/LEG ROOM (in.)	38.3/42.1	Cramped
INTERIOR SPACE (cu. ft.)	93	Average
CARGO SPACE (cu. ft.)	14.3	Average

Specifications may vary.

Prices

Model	Retail	Mkup
SE Coupe	15,870	9%
GT Coupe	19,070	9%
SE Sedan	16,070	9%
GT Sedan	19,470	9%

Competition

	POOR — GOOD	Pg.
Pontiac Grand Am	(no rating)	**199**
Chev. Monte Carlo	▮	127
Ford Taurus	▮	145
Honda Accord	▮	149

*Due to the importance of crash tests, cars with no results as of publication date cannot be given an overall rating.

Pontiac Grand Prix

This year the Grand Prix gets few changes. A theft-deterrent system, CD player, and the optional OnStar communications systems are some of the perks offered this year. The Grand Prix's dual airbags helped it perform well on the government's frontal crash tests, though side crash tests yielded only average results.

The Grand Prix is available in both coupe and sedan body styles with two trim levels: the base SE or the up-level GT. The standard 3.8 liter V6 engine gets a 5 hp boost to make 200 which should be ample power for this car, though you can choose a supercharged version of the same engine and get 240 horses.

The Ratings

	POOR GOOD
COMPARATIVE RATING	▢▢▢▢■▢▢▢▢▢
FRONTAL CRASH TEST	▢▢▢▢▢▢▢■▢▢
SAFETY FEATURES	▢▢▢▢▢▢▢▢■▢
FUEL ECONOMY	▢▢▢■▢▢▢▢▢▢
PM COST	▢▢▢▢▢▢■▢▢▢
REPAIR COST	▢▢▢▢▢▢■▢▢▢
WARRANTY	■▢▢▢▢▢▢▢▢▢
COMPLAINTS	▢■▢▢▢▢▢▢▢▢
INSURANCE COST	▢▢▢▢▢▢▢▢▢■

Safety

FRONTAL CRASH TEST	Good
SIDE CRASH TEST	Average
AIRBAGS	Dual (New Design)
ANTI-LOCK BRAKES	4-Wheel
DAY. RUNNING LIGHTS	Standard
BELT ADJUSTORS	None
BUILT-IN CHILD SEAT	Optional
PRETENSIONERS	None

General Information

WHERE MADE	U.S.
YEAR OF PRODUCTION	Third
PARKING INDEX	Average
BUMPERS	Strong
THEFT RATING	Average
TWINS	Century, Regal
GREEN RATING	Poor

Specifications

FUEL ECONOMY (cty/hwy)	20/29	Poor
DRIVING RANGE (miles)	441	Long
SEATING	5	
LENGTH (in.)	196.5	
HEAD/LEG ROOM (in.)	38.3/42.4	Cramped
INTERIOR SPACE (cu. ft.)	99	Roomy
CARGO SPACE (cu. ft.)	16	Large

Specifications may vary.

Prices

Model	Retail	Mkup
SE Sedan	18,795	8%
GT Sedan	20,665	8%
GT Coupe	20,415	8%

Competition

	POOR GOOD	Pg.
Pontiac Grand Prix	▢▢▢▢■▢▢▢▢▢	200
Chevrolet Lumina	▢▢▢▢▢▢▢■▢▢	124
Dodge Avenger	▢▢▢■▢▢▢▢▢▢	136
Ford Taurus	▢▢▢▢▢▢▢■▢▢	145

Pontiac Montana

Previously known as the Trans Sport, the Montana is twin of the Chevrolet Venture and Oldsmobile Silhouette. The trim levels are noted by wheelbase: regular wheelbase of 112 inches, or extended wheelbase at 120. This year the minivan gets power sliding doors on extended wheelbase models, some new colors, a sport performance package that includes all weather traction control and specially tuned suspension. The well-used second sliding door is available on models with both a regular or extended wheelbase. Dual airbags, side airbags and ABS are standard. There are five seating arrangements with a total capacity of eight. The standard engine is a 3.4 liter V6 which should proved ample power. Many comfort features are available including 17 cup holders! With good crash test results, the Montana is worth considering.

The Ratings

	POOR GOOD
COMPARATIVE RATING	▮ (position 3)
FRONTAL CRASH TEST	▮ (position 7)
SAFETY FEATURES	▮ (position 8)
FUEL ECONOMY	▮ (position 1)
PM COST	▮ (position 7)
REPAIR COST	▮ (position 6)
WARRANTY	▮ (position 1)
COMPLAINTS	▮ (position 4)
INSURANCE COST	▮ (position 9)

Safety

FRONTAL CRASH TEST	Good
SIDE CRASH TEST	No government results
AIRBAGS	Dual & Side (New Design)
ANTI-LOCK BRAKES	4-Wheel
DAY. RUNNING LIGHTS	Standard
BELT ADJUSTORS	Standard
BUILT-IN CHILD SEAT	Optional
PRETENSIONERS	Standard

General Information

WHERE MADE	U.S.
YEAR OF PRODUCTION	Third
PARKING INDEX	Hard
BUMPERS	Strong
THEFT RATING	
TWINS	Venture, Silhouette
GREEN RATING	Very Poor

Specifications

FUEL ECONOMY (cty/hwy)	18/25	Very Poor
DRIVING RANGE (miles)	538	Very Long
SEATING	7-8	
LENGTH (in.)	187.3	
HEAD/LEG ROOM (in.)	39.9/39.9	Vry. Cramped
INTERIOR SPACE (cu. ft.)		
CARGO SPACE (cu. ft.)	126.6	Very Large

Specifications may vary.

Prices

Model	Retail	Mkup
SE Reg. Wheelbase 3dr	20,840	9%
SE Reg. Wheelbase Sedan	22,380	9%
SE Ext. Wheelbase Sedan	23,190	9%

Competition

	POOR GOOD	Pg.
Pontiac Montana	▮ (position 4)	201
Chrysler T&C	▮ (position 3)	135
Dodge Caravan	▮ (position 3)	137
Ford Windstar	▮ (position 5)	146

The coupe and convertible models of this Cavalier twin borrow heavily from the Firebird's design, helping cater to young drivers looking for an affordable, sporty car. Dual airbags and ABS are standard. Standard daytime running lamps and optional traction control are great features. The SE coupe, sedan and convertible come standard with a 2.2-liter engine that is adequate. The GT coupe has a 2.4-liter dual cam engine with 25% more power. For '99 that engine gets new fuel injectors, exhaust manifolds, fuel injector rails, and a new catalytic converter. Ride is good on smooth roads, a little bumpy on anything else. Noise level is better than most competitors. Attractive styling, adequate performance and make the Sunfire attractive among inexpensive sports cars, but note the poor side crash test results.

The Ratings

	POOR — GOOD
COMPARATIVE RATING	■ (center)
FRONTAL CRASH TEST	■ (good side)
SAFETY FEATURES	■ (good side)
FUEL ECONOMY	■ (good side)
PM COST	■ (center)
REPAIR COST	■ (center)
WARRANTY	■ (poor side)
COMPLAINTS	■ (good side)
INSURANCE COST	■ (poor side)

Safety

FRONTAL CRASH TEST	Good
SIDE CRASH TEST	2dr Vry. Pr./ 4dr Poor
AIRBAGS	Dual (New Design)
ANTI-LOCK BRAKES	4-Wheel
DAY. RUNNING LIGHTS	Standard
BELT ADJUSTORS	Standard
BUILT-IN CHILD SEAT	None
PRETENSIONERS	None

General Information

WHERE MADE	U.S.
YEAR OF PRODUCTION	Fifth
PARKING INDEX	Easy
BUMPERS	Strong
THEFT RATING	Low
TWINS	Chevrolet Cavalier
GREEN RATING	Average

Specifications

FUEL ECONOMY (cty/hwy)	24/34	Good
DRIVING RANGE (miles)	435	Average
SEATING	5	
LENGTH (in.)	181.9	
HEAD/LEG ROOM (in.)	37.6/42.1	Vry. Cramped
INTERIOR SPACE (cu. ft.)	87.2	Cramped
CARGO SPACE (cu. ft.)	12.4	Small

Specifications may vary.

Prices

Model	Retail	Mkup
SE Coupe	12,595	7%
SE Sedan	12,595	7%
SE convertible	19,495	7%
GT Coupe	15,595	7%

Competition

	POOR — GOOD	Pg.
Pontiac Sunfire	■ (center)	**202**
Dodge/Plym. Neon	■ (poor side)	139
Mercury Tracer	■ (poor-center)	179
Subaru Impreza	■ (center)	207

Saab 9-3

The Saab 9-3 model line includes a coupe, a 5 door, and a convertible. A 2.0 liter turbo engine powers all models, though a 200 hp version comes with the SE models. Other models have the 185 hp engine. A 5 speed transmission is standard, and comes with a hydraulically operated clutch for easy use. Seats in the Saab are wider than earlier models, large trunk room and a large cabin space make for a comfortable ride.

For safety, the 9-3 offers dual front and side airbags for front occupants. This year Saab unleashes a whiplash protection system, which uses a padded head restraint to catch a passenger's head as it snaps backwards in a frontal collision.

The Ratings

	POOR — GOOD
COMPARATIVE RATING*	(no rating)
FRONTAL CRASH TEST	(no rating)
SAFETY FEATURES	■ (high)
FUEL ECONOMY	■ (low)
PM COST	■ (high)
REPAIR COST	■ (very low)
WARRANTY	■ (high)
COMPLAINTS	■ (mid)
INSURANCE COST	■ (mid-low)

Safety

FRONTAL CRASH TEST	No government results
SIDE CRASH TEST	No government results
AIRBAGS	Dual & Side
ANTI-LOCK BRAKES	4-Wheel
DAY. RUNNING LIGHTS	Standard
BELT ADJUSTORS	Standard
BUILT-IN CHILD SEAT	Optional(2)
PRETENSIONERS	Standard

General Information

WHERE MADE	Sweden
YEAR OF PRODUCTION	First
PARKING INDEX	Easy
BUMPERS	
THEFT RATING	
TWINS	
GREEN RATING	Very Poor

Specifications

FUEL ECONOMY (cty/hwy)	20/27	Poor
DRIVING RANGE (miles)	423	Average
SEATING	5	
LENGTH (in.)	182.2	
HEAD/LEG ROOM (in.)	39.3/42.3	Average
INTERIOR SPACE (cu. ft.)	89.6	Cramped
CARGO SPACE (cu. ft.)	21.7	Very Large

Specifications may vary.

Prices

Model	Retail	Mkup
Hatchback 3dr	25,500	5%
Hatchback SE 5dr	31,500	5%
Convertible	36,500	4%
Convertible SE	41,500	4%

Competition

	POOR — GOOD	Pg.
Saab 9-3	(no rating)	203
Audi A4	■ (good)	106
Merc.-Benz C-Class	■ (mid)	173
Oldsmobile Aurora	■ (low)	191

*Due to the importance of crash tests, cars with no results as of publication date cannot be given an overall rating.

Saab 9-5

The replacement for Saab's 9000, the 9-5 comes with a standard 2.3 liter 4 cylinder turbocharged engine, or an optional 3.0 liter 6 cylinder on the SE model. The 5 speed manual transmission comes with a hydraulic clutch to aid shifting, ABS is standard, as are driver and passenger front and side airbags. The Saab Active Head Restraint, also found on the 9-3, protects against whiplash in the event of a frontal collision.

Interior features include automatic climate control with separate temperature controls for the driver and passenger, heated mirrors, front and rear fog lights, tinted heat absorbing glass, and ample cabin space.

The Ratings

	POOR — GOOD
COMPARATIVE RATING *	
FRONTAL CRASH TEST	
SAFETY FEATURES	
FUEL ECONOMY	
PM COST	
REPAIR COST	
WARRANTY	
COMPLAINTS	
INSURANCE COST	

Safety

FRONTAL CRASH TEST	No government results
SIDE CRASH TEST	No government results
AIRBAGS	Dual & Side
ANTI-LOCK BRAKES	4-Wheel
DAY. RUNNING LIGHTS	Standard
BELT ADJUSTORS	Standard
BUILT-IN CHILD SEAT	Optional
PRETENSIONERS	Standard

General Information

WHERE MADE	Sweden
YEAR OF PRODUCTION	First
PARKING INDEX	Easy
BUMPERS	
THEFT RATING	
TWINS	
GREEN RATING	Poor

Specifications

FUEL ECONOMY (cty/hwy)	21/30	Average
DRIVING RANGE (miles)	505	Very Long
SEATING	5	
LENGTH (in.)	189.2	
HEAD/LEG ROOM (in.)	38.7/42.4	Average
INTERIOR SPACE (cu. ft.)	99	Roomy
CARGO SPACE (cu. ft.)	15.9	Large

Specifications may vary.

Prices

Model	Retail	Mkup
Base	29,995	7%
V6	33,750	6%
SE	36,800	6%

Competition

	POOR — GOOD	Pg.
Saab 9-5		204
Audi A4		106
Lexus ES300		163
Merc.-Benz C-Class		173

*Due to the importance of crash tests, cars with no results as of publication date cannot be given an overall rating.

Saturn SC

This year Saturn offers a 3 door coupe among its SC's. For all of its models, Saturn is trying to quiet its 1.9 liter 4 cylinder engine, with a new crankshaft, pistons, rods, and a cover over the timing chain. The new exhaust system is also quieter. The sleek looking SC includes standard daytime running lamps, standard dual de-powered airbags and optional ABS.

On the interior, the SC looks much like the SL/SW. Interior trim and controls are designed for comfort and ease of use. The engine delivers 100 horsepower which is not tops in this competitive market. Ride should be fairly smooth, though less so on rough roads. A fine product and a pleasant showroom experience are what you'll find at Saturn.

The Ratings

	POOR — GOOD
COMPARATIVE RATING*	
FRONTAL CRASH TEST	
SAFETY FEATURES	
FUEL ECONOMY	
PM COST	
REPAIR COST	
WARRANTY	
COMPLAINTS	
INSURANCE COST	

Safety

FRONTAL CRASH TEST	No government results
SIDE CRASH TEST	No government results
AIRBAGS	Dual (New Design)
ANTI-LOCK BRAKES	4-Wheel (opt)
DAY. RUNNING LIGHTS	Standard
BELT ADJUSTORS	Standard
BUILT-IN CHILD SEAT	None
PRETENSIONERS	None

General Information

WHERE MADE	U.S./Canada
YEAR OF PRODUCTION	Third
PARKING INDEX	Easy
BUMPERS	Strong
THEFT RATING	Very Low
TWINS	
GREEN RATING	Good

Specifications

FUEL ECONOMY (cty/hwy)	29/40	Very Good
DRIVING RANGE (miles)	417	Average
SEATING	4	
LENGTH (in.)	180	
HEAD/LEG ROOM (in.)	38.5/42.6	Average
INTERIOR SPACE (cu. ft.)	84.1	Vry. Cramped
CARGO SPACE (cu. ft.)	11.4	Very Small

Specifications may vary.

Prices

Model	Retail	Mkup
SC1 Manual	11,945	13%
SC1 Automatic	12,805	13%
SC2 Manual	14,505	13%
SC2 Automatic	15,365	13%

Competition

	POOR — GOOD	Pg.
Saturn SC		205
Dodge/Plym. Neon		139
Ford Escort		143
Honda Civic		150

*Due to the importance of crash tests, cars with no results as of publication date cannot be given an overall rating.

Saturn SL/SW

Just as with the SC, Saturn's sedan and wagon get adjustments under the hood to quiet the engine. Saturn's consumer friendly showroom and economical prices are helping change the car buying experience for everyone. The SL and SW come with standard dual airbags and optional ABS.

The dual over-head cam engine available on the SL and SW is more powerful than the base 4-cylinder model and only reduces fuel efficiency slightly. The raised roofline adds headroom which makes the sedan and wagon more comfortable, although the back seat is still tight for adults. The ride is good on smooth roads. Gauges and controls are well placed and easy to use. This economically priced car fares nicely with tough competition like the Ford Escort, Honda Civic and Neon.

The Ratings

	POOR — GOOD
COMPARATIVE RATING	▪ (7th of 10)
FRONTAL CRASH TEST	▪ (9th of 10)
SAFETY FEATURES	▪ (8th of 10)
FUEL ECONOMY	▪ (8th of 10)
PM COST	▪ (2nd of 10)
REPAIR COST	▪ (7th of 10)
WARRANTY	▪ (2nd of 10)
COMPLAINTS	▪ (5th of 10)
INSURANCE COST	▪ (4th of 10)

Safety

FRONTAL CRASH TEST	Very Good
SIDE CRASH TEST	Average
AIRBAGS	Dual (New Design)
ANTI-LOCK BRAKES	4-Wheel (opt)
DAY. RUNNING LIGHTS	Standard
BELT ADJUSTORS	Standard
BUILT-IN CHILD SEAT	None
PRETENSIONERS	None

General Information

WHERE MADE	U.S./Canada
YEAR OF PRODUCTION	Fourth
PARKING INDEX	Easy
BUMPERS	Strong
THEFT RATING	Very Low
TWINS	
GREEN RATING	Good

Specifications

FUEL ECONOMY (cty/hwy)	29/40	Very Good
DRIVING RANGE (miles)	417	Average
SEATING	5	
LENGTH (in.)	176.9	
HEAD/LEG ROOM (in.)	39.3/42.5	Roomy
INTERIOR SPACE (cu. ft.)	91	Cramped
CARGO SPACE (cu. ft.)	12.1	Small

Specifications may vary.

Prices

Model	Retail	Mkup
SL	10,595	13%
SL1 Manual	11,295	13%
SW1 Manual	12,295	13%
SW2 Manual	14,255	13%

Competition

	POOR — GOOD	Pg.
Saturn SL/SW	▪	206
Dodge/Plym. Neon	▪	139
Ford Escort	▪	143
Honda Civic	▪	150

The Impreza comes in two models: the L, as a sedan coupe or wagon, and the RS as a sedan or coupe. Few changes for this year include: more exterior colors and interior fabrics, a more powerful engine, and two improved transmissions. Standard on the Impreza are dual airbags, ABS is optional.

All-wheel drive now comes standard on all models, which should please cold weather drivers. The base model's engine is a 2.2-liter 4-cylinder engine that been given more horsepower and torque for 1999. A 2.5-liter, 15 hp engine is available on the coupe RS. On all models you have the option of new 4-speed automatic transmission, or a manual 5-speed. Front seats are comfortable; the back seat is the typical subcompact squeeze, and trunk space is only adequate.

The Ratings

	POOR ··· GOOD
COMPARATIVE RATING	▮ (middle)
FRONTAL CRASH TEST	▮ (good side)
SAFETY FEATURES	▮ (mid-good)
FUEL ECONOMY	▮ (middle)
PM COST	▮ (good)
REPAIR COST	▮ (middle)
WARRANTY	▮ (poor)
COMPLAINTS	▮ (mid-good)
INSURANCE COST	▮ (poor)

Safety

FRONTAL CRASH TEST	Good
SIDE CRASH TEST	No government results
AIRBAGS	Dual
ANTI-LOCK BRAKES	4-Wheel
DAY. RUNNING LIGHTS	None
BELT ADJUSTORS	Standard
BUILT-IN CHILD SEAT	None
PRETENSIONERS	Standard

General Information

WHERE MADE	Japan
YEAR OF PRODUCTION	Seventh
PARKING INDEX	Very Easy
BUMPERS	Strong
THEFT RATING	Very Low
TWINS	
GREEN RATING	Average

Specifications

FUEL ECONOMY (cty/hwy)	22/29	Average
DRIVING RANGE (miles)	337	Very Short
SEATING	5	
LENGTH (in.)	172.2	
HEAD/LEG ROOM (in.)	39.2/43.1	Roomy
INTERIOR SPACE (cu. ft.)	84.4	Vry. Cramped
CARGO SPACE (cu. ft.)	11.1	Very Small

Specifications may vary.

Prices

Model	Retail	Mkup
L Coupe AWD Manual	15,895	8%
2.5 RS Manual	19,195	8%
L Sedan AWD Manual	15,895	8%
L sport Wagon Manual	16,295	8%

Competition

	POOR ··· GOOD	Pg.
Subaru Impreza	▮ (middle)	207
Chevrolet Cavalier	▮ (mid-good)	123
Ford Escort	▮ (poor-mid)	143
Honda Civic	▮ (mid-good)	150

The Subaru Legacy includes the Brighton Wagon, Legacy L, 2.5GT, and the GT Limited. Between them you can choose between a sedan, coupe and wagon, each with various trim levels. The fresh styling the Legacy received in 1995 continues to make this car a good seller. ABS and dual airbags are standard across the board.

You have two engines to choose from: an improved 2.2-liter 4-cylinder or a 2.5-liter 4-cylinder. Both engines will deliver decent gas mileage. The Legacy also sports a new 5 speed manual transmission or a 4 speed automatic, your choice. All-wheel drive is standard on all the models. The GT model should please sportier buyers. Ride and comfort are both good and the Legacy performed well on government frontal crash tests.

The Ratings

	POOR — GOOD
COMPARATIVE RATING	
FRONTAL CRASH TEST	
SAFETY FEATURES	
FUEL ECONOMY	
PM COST	
REPAIR COST	
WARRANTY	
COMPLAINTS	
INSURANCE COST	

Safety

FRONTAL CRASH TEST	Good
SIDE CRASH TEST	No government results
AIRBAGS	Dual
ANTI-LOCK BRAKES	4-Wheel
DAY. RUNNING LIGHTS	None
BELT ADJUSTORS	Standard
BUILT-IN CHILD SEAT	None
PRETENSIONERS	Standard

General Information

WHERE MADE	Japan/U.S./Canada
YEAR OF PRODUCTION	Fifth
PARKING INDEX	Easy
BUMPERS	Strong
THEFT RATING	Low
TWINS	
GREEN RATING	Average

Specifications

FUEL ECONOMY (cty/hwy)	22/29	Average
DRIVING RANGE (miles)	405	Short
SEATING	5	
LENGTH (in.)	181.5	
HEAD/LEG ROOM (in.)	38.9/43.3	Roomy
INTERIOR SPACE (cu. ft.)	92.1	Cramped
CARGO SPACE (cu. ft.)	13	Small

Specifications may vary.

Prices

Model	Retail	Mkup
L Sedan 4WD Manual	19,195	9%
GT 4WD Manual	22,795	9%
L Wagon 4WD Manual	19,895	9%
GT Wagon 4WD Manual	23,495	9%

Competition

	POOR — GOOD	Pg.
Subaru Legacy		208
Ford Taurus		145
Oldsmobile Cutlass		192
Toyota Camry		213

Subaru Outback

The most popular Subaru, this car may soon find its way onto a police force near you. The base engine is a 2.2 liter 4 cylinder, but the 2.5 liter 4 cylinder will give you more power. You have your choice between a manual 5 speed or an automatic 4 speed transmission. Pick the 2.2 liter engine and the manual transmission and you'll meet LEV emissions standards. All wheel drive, ABS and Dual airbags are standard. This year the Outback gets a new grille, halogen headlights, new bucket seats, and comes pre-wired for keyless entry.

The Ratings

	POOR	GOOD
COMPARATIVE RATING*		
FRONTAL CRASH TEST		
SAFETY FEATURES		
FUEL ECONOMY		
PM COST		
REPAIR COST		
WARRANTY		
COMPLAINTS		
INSURANCE COST		

Safety

FRONTAL CRASH TEST	No government results
SIDE CRASH TEST	No government results
AIRBAGS	Dual
ANTI-LOCK BRAKES	4-Wheel
DAY. RUNNING LIGHTS	None
BELT ADJUSTORS	Standard
BUILT-IN CHILD SEAT	None
PRETENSIONERS	Standard

General Information

WHERE MADE	Japan/U.S./Canada
YEAR OF PRODUCTION	Fifth
PARKING INDEX	Easy
BUMPERS	Strong
THEFT RATING	
TWINS	
GREEN RATING	Average

Specifications

FUEL ECONOMY (cty/hwy)	22/29	Average
DRIVING RANGE (miles)	405	Short
SEATING	5	
LENGTH (in.)	185.8	
HEAD/LEG ROOM (in.)	40.2/43.3	Very Roomy
INTERIOR SPACE (cu. ft.)	96.8	Average
CARGO SPACE (cu. ft.)	36.5	Very Large

Specifications may vary.

Prices

Model	Retail	Mkup
Manual	22,495	9%
Automatic	23,295	9%

Competition

	POOR	GOOD	Pg.
Subaru Outback			**209**
Ford Taurus			145
Nissan Maxima			186
Toyota Camry			213

*Due to the importance of crash tests, cars with no results as of publication date cannot be given an overall rating.

Debuting in 1997, the Esteem has been redesigned for 1999. Changes include new sheet metal work, grille, fenders, and headlights. Three trim levels are available: GL, GLX and the GLX+, and the Esteem comes as either a sedan or wagon. The 1.6 liter 4 cylinder engine is standard on all models, and you can choose between the 4 speed automatic, or the 5 speed manual transmission. The small engine may lack race car power, but it gives good gas mileage, and the manual transmission passes TLEV standards. Later this year you'll be able to get a larger, 1.8 liter engine. Noise levels are comfortable inside and all models come with standard dual airbags, daytime running lamps, and optional ABS. The interior is tight as the car is nearly 20 inches shorter than the Ford Contour; trunk space will not be any better.

The Ratings

	POOR　　　GOOD
COMPARATIVE RATING*	□□□□□□□□□□
FRONTAL CRASH TEST	□□□□□□□□□□
SAFETY FEATURES	□□□□□■□□□□
FUEL ECONOMY	□□□□□□□□■□
PM COST	□□□■□□□□□□
REPAIR COST	■□□□□□□□□□
WARRANTY	■□□□□□□□□□
COMPLAINTS	□□□□□□■□□□
INSURANCE COST	■□□□□□□□□□

Safety

FRONTAL CRASH TEST	No government results
SIDE CRASH TEST	No government results
AIRBAGS	Dual
ANTI-LOCK BRAKES	4-Wheel (opt)
DAY. RUNNING LIGHTS	Standard
BELT ADJUSTORS	Standard
BUILT-IN CHILD SEAT	None
PRETENSIONERS	None

General Information

WHERE MADE	Japan
YEAR OF PRODUCTION	Fourth
PARKING INDEX	Very Easy
BUMPERS	Weak
THEFT RATING	
TWINS	
GREEN RATING	Good

Specifications

FUEL ECONOMY (cty/hwy)	30/37	Good
DRIVING RANGE (miles)	452	Long
SEATING	5	
LENGTH (in.)	165.2	
HEAD/LEG ROOM (in.)	39.1/42.3	Average
INTERIOR SPACE (cu. ft.)	97.9	Average
CARGO SPACE (cu. ft.)	12	Small

Specifications may vary.

Prices

Model	Retail	Mkup
GL Sedan Manual	12,199	5%
GLX Sedan Manual	13,299	5%
GL Wagon Manual	12,699	5%
GLX Wagon Manual	13,799	5%

Competition

	POOR　　　GOOD	Pg.
Suzuki Esteem	□□□□□□□□□□	210
Chevrolet Cavalier	□□□□□■□□□□	123
Dodge/Plym. Neon	□□□■□□□□□□	139
Honda Civic	□□□□■□□□□□	150

*Due to the importance of crash tests, cars with no results as of publication date cannot be given an overall rating.

Suzuki Swift

The Swift's small 1.3-liter 4-cylinder engine provides great fuel economy and stellar emissions ratings with the manual transmission. Because fuel efficiency suffers dramatically with the optional automatic transmission, stick to the standard 5-speed. Room for two is tight; the rear seat is really only for children. Handling is quick and precise, but crosswinds and large trucks can pose a problem.

Twin to the Chevrolet Metro, the Swift is inexpensive, but small so don't expect much room inside. ABS is optional, but dual airbags are standard. The starting price is under $10,000, you can get many options and the Swift comes with a great complaint rating. On the other hand, it's tiny, light and not a terrific handling car. This is basic transportation.

The Ratings

	POOR → GOOD
COMPARATIVE RATING	▒ (below middle)
FRONTAL CRASH TEST	▒ (good side)
SAFETY FEATURES	▒ (poor side)
FUEL ECONOMY	▒ (far good)
PM COST	▒ (poor-middle)
REPAIR COST	▒ (poor side)
WARRANTY	▒ (far poor)
COMPLAINTS	▒ (far good)
INSURANCE COST	▒ (far poor)

Safety

FRONTAL CRASH TEST	Good
SIDE CRASH TEST	No government results
AIRBAGS	Dual
ANTI-LOCK BRAKES	4-Wheel (opt)
DAY. RUNNING LIGHTS	Standard
BELT ADJUSTORS	Standard
BUILT-IN CHILD SEAT	None
PRETENSIONERS	None

General Information

WHERE MADE	Japan/U.S./Canada
YEAR OF PRODUCTION	Fifth
PARKING INDEX	Very Easy
BUMPERS	Weak
THEFT RATING	
TWINS	Chevrolet Metro
GREEN RATING	Good

Specifications

FUEL ECONOMY (cty/hwy)	39/43	Very Good
DRIVING RANGE (miles)	422	Average
SEATING	4	
LENGTH (in.)	149.4	
HEAD/LEG ROOM (in.)	39.1/42.5	Average
INTERIOR SPACE (cu. ft.)	85.8	Vry. Cramped
CARGO SPACE (cu. ft.)	8.4	Very Small

Specifications may vary.

Prices

Model	Retail	Mkup
Hatchback 3 dr Manual	9,099	7%
Hatchback 3 dr Automatic	9,749	7%

Competition

	POOR → GOOD	Pg.
Suzuki Swift	▒ (middle)	**211**
Honda Civic	▒ (poor-middle)	150
Hyundai Accent	▒ (poor-middle)	154
Nissan Sentra	▒ (middle)	188

This Toyota flagship in built in Georgetown, Kentucky—who would have imagined that twenty years ago? The Avalon comes in two trim levels, base XL and deluxe XLS, both with the same powerful 3-liter V6 and automatic transmission. Five adults will be comfortable, but don't count on fitting three adults comfortably on the front bench seat.

With more interior room and a higher price tag than the Camry, the Avalon is more upscale in design, competing with models like the Mercury Sable and Nissan Maxima. Dual airbags and ABS are standard. The Avalon gets only minor cosmetic changes for this model year. Its extra length makes the ride a bit smoother, but it weighs about the same as the Camry, so the handling is just as responsive.

The Ratings

	POOR ‹———› GOOD
COMPARATIVE RATING	Good
FRONTAL CRASH TEST	Good
SAFETY FEATURES	Above Average
FUEL ECONOMY	Average
PM COST	Poor
REPAIR COST	Poor
WARRANTY	Poor
COMPLAINTS	Good
INSURANCE COST	Good

Safety

FRONTAL CRASH TEST	Very Good
SIDE CRASH TEST	No government results
AIRBAGS	Dual & Side
ANTI-LOCK BRAKES	4-Wheel
DAY. RUNNING LIGHTS	None
BELT ADJUSTORS	Standard
BUILT-IN CHILD SEAT	None
PRETENSIONERS	Standard

General Information

WHERE MADE	U.S.
YEAR OF PRODUCTION	Fifth
PARKING INDEX	Average
BUMPERS	Strong
THEFT RATING	Average
TWINS	
GREEN RATING	Average

Specifications

FUEL ECONOMY (cty/hwy)	21/29	Average
DRIVING RANGE (miles)	463	Long
SEATING	5-6	
LENGTH (in.)	191.9	
HEAD/LEG ROOM (in.)	39.1/44.1	Very Roomy
INTERIOR SPACE (cu. ft.)	120.9	Very Roomy
CARGO SPACE (cu. ft.)	15.4	Average

Specifications may vary.

Prices

Model	Retail	Mkup
XL	24,568	12%
XLS	28,578	13%

Competition

	POOR ‹———› GOOD	Pg.
Toyota Avalon	Good	212
Buick Regal	Above Average	115
Mercury Sable	Above Average	178
Nissan Maxima	Below Average	186

Camry continues its reign as best a best seller going into this model year. You have your choice between three trim levels: CE, LE and XLE; and there are many option packages. Dual airbags are standard and 4-wheel ABS is optional. New this year is the option for side airbags for front occupants.

The CE comes standard with a 2.2 liter 4-cylinder engine with 133 hp. Most will prefer the more powerful 3.0-liter V6 engine with a slight loss in fuel economy. The handling is crisp and responsive. Controls are well designed and easy to use and the interior is comfortable for both driver and passengers. The Camry faces tough competition with the redesigned Accord and the popular Taurus, but the Camry remains the car to beat.

The Ratings

	POOR — GOOD
COMPARATIVE RATING	(mid)
FRONTAL CRASH TEST	(good)
SAFETY FEATURES	(good)
FUEL ECONOMY	(mid)
PM COST	(poor)
REPAIR COST	(mid)
WARRANTY	(mid)
COMPLAINTS	(mid)
INSURANCE COST	(mid-poor)

Safety

FRONTAL CRASH TEST	Very Good
SIDE CRASH TEST	Good
AIRBAGS	Dual & Side
ANTI-LOCK BRAKES	4-Wheel (opt)
DAY. RUNNING LIGHTS	None
BELT ADJUSTORS	Standard
BUILT-IN CHILD SEAT	Optional
PRETENSIONERS	Standard

General Information

WHERE MADE	U.S./Japan
YEAR OF PRODUCTION	Third
PARKING INDEX	Easy
BUMPERS	Strong
THEFT RATING	Average
TWINS	Lexus ES 300
GREEN RATING	Average

Specifications

FUEL ECONOMY (cty/hwy)	23/32	Average
DRIVING RANGE (miles)	509	Very Long
SEATING	5	
LENGTH (in.)	188.5	
HEAD/LEG ROOM (in.)	38.6/43.5	Roomy
INTERIOR SPACE (cu. ft.)	96.9	Average
CARGO SPACE (cu. ft.)	14.1	Average

Specifications may vary.

Prices

Model	Retail	Mkup
CE 4cyl Manual	17,038	11%
LE 4cyl Automatic	19,798	12%
LE V6 Manual	21,888	12%
XLE V6 Automatic	24,998	12%

Competition

	POOR — GOOD	Pg.
Toyota Camry	(mid)	**213**
Ford Taurus	(mid-good)	145
Honda Accord	(good)	149
Subaru Legacy	(mid)	208

For 1999, Toyota dropped the Celica GT coupe, leaving the GT liftback and convertible. Otherwise, no big changes for this year's Celica. The Celica is a mid-priced sports car, especially popular with women. Dual airbags are standard and four-wheel ABS is optional.

The base model GT gets a 1.8-liter 4-cylinder engine that's meek for a supposed performance car, although fuel economy is pretty good. The up-level GT convertible gets a slightly more powerful 2.2-liter 4-cylinder engine that's not quite as economical. The standard suspension handles well, but the sport suspension available on the GT is even better. The dashboard is functional and intelligently laid out. The interior has room for two; the rear seat is a joke. Low complaints make the Celica worth looking at.

The Ratings

	POOR — GOOD
COMPARATIVE RATING *	(no rating)
FRONTAL CRASH TEST	(no rating)
SAFETY FEATURES	▮ (mid)
FUEL ECONOMY	▮ (mid)
PM COST	▮ (poor side)
REPAIR COST	▮ (mid)
WARRANTY	▮ (poor side)
COMPLAINTS	▮ (good side)
INSURANCE COST	▮ (poor)

Safety

FRONTAL CRASH TEST	No government results
SIDE CRASH TEST	No government results
AIRBAGS	Dual
ANTI-LOCK BRAKES	4-Wheel (opt)
DAY. RUNNING LIGHTS	None
BELT ADJUSTORS	None
BUILT-IN CHILD SEAT	None
PRETENSIONERS	Standard

General Information

WHERE MADE	Japan
YEAR OF PRODUCTION	Sixth
PARKING INDEX	Very Easy
BUMPERS	Strong
THEFT RATING	Average
TWINS	
GREEN RATING	Average

Specifications

FUEL ECONOMY (cty/hwy)	22/28	Average
DRIVING RANGE (miles)	398	Short
SEATING	4	
LENGTH (in.)	174.2	
HEAD/LEG ROOM (in.)	38.3/44.2	Roomy
INTERIOR SPACE (cu. ft.)	77.2	Vry. Cramped
CARGO SPACE (cu. ft.)	16.2	Large

Specifications may vary.

Prices

Model	Retail	Mkup
GT Coupe Manual	20,111	12%
GT Coupe Automatic	20,911	12%
GT Convertible Manual	24,550	11%
GT Liftback Manual	20,536	12%

Competition

	POOR — GOOD	Pg.
Toyota Celica	(no rating)	214
Acura Integra	▮ (mid)	103
Ford Mustang	▮ (mid)	144
Mitsubishi Eclipse	▮ (poor)	182

*Due to the importance of crash tests, cars with no results as of publication date cannot be given an overall rating.

Toyota Corolla

The Corolla underwent a redesign last year and doesn't change much for '99. Safety was a priority with the latest redesign and the Corolla can come loaded with safety features. Dual airbags and daytime running lamps are standard; ABS and side airbags are optional.

A new engine is a 1.8-liter, 4-cylinder with 120 hp, which is more powerful than the previous 1.6-liter. The new Corolla's base VE is almost $1,000 less than last year's version. Yet, the Corolla still has lots of great features including a bigger glove box, a cloth-lined case for sunglasses on the dash, and a redesigned instrument panel with an optional outside temperature meter. Good crash test results, with front and side, contribute to the car's overall safety. But expensive repair, maintenance, and insurance costs hurt the overall score.

The Ratings

	POOR → GOOD
COMPARATIVE RATING	▮ (middle)
FRONTAL CRASH TEST	▮ (good)
SAFETY FEATURES	▮ (good)
FUEL ECONOMY	▮ (good)
PM COST	▮ (poor-mid)
REPAIR COST	▮ (poor-mid)
WARRANTY	▮ (poor)
COMPLAINTS	▮ (poor)
INSURANCE COST	▮ (poor)

Safety

FRONTAL CRASH TEST	Good
SIDE CRASH TEST	Good
AIRBAGS	Dual & Side (opt)
ANTI-LOCK BRAKES	4-Wheel (opt)
DAY. RUNNING LIGHTS	Standard
BELT ADJUSTORS	Standard
BUILT-IN CHILD SEAT	Optional
PRETENSIONERS	Standard

General Information

WHERE MADE	U.S./Canada
YEAR OF PRODUCTION	Second
PARKING INDEX	Very Easy
BUMPERS	Strong
THEFT RATING	Average
TWINS	Chevrolet Prizm
GREEN RATING	Average

Specifications

FUEL ECONOMY (cty/hwy)	31/38	Very Good
DRIVING RANGE (miles)	455	Long
SEATING	5	
LENGTH (in.)	174	
HEAD/LEG ROOM (in.)	39.3/42.5	Roomy
INTERIOR SPACE (cu. ft.)	88	Cramped
CARGO SPACE (cu. ft.)	12.1	Small

Specifications may vary.

Prices

Model	Retail	Mkup
VE Manual	12,218	9%
CE Manual	12,908	11%
CE Automatic	13,708	11%
LE Manual	14,868	11%

Competition

	POOR → GOOD	Pg.
Toyota Corolla	▮ (middle)	**215**
Chevrolet Cavalier	▮ (middle)	123
Honda Civic	▮ (low-mid)	150
Saturn SL/SW	▮ (middle)	206

This year the Sienna gets a second sliding door. As an option, you can get an automatic version of the door. The Sienna is Toyota's match for the Chrysler minivans, the philosophy being that if you can't beat 'em, copy 'em. The safety features are numerous. Dual airbags, height adjustable seats belts, pretensioners and 4-wheel ABS are standard. An optional built-in child seat is a must for parents.

The Camry's 3.0-liter V6 adequately powers the Sienna, but, not surprisingly gives poor mileage. Standard on this minivan is Toyota's tire pressure monitor. Using the sensors already in place for ABS, the vehicle calculates tire pressure based on rotational speed. A dashboard light alerts you when pressure is low—both a great fuel saver and safety feature.

The Ratings

	POOR	GOOD
COMPARATIVE RATING		
FRONTAL CRASH TEST		
SAFETY FEATURES		
FUEL ECONOMY		
PM COST		
REPAIR COST		
WARRANTY		
COMPLAINTS		
INSURANCE COST		

Safety

FRONTAL CRASH TEST	Very Good
SIDE CRASH TEST	No government results
AIRBAGS	Dual
ANTI-LOCK BRAKES	4-Wheel
DAY. RUNNING LIGHTS	None
BELT ADJUSTORS	Standard
BUILT-IN CHILD SEAT	Optional
PRETENSIONERS	Standard

General Information

WHERE MADE	U.S./Japan
YEAR OF PRODUCTION	Second
PARKING INDEX	Hard
BUMPERS	Strong
THEFT RATING	
TWINS	
GREEN RATING	Very Poor

Specifications

FUEL ECONOMY (cty/hwy)	18/24	Very Poor
DRIVING RANGE (miles)	441	Long
SEATING	7	
LENGTH (in.)	193.5	
HEAD/LEG ROOM (in.)	40.6/41.9	Roomy
INTERIOR SPACE (cu. ft.)		
CARGO SPACE (cu. ft.)	131	Very Large

Specifications may vary.

Prices

Model	Retail	Mkup
CE Sedan	21,428	11%
CE 5dr	22,318	11%
LE 5dr	24,358	12%
XLE 5dr	27,679	13%

Competition

	POOR	GOOD	Pg.
Toyota Sienna			216
Chevrolet Venture			129
Dodge Caravan			137
Plymouth Voyager			196

Toyota Solara

A spin off of the Camry, this all new sports car was a joint U.S.—Japanese engineering concept, built in Canada. The Solara comes with either a 2.2 liter 4 cylinder engine or a 3.0 liter V6. 5-speed manual transmission or 4-speed automatic is an option for both. Though built on the same platform as the Camry, changes made to the struts, springs, suspension mounts give the Solara a tighter, more responsive ride, with more control on corners. The Solara's quiet cabin is the result of filler in the roof and pillar panels and vibration dampening material within the cabin.

Safety features include standard dual airbags for front occupants, seat belt pretensioners, ABS on V6 models, and daytime running lamps. Front side airbags are optional, on all models, traction control is optional for the SLE.

The Ratings

	POOR ... GOOD
COMPARATIVE RATING*	(no rating)
FRONTAL CRASH TEST	(no rating)
SAFETY FEATURES	(good)
FUEL ECONOMY	(mid)
PM COST	(poor)
REPAIR COST	(poor)
WARRANTY	(poor)
COMPLAINTS	(mid)
INSURANCE COST	(mid)

Safety

FRONTAL CRASH TEST	No government results
SIDE CRASH TEST	No government results
AIRBAGS	Dual & Side (opt)
ANTI-LOCK BRAKES	4-Wheel
DAY. RUNNING LIGHTS	Standard
BELT ADJUSTORS	Standard
BUILT-IN CHILD SEAT	None
PRETENSIONERS	Standard

General Information

WHERE MADE	Canada
YEAR OF PRODUCTION	First
PARKING INDEX	Average
BUMPERS	Strong
THEFT RATING	
TWINS	
GREEN RATING	Poor

Specifications

FUEL ECONOMY (cty/hwy)	23/32	Average
DRIVING RANGE (miles)	509	Very Long
SEATING	5	
LENGTH (in.)	190	
HEAD/LEG ROOM (in.)	38.3/43.3	Average
INTERIOR SPACE (cu. ft.)	92.1	Cramped
CARGO SPACE (cu. ft.)	14.1	Average

Specifications may vary.

Prices

Model	Retail	Mkup
SE 4cyl Manual	18,638	11%
SE 4cyl Automatic	19,438	11%
SE V6 Manual	21,188	11%
SLE V6	24,988	11%

Competition

	POOR ... GOOD	Pg.
Toyota Solara	(no rating)	**217**
Dodge Avenger	(mid)	136
Hyundai Sonata	(poor-mid)	156
Pontiac Grand Prix	(mid)	200

*Due to the importance of crash tests, cars with no results as of publication date cannot be given an overall rating.

For 1999 the Golf is all-new. The five door hatchback gets 2.0 liter 115hp, 4 cylinder engine on all models. Dual airbags and daytime running lamps are standard, ABS is optional. Traction control is a great feature available on the some models.

All models come with 5-speed manual or automatic overdrive. In addition to the industry best 10-year/100,000 mile power train warranty, VW now includes all service, repairs and parts up the entire duration of the basic warranty of 2-years/24,000 miles. Unfortunately, crash tests are not available, otherwise this is a good choice.

The Ratings

	POOR ··· GOOD
COMPARATIVE RATING*	(no rating)
FRONTAL CRASH TEST	(no rating)
SAFETY FEATURES	▮ (good)
FUEL ECONOMY	▮ (mid)
PM COST	▮ (good)
REPAIR COST	▮ (mid-good)
WARRANTY	▮ (good)
COMPLAINTS	▮ (mid)
INSURANCE COST	▮ (mid)

Safety

FRONTAL CRASH TEST	No government results
SIDE CRASH TEST	No government results
AIRBAGS	Dual & Side (opt)
ANTI-LOCK BRAKES	4-Wheel
DAY. RUNNING LIGHTS	Standard
BELT ADJUSTORS	Standard
BUILT-IN CHILD SEAT	None
PRETENSIONERS	Standard

General Information

WHERE MADE	Mexico/Germany
YEAR OF PRODUCTION	First
PARKING INDEX	Very Easy
BUMPERS	
THEFT RATING	Low
TWINS	Volkswagen Jetta
GREEN RATING	Average

Specifications

FUEL ECONOMY (cty/hwy)	24/31	Average
DRIVING RANGE (miles)	660	Very Long
SEATING	5	
LENGTH (in.)	160.4	
HEAD/LEG ROOM (in.)	39.2/42.3	Average
INTERIOR SPACE (cu. ft.)	87.6	Cramped
CARGO SPACE (cu. ft.)	16.9	Large

Specifications may vary.

Prices

Model	Retail	Mkup
GL Sedan	13,495	8%
Wolfsburg Hatchback Coupe	15,275	6%
GTI VR6 Hatchback Coupe	20,235	8%

Competition

	POOR ··· GOOD	Pg.
Volkswagen Golf	(no rating)	218
Chevrolet Prizm	▮ (mid)	128
Ford Escort	▮ (mid)	143
Hyundai Accent	▮ (mid)	154

*Due to the importance of crash tests, cars with no results as of publication date cannot be given an overall rating.

It was a busy year for Volkswagen, who also introduces a new Jetta for 1999. Dual airbags and daytime running lamps are standard, ABS is available.

The Jetta offers a 2-liter 4-cylinder engine in the GL and as a choice for the GLS. The second engine for the GLS, is a 2.8-liter V6, which is the standard on the GLX model. All models come with 5-speed manual or automatic overdrive, and a 10-year/100,000 mile power train warranty. VW now includes all service, repairs and parts up the entire duration of the basic warranty of 2-years/24,000 miles. Handling is responsive, and the seats are comfortable.

The Ratings

	POOR	GOOD
COMPARATIVE RATING*		
FRONTAL CRASH TEST		
SAFETY FEATURES	■	
FUEL ECONOMY	■	
PM COST		■
REPAIR COST	■	
WARRANTY		■
COMPLAINTS	■	
INSURANCE COST	■	

Safety

FRONTAL CRASH TEST	No government results
SIDE CRASH TEST	No government results
AIRBAGS	Dual & Side (opt)
ANTI-LOCK BRAKES	4-Wheel
DAY. RUNNING LIGHTS	Standard
BELT ADJUSTORS	Standard
BUILT-IN CHILD SEAT	None
PRETENSIONERS	Standard

General Information

WHERE MADE	Mexico/Germany
YEAR OF PRODUCTION	First
PARKING INDEX	Very Easy
BUMPERS	
THEFT RATING	Average
TWINS	Volkswagen Golf
GREEN RATING	Average

Specifications

FUEL ECONOMY (cty/hwy)	24/31	Average
DRIVING RANGE (miles)	660	Very Long
SEATING	5	
LENGTH (in.)	173.4	
HEAD/LEG ROOM (in.)	39.2/42.3	Average
INTERIOR SPACE (cu. ft.)	87.5	Cramped
CARGO SPACE (cu. ft.)	15	Average

Specifications may vary.

Prices

Model	Retail	Mkup
GL	14,845	9%
Wolfsburg	16,500	8%
TDI	15,770	8%
GLX	20,955	8%

Competition

	POOR	GOOD	Pg.
Volkswagen Jetta			**219**
Acura Integra	■		103
Chevrolet Cavalier	■		123
Ford Contour	■		141

*Due to the importance of crash tests, cars with no results as of publication date cannot be given an overall rating.

The New Beetle is much more than the old bug. With standard front and side airbags for front occupants, it performed well in independent crash tests, though the government has yet to crash test the car. Volkswagen loaded the New Beetle with the current standard of safety features—virtually the opposite of its historic predecessor.

The New Beetle comes with a 2.0 liter 115 hp 4 cylinder, in-line gas engine or a 1.9 liter 90 hp 4 cylinder TDI, in-line diesel. The 2.0 liter meets LEV standards. Both engines come with a standard 5 speed manual transmission, with the option of a 4 speed automatic. A few luxury options are available including leather, heated seats and a sunroof. And don't forget the vase.

The Ratings

	POOR — GOOD
COMPARATIVE RATING *	(no rating)
FRONTAL CRASH TEST	(no rating)
SAFETY FEATURES	Good
FUEL ECONOMY	Average
PM COST	Good
REPAIR COST	Poor
WARRANTY	Good
COMPLAINTS	Average
INSURANCE COST	Average

Safety

FRONTAL CRASH TEST	No government results
SIDE CRASH TEST	No government results
AIRBAGS	Dual & Side
ANTI-LOCK BRAKES	4-Wheel
DAY. RUNNING LIGHTS	Standard
BELT ADJUSTORS	Standard
BUILT-IN CHILD SEAT	None
PRETENSIONERS	Standard

General Information

WHERE MADE	Mexico/Germany
YEAR OF PRODUCTION	Second
PARKING INDEX	Very Easy
BUMPERS	
THEFT RATING	
TWINS	
GREEN RATING	Average

Specifications

FUEL ECONOMY (cty/hwy)	24/31	Average
DRIVING RANGE (miles)	660	
SEATING	4	
LENGTH (in.)	161.1	
HEAD/LEG ROOM (in.)	41.3/39.4	Average
INTERIOR SPACE (cu. ft.)	84	Vry. Cramped
CARGO SPACE (cu. ft.)	12	Small

Specifications may vary.

Prices

Model	Retail	Mkup
Base	15,200	6%
TDI	16,475	6%

Competition

	POOR — GOOD	Pg.
VW New Beetle	(no rating)	220
Chevrolet Metro	Poor	126
Ford Escort	Poor/Average	143
Honda Civic	Poor/Average	150

*Due to the importance of crash tests, cars with no results as of publication date cannot be given an overall rating.

Volkswagen Passat

VW claims the Passat gives car buyers German automobile excellence with a low price tag. Safety features abound. Dual airbags are standard, as is traction control, ABS and side airbags. The GLS sedan and wagon have either a 1.8 liter engine with 4 cylinders, or a 2.8 liter V6. Both engines have a 5 speed manual transmission. The GLX model has a 2.8 liter V6 engine, and an automatic, Tiptronic transmission, offering the choice between manual and automatic gear shifting. All models can meet California's Transitional Low Emission Vehicles standards. Inside, the Passat has more interior room than its predecessor. Along with VW's industry best 10-year/100,000 miles powertrain warranty, VW now includes all service, repairs and parts up the entire duration of the basic warranty of 2-years/24,000 miles.

The Ratings

	POOR	GOOD
COMPARATIVE RATING*		
FRONTAL CRASH TEST		
SAFETY FEATURES		■
FUEL ECONOMY		■
PM COST		■
REPAIR COST	■	
WARRANTY		■
COMPLAINTS		■
INSURANCE COST		■

Safety

FRONTAL CRASH TEST	No government results
SIDE CRASH TEST	No government results
AIRBAGS	Dual & Side
ANTI-LOCK BRAKES	4-Wheel
DAY. RUNNING LIGHTS	Standard
BELT ADJUSTORS	Standard
BUILT-IN CHILD SEAT	None
PRETENSIONERS	Standard

General Information

WHERE MADE	Germany
YEAR OF PRODUCTION	Second
PARKING INDEX	Average
BUMPERS	Strong
THEFT RATING	Average
TWINS	
GREEN RATING	Average

Specifications

FUEL ECONOMY (cty/hwy)	23/32	Average
DRIVING RANGE (miles)	509	Very Long
SEATING	5	
LENGTH (in.)	184.1	
HEAD/LEG ROOM (in.)	39.7/41.5	Average
INTERIOR SPACE (cu. ft.)	95	Average
CARGO SPACE (cu. ft.)	15	Average

Specifications may vary.

Prices

Model	Retail	Mkup
GLS Sedan Manual	21,200	10%
GLX Sedan Automatic(5)	29,800	9%
GLS Wagon	21,750	10%
GLX Wagon	30,350	9%

Competition

	POOR	GOOD	Pg.
VW Passat			221
Buick Regal		■	115
Oldsmobile Cutlass	■		192
Toyota Camry		■	213

*Due to the importance of crash tests, cars with no results as of publication date cannot be given an overall rating.

Volvo C70/S70/V70

Despite the new name and smoother-out exterior, the sedan (S70) and wagon (V70) aren't radically different from the old 850. However, the C70 coupe's aggressive and sporty styling is a departure for Volvo and a convertible is available. Safety is still Volvo's strength. Dual airbags, side airbags, daytime running lamps, pretensioners and ABS are all standard. This Volvo did very well in the government's crash test this year contributing to its stellar overall rating.

The standard engine is a 2.4-liter, inline five that produces 168 hp. Turbo versions are optional and provide more power and all-wheel drive is available on the V70 wagons. Interior room is still roomy and comfortable, but five is a squeeze. The trunk space remains quite generous.

The Ratings

	POOR — GOOD
COMPARATIVE RATING	▮ (high)
FRONTAL CRASH TEST	▮ (high)
SAFETY FEATURES	▮ (high)
FUEL ECONOMY	▮ (low-mid)
PM COST	▮ (poor)
REPAIR COST	▮ (mid)
WARRANTY	▮ (high)
COMPLAINTS	▮ (low-mid)
INSURANCE COST	▮ (high)

Safety

FRONTAL CRASH TEST	Very Good
SIDE CRASH TEST	No government results
AIRBAGS	Dual & Side (New Design)
ANTI-LOCK BRAKES	4-Wheel
DAY. RUNNING LIGHTS	Standard
BELT ADJUSTORS	Standard
BUILT-IN CHILD SEAT	Optional
PRETENSIONERS	Standard

General Information

WHERE MADE	Germany/Canada/Sweden
YEAR OF PRODUCTION	Second
PARKING INDEX	Average
BUMPERS	Weak
THEFT RATING	
TWINS	
GREEN RATING	Poor

Specifications

FUEL ECONOMY (cty/hwy)	20/28	Poor
DRIVING RANGE (miles)	444	Long
SEATING	5	
LENGTH (in.)	185.7	
HEAD/LEG ROOM (in.)	39/41.3	Average
INTERIOR SPACE (cu. ft.)	79.6	Vry. Cramped
CARGO SPACE (cu. ft.)	13.1	Small

Specifications may vary.

Prices

Model	Retail	Mkup
S70 Sedan Manual	26,985	8%
V70 2WD Wagon Manual	28,285	8%
V70 AWD Wagon	34,420	8%
C70 Manual	38,995	11%

Competition

	POOR — GOOD	Pg.
Volvo S70	▮ (high)	**222**
Adui A4	▮ (high)	106
Lexus ES300	▮ (high)	163
Merc.-Benz C-Class	▮ (mid)	173

Volvo S80

The new S80 replaces Volvo's S90 and it's a giant departure from the boxy designs of old. The S80 offers either a 2.9 liter, 6 cylinder engine with 201 hp, or a 2.8 liter 6 cylinder twin turbo with 268 hp (known as the T-6). The list of safety features is no surprise for a Volvo: depowered airbags for driver and front passenger, side impact inflatable curtains, side impact airbags in all seats, safety belt pretensioners, daytime running lamps, and standard ABS. Even the base model comes fully loaded with luxury features like a security system with alarm, an anti-theft ignition immobilizer, dual zone electronic climate control, heated mirrors, cruise control, CD player, and simulated wood throughout the interior, and fog lamps. A strong competitor, but no crash tests results are available.

The Ratings

	POOR	GOOD
COMPARATIVE RATING*		
FRONTAL CRASH TEST		
SAFETY FEATURES		
FUEL ECONOMY		
PM COST		
REPAIR COST		
WARRANTY		
COMPLAINTS		
INSURANCE COST		

Safety

FRONTAL CRASH TEST	No government results
SIDE CRASH TEST	No government results
AIRBAGS	Dual & Side (New Design)
ANTI-LOCK BRAKES	4-Wheel
DAY. RUNNING LIGHTS	Standard
BELT ADJUSTORS	Standard
BUILT-IN CHILD SEAT	Optional
PRETENSIONERS	Standard

General Information

WHERE MADE	Germany/Sweden
YEAR OF PRODUCTION	First
PARKING INDEX	Easy
BUMPERS	
THEFT RATING	
TWINS	
GREEN RATING	Very Poor

Specifications

FUEL ECONOMY (cty/hwy)	18/27	Poor
DRIVING RANGE (miles)	475	Very Long
SEATING	5	
LENGTH (in.)	189.8	
HEAD/LEG ROOM (in.)	38.9/42.2	Average
INTERIOR SPACE (cu. ft.)	114.1	Very Roomy
CARGO SPACE (cu. ft.)	14.2	Average

Specifications may vary.

Prices

Model	Retail	Mkup
2.9 Sedan	35,820	9%
T-6	40,385	9%

Competition

	POOR	GOOD	Pg.
Volvo S80			**223**
Cadillac DeVille			118
Mazda Millenia			171
Merc.-Benz C-Class			173

Index

Airbags; *see Safety*
Anti-lock Brakes; *see Safety*
Auto Manufacturers, 84
Auto Safety Hotline, 34, 71, 77
Bumpers; *see Insurance*
Child Restraint Laws; *see Safety*
Child Safety Seats; *see Safety*
Complaints
  arbitration
    AUTOCAP, 78-9
    Better Business Bureau (BBB),
      75, 78
    legal aid, 76
    manufacturer's programs, 78
    state-run, 79
    ten tips for, 79
  NHTSA hotline/questionnaire, 77
  record-keeping, 75
  resolving, 75-6
  under warranty, 76; see *also Warranty*
  vehicle ratings (best/worst), 80
Consumer Groups
  Advocates for Highway & Auto
    Safety, 83
  Center for Auto Safety, 4, 61, 76,
    81-2
  Consumer Action—San Francisco,
    83
  Center for the Study of Services, 96
  Consumer Education and Protection
    Association, 83
  Consumers for Auto Reliability and
    Safety Foundation, 83
Corporate Twins, 18, 91
Crash Test; *see Safety*
Emissions Options, 43
Fuel Economy
  factors affecting, 42, 72
  EPA Figures, 45-8
  Green vehicles, 43
  octane ratings, 41
  oxyfuels, 42
  winners and losers, 44
Government Agencies
  Department of Justice, 83
  Department of Transportation (DOT),
    19, 75
  Environmental Protection Agency
    (EPA), 41, 44-5, 83
  Federal Highway Administration
    (FHA), 83
  Federal Trade Commission (FTC),
    56, 61, 75, 78, 83
  Highway Loss Data Institute
    (HLDI), 66, 69

National Highway Traffic Safety Administration (NHTSA), 61, 77, 83
  state attorney general's office, 76,
    85
Horn Location, 68
Insurance
  bumpers, 70
  deductibles, 68
  discounts and surcharges, 68
  Insurance Institute for Highway
    Safety (IIHS), 67
  no-fault, 66
  occupant injury statistics, 66
  reducing costs, 67-8
  repair costs, 70
  types of coverage, 65
Leasing
  questions to ask, 94
  residual value, 97
  types of, 96
  versus buying, 96-7
  versus financing, 97
Legal Action
  arbitration; *see Complaints*
  lemon laws, 78, 81-2, 85-88
Maintenance
  costs, 49-54
  dealing with a mechanic, 56
  keeping it going, 57
  operating costs, 9
  service contract, 55
  turbocharging, 55
National Automotive Dealers Association (NADA), 90
National Institute for Automotive
  Service Excellence, 56
Operating costs; *see Maintenance*
Policy Adjustments; *see Warranty*
  secret
Price
  auto brokers, 92
  avoiding lemons, 82, 90
  dealer mark up, 100
  negotiating, 89-92
  price shopping service, 92
  resale value, 93
Ratings
  explanation, 8-9, 99-101
  good choices, 8
Recall Information, 77
Repair
  complaints; *see Complaints*
  costs, 49-54
  dealing with a mechanic, 56
  payment by credit card, 56
  record keeping, 75

  under warranty, 59
Resale Value; *see Price*
Rustproofing, 60
Safety
  airbag deployment, 28
  anti-lock brakes, 30
  automatic crash protection, 26-7
  child restraint laws, 39-40
  children & airbags, 29
  child safety seats, 34-8
    locking clips, 34
    NHTSA hotline, 34
    product index, 36-7
    rear-facing, 38
    registering, 34
    tips on buying, 34
    tips on use, 38
    types, 35
  crash test
    explanation, 19-20
  future options, 98
  safety belts, 31
    myths and facts, 31
    state laws, 32-3
  vehicle ratings, 20-5
Service Bulletins, 61
Service Contracts, 55
Thefts, prevention, 69
Tires
  comparing, 71-2
  effect on fuel economy, 72
  heat resistance, 71
  longevity, 71-72
  NHTSA hotline, 71
  pricing, 72
  ratings program, 71, 73-4
  registration, 72
  traction, 71
  treadwear, 71
Warranty
  best and worst, 62
  comparing, 62-4
  corrosion, 60, 62
  dealer options, 60
  emmision system, 60
  expressed, 59
  full, 59
  implied, 59
  legal rights, 59-60
  limited, 59
  Magnuson-Moss Warranty Act, 76
  powertrain, 62
  roadside assistance, 62
  secret, 61, 81
  versus a service contract, 55, 60